PRAISE FOR *YOUNGER THAN THAT NOW*

"What makes *Younger Than That Now* remarkable is the remarkability of
the friendship . . . so authentic that readers of a certain age will wonder
how they ever survived it all."
—*Daily Journal*, Tupelo

"The book captures the hallucinatory days of the late 1960s, exploring
their ideas and different opinions on everything from the Vietnam war to
race relations to religion with some surprising twists along the way."
—*The Yazoo Herald*

"Their letters are filled with the confusion of growing up during a time of
change, intellectual debates on politics and religion, and updates on their
love lives. As much as Jeff and Ruth are different, they each cherish the
insight given to them by the other."
—*Booklist*

"A touching personal memoir . . . as well as a collective history of a
generation."
—*Delta Democrat Times*

"The lasting bond and openness between the two authors is the work's
strength. An example of how two people, going through crazy times, deal
with the business of living."
—*Library Journal*

"A rueful, sometimes funny look back at the dreams and excesses of the
'60s counterculture. Many readers will identify with the descriptions of
the era and the emotional roller coaster that marked the authors'
transition to adulthood, with all its compromises."
—*Publishers Weekly*

bantam books

New York   Toronto   London

Sydney   Auckland

younger

A Shared Passage

than

from the Sixties

that now

by Jeff Durstewitz

and

Ruth Williams

YOUNGER THAN THAT NOW

PUBLISHING HISTORY
Bantam hardcover / June 2000
Bantam trade paperback / May 2001

Grateful acknowledgment is made to the individuals, publishers, and other copyright owners for permission to reprint and quote from the materials listed below:
Letter by Jerry Greenfield reprinted courtesy of Jerry Greenfield.
Letter by Margaret F. Tuttle reprinted courtesy of Margaret F. Tuttle.
Letters by Vincent James Vito, Jr. reprinted courtesy of Dolores Vito.
Letter by Randall Williams reprinted courtesy of Randall Williams.
Lyrics to "I Feel Like I'm Fixin' To Die Rag." Words and music by Joe McDonald © 1965. Renewed 1993 Alkatraz Corner Music Co. BMI. Reprinted by permission. All rights reserved.
Lyrics to "OM" by Michael Pinder © 1964 (Renewed) by Music Sales Corporation (ASCAP) International Copyright Secured. All rights reserved. Reprinted by permission.
Lyrics to "He Ain't Heavy . . . He's My Brother" © 1969 by Harrison Music Corporation. Written by Bob Russell and Bobby Scott.

Library of Congress Catalog Card Number 99-053697

ISBN 0-553-38048-6

Published simultaneously in the United States and Canada

Bantam Books are published by Bantam Books, a division of Random House, Inc. Its trademark, consisting of the words "Bantam Books" and the portrayal of a rooster, is Registered in U.S. Patent and Trademark Office and in other countries. Marca Registrada. Bantam Books, 1540 Broadway, New York, New York 10036.

PRINTED IN THE UNITED STATES OF AMERICA

BVG   10   9   8   7   6   5   4   3   2   1

dedication

This is a book primarily about friendship, and it is dedicated to old friends everywhere. It is also dedicated to a particular group of kids who left the cosseted womb of high school between 1966 and 1972 to enter a world that was as insane as it was exalted.

During the writing of *Younger Than That Now,* the deaths of two of its best friends weighed heavily on us both. We will always be grateful to

Willie Morris   1934–1999
a generous man who held his light high to show us the way

Beverly Lewis Eames   1948–1999
an editor of gentle power and keen perceptions

Death is nothing at all. I have only slipped away into the next room. I am I and you are you . . . whatever we were to each other, that we are still. Call me by my old familiar name, speak to me in the easy way which we always used. Put no difference into your tone; wear no forced smile of solemnity or sorrow. Laugh as we always laughed at the little jokes we enjoyed together. Let my name be ever the household word that it always was. Let it be spoken without effect, without the ghost of a shadow on it. Life means all that it ever meant. It is the same as it ever was; there is absolutely unbroken continuity.

CANON HENRY SCOTT HOLLAND

*It is our inward journey that leads us through time—
forward or back, seldom in a straight line, most often
spiraling. Each of us is moving, changing with respect
to others. As we discover, we remember; remembering,
we discover; and most intensely do we experience this
when our separate journeys converge.*

—EUDORA WELTY
One Writer's Beginnings

contents

dear

whitey,

honky,

wasp,

bitch

1.   *J e f f*

idle hands

As you get older, you look back on how much you didn't know when you were a kid, and it makes you laugh. In some cases it makes you laugh till you cry.

In early 1969 Ruth Tuttle and I were seventeen-year-olds in far-flung corners of America—different countries, really—who thought we knew how things happen and why. There was at least some basis for these thoughts. We were reasonably intelligent, imaginative kids, comparatively well read and well schooled.

But your body, maturing so much faster than your mind and your emotions, deceives you as you begin to exit childhood. And one day the mirror shows your wondering eyes someone all too easily mistaken for an adult. What it doesn't tell you—not that you'd listen anyway—is that the act of growing up will take more time and inflict more pain than you can imagine, and that by the time it's done, you will be a patchwork of hidden scars and fractures.

Part of our flagrant hubris came of youth, the universal intoxicant. But it also came of membership in the nation's largest crop of children: the Baby Boomers. We were accustomed to society stretching and bending for us as we moved from coonskin caps and Ginny dolls to college, and we expected more of the same as our birthright. We were quite certain that this accommodation would be all for the better, and that we, the anointed ones, would bring about the flowering of all of humanity's fondest hopes.

Like most people, and certainly like millions of our postpubescent peers, Ruth and I were looking for love. And we found it with each other, except that it wasn't the kind we expected. But our mind-love, in many ways greater and better than the sweaty and transitory variety, helped sustain us through any number of dizzying amours, bitter disappointments, personal and generational delusions, divorce and death. All through this hard passage from youth to middle age, we wrote to each other and saved the letters, hundreds of them. We clung to them because we knew they contained something priceless—the keys to our souls, the record of who we were and who we were becoming.

It has been said that the gods first make people crazy before they bring them low. But in the case of Ruth and me, it may be more true that they made us bored before they enlightened us. It all began with a silly prank.

It was a Friday afternoon in February of 1969, eighth period, and my usual crew—Vinny Vito, Dave "Feldo" Feldman, Jerry Greenfield, Ben Cohen, Judy Vecchione, Sue Ball, Ronnie Bauch and a few others—had assembled in the office of *Hoofbeats,* the student newspaper of Calhoun High School in Merrick, Long Island. We'd reached the winter doldrums of our senior year, and we were seriously bored.

Into this hotbed of ennui dropped a seed: the latest newspaper from a high school in Yazoo City, Mississippi. It was one of several exchange papers we received, and as each school sent us its latest issue, I'd scan it with gimlet eyes. *The Yazooan* was something of a joke around the office, not for its poor quality—it was quite well written and edited—but because it was from a place that had the nerve to call itself Yazoo City. The name in itself was enough for a laugh from us worldly "Noo Yawkas," and the fact that this jerkwater burg was located in Mississippi, the most backward state of the whole impossibly retro South, was also comical. But Ben pointed out two additional provocations in the latest issue.

As editor of *Hoofbeats,* I was most affronted by the first: The student featured as the "Senior Pic" on *The Yazooan*'s front page was none other than its editor, Ruth Tuttle. But my outrage was tempered a bit by the fact that this miscreant Miss Tuttle seemed quite smashing, judging from her photo. The second crime occurred in an ad for the Toggery, a clothing store. The ad featured a smirking Yazoo football hero, Mike Bagwell, with an exhortation to "Be a stud like Mike Bagwell in your Toggery shirt, Higgins pants and Bostonian shoes." A *stud* like Mike Bagwell? Obviously, these Yazoo yahoos needed some acculturation.

I began a letter in mock indignation, and soon we were passing it around, each laughing and adding a section. We roasted Ruth, the improbable Yazoo City, its miserable high school and the insufferable Mike Bagwell—not to mention the shit-kicking, night-riding South itself. Mississippi was, after all, the state that hadn't yet ratified the Thirteenth Amendment, which abolished slavery. It also was where three civil rights workers had been murdered only a few years before and where Medgar Evers had been shot down in sight of his family. Whites in Mississippi had a lot of grief coming, and we were only too happy to provide it. Scrawled over two sides of notebook paper, the letter contained every snide slam we could think of, plus tongue-in-cheek references to ourselves as despicable Jew Commies and self-righteous bastards and bitches.

But it was perhaps less of a joke for Judy, a brilliant girl with long, dark hair and snapping brown eyes. Her reference to burning crosses came of her deep commitment to the Civil Rights movement, of which she was already a veteran. The daughter of activist parents, she had been to Washington to hear Martin Luther King, Jr., and the opportunity to lash out at the Deep South fired her up. (Twenty years later, working for WGBH in Boston, she would produce a segment of the award-winning *Eyes on the Prize*, a documentary of the movement.) For my main man, the ever thoughtful Vin, it wasn't a joke either; he'd studied Malcolm X in a sociology class, and though raised in the white working class, he strongly identified with Malcolm's philosophy.

The rest of us just skylarked through it, one-upping each other with puns, put-downs and in-jokes. We each signed it. Then eighth period ended, the laughter died down and it was time to go home. I made a show of addressing an envelope and putting a stamp on it, but I doubt anyone thought I'd actually put it in the mail.

I carried the letter around with me for several days, inwardly debating the pros and cons of sending it. What was the worst that could happen? Ruth Tuttle might be too stunned to reply, in which case there would be no further sport, but no downside, either. Of course, she might take it to her principal and demand redress of Yazoo's honor, not to mention her own and the South's. What might happen then? Would he call our principal, or fire off a nasty letter? If he did, who cared? We were the cream of our class; we all would be graduating soon anyway. At most, Mr. Jordan might make us write some sort of bogus apology, which could turn out to be nearly as much fun as the original.

Finally I found myself standing at the mailbox across from my house. I hesitated, thought, *Aw, what the hell?* and dropped the letter in. The faint "thunk" it made when it hit the bottom of the empty box hinted nothing of the awesome workings of fate, and I whistled as I went about my many adolescent offices afterward.

If anyone had told me that I'd just done something that would profoundly change the course of two lives, I would have thought they were at least as crazy as me and my friends.

2.   Ruth

it wasn't the second coming, but it felt like salvation

While the Yankee North shivered and shook, getting no respite from winter, in February 1969 Mississippi already enjoyed the tight embrace of a seductive springtime. Tiny drops of moisture sparkled on budding azaleas, and a warming breeze made the daffodils, which had opened only that morning, bob beneath their blankets of cobwebs. Mississippi air rolls up in great waves from the Gulf of Mexico and is so pure that it can cause euphoria. So I lingered on my front porch, breathing it in for several long minutes before skipping down the front steps toward Yazoo City High School.

I was being seduced by a letter I thought was extraordinary: a gift from God, a miracle I had earned with tearful prayers and sleepless, long nights. Never mind that it was confrontational and offensive, from a group of high school seniors I had never met, who lived in the far-off ether of suburban New York City. The hunger of a starved mind is as acute as a bellyache, and this letter had somehow eased that pain for me.

I crossed the bayou that runs from Brickyard Hill to the Yazoo River, where Gypsies had camped in the early 1900s. But no one built fires or slept beside it any longer. Now it was dark and overgrown, frequented only by dogs and snakes. On the other side was Campbell Street, named by my great-grandfather, Tom Campbell, after himself, and the old Butler and Haverkamp houses. The elderly ladies who lived in them could often be seen rocking on their porches, pale, small, white-haired, watching. Today, only Mrs. Haverkamp was out, and I waved to her as I approached. She hoisted her lace handkerchief gaily from its nest in her lap and beckoned me onto the porch. "How's your momma?" she asked.

"She's fine," I answered, looking for the little flask that was usually tucked in a bag by her rocking chair. Its sterling silver skin winked at me as she rocked back and forth, from shadow to sunlight, shadow to sunlight, the cane chair clicking and creaking, her little feet tapping each time they gave another push.

I had first met her in 1963, right after we moved to Yazoo, where my mother had been raised from birth by her Aunt Ruth. The young president,

John Kennedy, was alive then, planting the seeds of disastrous conflict in Vietnam, and Martin Luther King, Jr. was a respected Atlanta minister with a growing national following. My great-aunt Ruth's Victorian house on Jackson Avenue, where my family lived, had not been remodeled then. It had the faded wallpaper of my mother's childhood, and of her aunts' and uncles' before her, and the marks of their grimy, tiny hands.

But by 1969 all of those people and things had become history, except for Mrs. Haverkamp. She rocked placidly on her shady porch, her old-lady eyes turned expectantly up to mine.

I usually stopped to visit. But that sunny February morning I walked on. I didn't want to waste time with someone whose surprises seemed all used up, especially when my own life was suddenly so full of potential. The act of being young is possible because inexperience wraps us like a hard shell. When we move on into life, the shell is stripped away by deaths, illnesses and missed opportunities, so we begin to feel pain almost in anticipation of a loss. But at seventeen, I was so calloused with innocence as I walked away from Mrs. Haverkamp's porch that I couldn't hear the rending of fragile ancestral ties with those women and men long dead, who began their lives in the nineteenth century and who handed down to me their unshakable childlike faith in God, their constancy, Scottish practicality, flawless social graces and their love.

No one was waiting for me at school—no eager girlfriend ready to hear the latest gossip or amorous boyfriend wanting to hold my hand before the eight o'clock bell. My friends were, as usual, paired off with their beaux, letter jackets carelessly tossed over their shoulders like plunder. A few of them waved as I walked by. Dell Gotthelf, who spoke to everyone, trilled out a cheery "Hey!" Most Beautiful and Miss YHS, she had made it a vocation to be unflappably pleasant. She was the Ronald Reagan of Yazoo City High School.

I went inside the building. As editor of *The Yazooan,* I was allowed in before the bell. *The Yazooan* office was on the second floor, where it had been since Willie Morris was its editor in the fifties, behind Mrs. Omie Parker's former classroom. As time marched by for others, Mrs. Parker had seemed to stay the course, coloring her raven hair to hide the gray and returning like a swallow to her worn desk, year after year. She had continued working well past the time she could have retired, and I accepted it as a personal benediction that her last year as a teacher was my first in Yazoo City High School.

"Miss Tuttle," she had said to me one day, "I expect you to achieve greatness in your high school career, which is no less than your Aunt Ruth would expect, if she were alive today." Then she had ratcheted the challenge even higher by describing Willie and his transcendent rise to the aerie of publishing. Then editor of *Harper's* magazine, he was established early on as the giant against whom I would have to measure my own stature as a writer.

The Yazooan room couldn't have been more removed from the hormonal hustle of my peers. The gray-green cubicle had become a sanctuary on those occasions when I slipped out of class to write an article or meet a deadline, and it saved me from having to stand alone in the hallway between classes. That day, I carefully closed and locked the door before I pulled the letter out of my algebra book and sat by the window to read it again.

It had arrived the afternoon before, finding its way to me in physics class—the purgatorial low point of another soporific day at Yazoo City High School. The school secretary had made an announcement over the school's PA system: "Ruth Tuttle, please come to the office and pick up your mail."

At the time I was morosely mulling the relationship of velocity to torque, not suspecting that a significant amount of emotional and mental torque was about to increase the velocity of my life. I marked the place in my textbook and stood up to go to the office. "Where do you think you're going?" the physics instructor, Mr. Richardson, asked, his voice low and threatening. The class, already quiet because no one dared talk in his classroom, now became deathly still as well.

He and I didn't like each other. Our problems had begun that fall, when I interviewed some of the school's new black students for an article in *The Yazooan*. They were the first voluntary pioneers of integration, before it became mandatory in 1970. Their dignity and desire to learn, despite being under constant surveillance, had gained my respect. Debbie Nicholas and I even went so far one day as to admit to each other that some of the colored students were "just like us," and that Pamela Harrison, who was the daughter of the black dentist, dressed better than we did. We marveled at these realizations.

In 1969, Yazoo City was beginning to bend toward the end of racial segregation, hoping not to break. There was fear, a certain sense of both races walking a fine line. And there were resentments that couldn't be spoken within hearing of federal lawyers, or the media, who would soon be picking the bones of my old town for signs of trouble.

I had submitted the interview to Coach Rush, the principal, for approval, like every story we published. So far, he'd never questioned anything, so I wasn't worried. But that same afternoon, Mr. Richardson—who was also assistant principal—came to fetch me from my fifth-period English class. When I joined him in the hall outside the classroom, he glowered at me, a cold, hard, come-to-Jesus look.

"What's going on?" I asked. But he just hunched his shoulders and silently marched down the hall, fists clenched in the spacious pockets of his worn khakis. I fell in a few paces behind, following him to the principal's office, my face burning with embarrassment. I, the teachers' pet, had somehow made a mess, and he had the air of a man who knew the best use of a newspaper.

In Coach Rush's office I found the paper's faculty adviser, JoAnne Prichard, waiting for us. Mr. Richardson came in, then closed the door. Mrs. Prichard sat facing Coach Rush, her classic profile outlined by the bright light from the window. Her mouth was set and her brown eyes seemed even darker than usual. When I sat down next to her, she and I exchanged a look. I saw consternation and defeat in her eyes.

Coach Rush began to tell me that the interview was too controversial. "This is the sort of thing that could get people riled up. We've got to keep our heads down."

Mr. Richardson said, "Why would a white girl *want* to interview a colored boy? What do you see in this boy?"

I was embarrassed, and felt I had been caught red-handed, because I had indeed found something appealing about that student. Then I became angry for being made to feel guilty. I had been impressed with his wonderful intellect and love of books, which was what I had said in the article. Perhaps Mr. Richardson equated respect and admiration with sexual attraction. Or maybe he couldn't accept anything complimentary that was said about a black boy. It was the same bigotry I had lived with and witnessed all my life, yet this was the first time its sharp edge had cut me. I said, "He's a smart person. It doesn't matter if he's black."

" 'It doesn't matter,' " Mr. Richardson parroted, making my words sound ludicrous. "Well, it matters a lot to some who be your betters."

"Now, George," Coach Rush said. "I'm sure Ruth's going to cooperate with us." His hands were trembling.

Mrs. Prichard spoke up. "Why don't *you* edit the interview, Coach Rush? Then we'll either use the article like you want it or leave it out."

Relieved, Coach Rush smiled and said, "Well, what a fine idea. That's what we'll do." Mrs. Prichard and I left quickly, before the cease-fire could be broken, and Mr. Richardson sat by the door as we went, his face a mask, hands resting on his knees. His eyes followed me as I hurried past him.

When the edited article came back to us, my glowing compliments for the black students were gone, as were all my editorial remarks about integration and all references to skin color. It was essentially as though I had interviewed white students about their hobbies and what they wanted to be when they grew up. "Well," Mrs. Prichard said, "in a way that's a victory. They're being treated just like any other students." We ran the article as he had edited it.

But I persisted in trying to do an end run around the line that had been drawn between myself and the administration. Graduation was only a few months off, and I was already enrolled in the honors program of a fine Virginia women's college, Mary Baldwin. I didn't think anyone could hurt me.

But later, when Coach Rush became ill, I found myself in constant conflict with Mr. Richardson, who relentlessly inserted his malevolent red pencil into most of my editorials. Another one of my teachers, Mrs. Clark, became his staunchest ally. The next year she took over *The Yazooan* from Mrs. Prichard and destroyed decades of back editions, including those I had worked on. She was trying, I was told, to rid the school of a bad influence.

Mr. Richardson's most potent weapon was humiliation. In January he made me stand by a window in front of the class to watch as a batch of opinion polls I had circulated was burned outside on the lawn. While my classmates whispered and tittered behind me, I stared into the schoolyard below. Bundles of mimeographed paper were being dropped into a rusty oil drum. Flames jumped up to greet each new batch and the janitor occasionally stirred them with a broom handle. I blinked hard, holding back bitter tears before they ran down my face.

Then Mr. Richardson left the room, and I defiantly went back to my chair. As the other students looked at me nervously and watched the door for his return, I sat reading a novel, determined to defy him in this small way at least. I didn't realize he was about to make my humiliation complete.

The school's PA system crackled on. "Any student who still has a copy of Ruth Tuttle's unauthorized poll should hand it to a teacher before the end of this period. Teachers are instructed to deliver these polls to the side lot, where they are being burned," Mr. Richardson said.

To my knowledge, he succeeded in destroying every copy of the poll, but I remember these eight questions from it: 'Do you believe in God? Have you ever used marijuana? Are you still a virgin? Have you ever used LSD? Do you drink alcohol? Do you smoke cigarettes? Have you ever heard of Vietnam? Do you support integration?'

That night at dinner my father gave me a long, dark look. "We need to talk," he said. I just nodded. The rest of the family ate quickly and left us alone with a tableful of dirty dishes. "Why didn't you tell me about this poll?" he asked, leaning forward.

It was an unexpected question, assuming as it did that we were regular confidants. The reality was that I never told him anything. My external life was a carefully controlled structure of independence. I never asked for advice or guidance. I never shared my feelings. I went to church every time the doors opened. I read my Bible. I sought refuge in the one thing I knew he stayed clear of: religion. Through its protection, I enjoyed a precious solitude filled with teeming secret thoughts of boys and insolent plans for the future.

When he drank, which was almost nightly, his charming and sociable nature became intrusive. It often embarrassed me. He might walk into my bedroom without knocking, or stand behind me when I was practicing the piano and say, "Play me a love song." I had his collection of 1940s sheet music, and as I stumbled through "Ebb Tide"—the only one I knew passably well—he'd sing the lyrics. Daddy had a gorgeous tenor voice, and when he sang, a yearning emotional quality came through. At those times, I felt his desperate loneliness, the kind that is bred in childhood by violence and poverty. That may explain why I remember those duets as fearful, throat-constricting forays into danger. I was terrified of being lost in Daddy's dark memories.

He seemed to be battling some vicious, internal monster. His weapons were his warm heart, keen intelligence and love of fun, but sometimes they weren't enough. Then he gave the monster a sacrifice of pain from one of his children, pain inflicted with an open palm or shaming words.

As a child, I had tried to console him, telling him to pray to God if he wanted to be happy, but as I got older, I feared there was a gaping spiritual wound through which all of his goodness would eventually slip away.

When he asked about the poll, I was afraid. "I guess I forgot to mention it," I said lamely.

"Tell me about it now." He lit a cigarette and waited. A long ash was hanging off the end of it before I started talking.

"It was just a story idea for *The Yazooan*. No big deal." I swung my long hair over my shoulder and looked away, but he took my chin and forced me to look at him.

"Why did you do it?"

I saw he wasn't going to relent, and flight was out of the question, so I told him about how things were changing in Yazoo City—drugs, alcohol, cigarettes, Vietnam, integration—and how I had wanted to document it. I used cold, scientific terms to keep him from suspecting that I was interested in experiencing some of these things.

"What about the sex question? Wasn't there a sex question?" he asked.

"Yessir."

"What was it?"

I sat silent.

"There's nothing a father and daughter can't talk about," he said, leaning closer.

"I'll have to pray about it first," I whispered, staring at my hands. That, finally, made him mad.

"You do that. You pray about it," he yelled. "Then when God tells you what He thinks, you tell me. In the meantime, we're gonna keep having these talks until I get a little respect in my own home."

"Am I going to be expelled from school?" I asked. I felt braver, because I had moved him to familiar territory.

"Mr. Richardson agreed to let me handle this," he replied. Then, pointing his finger at me, he said, "No more of these polls, or articles, unless I read them first."

After that I felt trapped by my father's ultimatum and persecuted by Mr. Richardson. The strange letter that arrived a few weeks later gave me a perfect, and secret, way to escape both of them.

When I picked it up after physics class, the plain bond envelope appeared innocuous at first, but then I saw the New York postmark and my heart raced. I slit it open with the school secretary's letter opener and peeked inside at the greeting. "Dear whitey, honky, WASP, bitch." What could it mean? Carefully, feigning boredom, I handed the letter opener back to the curious secretary, put the envelope into my purse and walked quickly away from the principal's office.

Students flowed around me on both sides as I plowed through the hallway to the gym. It was empty, and I climbed to the top row of bleachers to make sure no one could interrupt me. The smell of sweaty gym clothes hung in the air, so I held my nose as I read.

The letter was a single sheet of notebook paper, covered on two sides with an assortment of messages in different handwriting. Cuss words caught my eye. Profanities and unfamiliar terms like "WASP" and "Jew Commie" gave me a sense of unreality. But there were backhanded compliments, too: Someone named Jeff called me a "nymph" and a "Southern belle." *This guy Jeff seems interested in more than my editorial policy,* I thought. The signatures at the end—"Groin," "Vinny," "Bennett Cohen," "Feldo," "Suzy Q," "Judy Vecchione," and of course "Jeff Durstewitz"— were like a choir of sirens singing an irresistible song of emancipation to me. Who were these people with the strange names? Why had they singled me out? My trusting child's heart immediately opened to the possibility of divine intervention. There had to be a reason behind this, something I couldn't know.

That night I wondered over the origins of the slanders they had written against me, their unknown victim. They had accused me of bigotry, conceit and racism, and even hinted that I was a murderer through my assumed complicity in Ku Klux Klan lynchings. And I was puzzled by questions about Mike Bagwell and me "making out." When had I ever been associated with Mike Bagwell? He the football hero, Mr. YHS, and I the brainy wallflower? I pored over the various scribblings and began to sort them out.

I showed the letter to only one person, Alice DeCell, the assistant editor of *The Yazooan*. She advised me to turn it in to Coach Rush when he returned, and strongly urged me to tell my parents so they could take steps to defend me. She was unyielding in her vilification of the dastardly Yankees who had written it. But I was impatient with her conservatism and respect for authority. *Why not write back?* I asked myself. *What harm could it do?* And there was also this: I was attracted to the danger of it. As I reread the letter, I found myself drawn again and again to the section by Jeff. He wrote passionately. Whether his ardor extended beyond offensive social commentary I didn't know, but I intended to find out.

A fantasy was born. How many dateless Saturdays—they were all that way for me then—could I spend in romantic contemplation of a secret beau? Maybe we would never meet, but I could fill lonely hours with imaginings of what it would be like if we did. The letter I wrote to Jeff was suffused with desperate hope, carefully camouflaged in outrage. I rewrote it several times, trying to leaven reprimand with coquettishness. Then I mailed it.

3. Jeff

mail and femail

The letter that arrived in Merrick a few days later was addressed to me in a measured, graceful hand. I found it among the items in my *Hoofbeats* mailbox. When I saw the return address, I bounded up to the newspaper office on the second floor, taking two and three steps at a time, and locked the door behind me. So she'd chosen to respond to me, and not to Mr. Jordan. What a relief! I tore the letter open.

February 27, 1969

Dear Jeff,

I'm writing to thank you and your friends for your concern over the condition of my ego. However, I'm quite capable of coping with it myself and I could care less whether or not you approve. If you're really concerned about my welfare, I have plenty of other things you can help with. Anyway, let's get the facts straight. The Sr. Pics are chosen by **The Yazooan**'s *sponsor and other qualified persons. I have nothing to do with it and unfortunately, Sr. Pics isn't exactly a huge honor. It's not like winning the Miss America contest. So you see, you wasted ink, paper, stamp and time on a useless cause.*

You called yourself "self-righteous." As much as it hurts, I have to agree. Letters like the one I received are the product of small minds—if you'll excuse a trite phrase—and it hurts me to find that such minds exist within my generation.

I didn't mind reading about my lack of modesty, or about how intellectually superior you and your friends are, but the sickening part was all of your choice adjectives. I don't know what God and people mean to you, but they both mean very much to me. Using a vocabulary like you did was offensive— to put it mildly. You seem to have little consideration for either people or God. Well, you look after your own life.

At first I was angry and bewildered. Why would nine or ten people want to send something like that to a person

*they've never met, seen or spoken to? Well, why would I
write back? Don't know, but we're so obviously different, it's
interesting.*

*Jeff, have you noticed that your capital letters are rather
elaborate? That's a sign of an intricate personality and the
desire to assert yourself.*

Since everyone seemed so curious—I **don't** *think New
Yorkers are Jew Commies (whatever that is) and I don't know
if Mike Bagwell can make out well or not. How about you?
And how about the rest of your friends?*

*Well, I hope to hear from Merrick, New York, soon. This is
the end of my letter. If I never hear from you again—it's been
nice knowing you. If I should be so lucky as to get another
jewel in the mail—great!*

> *With Love,*
> *Ruth Tuttle*

I'll never forget how hard Ruth's reply hit me. I read it countless times during the next few days, marveling again and again at its graceful cadences,
its masterly phrasing, its humanity and maturity—all qualities that had
been missing from my letter. One phrase in particular stood out: ". . . it
hurts me to find that such minds exist within my generation." What a great
line! She'd made me feel like a worm, and I knew that anyone with that
kind of skill was worth cultivating.

And there was something else, something delectably coy in the transition on the second page, the part that said, ". . . we're so obviously different, it's interesting." And then she'd gone on to find something alluring in
my capital letters. It was inescapable: She was one hell of a smart, good-
looking babe, and she wanted to get to know me better. Hot damn!

I felt like a jerk for sending her such rubbish and wanted to make
amends. But more than that, I wanted to overcome a bad beginning and
get something going with this intelligent girl I'd miraculously stumbled
upon. After several days, I sent my carefully considered reply.

March 3, 1969

My dear (if I may take the liberty) Ruth,

I don't know exactly what to say at this point.

*I suppose I should elaborate on the conditions which pro-
duced the first opus. My friends and I congregate in the* **Hoofbeats** *room during eighth period to fool around. One day, one
of my managing editors, who signed himself "hirsutely" since
he wears a beard, was reading through your paper when he*

noticed your "Senior Pics" article. I pointed out the fact that you, one of the subjects, were also the editor in chief of the newspaper. We decided to write you a letter deploring your conceit. I know it was an immature thing to do, but you must understand that I wasn't responsible for anything that was not on the first side. I realize a few of us went a trifle "hairy."

Your letter gave me quite an insight into your character. I think that if you had seen the glee and fiendish pleasure that each of us took in adding his or her own two cents, you might have enjoyed it. I mean, selection system notwithstanding, I could not conceive of any editor having himself as the subject for an article like that. We were doing our best to be offensive, with the possible exception of myself. I really didn't intend to insult you; it was more of a questioning.

This explanation over, allow me to apologize. We saw "Yazoo City, Mississippi" and stereotyped you immediately as some sort of prototype Southern belle–racist–white Anglo-Saxon Protestant, which I realize was completely unfair. The reason I'm apologizing is mainly because I sent it. I suppose the others would feel the same way, if I had let them read your letter.

It was a case of mass frustrations being taken out on an innocent individual. We're all pretty concerned about things like racism and the college disorders, and you were a natural target. Again, please accept my apologies.

I don't know how you might take this (possibly as an insult), but your letter makes me feel that I like you. I wasn't expecting a sincere, intelligent, and very sensitive person to write back at all.

Incidentally, that part about "Jew Commies" was written by an extremely bitchy Irish Catholic. . . . I honestly think she was jealous of you. The term comes from our ideas as to what your initial reaction would be—something like "Oh those lousy, despicable Jew Commie bastards!" I guess it just seemed like a funny thing to say. Actually, it's kind of amusing since I'm pretty much a WASP myself. I was brought up as an Episcopalian, which brings me to a point in your letter—I'm sorry if my use of the word "goddamn" offended you, but to some extent, your inferences as to my godlessness are entirely correct, especially if you substitute "religion" for "God." I have utter contempt for organized religion and most priests, pastors, ministers, rabbis, or whatever. I think religion (organized) and its proponents are among the biggest drags and contre-temps that society has ever encountered. I stopped going to church when I was around fourteen, and have since then been very heavily influenced by Buddhist and secular philosophical thought, but I do believe in God, although my abstraction is probably very unlike your abstraction.

I have so much to say to you, but it looks as if I've already provided quite enough for any further study of my handwriting. I don't know much about it, but offhand I would say your handwriting is very beautiful.

I know I've been a trifle verbose, but your letter really turned me on.

I would like to know how you feel about things in general—also, I would like to be forgiven for my poor taste in sending you the first letter. And please don't be offended by my usage of certain terms. It's not meant to shock, insult or impress you—it's just the way I speak.

This may sound a bit strange (then again, I don't suppose I've done anything normal concerning you so far) but I'd really like to have a picture of you. Also, your phone number.

Please write as soon as possible, Ruth—I'm really interested in what you have to say or think—maybe it would do us both some good. And try to forgive and forget my sins of the past. . . .

> Yours (with much sincere respect, and,
> if I may take the liberty, affection),
> Jeff Durstewitz

March 6, 1969

Dear Jeff,

Well, here we are attempting at least a small reconciliation of North and South, Yankee and Rebel. It seems like we're succeeding. Anyway, I'm ready to try if you are. I'm fixing to tell you something typical. My mother is an ardent Southerner—to her New York State is the same thing as a Communist concentration camp—and she got upset over the "New York" in the return address on your letter. Now she keeps asking me if I don't have "something to tell her."

I was pleasantly surprised to find that there is a boy who writes interesting letters. Congratulations! You are one of few.

I gathered that you are concerned over the plight of

negroes, so maybe you'll be interested to hear about the negroes in Yazoo City. In my high school of 700, we now have 35
negroes and two negro teachers. About once a week, a negro
and a white have a fight in the hall, usually caused by the
same troublemakers. (Personally, I like some of the black students better than I do most of the white ones. Still, I'm a
product of my environment and I doubt that I'll ever reach
the point where I can ask a negro over to my house, or even
become close friends.)

I guess my attitude is more liberal than most of my
friends'. I really believe that negroes get the short end of the
deal and that they deserve a better chance, but when the
black cook who has been in my family for seventy years (since
she was born) persists in calling me "Little Miss Ruth" and
takes all my old clothes home to her grandchildren, it becomes difficult to get on the same level with a black. I feel
rather like a feudal lord must have felt.

Did you know that negroes like Kay call the negroes who
go to Chicago or who advocate Black Studies—niggers? The
term didn't originate with Southern whites, but with Southern
negroes who felt themselves superior to others of their race.

When I read your letter, I didn't get emotional until I
reached the "religion section." You see, what I've found with
God is by far the most important part of my life—it **is** my life.
I really make contact with God. My "abstraction" is **not** an
abstraction but a real spirit. He's constantly showing me new
things so I always have plenty to say about Him. For instance,
the newest thing in my life is you. I bet you hadn't thought
that God was using you to make me clarify my own thoughts.
Your letter is already making me examine my own feelings
about a lot of things. It's a new experience writing to someone
so completely different from me—or maybe I should say
someone with a completely different background.

I do want to say this: I like you, too.

I'm enclosing two pictures. Neither one looks like what I
think I look like, so see if you can find the happy medium.
I'd like to have a picture of you, too. Where are you going to
college? I'm going to Mary Baldwin in Staunton, Virginia. I
can't wait to leave the closed society of Yazoo City. This town
is stifling.

Sunday, March 9, 1969

Dear Ruth,

As soon as I got home from work I found your letter and read it. You stimulated my mind so much, it was really wild. Now it's 2:45 A.M., after a 10-hour workday and a night of fast dancing and blasting around, and I have to write to you, now.

Ruth, you're so beautiful. I showed your picture to some of the people who wrote you the first time and they were pretty impressed.

I think I'll have to begin with your religion section. I sincerely wish you had gone into more detail about your relationship with what you call "God." It intrigued me quite a bit. It seems that you have established some sort of one-to-one relationship with Him. I don't understand. I think of God as a primal, omnipotent, omniscient, omnipresent spirit, or embodiment of all nature—in other words, a genius or prime mover behind everything, sort of the life force of the universe. As you may have guessed, I don't have a picture of God in my mind. I think that anyone who envisions God is, in fact, limiting Him to the sphere and scope of human imagination. And what is "human" except "higher animal"? In other words, anyone who "sees" God is actually putting him within the scope (albeit the zenith of the scope) of the intelligence and imagination of an animal. I can't accept that.

Please don't get the idea that I'm trying to destroy or undercut your beliefs by saying these things. It's just the way I feel, but I wish you would tell me more about it.

And tell me more about yourself: How do you dress? What kind of music do you dig? Are you short or tall? How do you usually wear your hair?

I'm about 5'8" tall, with a slight build. I weigh around 125, although I'm kind of "wiry" from doing stock work in a delicatessen a few years ago (nothin' like stock work to build a man up!). I have blondish hair, with very blue eyes and kind of bushy eyebrows, though not too much so . . . long thin sideburns and longish hair. I guess my features are fairly English looking, though strongly tempered by my German and Irish parents. I can't send you a picture of myself because I don't have one that's less than two or three years old.

I dig most of the new sound in rock, except pop rock (like Gary Puckett) and infant rock (like the 1910 Fruitgum Company). My favorite groups are the Lovin' Spoonful, Bee Gees, and Jefferson Airplane, though not necessarily in that order. Musically speaking, I've played drums and sung in a few rock bands and I'm also a member of the Calhoun High School Choir, which is one of the 10 best H.S. choirs on the Eastern Seaboard. I think school and the marking system in particular are irrelevant to most of life. Maybe that's why I don't dig school too much.

This letter-writing business is so frustrating. I wish I could see you. The thing about seeing you, though, is that I'll probably become turned on physically, which I gather you would feel uncomfortable about? You didn't mention how you feel about sex at all, and I would really like to discuss it. I think there is almost as much misunderstanding and deceit (not to mention honest ignorance) around the topic of sex as there is in religion.

You know, in reference to your "negro" section—you really can't expect Kay to say anything else about the blacks who want to break out. She is, if you'll pardon the expression, like a housebroken pet. I wouldn't expect her to say anything else any more than I expect my dog to urinate on the floor. But what would you do if my name was Jeff Smith, and I informed you in this letter that I am actually a black man? How would that affect you? If you can honestly say that it wouldn't change things, then you are not prejudiced. If not, then you have a job to do.

March 12, 1969

Dear Jeff,

Let's make a promise that if we ever offend each other, we won't stop writing and we'll discuss it.

Your last letter upset me, kind of. I know that boys are supposed to always have sex on the brain, but I was still shocked when you brought it up. What I mean is no one talks about it here—not boys and girls anyway. My mother would kill me if she knew we were talking about it. She'd say I'm leading you on.

But you did get me thinking, so here's my Tuttle Manifesto on Sex:

I like sex, especially kissing and hugging. Sometimes I think I like it too much and I'll get "in trouble" some day because I'll lose my head and go all the way. What I really want is to fall in love and get married before I do that. But I'm not

*a prude, I promise!!! I do think it's important for the boy and
girl to get to know each other first, and I don't like being
pressured. I guess the most important thing, though, is that
the person I fall in love with will have to love God more than
he loves me.*

March 15, 1969

Dear Ruth,

Good God!!! *Your letters turn me on so much. This is so
frustrating! All I can do is look at your picture and wish that
we were alone someplace together. It's really wild, how I feel
about you. Very hard to put into words. But with each letter,
I'm getting to know you that much better, and I'm getting
more and more convinced that I'm going to* **have** *to meet you
one day. Maybe I can go down there over the Easter Vacation.
The only thing is, you'd have to promise me all your spare
time—that's quite a trip.*

*Ruthie, you surprise me every time you write! And so far,
it's been nothing but pleasant surprises. Your "Tuttle Manifesto on Sex" was quite enlightening. I had you pictured in my
mind as some sort of a nun in your private little religion. It's
kind of a relief to find out you're normal. I think my own atti-
tudes on sex are fairly normal. I don't think there's* **anything**
*wrong with any kind or type of sex; unless, of course, it's
forced. The only "sin," in my book, is when someone is hurt
by it. For instance, to have an illegitimate child, I think, is
wrong because it invariably hurts the child and usually hurts
the mother as well. But as long as there is agreement in performing any sex act, and no one is hurt because of it, I don't
think anything "wrong" is involved. That includes pre-
married. For instance, if a girl and myself agree that we
would like to copulate (and I would make sure that she had
no sex hang-ups before doing anything) I think that we are
mature enough in our minds and bodies to know what we are
doing. I personally don't think marriage should have too
much to do with it.*

*I think the whole idea of virginity at marriage is kind of
ridiculous. I'm not a virgin, so how can I expect my wife to be
one? And furthermore, there is no possible way she can* **prove**
*if I am a virgin or not—so how the hell can I expect to look
for her "proof" on the first night? I think it's pretty stupid.
(Not to mention unfair.)*

If I ever do get to see you, Ruth, I'm almost positive I'll want to have sex with you (especially if you're as sexy as you look). But at least neither of us can say we don't know each other well enough!

O.K. That's enough on sex.

By the way, I was going to ask you the same thing. If I ever offend you, please don't stop writing, just tell me why.

I don't think you're digging what I said about God, Ruth. I still can't believe in a personal God. I see God as an impersonal manifestation of the universe. Jesus, along with Lord Buddha and Mohammed, I regard as sort of an angel put here as an example of how men should act. I believe in evolution and natural selection and feel very strong'y about reincarnation. I don't understand what you mean about the person you fall in love with having to love God more than you. But I can truly say I love nature—which I think is the physical embodiment of God's spirit. How would you feel about that?

*Now let's get the dates straight—**exactly** when is your Easter Vacation?*

Well, write back soon, doll—and try to think of me as much as I do of you.

4. Ruth

swept away

I walked home from school for our midday dinner every day, always hoping a letter from Jeff would be lying under the flower arrangement on the dining room table. When it was, which was often, I would run upstairs to read it in my room, safely removed from prying eyes. I still associate the smell of fried chicken with the feel of a fat envelope from Merrick, dripping with forbidden revelations, hinted-at sexual liaisons and adolescent hubris. But while I had readily succumbed to the romance of the situation, the boy who now occupied all my fantasies was an enigma.

March 26, 1969

Dear Jeff,

I just can't grasp the things you say and I can't believe you're really saying them. I mean, I know what I feel, and to me God is the center of the universe. The way you talk about God . . . it tears me up to realize that God just isn't important or real to you. I find I've reached the point where I care about you. You've become an important person to me and I want you to have everything beautiful in your life. Don't you feel deprived of something? Or do you even understand what I mean? I think I'd marry a negro, or go on a march for negro rights if you'd just comprehend—no, I mean feel—what I'm saying.

We are badly in need of talking instead of just writing.

You said something about me thinking of you. Well, I can't think about you any more than I already do. Think, talk and write about you. If we don't get together sometime soon, we might be able to travel on thought waves.

We don't have an Easter vacation. (I think Good Friday is a Catholic thing.) Yours is next week? I can't believe it's so soon. I'll just take off from school. Please come. You don't even have to inform me of the exact day you'll get here. Just send a note that says, "I'm coming," and I'll be looking for you.

When *(I won't say if)* you get here, I'm taking you out to
my farm and putting you on a horse. Then we can round up
cows and scare the chickens the negroes keep. Maybe we can
even go slumming and talk to the pickaninnies—little black
children—if they act friendly. Sometimes the negroes are
pretty hostile. They walk right over you when you pass them
on the sidewalk. Sometimes they stand in the middle of the
street and dare you to run over them and shout obscenities at
passing cars. Well, you'll see when you get here.

I hope we'll see each other soon, but I realize that there
are quite a few miles between here and New York—darn it! Be
careful if you come.

My life became centered on reading Jeff's letters and writing my replies. I
poured every ounce of my girlhood strength into forging an unbreakable
emotional link with Jeff through our letters. But I never actually believed
my Northern knight could rescue me in a more tangible way by materializ-
ing in the flesh, which may be why I wasn't quick to shatter the newfound
calm of my life by asking for permission for his visit. As I came to find out,
however, nothing could stop the seventeen-year-old Jeff Durstewitz. He
had marshaled a small but impressive troop of fellow campaigners and was
set to proceed, like Sherman, into the heart of the Southland. I was weak
with anticipation.

March 27, 1969

Dear Ruth,

*I'm writing this early Thursday morning before school, so
I don't have time to say anything but the essentials. I'll call
Saturday night, probably around 11:00. My friends and I plan
to leave Sunday morning. We should get there by Tuesday
evening. If they don't take me all the way, which I'm pretty
sure they will, I'll call you from wherever I am. My friends
would also like to be able, if possible, to use your shower and
bathroom-type facilities on Tuesday. I'll speak to you more
about it Saturday night, but it's sort of one of the conditions
of my getting down there. So anyway, I'll speak to you then.
Please be home!*

Thinking of you—

I tried to get permission for Jeff's visit from my mother. She knew, as I did,
that my father would have the last word, but I had been hoping to at least
get her moral support before I asked him. She listened to me in silence,

making a few negative clucking sounds when I said, "Jeff's the first boy who's ever understood me. I feel like I've known him all my life."

"What does his father do for a living?" she asked.

"Um, something with boats," I said lamely, not having a clue about what a merchant seaman did. "He's gone most of the time."

"I think you're being very foolish," she said, "to get your hopes up about this boy. I'm afraid he's going to be a big disappointment. You may think you'll like a Yankee boy with radical ideas, but he'll just embarrass you in front of your friends. You're forgetting who you are."

I gave up on her. If Daddy said yes, she would go along and be a charming Southern hostess, no matter how unconventional she found the situation. I approached him after lunch. He was in one of his disarmingly pleasant moods, and I knew from experience that I had caught him at a good time.

"This is important to me, Daddy," I said. "Jeff's different from the boys around here. He's really, really smart."

"Too smart, if you ask me," he said, his demeanor suddenly darkening.

"I thought you would understand," I wailed.

"I understand you've waited until the boy's already on the road," he yelled, making the ice cubes in his glass tinkle. "What am I supposed to do, say, 'Go home' after he's driven all that way? Why am I always the one who has to impose discipline in this family?"

"But, Daddy," I said, "don't you want to meet someone different? Haven't you ever met anyone from New York?"

"Of course I've met people from New York," he said quickly. I had offended his gregarious nature. "I know they're not monsters."

"Well, then . . ."

"I get your point," he said as he flapped his hand in the air to hush me up. "But you're not missing any school because of this Jeff."

"I'll take them with me," I said quickly.

"Them?" he asked. But I knew I had won and I gave him a rare, heartfelt hug of appreciation before I broke the news about our other two guests.

5. *Jeff*

whalin' with rocco

Jerry Greenfield, Dave Feldman and I were more or less asleep when we shoved off from Feldo's house that crystal morning in late March. I had closed the deli the night before, and Feldo had been busy till late with last-minute checks on his car. Jerry said little as we prepared to leave. Perhaps he suspected that we'd cozened him—which, in fact, we had.

He'd been quite firm about not wanting to go into the Deep South—Tennessee was far enough, and he wasn't even sure about that. Mississippi was definitely out. Hadn't those Jewish boys and a black guy been killed there a few years before? Jerry had no desire to risk his life in the pursuit of some romantic fantasy of mine. In order to get him to sign on, Feldo and I had ostensibly agreed that they would drive me only as far as the Mississippi border, after which they'd do some camping in the Great Smokies on the way back to Merrick. I would make my way to Yazoo by bus, then fly home from Jackson.

But Feldo and I planned to drive all the way to Yazoo and take Jerry with us. We knew it was for his own good—just another part of the loosening up that Jerry, a straight-A type, so clearly needed. Besides, what danger could possibly befall us? We had a bona fide invitation from a genuine Southerner, and it wasn't as if we were planning to lay siege to Jackson. Feldo and I had decided a few nights before, while discussing our Jerry problem, that we'd break the facts to him when we were well beyond range of his being able to back out.

Feldo's car, a 1963 Beetle, was one of the more venerable units in the Feldman family Volkswagen fleet. Feldo had tried to soup up the engine with a Judson supercharger, but it hadn't panned out. The supercharger had made the old Bug step lively—relatively speaking—and sound like a 'Vette. It had even caused unsuspecting pump monkeys at gas stations to crane their necks looking for the killer machine. But ultimately it had only one significant effect—cutting Feldo's gas mileage. He'd removed it a month or two before.

Still, we had a lot of fun with the supercharged Devilbug; we'd pull up next to muscle cars and roar the Bug a bit, as if we actually had something under the hood. Then, when the light changed, they'd screech off and leave clouds of rubber on the mistaken assumption that we were after them. Typically we'd be in a right lane, and we'd turn and putter on our merry way as the victims made fools of themselves. In case these tactics offended the wrong motorhead, we carried a heavy club in the Devilbug— the Whalin' Stick.

But something told us we'd have to tone down our act if we were going to take it to Yazoo City. So Feldo had reluctantly peeled off the yellow vinyl polka dots he'd applied to the Beetle's red shell. You could still see where they'd been, though, because they'd left darker spots on the paint. We debated at length whether the yellow plastic flowers attached to the antenna should come down, but decided not to touch them. Flowers were, after all, our generational insignia. We even debated removing the Bug's yellow longitudinal racing stripes, but Feldo drew the line at that. "I'd have to redo the paint job, Durst," he said, "and I ain't got the bread."

Feldo picked me up the morning of the big day, the two of us bleary but excited as we loaded my stuff into the Bug's tiny front boot. Then we drove over to Jerry's to collect him and his bag, and returned to Feldo's to stuff his camping gear into the remaining space in the back and get a jug of coffee from his mother. Our parents hadn't forbidden the trip, I think, because we had the invitation (they didn't know, as I didn't, that it was only from Ruth, not from her parents), and because there were three of us. Actually, it was more like three and a half, since Feldo was a very mannish boy. With his piercing eyes, bulging biceps and extraordinary wit and charm, he could either pulverize an adversary or mesmerize him, depending on his mood. Having him on board made the whole venture seem more plausible.

We got staccato last-minute instructions from Feldo's father and words of encouragement from his mother, whose blue eyes glistened as she waved good-bye. Then, in high spirits, we were off, the overladen Bug laboring to keep up with the sparse but fleet traffic. In about an hour we crossed the Verrazano-Narrows Bridge to Staten Island. To our right loomed New York, city of cities, sparkling and coldly enticing in the morning light. But we had set our sights south, toward its tiny antithesis, Yazoo City.

Five or so hours later we were at the start of Skyline Drive, and it may have been there in Virginia, amid the hairpin turns and breathtaking scenery of the Blue Ridge, that we let Jerry have the shocking truth about our destination. He didn't carry on a lot, although he did shake his head over and over again, muttering, "I can't *believe* you guys! I just can't *believe* it." We may have felt a twinge or two of guilt, but it would have been against our code to apologize.

Instead we broke into a chorus of our theme song: "Whalin' with Rocco." Rocco was a minor mafioso I worked with at the deli. A muscular, retired thumb twister, he had a wife with the face of a Sicilian gargoyle.

But she was, he always insisted with a lewd twinkle in his eye, "built like a brick shithouse." Rocco loved to sit us down and tell us about his macho exploits ("and then I nailed the dirty rat bastard—baBOOM!") along with the true facts of life. So now, in his honor, we sang (to the tune of "Waltzing Matilda"):

> *Whalin' with Rocco, whalin' with Rocco, we'll go a whalin', o Rocco,*
> *   with you.*
> *As we whaled and we whaled, and we kicked the shit out of*
> *   everyone—*
> *We'll go a whalin', o Rocco, with you!*

We turned to see if Jerry was singing along, but he'd fallen asleep. Feldo said: "Guess he's not gonna try to jump out of the car, huh, Durst?" I agreed, and we sang another chorus. Feldo particularly liked the chorus, because he got to narrate: "Now, kids—let me tell you a thing or two about this man named Rocco . . ." while I crooned the refrain softly in the background. When he ran out of "bu'shit," as we called it, I'd narrate and he'd croon.

We drove farther and farther down the spine of the Appalachians, careening through high passes where Yankee and Rebel armies had chased each other a century before, although we were oblivious to any history but our own.

Feldo banged the outside of the door with his huge left paw as he drove, keeping time to our singing or the radio. Jerry spent most of the day either asleep or in deep denial in the backseat, but he did lighten up once or twice for a singalong. His main fear, as we got deeper into the South, seemed to be that we'd be found out for Northern agitators and set upon by hooded Klansmen. Feldo and I scorned and scoffed, but we couldn't talk Jerry out of his funk.

By the time we stopped at a motel outside Knoxville for the night, he was having a full-blown crisis and didn't want to get out of the car. Feldo and I swung into action: Informing him that we were in fact Israeli commandos, we leaped out of the Bug with imaginary Uzis blazing, clearing a wide swath of Klansmen from the car to our room. "Out of the car!" I barked to Jerry, who was smiling in spite of himself. "Quick, Herr Groinberger, we can't hold them off forever," added Feldo.

Crouching and firing, we backed in behind Jerry, who by this time had found a spare Uzi and was laying into the Klansmen himself. Wave after wave they attacked, poor fools, as we gleefully mowed them down, occasionally lobbing a grenade out the front door or spraying fire from the bathroom window. The fight lasted only minutes, but by its end Jerry was laughing.

After we ate I called Ruth, and I told her we were psyched to be about halfway there (or so we thought), and that she could expect us after dinner the following night.

We had breakfast early the next morning in the motel restaurant, but afterward, as we loaded the car and prepared to plunge into the Deep South, Jerry's misgivings returned. He looked grave as we asked directions of the motel's affable proprietor, Juan Fugate, but his expression lightened when Juan revealed that he was a Sephardic Jew. Jerry couldn't believe it; here we were in Tennessee, yet we'd been sleeping under the roof of a landsman all along! We asked Juan if he'd had any trouble with the local Klan, and he laughed. "No trouble, boys. They're not so bad once you get to know them."

"Get to *know* them?" Jerry was incredulous.

"Sure," Juan laughed again. "I cater their annual dinners."

No matter what we encountered in the South, Jerry was prepared for it now.

6. Ruth

lady-in-waiting

Where was Jeff? It was April Fools' Day, and as the day stretched on I grew afraid that I was going to be the fool. Alternating between hope and devastation, I spent the late afternoon staring out my bedroom window, watching for him. Then, about seven, the phone rang.

It was Jeff. Our conversation was matter-of-fact on his part and breathlessly whispered on mine. He said he was calling from Birmingham and they wouldn't arrive until ten. I begged him to drive faster. I knew that ten was a completely unacceptable arrival time—on a school night, with four students in the house—I had two sisters and a brother—plus a father who rose at five every morning to head for the country and his cows. "Can't you get here sooner?"

"We'll be together soon enough," Jeff consoled me. "Don't worry about that."

My hands were trembling and my heart racing when I hung up the phone. "We'll be together," he had said. Jeff was really coming. It was the first time I believed it.

"Was that the boy?" my father asked. Like a giant shadow, he had suddenly appeared behind me.

"Yeah."

"Yes sir, young lady."

"Yes *sir*, that was Jeff." I tried to look nonchalant. "They'll be here soon."

"Well, I hope you don't think your mother and I are going to go to bed and leave you up waiting for them," he said—the very thing I *was* hoping for.

"I'll be upstairs—*studying*," I said disdainfully.

"Good idea. And when the boys get here," he went on, pointing his finger at me and giving me a meaningful look, "you let me handle things."

Momma followed me upstairs. "I hope you understand," she said, "that we expect you to be a perfect lady with these boys. It's up to you to set the standards. If you let them know, once and for all, that you're a good girl, they'll mind their manners." Her words found my own doubts and twisted them, and for an instant I felt as though I'd left my body to become a dispassionate observer. What I saw was a doubtful, slump-shouldered girl and a pursed-lipped woman, turning away from each other and the intimate discussion they both wanted to avoid.

I had only a vague notion of what was involved in "going all the way" except that it led to pregnancy. In fact, I didn't know anyone other than my parents or my friends' parents who'd ever had sex, and I seriously doubted that they even did it after they quit having children. So, what scared me most was that I thought I might *want* to have sex. (I had bragged to a friend that Jeff and I were "lovers on paper," never believing I might have to live up to my words.)

Indeed, what was I expecting? What had I led Jeff to believe? How, oh how, could I have been so brazen? Everything fell in a jumble in my brain. My secret boyfriend and his strange ways were going to be exposed to the harshest scrutiny.

But, as horrifying as these thoughts were, before long I forgot them and was once again spinning daydreams: Jeff and his friends coming in the front door, calm and dignified, wearing Brooks Brothers suits and carrying two beautiful bouquets of flowers—one small, romantic knot of wildflowers for me and a large, extravagant spray of roses for my mother. Jeff would step forward and hand my father a fifth of bourbon—Rebel Yell, of course—and say, "Sir, it's an honor to make your acquaintance." Then, social obligations over, he and I would look at each other for the first time and exchange a secret look that said, "You're everything I expected."

I envisioned this and other delightful scenarios, retrieving once again the romance and anticipation that had sustained me for more than a month, until I fell asleep, head on the windowsill, with a white satin quilt wrapped around me like a rosebud.

7. Jeff

hold on, i'm coming

It was dusk when we stopped for gas just past Meridian, Mississippi. Feldo executed one of his trademark power turns into the filling station, whipping us around so sharply that we nearly clipped a big sedan sitting in the opposite lane. I turned to see if we'd lost any paint and noticed that the other car had a small gold star on the door, darkened glass and a blue cherry on the dash. "I don't think you should have cut that so close, Feldo," I said. "He looks like a cop."

But the car went on its way, and we busied ourselves filling the tank and poring over a map. Our route seemed fairly straightforward until we got to Newton, where we'd have to start threading a maze of country roads, skirting the Ross Barnett Reservoir north of Jackson before hitting Highway 49 at Bentonia, south of Yazoo. From there it would be straight sailing to Ruth's house.

The Devilbug was downright sluggish with a full tank, and we cursed as it wheezed and strained through the darkening hill country of eastern Mississippi. But later we were thankful for this sloth, which kept us from breaking the speed limit. By eleven, we were pressing westward past Newton into the inky blackness of an overcast night. We began to feel punchy as we sputtered down the main streets of tiny towns, like distance runners who've "hit the wall" but can't stop. Around midnight we found ourselves in Forest, population 634, which wasn't on our itinerary.

"Feldo," I pressed, "admit it: You have no idea where we are." He replied icily that he knew exactly where we were and that I, the would-be Romeo, should keep my jerkin on. But Jerry, scrunched over a map in the backseat with a flashlight, sounded dubious. "We're not supposed to be in Forest, Feldo," he said. "I'm not sure where we're supposed to be, but I know it's not here."

Feldo drove on, sticking his head out the window for a better look at the sparse road signage and making rights and lefts until we found ourselves back in Forest. "That's it!" I said. "Pull over and let's try to figure out where the hell we are."

Demoralized, Feldo pulled over. "Too bad there isn't a cop around here," Jerry joked. Feldo's face brightened as he checked the rearview mirror. "Hey, lookie there, guys—a cop! Who *says* there's never one around when you need one?" We turned and saw a blue light flashing.

Giddy with fatigue, we couldn't believe our good fortune in finding—or being found by—a helpful gendarme. We didn't realize it was the cop from the gas station, who had been tailing us for miles. As Feldo got out and started to walk back to the prowl car, Jerry and I whooped: "Go get 'em, Rocco—don't take any crap from that cracker, hear?" I joyfully shook the Whalin' Stick inside the car, sure we would be on our way soon.

Feldo was gone for about a minute; when he returned, his face was ashen. "He wants us in the squad car, guys—now." Our smiles frozen, we got out and headed back with him. "He just doesn't seem to understand me," Feldo said.

We got in the car, Feldo in front, Jerry and I in the back, and the interrogation began. "Nayuh—whayuh deed y'all bwahs suy yeeoo was comin' fum? Ayund haa come y'all ain't in skewel lahk the keeyids dayown heeah, huh bwahs?" We'd spoken with Juan Fugate and a few other Southerners that day, but we'd never heard a true-grits accent before. We desperately needed an interpreter. "You bwahs been chacked yet?" the deputy asked. Feldo and I looked at each other in alarm—neither of us had the slightest idea what he was talking about.

"Excuse me, officer?" Feldo asked, doing his best to appear respectful and cooperative. The deputy's oversized revolver glinted silvery in its holster, and a shotgun's nose poked out from under the seat near my feet. Hillbilly music poured from his radio. At one point, Feldo's earnest answers prompted him to shout: "Naa tha's a crocka *bull-shit—BULL*-shit!" After another fruitless exchange, he scowled at Feldo, then threw his pen against his clipboard and said, slowly and distinctly: *"Don't ah spake Ainglish, bwah?"*

For once in his life, Feldo was at a loss for words. That was the very problem: The guy didn't seem to be speaking English. What was the penalty for failure to communicate with a Mississippi cop? Like Paul Newman in *Cool Hand Luke,* which later would become Jerry's favorite movie, we were trapped in an untenable situation. I had visions of lurid headlines on Long Island: "Three Merrick boys lost, feared dead in Mississippi." The deputy, after all, could take us to a lockup, or to some godforsaken swamp where an unfortunate "accident" might occur.

Feldo gamely tried once again to explain our story: We weren't in school because we were on Easter break, which was a real vacation in New York, though not in Mississippi, and we were on our way to Yazoo City at the invitation of the Tuttle family, with whose daughter, Ruth, we were friends. Durst, here, was the editor of his high school newspaper, and

Ruth was the editor of hers, and they'd been corresponding. We hadn't run away from home, and the officer—who scowled through this entire recitation—could verify our story. We'd already supplied Ruth's phone number and our parents' numbers, but the deputy didn't seem interested in using them. He did, however, relay quite a bit of information over the radio, much of which we couldn't understand.

8.   Ruth

outside agitators

About 2 A.M. the phone rang, and I had my hand on the receiver before I was even awake. But my father had already answered the phone downstairs. I stood barefoot in the cold hallway, listening on the extension while he talked to a stern-voiced man.

"Mr. Tuttle?"

"Yes, this is Doug Tuttle."

"I'm with the Scott County Sheriff's Department."

Daddy didn't say anything. But I knew he was listening hard.

"My deputy's got three boys here, sir," the lawman said, with strong emphasis on "three," "who claim to be coming to visit your daughter."

"That's right." My father sounded cautious. "We were expecting . . ."

"But these here boys be from New York," the man interrupted. "I'm thinkin' they might be outside agitators."

"Well, now," my father said, laughing slightly under his breath as though he and the man were about to share a joke, "those boys are telling the truth. My daughter invited them to visit—you know how teenagers are—and we've been expecting them. I'm sorry you had to be bothered."

"I hope you know what you're doing, Mr. Tuttle," he said. "The deputy says these boys look like they're up to no good."

"No, now they're harmless, 'cept that they've wasted your time," Daddy said. "Could you give me your name and address? I know my wife will want to write and thank you for looking after them."

"No need for that, Mr. Tuttle. Just doing my duty." Something seemed to have been resolved. "How you folks doing up there in Yazoo City?"

"Just trying to raise a few cows and keep track of ol' Archie Manning. How 'bout you?" Before they hung up, Daddy knew his golf handicap, the make of his pickup truck and what his wife's maiden name was. If anything happened to Jeff and his friends, we would know where to look.

I quietly hung up the receiver and tiptoed back into my room, but not quickly enough to get situated in bed before my father came in. "Do you know who that was?" he whispered, my conspirator in a crime gone wrong. "A sheriff. Those friends of yours have really gotten into some trouble now. Oh, God, this was a bad idea."

"They're gonna be okay, aren't they?" For the first time I felt scared.

"I don't know," he said. "Do you know their parents' names, in case I have to call them?"

I shook my head no, wide-eyed at the implications.

"Stay in your room. Don't you dare move when they get here—*if* they get here."

Jeff

The standoff went on, minute after eternal minute, Feldo doing his best to interpret and answer the deputy's questions, I seeking to buttress his story with details and affirmations whenever I could.

Jerry, sitting to my right in the backseat, hadn't said anything for a long time, and I realized with a sinking, guilty feeling that he was probably petrified. I put off looking at him, afraid to find him silently crying, maybe, or staring at me with cold hatred. When I finally did, I got a shock: His face was lit by a big, smart-alecky grin, and he was quietly snapping his fingers and tapping his feet in transparent mockery of the deputy's shitkicker music. He looked me right in the eyes and seemed about to say something cocky. I turned away, not wanting to provoke him, but I made a mental note to strangle him if we ever got out of this alive.

Finally, the deputy just let us go. It seemed like a miracle. We didn't realize he had verified that we really did have a fair damsel waiting in Yazoo City. We got back into the Bug, Feldo and I sobered and quiet and Jerry laughing and chipper. "How'd you like that music, Durst?" he asked as he climbed into the back. "Cool, huh?"

I unloaded on him: "Are you crazy? That cop could have done anything with us. We're probably lucky to be alive!" Feldo nodded solemnly in support, but Jerry waved his hand. "Nah. They've got to give us a phone call. I'd have called my dad, and he would have gotten us a lawyer. We didn't break any laws, so they couldn't have done anything to us."

We argued awhile longer, but in the end Feldo and I gave up on Jerry and just counted our blessings. A few hours later we found ourselves, mortally tired, turning onto Jackson Avenue in Yazoo City. Somehow the Devilbug had taken us unerringly from Forest to Ruth's door, although we never did get directions from that cop.

Ruth

Just before dawn, I heard the doorbell, then muffled voices. I pulled on my blue fleece robe and walked, barefoot, to the landing. This, finally, was going to be the grand moment. I took a deep breath before slowly descending into the dimly lit foyer below.

But with each step I took, reality poked bigger and bigger holes in my daydreams. The boys had dragged a mountain of duffel bags, loose clothing and even some mangled foodstuffs into the living room. They were the most bedraggled bunch of bleary-eyed travelers I could have imagined. They were even beyond my worst imaginings, because everything about them, from hairstyles to shoes, was inconceivably foreign. My father looked slightly hysterical as he pumped their hands and slapped them on their backs. And when he turned toward me, I saw relief in his eyes, quickly followed by something else—gentle pity, a cloud of concern.

He stepped out of the way and, finally, I got a close look at my visitors. Only one was blond with blue eyes, and after a brief glance I had to look away. The sweet intrigue was over. In a hallucinatory dream he began to shrink before my eyes. Though his face was that of a poet—a delicate, sensitive and intelligent face tinged with fatigue, a face I could have loved— he was too short. He looked either horrified or petrified with fear and his eyes darted desperately toward his friends.

Then a hunk of a boy with a commanding and flamboyant presence stepped forward and offered me his hand. He had piercing green eyes and a shock of black hair that seemed to writhe in tendrils like Medusa's own locks. Muscles rippled in his arms. "Hi, I'm Jeff."

I had a brief hopeful moment. Maybe he *was* Jeff?

Then the real Jeff, the one with the sensitive face, touched my shoulder and I turned. Intensity crackled off of him when he said, "This is Dave. I'm Jeff." I shook his hand without meeting his eyes.

Jerry stood apart from us, smiling with a wry expression that seemed to say, "So, isn't this a mess?"

Jeff

When we pulled up to Ruth's house, I was astonished at its size and grandeur. *It's a mansion,* I thought to myself as we stumbled up the front steps. To someone who'd been raised in little Long Island boxes, it suggested that I'd soon be romancing an heiress.

We rang, and the door swung open. Standing in the doorway was Ruth's father, a beaming giant of a man who seemed on the verge of laughing out loud as he surveyed us. This seemed somewhat odd, but I didn't dwell on it, given the circumstances. We shook hands, Mr. Tuttle pumping our arms and slapping our backs with an almost manic intensity, and then I looked over his shoulder. A wide, paneled wooden stairway, which ended in a classical column instead of a newel post, descended into a large foyer with a black-and-white tile floor, and I was quite struck by the opulence of it all. My eyes stopped halfway to the first landing; standing there was a slender, wide-eyed girl I knew must be Ruth. I'd expected that she would be about my height and had worn my favorite old tan suede boots on purpose for this occasion. Although they were beat up, they had the tallest heels of any shoes I owned, and I wanted to be sure that I measured up.

But when Ruth glided to the bottom of the stairs, I could see that the boots weren't going to be nearly enough. She went over to Dave and Jerry first, and I was shocked to see that she—with bare feet—was slightly taller than Feldo, who had a good two inches on me. Feldo, moving smoothly to take full advantage of my confusion, stepped up to Ruth with a rakish grin and said, "Hi, I'm Jeff."

I tried to be a sport and laugh along with Jerry, but inwardly I was stunned. Then she was in front of me, and though I stood as tall as I could, and though she was slouching a bit, she towered over me. She was willowy and attractive, with a warm smile and sparkling brown eyes, but I was oblivious to her charms. Feldo came over and clapped me on the back in commiseration. He and Jerry exchanged looks, and Jerry shook his head and smiled.

A few minutes later we brought in our bags and were bivouacked, Dave and Jerry upstairs and me in the parlor, which was to become my room for the week. With the lights out and the house quiet, I went over in my mind again and again the letters in which we'd exchanged physical descriptions. I had said I was about 5' 8" (which was a stretch, although I believed it at the time), and she had answered: "I'm tall, too—about 5'8"." Had she lied on purpose? But why? It just didn't jibe with my image of the girl I'd come to adore. The most promising affair of my young life had fizzled before it had properly begun, and here we were planning to spend the next week under the same roof! Marveling at life's unfathomable cruelties, I finally fell asleep.

belle for a day

I thought I would rather die than ever get out of bed again. What was I going to do? At seven Momma was knocking on doors and rousting everyone out, and panic began to overtake me. My only recourse was to pretend everything was fine.

In keeping with that plan, I put on a fitted, shell-pink linen skirt and a delicately top-stitched beige blouse with mother-of-pearl buttons, and beige pumps. It was a grasp at dignity, for I was sure that when I got to school, I would be facing the social equivalent of the gallows.

I went downstairs with my head up. But my despair deepened. "Good morning, honey," my mother chirped, obviously no longer worried about me losing my heart, or my virginity. The scene at the breakfast table was even more alarming. My sisters sat transfixed by the New York boys, whose clothing and bantering palaver were both incomprehensible. I sneaked a look at Jeff. He studiously avoided eye contact.

He wore black bell-bottom jeans and a pair of brown boots. His belt was about three inches wide and had a heavy round buckle. His hair hung down in blond curls to the top of his glasses, to which he had affixed flip-up sunshades. But the most memorable thing about Jeff's outfit was the white T-shirt he wore under his long-sleeved striped shirt. I could actually see it above his top button, and to me a white T-shirt was underwear.

Dave wore black jeans with a skin-tight black shirt, and his hair stood out wildly from his head. Jerry could have passed Mississippi muster in his short-sleeved, pin-striped shirt and narrow belt except for two things: His sideburns stretched to his jawline and he, like Dave, had on high-top tennis shoes. But Jerry's brown pants were tucked neatly into the tops of his shoes, a fact I noted with gratitude. I walked next to him on the way to school.

Behind us, puns and wisecracks were flying between Jeff and Dave as they commented on everything from the warm weather to my English setter, Mr. Ginger. Their wordplay was razor sharp and, because of their heavy New York accents, I had to pay close attention. But once I got the knack of it, I managed to get in one or two zings of my own that provoked a quick riposte and a wink from Jeff.

Regret and anger welled up in me. This just wasn't fair. I'd often imagined this day as a triumph. It was supposed to be our first day as a couple, when I would show up at school with my spectacular boyfriend, who had driven all the way from New York to see me. Now, I was facing ridicule instead.

I stopped next to my friend Patty Woodell and her boyfriend, Lee Erickson. Patty had endured the weeks of waiting with me, listening in wonderment to my grandiose descriptions of Jeff. I had called him my dream man, a genius, a Greek god. Now, in a barely audible voice, I said to her, "Well, here they are."

"Oh," Patty shrieked, "it's the Yankees! Which one of you is Jeff?" She looked expectantly at Dave. I hurried to make things clear.

"This is Jeff. Jeff, this is my friend Patty. She's Miss Yazoo City."

"Oh," he said. "A VIP."

Patty covered her confusion with a bright smile, and in her most sincerely insincere voice she said, "*I* knew that. You *had* to be Jeff, honey. *Just like Ruth described you.*" Then she gave my arm a squeeze that said "Too bad! He's so sho-o-o-rt!" and handed me a Hershey's Kiss, my consolation prize, I guess. We moved on. A crowd was gathering. At least that part of my fantasy was coming true.

There were shocked faces, and some conversations were stopped in midsentence. Fingers were being pointed in our direction from the redneck contingent at the other end of the covered walkway in front of the school. Protectively, I put my hand on Jeff's arm and guided him through the crowd, noticing that Jerry and even Dave were following as close as they could, forming a kind of phalanx. That's when I realized how bizarre this was for them, too. It was the first time I believed they hadn't *tried* to look different. They *were* different.

From then on, I found refuge in my well-established role of rebel. I accepted every startled glance as a personal tribute, every frown as another incentive to show off this strange trio of adventurers. I was delighted each time they had to ask for a translation of a Southern drawl, and laughed at my friends' attempts to understand their New York accents. Unlike me and the other A students at Yazoo City High, who viewed our brains as a social curse, my visitors were profligate, throwing intelligence around the way a rich Texas bride spends her daddy's money.

The visit was documented on the second day when the four of us were photographed together for the front page of the *Yazoo City Herald*. Under the picture was the caption:

VISITING HIGH SCHOOL JOURNALISTS
Yazooan Editor Ruth Tuttle chats with New York visitors
Jeff Durstewitz, Jerry Greenfield and Dave Felt [*sic*].

We all looked gravely subdued except for Jerry, who was smiling, or smirking, at some private joke. But our expressions could have been due to the news we had received right before the photograph was taken. Coach Rush had told me to take the boys home and not to come back with them again. He said a group of students had roughed up my friend Debbie Hill in the hall and issued a warning: "You'd better tell Ruth to get rid of those nigger lovers, or we will." Never one to take a stand, Coach Rush decided to do what they wanted.

The next morning, Dave and Jerry left for Merrick, and we had hardly waved them away from the curb before Jeff tried to start a prickly conversation with me, one we wouldn't finish for twenty-six years. He said, "You must be taller than five-eight." *And you must be shorter,* I thought, but didn't say, offended that he would be so impolite as to drag such a sore subject into the open.

In fact, my feelings about our supposed miscommunication were so conflicted, and bordered so closely on anger, that I saw only one way to avoid the inevitable accusations such a conversation would lead to: I refused to discuss it, resorting to a giddy "Who cares?" laugh and dismissive shrug of my shoulders. I also began to drop hints about other boyfriends, and hot dates, which were pure fabrications. I didn't want him to think he was the only thing I had going, even if he was, because while I didn't find my Northern knight that week, Jeff did find his Southern belle.

1 Q. *Jeff*

strangers in a strange land

It was sunny the morning after we arrived, and by the time I was fully awake my bitter regret had been replaced by a sense of anticipation. Ruth and I may not have been meant to be sweethearts, but I still had an adventure in progress and I planned to make the best of it.

The first thing I noticed about Yazoo City High School was that all the guys were dressed in a style we called "colleege" (shorthand for "collegiate"): pressed chinos, dress shirts, letter sweaters and penny loafers. And all the girls looked like blue-eyed, blond models for Breck shampoo. There seemed to be no "ethnics" to speak of in Yazoo City, with the exception of a smattering of Armenians. Interspersed with names that all came directly from the Civil War—Hood, Lee, Hill, Davis—was the occasional Bubba Bagdikian.

But there didn't seem to be any Polish or Italian names, and only a few Irish and German ones. It was as if we'd stumbled into a time capsule of an earlier, ethnically pure, white America, the country that the Know-Nothings had tried to preserve against waves of Irish and German Catholics in the 1840s and '50s.

We went to classes with Ruth that morning, Feldo and I dueling through them just as we did at Calhoun. It was a game we played: Who could compromise a teacher's control of the class the most? We boiled over about the Vietnam War in a history class, Feldo insisting on an immediate pullout, while I argued that Nixon's policy of gradual disengagement should be given a chance. Jerry said little, but anyone who assumed that he didn't know at least as much as we did would have been dead wrong. Grandstanding just wasn't his style.

Toward the end of the morning we went to the *Yazooan* office, a beehive of activity presided over by Mrs. Prichard, the faculty sponsor. She was a stunningly beautiful young woman, and I wasn't surprised to learn that she'd once come close to winning the title of Miss Mississippi. I was having a hard time taking my eyes off her when I noticed Jerry focusing on something—or someone—nearer at hand.

Standing next to me was a girl so fine that I felt myself undergoing a kind of benign cardiac arrest. It was a state in which breathing, thinking, talking—all the normal physical and social functions—are subsumed into mute wonder. I don't know how long I lingered in that dream state, but when I finally glanced at Jerry, I could tell she'd had the same impact on him. She had long hair the color of sunshine, big, strikingly blue eyes, a soft, slightly pouty mouth and a good-humored smile that could easily turn wry on you. She seemed to be telling us something droll, but her Dixie lilt was nearly impenetrable. It didn't matter, because I was much more interested in looking at her than in listening to her. She was about 5'4", and her hourglass form represented the zenith of female architecture. But perhaps the most enchanting thing about her was the way she was holding her books. She had propped several texts, all askew, on top of a notebook crammed with papers hanging out every which way, all pinned precariously against her side. She seemed totally caught up in what she was saying, the opposite of the *femme fatale* she could have played so effectively.

The girl, whom Ruth introduced as Alice DeCell, was laughing and telling us we would have gotten quite a different response if we'd sent our first letter to her. Then suddenly she lost control of her books and papers and dropped them in a mess on the floor, never pausing in her monologue as she knelt to gather them up. Jerry and I exchanged glances, and Jerry said quietly: "I saw her first, Durst." As we bent to help, I was thinking: *Yeah, Jer, but you're going home soon.*

At noon we went back to the Tuttle house for a big Southern feast. The four of us, along with Ruth's mother, father, sisters and brother, sat around the big table in the dining room and chatted reasonably freely, given that we boys were on best behavior. The great novelty of the meal for me was Rita, the Tuttle family's cook. I'd never been waited on by a servant before, and it felt strange—pleasant and embarrassing at the same time. Part of me wanted to help Rita bring in the food and take away the empty dishes. But I managed to sit tight.

Mrs. Tuttle asked us what our daddies did. Our answers showed, I believe, that we brash Yankees had already breathed deeply of the Old South. Feldo, for instance, usually flaunted his working-class origins, proudly telling people that his dad was a fireman and an ironworker. Yet now he told Mrs. Tuttle that his father was "an employee of the City of New York." I usually told people my father was a sailor. But now I found myself saying that he was "a staff officer in the merchant marine." The idea that our parents might not be socially acceptable never would have occurred to us in Merrick. Jerry's father was a stockbroker, so he was home free.

One of our classes that afternoon was taught by a black teacher. This was more a novelty for us than we let on, because Calhoun didn't have any teachers of color. The teacher, Mrs. Baker, gamely tried to present a class on race relations, and we were shocked by the response from her all-white class. They baited her—and us—subtly and not so subtly, one student casually remarking that it would be easier to relate to blacks if they didn't smell so funny. Feldo sat with his head downcast and his hooded eyes blazing, a fist up in the air, waiting for his turn to demolish Jim Crow logic once and for all. But his turn never came; Mrs. Baker wisely ignored him.

His comments might well have touched off a fight, because there was a rejectionist front forming—a group of students who wanted us out. I told Ruth later that I thought Mrs. Baker, who'd even had to defend her teaching credentials to the openly skeptical class, was an Uncle Tom for not dealing more firmly with the racists. Of course, that was an easy call for me to make; I was flying north at the end of the week.

Appalled as we were by some of what we encountered at Yazoo City High School, we also enjoyed the attention we were getting. At one point, we regaled some of Ruth's friends with a display of Yankee speed-talk in *The Yazooan* room, clipping syllables like fingernails. And Feldo and I were also slinging strings of puns, so we might as well have been speaking Urdu. "Kin yeeuw understayund thayum?" said one dismayed Mississippian. "Ah cayunt understayund a woord theyur sayin," marveled another.

Alice joined us after school and we five crammed into the Devilbug to "drag Grand," having been told that this was *de rigueur* for a Yazoo afternoon. We drove for a while up and down the wide boulevard with its circular park and well-to-do homes, waving like visiting astronauts—which, in a sense, we were, although not from exactly the same planet—and teaching Ruth and Alice how to run a Chinese fire drill at red lights. These Southern belles, I noted with great satisfaction, seemed to fit right in with Rocco's rollicking crew.

The next morning we strode the halls of YHS like carpetbaggers, having developed a small coterie of friends and having begun to get the hang of communicating in Southernese. We all went to Alice's house for lunch that day, and Feldo scored easy points with her younger brother, Brister, by casually pressing with one arm a set of weights that the younger boy could barely lift with two. Alice and Ruth, taking their cue from Brister's honest awe, gleefully played up to Feldo as if he were God's gift to Southern womanhood, and I found myself smiling. The visit seemed to be going incredibly well despite its disastrous beginning. I had found the embodiment of my dreams in Alice, and I sensed that I wouldn't have to give up Ruth's friendship to win her.

It also seemed that Alice's parents, far from being put off by the marauding Yankees, were delighted that Alice had fallen into our orbit. Her father, Herman DeCell, was a Harvard-educated lawyer and respected state senator who was holding the middle ground between the state's forward- and backward-looking forces. Her mother, Harriet, was an outspoken high school teacher who'd also been educated up North. They had many Northern friends, Alice told us, and had sent her to camp in Andover, Massachusetts, where she had made friends with a girl from Merrick. It was an acquaintance that would be important to all of us a few months later.

On our way back to the high school, my plans solidified: I would have a talk with Ruth, then make my move with Alice. I had to work quickly, since I was leaving in four days, but I wanted Ruth's blessing. I felt I owed her a big debt. It was because of her, after all, that I'd undertaken this incredible odyssey and met Alice. What I didn't understand—perhaps because I was just a heedless boy or because Ruth was such a good actress—was her keen disappointment in our relationship. If I had known how close I came to losing her that first week in Mississippi, I would have moved much more cautiously.

When we got back to YHS after lunch, storm clouds had gathered. Ruth was called into Coach Rush's office as soon as we entered the building, and she came to tell us shortly afterward that we were being thrown out.

We picked up Alice after school and meandered around town, eventually ending up at Coach Rush's house, where we drove up onto the lawn and honked and hooted, shaking the Whalin' Stick and threatening to whale him if he dared to show his face. Luckily, no one was home.

That night was Feldo and Jerry's last in Yazoo, and they were a bit downcast at the prospect of leaving. But I was anxious to see Jerry go, even though he'd reluctantly ceded the "rights" to Alice to me that day, admitting that rights you couldn't enforce weren't worth much. We dragged Grand and drove deep into the Mississippi Delta that night before knocking off so Jerry and Feldo could get a full night's sleep. The next morning they were off, leaving me alone—at last—to pursue my double agenda.

One of the most astonishing things about Alice, I'd come to realize, was that she didn't have a boyfriend. I knew that if she'd been at Calhoun, she'd have had her choice from a swarm of suitors. But here—perhaps because she was seen as too brainy, or perhaps because her mother was a formidable teacher through whose classes most boys at Yazoo High had to pass on their way to graduation—she'd been virtually ignored by the opposite sex. For me the situation was almost too good to be true.

The next night Ruth and I went with Alice and some of her friends to see Franco Zeffirelli's version of *Romeo and Juliet*, which was playing in Jackson. It was a flawed experience: Some yahoos in the audience managed to turn the film into a vulgar farce. But I was promised recompense by way of Shakey's pizza. The honor of the South at stake, Alice brashly assured me that this was the real article, as good as any I'd get up North.

I could hardly believe my eyes when the alleged pizza arrived. Our party of six had had to order four pies because they were so puny. And they tasted like paste and ketchup on cardboard. "Isn't it good?" Alice asked between bites, her eyes shining with pride. "Have some more." I held my fire for love's sake, but I made a mental note to introduce Ruth and Alice to the real thing at Spertino's in Merrick when—not if—they came up. As for Shakey's, it later became a post office.

Ruth and I got back to her house after midnight, and for the first time the two of us were alone. The house was dark except for a light in the kitchen, and it seemed as good a time as any to have our Big Talk. It was a brief conversation that began somewhat awkwardly but got easier by the minute. I said I felt we could become really good friends, and she hastily agreed, adding that that was what she, who already had several boyfriends, had had in mind right from the start. She smiled, and we hugged briefly before she went upstairs. I hit the sack that night vastly relieved.

The next day, I called Alice and asked her for a date, trying to sound as casual as I could. She immediately said yes, and we made plans to see *To Sir, With Love* at the nearby drive-in along with a few of her friends. When I told Ruth, she seemed amused at my taking an interest in "little ol' Alice," to whom she tended to refer patronizingly, as if Alice were one of her younger sisters. This was the confirmation I was looking for: Now I felt free to pursue Alice at full tilt.

It didn't strike me until we pulled into the drive-in that *To Sir, With Love* was an odd choice for a Deep South showing. Arrayed around us were good ol' boys and their good ol' girlfriends, ready for a night of heavy necking and submarine racing, all of whom were about to see—assuming anyone was actually watching the movie—the fair-skinned Lulu make eyes at Sidney Poitier. When Lulu, in her miniskirt, planted a kiss on Poitier's ebony face, all hell broke loose in the parking lot. Engines roared to life and revved up angrily, horns honked and several patrons almost collided in their haste to exit. Alice seemed embarrassed by the reaction.

On the way home, I put my arm around her in the backseat and she leaned against me. When we got to her house, I walked her up to her front door, where she obligingly closed her eyes and waited. I gave her a brief but tender kiss on the lips—I didn't want to overdo it—and floated back to Ruth's house.

In the morning I called on Alice again, and while I was waiting for her, the impish Brister told me he'd seen our kiss on the doorstep. "You know," he said, "she's never been kissed before. That was her first time." Alice, who was coming into the room, grabbed a pillow off the sofa and flew at him, bashing away as he gleefully shouted, "It's true! You know it's true!" before escaping. But she didn't deny it, and I was filled with a kind of awe.

On my last evening in Yazoo, Ruth and I went to see her horses. The whole family got into the big Olds 98 and drove across the tracks into what was colloquially known as Niggertown. Its squalor shocked and sickened me. Ramshackle hovels, obviously lacking electricity and plumbing, stood on stilts. Tiny, half-naked tots and scrawny dogs skittered about on spindly legs, and some of the children—whom Ruth had provocatively referred to as "pickaninnies" in a letter—had runny eyes and distended bellies.

The pasture was at the end of this street of shanties, and Ruth's sleek horses whinnied their thanks as we fed them carrots and patted their noses. I liked horses, but I couldn't help looking over my shoulder, aghast at this wretched Third World scene in my own country. Then Ruth came near and looked me in the eyes. "I know what you're thinking," she said quietly. "And you're right. It *is* terrible, isn't it?" A little while later, we all piled into the air-conditioned car and drove off, leaving the horses—and the pickaninnies—staring after us.

11. Ruth

friendship begins

Though Jeff and I talked about our future relationship that night after *Romeo and Juliet,* it didn't quiet my sorrow at the way things had turned out. I knew the rules now. I knew we could go on as friends. But none of that helped me deal with the reality of having to watch as he found, with Alice, the exhilarating sweetness I had expected for myself. I realized we didn't want each other that way and that I was an equal partner in that decision. But I still felt a loss. Why couldn't he have been what I expected?

I woke up on Saturday to a lackadaisical rain—a slow, warm drizzle that would intermittently slack off. I went downstairs, dragging a little from the weight of my sorrows, and found Jeff at the kitchen table with my mother. He looked like an Irish pasha, his blue eyes twinkling, his face eager as he accepted a plate of bacon and eggs from her. He seemed to beam with contentment.

I sat next to him and picked at some grits while we discussed what we would do that day, his last in Yazoo.

"You've got to see the cemetery," I suggested. "It's old, and beautiful, and a nice walk." I hoped the ancient glory of the place would affect him as it did me.

"Sure," Jeff said, "but let's get Alice to meet us." Exasperated, I handed him the phone and went to get my purse. I had taken all of his letters out of it the night before, thinking that reading them again would help me accept what had happened. I had been prepared to take a morose journey into what might have been. Instead, I had found myself laughing out loud at the rude and infamous first letter. The passages signed by "The Groin" and "Feldo" were, like them, outrageous and fascinating in their intellectual sleight-of-hand. It made me a little happier about the way things had turned out.

I had put that letter back in my purse, thinking Jeff could describe the other people who had signed it. *Maybe I'll even go to Merrick and meet them in person,* I'd thought, then fell asleep spinning schemes of a trip to New York.

We walked out the back door just as the sun came out of the clouds. It stayed with us all the way to the cemetery, and we chatted in a polite, if dispassionate, way as we walked. Inside the cemetery's wrought iron entranceway, I stopped by one of the graves and laid my hand on the headstone. It marked the grave of my mother's beloved first husband, David West, who died at twenty-five of a wasting neurological disease. It was a horror she still couldn't fathom and wouldn't discuss with me. Yet she retained the innocent wonder of youth and was the first to laugh when we all sat around the table telling stories. Perhaps that was because she lived in the land of her childhood, with its loving ghosts in every corner of the old house. But sometimes I'd catch an expression on her face, an awareness, perhaps, of how thin a membrane there is between life's tragic winnowing and its blessings. Hanging on to joy was her defiant victory.

"This is a mysterious old place," Jeff said.

"Wait until you see this." I led him to a neglected grave. In the 1800s a "witch" had tormented the people of Yazoo City, and they repaid her in kind. After she died, the city fathers had an iron chain put around her cemetery plot so she couldn't do what she had vowed: rise from the grave and destroy the town. In 1904, when most of Yazoo City's downtown burned to the ground, it was discovered that one of the links was missing from the chain. A legend began then that she had escaped and carried out her curse.

Jeff and I stood over the plot with its now rusting chain—still missing a link and still hooked to four metal cornerposts. There was no marker. Untended grass and weeds almost obscured the links of the chain, and an ancient cedar tree had dropped a rotten limb across the grave. I felt lost. All the adolescent hope and love that this boy had sparked in me weighed me down. It was a kind of suffocation that I struggled to get past.

I pulled out the letter and said, "You know, I thought this was an awful thing at first, but now I'm growing fond of it."

"I guess I understand that," Jeff said.

"You do?"

"Well, yeah. Even though it's a huge pile of crap, it *is* the thing that brought us together."

"As friends, you mean." I said it sarcastically. I couldn't stop the bitterness from creeping out.

He looked startled, and I saw a shadow of confusion cross his face. This was a guy who made friends for life. I had only a glimmer of that then, through my acquaintance with Dave and Jerry, but it was enough to keep me silent. Friendship—I could consider it, although I didn't embrace it at that moment. The dregs of our romance, however, I left forever with the witch.

I changed the subject, mentioning my notion of a visit to Merrick. That perked him up. "Maybe Alice can come with you?"

"Um-m."

It started to rain again. Jeff and I ran under the dense overhang of the cedar tree to wait out the downpour, and I saw that a few drops had made the ink run on the letter. I hastily stuffed it into my purse. The rain got heavier, and we were glad when Alice came driving up in her mother's brown and gold Pontiac station wagon. I made a dash for it with Jeff, but something—perhaps the wind, or perhaps the witch—caused the letter to fall out of my purse.

I didn't realize it was missing until several days later. I looked for it everywhere, thinking I must have lost it at school or left it in Alice's car, but it didn't turn up. All I had was the envelope, smudged by raindrops. Then one day during lunch break, I carried a sandwich to the cemetery and went to sit by the witch's grave. There, on the cornerpost like a cap of papier-mâché, were the letter's remains. I recognized the blue lines of Jeff's notebook paper, but all the writing had been washed away. I peeled it off and carried it home. Eventually I threw it away, because the words—its power—were gone. I've always believed they went to reside with the witch, who has thus far kept them for her own amusement.

When it was time for Jeff to leave, I was relieved. The emotional gauntlet of the previous week had worn me out, and we had failed to connect in person as we had on paper. But I got up earlier than usual the morning we took him to the airport, and pulled out Aunt Ruth's old Underwood typewriter. I had a deadline to meet for *The Yazooan,* an editorial on Jeff, Dave and Jerry's impact on Yazoo City. I wrote quickly, emotionlessly, of their visit as a kind of sociological study. "Though the boys," I summed up, "had many compliments about Mississippi, they didn't become Southern converts. They left with jumbled impressions of good and bad. They were pleased to find that not all white Mississippians could be grouped in the 'redneck WASP' category." I dashed off a headline—"New Yorkers Whale Yazoo City"—then dressed for the drive to Jackson.

On the way to the airport, my father took us to lunch at the Green Derby Restaurant on Highway 80 in Jackson, where we all ordered sixteen-ounce T-bones and baked potatoes with sour cream and chives. I don't remember what was said as we sat in one of the black Naugahyde booths, eating oversized yeast rolls and watching Daddy charm the waitress. I do remember the emptiness of my feelings as I prepared to end what, up to that point, had been the greatest experience of my life as well as one of its bitterest.

I was silent and despondent during the ride home from the airport. My mother tried to catch my eye several times and engage me in conversation, but I stared relentlessly out the window. I knew she felt sorry for me, and it made me furious. "Well, I guess that's that," she said once. I shrugged and kept staring at the kudzu along Highway 49. I saw my father give her a glance.

About ten miles from home, he said, "They were an interesting bunch of boys." I saw him looking at me in the rearview mirror and shifted around as if to get a better view of Little Yazoo's cluster of gas stations. I wasn't going to discuss it.

When I had said good-bye to Jeff at the airport, I felt just the way my mother did: "That's that." Never mind that we'd hugged warmly, and promised to keep writing, and even planned a visit, with Alice, to Merrick. I still didn't know what to do with the ragged remnants of our love affair. The real Jeff seemed only a stand-in for the mysterious boy of letters, the one I'd fallen in love with, the one that still felt as real as life to me. That boy wouldn't have replaced me so quickly with Alice.

The fact that my parents' glances were filled with concern and understanding only increased my anger and pain. They seemed to feel they had won some moral battle for my heart. As we turned onto Brickyard Hill, I finally spoke up. "You know, I'm going to Merrick to visit him. This isn't over yet."

My mother's sympathetic expression vanished. "We'll just *see* about that, young lady."

A few days later a thank-you note arrived from Jerry. My parents both read it, standing in the kitchen before dinner. "Nice boy," Momma said and didn't offer to let me read it. Later that night I found it in the gold-enameled trash can in her dressing room, and retrieved it.

April 5, 1969

Dear Mr. and Mrs. Tuttle,

We left in such a hurry that I'm afraid I didn't have time to tell you how much I enjoyed the visit with you and your family. I realize how busy you both must be, so I especially appreciate your taking the time to give us such a happy time. I know now what people mean when they talk about real Southern hospitality. The meals were true examples of culinary masterpieces; even your leftovers were fantastic.

In addition to this, the factor which made our stay most enjoyable was the atmosphere which pervaded your house. Your entire family made us feel at home as though we really belonged. I just hope we didn't inconvenience you too much.

I'd like to say that I'm sorry if we offended anyone with our appearance (hair length mostly) or our ideas. That was the furthest thing from my mind. We might have seemed strange to you, but if you Southerners (not you personally)

accept us as people, things would get along much better.
Thank you again.

Sincerely yours,
Jerry Greenfield

My heart ached because he had seen the warmth and charm of my old home, because my family had made me proud of them, because Jerry hadn't been deceived and had dared to challenge—ever so gently—our bigotry. His note dissolved the bitter husk of my disappointment, and when a letter arrived from Jeff, I tore into it eagerly.

April 9th and 10th, 1969

Dearest Ruth,
      1500 miles and a few days later, and I'm still having trou-
ble believing that it all happened. And now it's over!! I had
the weirdest feeling at the airport while I waited for Dave. I
felt as if I had left a whole different world and come back to
my own, all in the space of about four hours.
      I've been telling my friends about the trip and I think I'm
succeeding in giving them some idea about conditions down
there. Yesterday my brother said that he hadn't eaten any
lunch because he "wasn't interested" in the bologna in the re-
frigerator—and today I saw this ad in the **Atlantic Monthly**
about a Mississippi relief fund—it had a picture of some
starving black children and had something like "Walk through
any Mississippi Delta town and look around you." You know
which Mississippi Delta town I was thinking about. Anyway, I
showed the ad to my brother and explained it to him. I hope
he doesn't turn down any more bologna sandwiches.
      I really miss everyone. I doubt if I can thank you enough
for inviting me down. It was definitely one of the high points
of my life! I mean that.
      Say the word and I'll tell my mother to write your parents
a letter inviting you up here. If you can just explain to them
how great it was for me to visit you, maybe they'll understand
more why you want to go. Also, you can tell them that any
fears they may have on your behalf are groundless. I don't
know how you feel exactly, but I feel more like your far-
removed brother than anything else. You would have your own
room, of course.

Write soon, dear. I miss you.

Hugging his letter to me, I sat by my window and realized that a compelling connection still existed between us, if only in the realm of pen and paper. I felt certain nothing could ever stop us from writing.

April 15, 1969

Dear Jeff,

I've turned into a whole new person since your visit. I can really see your points about the negroes. Sometimes I feel like screaming, "Quit scraping and bowing and stand up for your rights. No one is going to just hand them to you because they're all blinded from 300 years of prejudice!" The problem in Yazoo is on both sides. Anyway, I'm developing a Yankee philosophy. But, besides turning into an integrationist, I'm fine.

Be good, "keep the faith," whale N.Y. and **get me there to do it with you!**

survivors

ruth's choice

June Cleaver is daintily spreading mayonnaise on the Beav's white-bread sandwich. He suddenly bursts into the kitchen. "Hi, Mom."

She adjusts the pearls at her neck. "Beaver, what's that on your shirt?"

"Just some neat mud and stuff."

The hapless Beav ducks his head and tries to make a quick getaway.

"Beaver, go straight to your room and change your clothes."

"Aw, Mom!"

Another family emergency is handily dispatched.

I was never a fan of *Leave It to Beaver*. I felt wistful and inadequate in the face of the Cleavers' perfect family life. Nothing bad ever happened to them. We never saw Beaver and Wally getting drilled on what to do in case of a nuclear attack. Or June and Ward discussing who would shoot the neighbors if they tried to break in to the Cleavers' bomb shelter on the fateful day. Yet the Cold War raged during the entire run of that show, as insidious as a dry drunk. While repressed, real-life sixties families were beginning to pop apart like scum bubbles on the surface of a Mississippi cow pond, the Ward-and-June propaganda machine made us forget what an impossible dream it all was.

In 1962, when I was ten, my family moved to San Mateo, California, from Texas, where I had been born, just as the Cuban Missile crisis was playing out. In my new home, I thought constantly about how to stay alive in a nuclear holocaust, but was completely unprepared for the emotional one that did happen.

One cool morning in October, with Russian missiles pointing at the nation's borders, I finished my preparations for surviving an A-bomb attack. My friend Carolyn Corn and I had evacuated our dolls to her playhouse that morning and hidden a jar of water under a floorboard with some blankets. I was sure we'd be okay there. A paper sack containing two apples, a banana and some potato chips I'd stolen from the pantry was on the floor next to me. As an afterthought I'd thrown in my Girl Scout knife. I was wearing white Keds, white shorts and a yellow dotted-swiss blouse with sweetheart sleeves. A pink nightgown was tied around my waist. No one had asked me why.

I stretched out on the floor of our living room and propped myself up on my elbows to look out the picture window. The sky was clear, but I scanned it nervously, searching for the mushroom cloud that meant I should bolt and run six blocks to Carolyn's house.

I could hear my parents talking in the kitchen. They had been in there since lunch with checkbooks and bills spread on the counter between them. This was unusual, so as I watched the sky I kept one ear cocked to learn what was going on.

"What do you want?" my mother asked my father. "Just tell me."

A chair creaked, but he didn't say anything.

"Doug, I don't understand."

"That's the problem."

"You say we don't love you, but we do. The children and I do."

I crept quietly into a burgundy velvet wing chair to hear better.

"I'm leaving," he said. "I have to."

"What will I tell the kids?" she whispered. I was straining to hear them.

"I want Ruth and little Doug to live with me. The baby and Patty need you."

The thumping of my heart seemed loud enough to get their attention. Didn't they know I was listening? Wouldn't they stop if they knew? How could they be doing this *now*? The whole world seemed suddenly full of irrational grown-ups. Dropping bombs. Scaring their children. Destroying the world.

"Okay," my mother said. *Okay? Okay for me to go in my room, pack a bag, leave our home and live with Daddy?* "But we should ask Ruth. She's old enough to make up her own mind," she added.

No, don't ask me, I prayed. *Don't make me choose.*

I heard my father's footsteps as he came to find me. I wanted to run away, but couldn't move. The best I could do was sit up and bite the tops of my knees to stifle the tears that were already flowing. He came around the corner.

"Oh, Daddy."

He knelt in front of me. *Don't ask me. Don't ask me.*

Taking one of my hands, he held it for a moment. He was crying, too. "I'm going," he said.

"Why?"

His dark head fell and rested against my forehead. I could smell Old Spice. Then he stood up, frowning, the angry and moody Daddy who made us children afraid. He didn't look at me again before turning and walking quickly from the room, a deserter.

I didn't hear him say anything more to my mother, just the sound of the front door closing and the car starting. In a few minutes I went where she still sat, hunched over the counter, a check in her hand. But instead of running to her for comfort, I consoled her. There had seemed to be a child looking out from behind her soft hazel eyes, a child much younger and more vulnerable even than I was. We held each other tightly, rocking back and forth in the kitchen. I thought for the first time that she was a small person, not realizing that it was I who was getting so big. We stood eye to eye.

"Don't tell your brother and sisters," she said. "Maybe he'll come back soon."

"What are we going to do?"

"Pray for him, sweetheart. That's all we can do."

This was a revelation, to think of my father as in need of prayer, or help of any kind. Yet in an instant he had been transformed for me into a kind of lost soul, one who had condemned his wife and children to a parallel hell of uncertain finances, lonely vigils and painful secrets.

That night, Aunt Ruth called from Yazoo City. As usual we all clamored to speak to her, giving my mother only a few minutes to talk to this spinster who had raised her. Their conversation was light, even cheery, and I kept watching my mother, wondering when she was going to break the news, wondering when we could go to Yazoo City, the safest place I knew.

The receiver was passed from child to child, and while I waited my turn Momma pulled me aside. "Not one word about your father."

"But Momma, Aunt Ruth could help."

"Not a word. Promise me." I promised and took the phone.

"Hi, Aunt Ruth," I yelled into the receiver. She had been almost totally deaf since she was seventeen. But that hadn't stopped her from becoming Mississippi's first woman lawyer in 1912, or from making a substantial amount of money from the invention of an eraser bed for Underwood typewriters. A self-described old maid, Aunt Ruth's life gave dignity and a certain desirability to going it alone.

Her voice was tired, though, and even to my ten-year-old ears it sounded frail. Diabetes later in life had sapped her strength ("I miss the warmth of sugar," she'd written my mother) as well as taken most of her sight. But she was still plying financial waters, unwilling—or unable—to accept retirement. I felt a familiar spark of interest when she said, "The stock market is up. Are you ready to read the reports to me?" This was our ritual.

I got the afternoon paper and turned to the stock report. For the next ten minutes she called out company names and symbols from memory, and I scanned the tiny printed columns, calling out, "Up! A quarter" or "Down, an eighth."

She would occasionally make one of her strange pronouncements. "That one'll split soon" or "Fruehauf should have a dividend due."

My chest began to hurt, a hard lump grinding just beneath my voice.

Aunt Ruth, help us! I wanted to cry out. I thought of her sitting in the lofty upstairs parlor of her childhood home, the ancient pecan trees towering overhead. I could hear the Lennon Sisters crooning on the big black-and-white television set, and it made me yearn for her stern Presbyterian demeanor and her dry, tight-lipped kisses. The remembered smell of moldering books and aging cypress that pervaded the old house brought tears to my eyes. But I didn't share our secret with her.

For six more months we remained encamped in our rented, low-ceilinged California house, waiting for my father to come back.

The boxes that had been in the garage since our move from Corpus Christi that summer, when we had arrived full of hope about living in the promised land, never did get unpacked. Sometimes I'd peel back one of the flaps and peek inside at the evidence of our former life as a family. A swing set. A box of dog clippers and a collar with the nametag of our poodle Brigitte, who had been hit by a car not long before we left Texas.

Then one day in spring I found something else in the garage: cartons of dyed Easter eggs, chocolate bunnies, plastic eggs with dollar bills inside and a note.

> *Sorry I had to deliver these a day early.*
>
> *The Easter Bunny*

Patty, Doug and I ran eagerly from treasure to treasure, marveling at the eccentric ways of the California Easter Bunny, who left his eggs in the garage. I was in the thick of the celebration, still a firm believer in all things magical, until I saw Momma sadly take the note and go inside.

Daddy? Was all this from him? No Easter Bunny at all, just my father alone in a kitchen somewhere coloring eggs? I picked up a stuffed rabbit and stared into its lifeless eyes, wondering why he didn't want to be with us anymore. *What did we do to him?*

My mother drove our pink '59 Thunderbird practically onto the curb at the sight of a black teenager holding hands with his white girlfriend. I swiveled around to get a better look.

"I can't believe they let that sort of thing go on here. California! It wouldn't be allowed in Mississippi," she said.

"They're just in love," I volunteered. Surely this would clear things up for her. But she cowed me with an incredulous searching look, a "What's become of my real child?" glare, that told me it wasn't the right thing to say at all. I turned to look at the couple again. The boy pulled his girlfriend up against his chest and she laughed a little before offering him her lips. I watched, wide-eyed.

"Don't look at *that*," Momma gasped at me as she sped through a red light. A brown Chevy slammed on its brakes and a pedestrian yelled, "Woman driver!"

I pondered that *"that."* She'd said the word as if she were spitting out bile, and its bitter aftertaste came not from the passionate kiss I had witnessed, but rather from the boy's skin color, so dark against the girl's white arms around his neck.

It's a bad thing? I asked myself, hefting its oppressive weight. The black people I'd known had taught me to tie my shoes, taken me to the zoo, cooked my meals. My beloved Gladys—our maid in Houston—I had once called "Mother."

"You just call me Gladys, honey. That's good enough," she'd told me.

"But Gladys, I love you. I have to call you something special."

"Come here, child." I climbed into her lap and rested my head on her soft breast. Her uniform was white and starchy under my cheek. She picked up a new bottle of milk from the counter and pulled off the cardboard tab. Her dark brown hands were callused, but very gentle, and I thought of how nicely she could tie a hair ribbon. She had taught me to tie my shoes the same way. Then she poured yellow cream off the top of the milk into a small glass and handed it to me, holding me while I drank it, and humming a deep, throaty melody.

Having known nothing but love and kindness from black people, I found my mother's scorn bizarre. And since I had just learned that grown-ups weren't infallible, I felt comfortable disagreeing with her. I kept these thoughts secret, but I was, more and more, making my own choices about the way the world should work.

"We're going home," my mother was saying next to me.

"I have to go to school," I protested.

"No, I mean we're going *home*."

Home, of course, meant Yazoo City and Aunt Ruth, who had raised my mother from birth. The only thing we had of my real grandmother—Ida, Aunt Ruth's sister who had died of complications from childbirth—was a faded 1910 photograph.

A month later all our belongings were packed up and sent to Mississippi, though not, I'm sure, just because of *that* incident. Momma had simply borne all she could stand. As soon as the movers finished loading the truck, we would get on a plane to Houston, where my father's parents, Nanny and Dodo, lived in a rambling house outside of the city on Lake Houston. Nanny had talked Momma into stopping off for a visit. I remember Momma saying to her during a phone call, "I don't understand him either, Mother."

Nanny almost always got her way. She was a powerfully built woman, almost six feet tall, with a personality to match. And, since she weighed over three hundred pounds, I never knew if she was going to smother me with rolls of fat or just squeeze the life out of me when she swept me into a breath-grabbing bear hug. Dodo was the exact opposite: quiet, reserved and deliberate. His favorite pastime was reading the dictionary.

Daddy and my brother, Doug, whom we called Duddie, were going to the Grand Canyon and we were going to Houston without them.

I took Duddie aside and gravely counseled him not to let our father keep him. "Momma needs you more than he does."

"But he's taking me to the Grand Canyon!" he protested. He was six and had big blue eyes and wavy, golden blond hair—a cruel joke on Patty and me, who had brown eyes and straight brown hair, and were condemned as toddlers to the recurring torture of the permanent wave.

"You're a selfish little boy," I hissed, grabbing as big a hank of Duddie's golden strands as I could and pulling. "You'll probably fall into the Grand Canyon and die." He started to cry and I quickly walked away to escape into the hills behind our house, where I waited, sitting on a rock outcropping and staring into the valley below. The smell of sage has triggered melancholy in me ever since.

When I thought they had gone, I struggled back up the path past turquoise-streaked boulders. But I saw that Daddy was in the backyard looking for me. He stood in the middle of a bed of last season's snapdragons, prodding the brown stalks with his foot. Perhaps he was remembering how we'd planted them together, how a nest of rattlesnakes had been routed out by our digging, how I had run screaming into his arms. A cigarette hung from his lips and his Rat Pack hairstyle was mussed from a long day of packing boxes.

"I hope you're happy," I spat out when I trudged past him. He laid his arm across my shoulder and tried to draw me to him, but I struggled free and he let me go. In a few minutes I stood in the front yard, holding baby Margaret and watching as Momma handed him Duddie's suitcases. Patty, the dark-eyed child who had inherited Daddy's temper, stood angrily at my side with her arms crossed on her little chest, her face a study in rage. She'd already gotten one spanking that day for insolence. But it must have been hard for her, seeing Duddie leave, because he was her particular playmate in the family. Their high-pitched screeching and giggling were the background of all our lives.

Then Daddy drove away with his only son, who looked small and scared, hunched down in the passenger seat with his arms around a snot-stained teddy bear.

They were waiting at the airport in Houston when we arrived three days later. My mother exclaimed with surprise when she saw them standing on the runway at the foot of the stairs.

Nanny put us kids onto roll-away beds in the living room and ushered my father into the big guest room with Momma. The next morning Patty and I found Nanny beaming, propped up on pillows in her twin bed with her satin bed jacket and its many ribbons flowing around her. She beckoned us to climb in beside her. I was soon struggling to escape from her overweening kisses. But each time I reached the edge of the bed, she caught me, tickling and pulling me end over end into her big breasts, where I would gasp with laughter and lack of oxygen.

She and Dodo chain-smoked that morning while they watched *The Price Is Right* from their cigarette-scarred recliners, and by the time Daddy and Momma finally came, sheepishly, out of their bedroom, a cloud of smoke was floating in the rafters. No one made any big announcements, but when we left a few days later for Mississippi, Daddy was driving. I felt my prayer, repeated endlessly since he had left us, "Please, God, make Daddy love Mommy again," had been answered. I just didn't know how much was God's doing and how much was my big Nanny's.

In Yazoo City, powerful ancestral ties began to bind Margaret Tuttle and her children, though ultimately they would not hold my father. Even that first summer he was often gone, tending to his new sales region in Texas, a promotion. And when he was with us, Daddy would sing "I Left My Heart in San Francisco." He even asked me to learn to play it on the piano, which I refused to do. But it became the Tuttle family's theme song anyway, because we had all left our hearts in San Francisco, where the unquestioning love that grows from a family's unity was lost forever. We had it once, and I remember it, though my sisters and brother do not. It is one of the secrets that Momma and I share.

My Ancestors Were My Constant Companions

My sister Patty and I lay curled tightly under our quilts, the big fans making a soothing "whooo" in the background. Even though it was summer in Mississippi, the sleeping porch of Aunt Ruth's old house was always cool.

She sat on the edge of my bed, singing us to sleep.

> *Hark! Tis the shepherd's voice I hear, out in the desert dark and*
> *drear.*

Calling the sheep who've gone astray, far from the shepherd's
  fold away.
Bring them in! Bring them in! Bring the wanderers from the fields
  of sin.
Bring them in! Bring them in! Bring the wandering ones to Jesus.

As she sang, her old-lady voice cracked and trembled, but the fervor came through loud and clear. I held her hand tightly and lay there listening in the moonlight, mesmerized by an illustration on the wall of Little Black Sambo chasing a tiger around a palm tree.

That night I dreamed of pancakes drenched in tiger butter, and of black native children touching my white skin, trying to turn me into a bowl of milk.

Six months later Aunt Ruth was dead.

I wasn't allowed to go to the funeral, but afterward Daddy took me to her grave and I pulled a pink carnation from the flowers that flowed onto the adjacent tombstones of her mother and father and brother.

"Try to remember her like she was," he said to me as we stood there. "Do you have any questions?"

"No." I had no questions, only thoughts of wanting to join her, of being unable to go on without her. He was no comfort, so obviously unmoved himself by the death of the woman who would leave his wife a fortune. And my mother had not offered me consolation, perhaps needing all that was available for herself, grief rendering her a stoic. She went quietly and gently about the details of laying her aunt to rest, she who knew her best of all, who had spent what I jealously saw as carefree years under her care. No, she couldn't understand that I had lost the only person I trusted. Or maybe she did know, but didn't see the worth of my loss when measured against her own.

I tried to feel Aunt Ruth beneath the flowers that lay five feet deep on the freshly mounded dirt of her grave. But flowers and Aunt Ruth didn't go together. Better if it had been yellow legal pads, or oil derricks piled up over her, or Bibles. The flowers worked as a repellent, and I fled the spot, returning to her house—now our house—to pillage the papers in her desk. I found the comfort I sought, a note she'd written to herself a few years before.

Today I feel life has just started and that I have many things
to accomplish before passing on to the great beyond from
which no mere man has returned to live again in this world,
except Lazarus, who failed to expire on death, so have always

felt that death is a mysterious deep sleep until Judgment Day,
when bodies will be resurrected from the grave and each
judged according to his life as lived in this world for the eter-
nal life in Heaven.

I put on one of her blouses and pressed the carnation between the pages of
my Bible. Then I lay on the floor of my bedroom and pulled the emotional
tissue of memory around me, and prayed for myself, who felt lost in a
lonely world.

It seemed remodeling began almost immediately, and I flew—leaving
smudges of grief like a chimney swift trapped in the house—from room
to room, watching the old mantels pried from the walls, seeing bland
Sheetrock covering rose and hollyhock wallpapers. The sleeping porch lost
its leaded glass window that could be opened to spy on the stairwell. The
"raw head and bloody bones" closet upstairs was painted and shelved, no
longer a terror for small children. And Aunt Ruth's mannish suits and
whalebone corsets were bundled off along with her mother's Victorian fur-
niture to Kay, her maid and cook for over forty years, and now ours. Elizabeth Thompson Campbell's nineteenth-century dowry ended up in a dark
two-room shack, perched high on Brickyard Hill, that Kay shared with her
husband and daughter.

The echoes of ancestral furnishings, the dense rugs, the heavy draperies, linger like lost friends in childhood memories. Even now, I see them
every time I walk through the old house. So in a way, I continued to live
with Aunt Ruth, the ghosts of her parents, Elizabeth and Tom, my long
dead grandmother Ida, and the "raw head and bloody bones" creature that
I'm sure still haunts the attic, walled up behind shelves of linens.

That

"I don't know how your father can do this to me," Momma was saying as
we drove to Jackson. Only an emergency would have caused her to take me
with her, because she'd interrupted my eighth-grade algebra class and gotten me out of school. She navigated up and down the kudzu-covered hills
to the Jackson airport, fretting about "the race question" and Daddy's involvement in it.

Of course, she rationalized, it was because of "this darn job." Daddy
had been asked by Owen Cooper—Yazoo's leading employer and friend of
future president Jimmy Carter—to spearhead the revamping of Head Start
in Mississippi. Since then my father had shuttled back and forth between

Washington and Mississippi, carrying messages and money from Sargent Shriver to moderate white Mississippians who wanted the program to work, but not by putting money into the hands of out-of-state "radical negroes." There were many black Mississippians who supported Shriver's initiatives, too, believing federal largesse should be spread among citizens of the state. It was a divisive time for both blacks and whites.

Daddy had built a statewide coalition of County Supervisors and driven almost every road in Mississippi, making black and white friends along the way. An incident with the Ku Klux Klan, the brutal beating of a black field organizer who was traveling alone, had shaken everyone up a few weeks before. But that was the sort of excitement my father thrived on. "Always good in a crisis," Momma liked to say about him. I had modified it to "Always in a crisis."

I don't think he was particularly enlightened about racial matters. We didn't discuss them at home and he was certainly no crusader. On the other hand, I never heard him haranguing or race-baiting as some of my friends' fathers did. The word "nigger" wasn't used under any circumstances in our family. My father says he simply believed in assessing individuals on their own merits, and I think that's what enabled him to work so close to the heart of racial divisions. But even that level of tolerance was rare among whites in 1960s Mississippi.

Being the wife of such a man was, however, not always to my mother's liking. "You're probably going to have to shake this colored man's hand, too," she said, a doting mother warning her unsuspecting child of life's unpleasant potholes. I thought for a while about it, and about the belief, still common among my friends in Yazoo City, that the blackness could rub off. But by this time I was rebel enough to know I'd shake the man's hand, and do it gladly, if it upset my mother.

Daddy was waiting for us in the airport lobby. He was garrulous and laughing, with his tie half off and his suit coat thrown over one shoulder. The black man stood quietly, his tie perfectly knotted and his coat buttoned.

They'd been waiting awhile, but Momma dragged her feet as we approached. Then, stiffly, like a prisoner in front of a firing squad, she extended a gloved hand. The man held it very briefly and said, "So nice to meet you." I saw her surreptitiously wipe it on her skirt when he dropped it, and she reached for me. She was trembling.

She's scared, I thought.

I recalled my great-aunt Fanny's stories about how her father, when he was five, had been lifted onto Robert E. Lee's horse, Traveller, while the general took a drink of water from the family well. I remembered the old Southern resolve, "Forget, hell!" and wondered how many stories that boy, my great-grandfather, had told my mother of Civil War glory and carpetbagger injustice, black servitude and white supremacy. When had she had any relationship with a black person except as a beneficiary of his or her labor? Or as the dispenser of feudal largesse?

Yet here she stood, having just offered her hand to a middle-class black man, her husband's equal in the workplace. No wonder she trembled. She had defied two hundred and fifty years of familial programming. It was an act like so many others that were beginning to happen across the South: the previously unthinkable made commonplace.

Boldly, I held out my own hand, though the man had already turned away. He felt me brushing his sleeve and turned back to me.

"This is my daughter, Ruth," Daddy said, winking at me.

"I'm so pleased to meet you," I said, and the man smiled broadly as he took my hand in both of his and pumped it up and down. His grip was strong and warm. I was conscious of my mother's protective hand on my shoulder, giving me the slightest tug to step back next to her, and I shrugged it off.

My father left to make some phone calls. The black man and my mother talked about the weather for a few minutes, then she asked where he lived.

"Here in Jackson," he said. "Just around the corner from Medgar's house."

"Medgar?" I asked.

"Medgar Evers. He was gunned down in his driveway there, less than a year ago."

"Why?" I asked.

My mother shifted uncomfortably.

"NAACP. He worked for the NAACP." I saw a flicker of something in the man's eyes. Contempt? Disbelief? I couldn't say. But I began to feel ashamed of myself. Somehow inappropriate. We all just stood there in silence. When Daddy got back, his face was beet red.

"I thought we'd get a bite to eat," he stammered, "but I can't find a single place in Jackson that'll serve us, unless you know of one?" He looked hopefully at his associate, whose own face had gotten tight.

"No, no I don't," he said.

They both looked at my mother, and I saw her lips press together. No invitation to a home-cooked meal would be forthcoming.

With cool dignity, the man excused himself and said he'd find his own way home. We three marched silently to our car, and my parents didn't say a word to each other the whole long drive back to Yazoo City.

Small Talk

I held on to the dashboard with all my might. Sue, on my left, was flung into me when the truck took a sharp turn off Grand onto Highway 49. My teeth were chattering with fear.

The driver had had two beers, but I didn't think he was drunk. Instead, I thought he had gone insane, an instantaneous madness that had arisen when I'd asked him a question about Vietnam.

The afternoon had started out so peacefully. Sue and I, high school juniors now, had been dragging Grand in my Camaro, sipping Dr Peppers and talking about boys. I wanted a boyfriend *real bad,* and I thought Sue could teach me the tricks that would get me one.

There were several obstacles I had to overcome. Being so tall was one, of course. Being a brain was another. But neither of those, I felt, was the real problem. It grew from some dark and serious place in me that made me incapable of the flirtatious small talk that can smooth over rough spots in a teenage conversation. Sue tried to teach me the art of chitchat. But when called on to perform, I always drew a blank, coming up with nothing more beguiling than "What do you think of Mrs. Jenkins as a teacher?" at which point Sue would salvage the situation with "Last week in her class my hair went completely flat. You know, this part right here with the blond streak?" I felt absurdly grateful for her tolerance of me. She taught me everything I know about face creams, mascara and foundation makeup, and what I learned from her about organizing a wardrobe was a formidable professional tool in the eighties. But that day in 1968, even Sue was speechless.

We'd seen this guy in the Quik Stop when we were buying our Dr Peppers. "Catch an eyeful of that," Sue had whispered to me at the cash register. We knew almost every boy in Yazoo, by name if nothing else, but occasionally a boy from another county, a planter's son or a college boy home for the weekend, would show up and pique our interest.

Sue sauntered out to the parking lot behind the stranger and was soon leaning against his red truck, laughing and flirting. When I joined her she asked, "Wanna go for a ride with this guy?"

"Sure." We climbed into the cab and his sister got in beside us. Then the truck headed up Grand.

I knew almost right away that we'd made a bad decision.

"Look at this," the young man said, holding a blue-gray pistol flat on the palm of his hand.

"It's pretty," Sue squeaked out.

"Fucking A, man. It *is* pretty. Pretty powerful."

"Where'd you get it?" I asked him.

" 'Nam. I got it in Vee-ut-nam." He laughed. But it was a mirthless, smirky laugh. He laid the gun in his lap.

Having forgotten again how to make small talk, I asked that question: "Did you kill anyone?" He looked at me as if I were a three-hundred-pound bully who had just punched him. It was a scared, vulnerable look, quickly washed away by emotional bedlam. But I'd seen in it some of the reality of Vietnam, which until then had been no more to me than a list of casualties and exploding palm trees on the nightly news.

He slammed his hand onto the steering wheel several times. We took a corner on two wheels. His sister, wedged between me and the door, began fumbling in the glove compartment. She shoved a box of ammunition to one side and it broke open, spilling small, pointed shells under my feet. I bent to scoop them back into the box. When I sat up, she was holding what looked like a half-smoked cigarette. She lit it.

"Give him this," she told me. Sniffing a sweetish odor, I passed it to Sue, who gave it to the boy. The gun fell to the floor and began sliding back and forth. Gingerly, I picked it up and quickly stowed it in the glove box.

As cloying smoke filled the cabin, a measure of calm returned. Our driver's moment of insanity seemed to be over. He pulled onto the gravel shoulder of Graball Road and turned off the ignition.

"Man, what a bummer. I think I had a flashback," he said. The joint was now only a nub, and he took a last, long drag off of it, holding the smoke in his lungs until it finally sneaked out in a series of snorts and gasps.

"You okay?" the boy's sister asked him.

"He's crazy," I whispered in Sue's ear. "Let's go get my car."

I was deeply distressed by our encounter with that simple Mississippi boy, who'd had his life ripped from its moorings in Vietnam, and the memory stayed with me.

In another year or so, I would begin trying to shoulder some of the burdens of ending the war. But that day, Sue and I bought some more Dr Peppers and started dragging Grand for other, less damaged goods.

I can't say exactly when I decided to discard the dusty hand-me-downs of my Mississippi ancestors, for I loved them dearly. But I was uncomfortable with bigotry and privilege, disturbed by the specter of Vietnam, and saw that most of the people around me were not. Perhaps I am mistaken in remembering I had choices. Maybe there was no other choice for me except to go away.

I know that at the end of my senior year a plane ticket to New York *seemed* like the only way out. I pinned my hopes on getting it, and on Jeff, a boy about whom I still knew very little. I did wonder why he kept writing me, tenaciously reshaping our tattered teenage romance into friendship. Mostly, though, while my friends celebrated the end of high school at dances and parties, I sat at home and dreamed of the Big Apple.

13. *Jeff*

going it alone

I woke up to a noise I'd never heard before, a gasping, racking, liquid sound that finally roused me out of my snug bed in the little open room between the kitchen and the parlor. Clutching my faithful Foxy-doodle, whose orange and white fur was already soiled and pilling and whose shiny black plastic nose had fallen or been gnawed off, I made my way slowly through the dim apartment toward a single light in the living room. It was the middle of the night, and I couldn't understand why my mother would be up.

I heard words: "My baby, my poor baby, my poor Keithy, oh my poor Keithy," but they sounded strange, lyrics in a moaning singsong. Was it really my mother making these sounds? "I want my baby back, bring my baby back, bring him back, please, God, please. . . ."

She was sobbing—great, heaving sobs amid gasping intakes of breath, her tears flowing down between the wet fingers she held to her cheeks. In one hand she clutched a handkerchief, and as she saw me coming she started slightly, then dabbed at her nose and mouth.

"Mommy, why are you crying?"

She didn't answer at first, although she put a hand on my shoulder while she tried to collect herself. Finally the racking of her slender body eased somewhat, and she was able to look at me, her eyes brimming.

"My baby, my little Keithy, your little brother. I miss him so much, and I wish Gawdy hadn't taken him away and made him an angel. I want him back, I want him back, poor Keithy. . . ."

The strange baby, my brother, had hardly been home with us during his brief life. I wanted to feel as sad as my mother, wanted to cry with her, but I couldn't.

"But Keithy is with Gawdy and the angels, Mommy . . . isn't he?"

She didn't answer for a long time, just cried and moaned and rocked slightly in the stuffed chair, her eyes closed. After a while she took me on her lap, but when I said, "Come be my Mommy," she didn't respond with a delighted hug and a smile as she always had. After a while I climbed down from her lap and took Foxy-doodle back to bed, thinking about Keith.

He had been born with Down's syndrome, as I learned later, and I heard strange, forbidding words when the grown-ups spoke of him—words like "retarded" and "mongoloid." Dr. Wilkins had told my mother that "it was probably just as well" that Keith had died of pneumonia after a year of living mostly at the hospital, since he would never be a normal child. But that—and the fact that he was now with God and the angels—hadn't seemed to ease my mother's grief.

Maybe she was so sorrowful because Joe had failed to save Keithy. I knew she wished that her first husband hadn't died so young. Joe, the lanky, smiling French-Canadian golfer my mother had married during World War II only to discover he was dying of tuberculosis, was a kind of unofficial guardian angel. He was always "watching over us," my mother said, and if anything bad was about to happen, he would protect us.

Of course she never mentioned him during the three or so months out of every twelve that my father was home. And although I wanted to believe in Joe, since he seemed to be a kind of spiritual father to make up for the persistent absence of my real one and because my mother seemed to place so much stock in him, I knew now that he wasn't always able to save us from evil.

After a while my eyes closed, and the muffled sounds from the living room began to lull me to sleep. Soon I was dreaming of my brother, with his odd unsmiling face, flitting about among the trumpet-playing angels. Would he be happy with them? Would they be able to make him smile?

In later years I came to the conclusion that Keith's brief life and early death marked the death as well of most of the love my mother had felt for my father. She had had terrible relations with his mother during the pregnancy, and she had read an article to the effect that stress could cause mongolism, so she always blamed her mother-in-law for Keith's condition.

Right or wrong, she never forgave my grandmother—or my father for not intervening and shielding her from his mother. And for being out to sea most of the time.

Armageddon Now

"How long do you think they'll go at it this time?" I said to my brother, Jim, trying to lighten things up with a bit of foxhole humor. But my question was drowned out by the familiar sounds of marital hell from downstairs—the hysterical screaming, the insults, the stammered shouts in reply, the shattering of glass and crockery (but never, thank God, the sound of blows). I'd closed two doors—one at the bottom of the stairs and one leading to my room—to prevent the awful noise from reaching us, but it had gotten through anyway. It was the same every time Dad came home.

I thought wryly of the nursery rhyme my mother had taught me years

ago in the dim cloister of our first home in Queens, a rhyme she would re-
cite whenever some kid in that roiling ethnic cauldron made me cry:

Sticks and stones may break my bones,
but words can never harm me.

But words have a way of hurting far more than sticks and stones, and the
rabid words my mother periodically aimed at my father—the poisoned fruit
of her realization that she would have to bring up his children virtually
alone—had hurt me and my siblings at least as much as they had hurt him.
Had my parents ever been happy together? Wasn't it even possible that this
endlessly repeated misery was a form of happiness for them?

My mother had confided in me many a time throughout my childhood,
from the earliest days I could remember, enlisting me in her lonely battle
for the emotional goods she felt she had been denied.

"He told me he'd give up the sea and get a normal, decent job like
other men. But now I'm married to a man who's gone all the time, and you
don't have a real father. I wish I could get out of this stinkin' mess." I assumed she meant she would take me, and later my siblings as well, when
she left, if she ever did. But she never said that. Perhaps she thought it was
so obvious it didn't need to be said.

I never knew what to say when she reeled off her complaints: My father didn't send enough money home; he had said he would become an
Episcopalian, as my mother had, to bridge the gap between her Catholi-
cism and his Lutheranism, but he never had. Another broken promise, another reason to get out.

There was a lull in the fighting, and we heard the lower door open
and close, then light footsteps on the stairs. In a moment there was a
knock, but Jim, who was nearer the door, was too shell-shocked to move. I
walked over and opened it for Deb, the youngster of our family. She said
nothing—it's hard to converse when your guts are wrung up tight like a
dishrag—but looked me in the eyes as she came in, wanting assurance that
we would survive this one, too. "They're quiet now," I said. "Maybe it's
over."

Deb and Jim looked at me, wanting to believe. Then we heard Mom's
battle cry: "I'm getting out of this stinkin' mess!"

"Oh, quit your goddamn complaining!" Dad roared. "You never had it
so good!"

Good-natured, trusting and a decorated veteran of the Pacific campaign in World War II, he wasn't a bad man by any means. But he was a
loner by nature, someone who needed his own clearly defined space in
which to sort things out. He wasn't sullen or unfriendly—in fact, he smiled
readily and addressed people he met as "friend"—but he was the opposite

of gregarious, and he gave up working on glamorous liners like the *Independence* and the *Constitution* because he couldn't play the purser's role of social director. On the freighters where he settled in for good, ships with names like *Export Builder* and *Export Adventurer,* he could keep the ship's books, act as its medic, shopkeeper and paymaster, and mess with the other officers in the wardroom without being at the beck and call of hundreds of demanding passengers. It was his ideal job, and he would stay at it, with only a few interruptions to look for work on shore, for nearly forty years.

Mom did her best to give us a good upbringing, exposing us to great music, art and as many books as we could read. What she wasn't able to provide was the stability that a good parenting partnership can create. She knew she couldn't do the job alone, but she couldn't get any help, which caused untold frustration and friction.

Typically the fights began innocently enough; Dad would question an expenditure (my mother spent money freely, whereas my father was pretty careful with a buck), or he would receive a letter from his mother. Then the air in the house would subtly begin to thicken. Sometimes, wrapped up as we were in our own childish and adolescent lives, we wouldn't even see it coming.

But when the storm clouds started to gather—the heavy silence between them, the slamming of doors and cooking gear, the look of righteous determination on the old man's face as he prepared to fight what he considered the good fight—we knew we were in for it once again. But knowing gave no comfort. There was nothing you could do or say to avert it, and there was no getting used to it. The only way to survive was to escape.

Our family life, what little there was that included all five of us, wasn't all hell. Sometimes we behaved relatively normally, going upstate on two-week vacations to Letchworth State Park with Nanny and Pappy, my mother's parents, or piling everything into our balky old Rambler station wagon and heading for the beach. But even there, my father would go off on his own as soon as possible. A strong swimmer, he'd wade out to the point where only his head and shoulders showed, then he'd start his steady, slow breaststroke up and down the shore, swimming for three and four hours at a stretch. My mother, who didn't swim, was left on the beach with three kids to look after. On lap twenty or so she would turn to me, the oldest child, shake her head despairingly and say, "Even when he's home, he's not here."

There was a crash and a screech downstairs. "Well," Jim said, "that's it. I'm going." He got up and walked quickly out of the room and down the stairs. In a moment he was out the front door and heading around back to the porch to get his bike. I was planning to split, too, but I felt bad about leaving Deb, who was too young to go out without permission.

"You can stay here till it's over," I told her. "Listen to records or whatever. Try to ignore it. I'm going over to Vin's house."

"Okay," she said without much conviction. Her blue eyes were moist; she looked like a hunted beast.

I had been the de facto man of the family for years. I had looked after my siblings from the age of nine and I often rode herd on them now, in my late teens. But while I probably was too hard on my brother, I had a soft spot for my baby sister, the infant I'd insisted on holding in the car on the way back from the hospital when she was born. I knew she'd survive this reprise of what I called the Battle of the Bulge—my brother and I had. But her room, unlike ours, was on the first floor, right next to our parents' bedroom. She wouldn't be able to go back to it for hours.

"Don't worry," I said, chucking her under the chin. "I won't be gone that long. Maybe when I get back I'll be able to get the car and we can go out for a soda or something like that. If I can't, I'll ride you on my bike. Okay?"

"Okay," she said again, heading for the bookcase Pappy had built into one of the walls of my room. "See you later."

I closed the door behind me, flinching as an unearthly scream issued from below, followed by a roared "Jesus Christ! Are you crazy? Are you out of your mind?" For a moment I considered checking on them to make sure nothing truly awful had happened, but then I shrugged, straightened up and headed down the stairs.

Hard Cases

The suburbs were the great white hope of the great white proletarian masses after World War II. Though they seemed pristine—incubators for the Baby Boom, orderly rows of new houses mushrooming across the truck farms and oak forests of Long Island soon after the boys came home—they were, after all, only one step removed from the city itself. And New York was big, ugly, scary and dirty.

The people who made the potato fields sprout with children were still city people—often only one generation removed from the boat people who had brought their families over the ocean. And their children in many cases had spent their early years in the hard, faceless city itself, as I had. Almost none of us had known the "it takes a village" ethic of small-town America, and many of us were very rough cases indeed.

I don't think I was one of the worst, but I know I wasn't one of the best, either. I was a risk taker, a daredevil, the kind of kid who would gleefully run right to the edge of disaster to impress his friends or get a laugh. When I was six or seven, I leaped off my brother's changing table and swung on the dining room chandelier after watching a Tarzan movie on TV. Luckily, I didn't weigh enough to bring it down. But I wasn't in awe of danger—or authority. And, since my father wasn't around to tan my hide and my distracted and overwhelmed mother was the very opposite of a steady disciplinarian, she lost control of me very early on.

Once, when I was about nine, on a visit to my grandparents' house on Eighty-ninth Avenue in the Woodhaven section of Queens, I ran the cramped streets of my old neighborhood with my friends and learned a new word.

"Cocksucker! Kaminsky is a cocksucker!"

My friend Stevie was taunting his neighborhood enemy, and while I was filing away this new term for rapid and devastating deployment back in Malverne, they got into a shoving match. Kaminsky, a somewhat smaller and less pugnacious boy, ran away in tears, and Stevie was basking in his triumph when old man Kaminsky came rumbling down the block in his undershirt, grabbing my horrified friend by the shoulder and shaking him roughly as he demanded who the hell Stevie thought he was, pushing his son and calling him a name like that.

Stevie, in tears, ran and got his own father, a stocky railroad man, and the two men were soon shouting and shoving each other in the Kaminskys' doorway before they vanished inside. A few minutes later, to our astonishment, Stevie's father left the house smiling, and the two men shook hands and laughed at how close they'd come to blows. Stevie was deeply disappointed.

"I thought my old man was going to kick the shit out of his old man," he confided. "And Kaminsky's *still* a cocksucker." We laughed, then ran to join the rest of the gang, who were hanging out in an unused garage across from the back of a large commercial bakery. The guys were grinning as we joined them, their eyes gleeful and their mouths stuffed with warm white bread. The game was to run across the street and grab a loaf off the unattended loading dock, and one of them, looking pointedly at me, said that anyone who wouldn't do it was a pussy faggot. Soon I had my own loaf, most of which became ammunition in a food fight.

My family had moved out to Malverne, a village just over the Nassau County line that separated suburbia from the city, when I was five years old. I had a relatively happy childhood there—Little League, Cub Scouts, the woods with its lazy, turtle-filled stream across the street from my home. I had a huge room all to myself on the second floor, but on hot summer nights I slept on the side porch. It was there that I'd listen to Red Barber and Mel Allen turn Yankees games into radio ballet and read, five or six times, *The Kid Who Batted 1,000.* With cars whizzing by on Ocean Avenue thirty feet from my head, I'd drift off on the chaise longue, the traffic sounds gradually becoming the crowd noise in my baseball dreams.

The county decided to widen Ocean Avenue in the early sixties, which meant that our side yard would be cut in half and the already heavy traffic flow would increase. That, my parents said, meant we had to move. But there was another, darker, reason for the move. There was a shantytown on the other side of Ocean Avenue, and when I was in fourth grade a court ruled that the children of the migrants who lived there could no longer be confined to Woodfield Road School. Now these black pupils would come to our school, Lindner Place, bringing wrenching problems of assimilation and sparking white protests that were shown on national TV.

I befriended one of these waifs of social justice, a boy named Bradley, sitting next to him and helping him read books about World War II in the school library. He or his clothes had a slightly astringent scent I couldn't name—perhaps lye soap—but he was a friendly, likable kid with a ready smile and a great thirst for knowledge. He and I walked home the same way from school, and once I invited him in for cookies and milk.

When I led Bradley into our house, feeling something like the prince showing off the palace to his pauper pal, I saw my mother's eyes widen. But she played it cool for once, leading us into the kitchen, where my Irish grandma, who generally referred to blacks as "jigs" or "jigaboos," was sitting.

"Hi, Nanny. This is my friend Bradley from school," I said, grabbing a glass of milk and a few cookies. I watched her reaction. After an involuntary start and a sharp intake of breath, she rose quickly from the table and said: "Adelaide, I think we'll be going. Where *is* he now?" referring to Pappy, who was fixing something in the basement.

Later that night my mother got a much stronger reaction from a neighbor whose son was a playmate of mine. I don't know how she'd heard of Bradley's brief visit, but she was furious about it.

"I don't know about you, but *I* have no intention of seeing the niggers take over Malverne," she told my mother, her hands on her hips and her eyes narrow. "I think you should forbid Jeff to associate with nigger children or invite them into your house, because if you don't, this neighborhood could go like *that*," she said, snapping her fingers loudly.

She had made the mistake of talking down to my mother, who may not have wanted me to associate with Bradley, but who now went into reverse. She heard the neighbor out, looking concerned but saying nothing definitive. Then she showed her the door and turned on her heel, her jaw set and her eyes flashing. She was silent as she steamed past me, but the point was made; inviting a black kid into our house would cause a tremendous fuss. I never did it again.

One morning in September of 1962 I woke up and found myself in Merrick, five miles farther out on the Island, a stranger with a weird-looking last name. Merrick had no blacks nearby and no possibility of an integration crisis, although many of the surrounding towns—Freeport,

Uniondale, Hempstead—had large black populations and saw a lot of trouble, especially after Martin Luther King, Jr., was shot.

But while I didn't have to deal with the effects of racial integration anymore, my social integration went badly. The smart kids among my new sixth-grade mates didn't accept me, and, perhaps out of spite for the move I hadn't wanted to make, I gravitated toward several delinquents who'd been left back two or three times each. It was with them, at the age of eleven, that I had my first real taste of carnal knowledge.

I had a paper route at the time, and at the end of my rounds one day in late spring I came upon Masterson, a punk from my class, and four other guys trying to persuade Yolanda Markov to service them in the wooded margin behind a nearby school. Yolanda, an intelligent but emotionally disturbed and physically mature girl of fourteen who played the role of local floozy, lived close to me, although we were now about a mile from our homes. She almost never said no, but this time—pleased as she was by the attention—she was begging off, claiming she had to get home to start supper for her widowed mother.

Masterson seized the initiative when I pedaled up.

"Look, Yolanda," he said, "here's Durstewitz. He can ride you home when we're done, so you don't have to worry about being late."

Her resistance, never very convincing, crumbled, and we all headed for the woods. It must have been obvious to anyone looking on that Yolanda was about to accommodate a party of six, like an extra-large pizza. But, as in the city, no one looked, or at least no one bothered to intervene. I couldn't believe my good fortune; I was about to be initiated into the mysteries of the flesh at age eleven, and all because the *Long Island Press*'s route manager had been desperate enough to hire a runt like me.

Yolanda, a sexual trouper, got through what followed by pretending that one of the boys, big, baby-faced Bo Roberts, was her boyfriend. She stroked and fellated him, but try as she might to coax him, Bo couldn't or wouldn't perform in front of a crowd. Several of the others had no such inhibitions, although each waited his turn with more decorum than he usually showed on the school lunch line. Finished, each one jumped up, vastly pleased with himself, zippering and grinning as I sat wide-eyed, fondling Yolanda's outsized breasts. She invited me to jump aboard when the last of the older guys was done, but I declined, not having reached puberty and not wanting to embarrass myself.

Two years later, after my voice had changed, I had another close encounter with Yolanda. I'd been at her door one afternoon, trying to wheedle my way in, when a carful of beer-guzzling guys pulled up for what was obviously going to be another gang bang. Yolanda, waving gaily from the stoop as if she were about to go on a dream date, told the guys she had to be home by 4:30 at the latest. Then she got into the car, and they all roared off.

I came back to Yolanda's at about 4:45, figuring there might be a window of opportunity before her mother got home. I rang the bell, and she answered the door in a towel, fresh from the shower. She gave me a "you naughty boy" smile, let me in and actually said, "Let me slip into something more comfy." She left for a few moments, then reappeared in a filmy blue peignoir and sat on the couch next to me. She had the TV on—Shirley Temple singing "The Good Ship Lollipop"—and as I feverishly pulled her nightie up, she paid very little attention to me. She lay back and let me feel, suck and hump all I wanted, but for some reason she didn't want my virginity on her conscience.

"You're too young!" she kept saying, frowning indulgently. With my pants down and Shirley Temple capering away, I finally parted her legs. But she frustrated my frenzied thrusts with expert muscular control.

Finally, sighing and shaking her head as if to say, "You asked for it," she relented, and I had the sensation of falling through a trapdoor. While I gyrated up and down like a dog, she calmly counted out loud to thirty-six or so, continuing to watch the TV all the while. Then she shouted: "Get out! Get out!" I did, and she coolly handed me a tissue for the mess on my leg. She smiled at me like some kind of sexual fairy godmother and said she hoped I was happy.

It had been a decidedly mixed blessing, this premature penetration, as I found out when I went home that day. My mother turned my triumph into ashes, scowling as if I were the lowest form of vermin and grilling me about where I'd been. She didn't accuse me directly of visiting Yolanda, but it seemed she knew—perhaps one of the neighbors had seen me at the siren's door and called. I admitted nothing, but eventually felt very guilty about those thirty-six seconds of pleasure.

There were other bad experiences, too—the worst of which came literally at the hands of one of our new neighbors in Merrick, who was a Boy Scout leader and a pillar of the church. He invited me to join his troop, which his son, Charley, also belonged to, right after the move from Malverne. My mother encouraged me to do so, thinking it would help me adjust.

I was a bit nervous as I walked to my first patrol meeting with Charley, hoping I would fit in but dreading having everyone mangle my last name again. Two brothers, Joey and Pete, were the patrol leader and assistant patrol leader, and we went in through the back door of their home. Charley said hello to their mother, who was making supper in the kitchen. I said hi, too, but didn't introduce myself. Then, my mouth watering from cooking smells, I followed Charley down the basement stairs.

Joey ignored me except to mention that there would be a demonstration for new members. After a bit of patrol "business" that was mostly horseplay, the demo began. He and his chubby brother, Pete, walked over to a well-lit corner of the basement, where Pete dropped his khaki pants and shorts and bent over. Then Joey buggered him, to the patrol's enthusiastic cheers. As he humped, he looked at me, grinning broadly. "Now you know how we do it in the Boy Scouts!" he said.

The other boys clapped and whistled until Joey seemed to have an orgasm, then Pete straightened up and pulled his pants up. I was still reeling from this exhibition when Billy Barnes reminded us we had an overnight coming up soon. "And I know you guys want me to bring along my little sister, like I did before, but it ain't gonna be free this time." After he assured the guys that he could smuggle her in with no trouble, spirited bidding began for her companionship.

Charley was grinning when we left the meeting a while later. "Some patrol, huh?"

I quit the troop soon after that, but I didn't manage to elude Charley's father, a flaccid-looking little man with fair, blotchy skin and thinning hair who seemed to experience a kind of exaltation when talking to his son's friends. Mr. Twitch, as I called him, lived with his wife and two kids in a filthy dump of a house that was a free-vice zone when Mrs. Twitch wasn't there—you could smoke cigarettes, jerk off and sniff glue, as Charley did. I went over one summer afternoon for a circle jerk with Charley and one or two other guys, not realizing that Mr. Twitch was there. We were all whacking away when he suddenly came over to me.

"Here," he said, looking me in the eyes, his face the grinning, very bothered face of lust itself, "let me show you how. Oh, it's so nice and hard, isn't it?"

I was astonished and too appalled to speak at first. I couldn't believe what was happening. Time seemed to stand still amid the heat and stench of the place, and sweat popped out in beads on my brow.

"I don't want to do this," I finally managed to blurt out. Then I ran out of the house, feeling angry and defiled and wishing that my father was around to kick the shit out of Mr. Twitch. Now I was beginning to understand the word my city friend Stevie had used. Mr. Twitch, I realized, was probably a cocksucker.

The Great Escape

When I returned home from Yazoo City, I felt my life had finally attained escape velocity. I had proved I could actually exit the mess my mother had complained about for so long. The trip—my major solo flight from the nest and my first airplane flight as well—had been a spectacular success in every way.

Still, I knew I couldn't have left my parents' orbit without the help of

my main men, the friends who had thrown me a lifeline during the dark junior high years, when I was caught between a monsoon of hormones and
the scant comfort of home and hadn't been quite sure I was human. Without parents I could talk to, I'd nearly gone astray many times.

My friends, beginning with Vin and with various male and female additions and subtractions along the way, had coalesced into a tight support
network by the end of my senior year in high school, and it seemed life
could hardly get better. I had even received my father's permission to use
five hundred dollars of my deli earnings to buy a car, on the condition that
I had to sell it and apply the money toward tuition in September. Having
my own wheels meant I could leave the house—and the psychic holocaust
that always marked the last days before Dad went on a foreign voyage—
whenever I chose.

Vin called soon after I got back from Yazoo City.

"Durst," he said, "you've got to tell me about this Mississippi thing.
Jerry and Feldo have been babbling about it ever since they got back, but I
want to get the whole story from you, assuming you can still talk." Obviously, he'd heard about the lovely Alice.

Ten minutes later, I was sitting on the guest bed in his garretlike room
waiting for him to bring some snacks upstairs. Outside in the warm spring
air, the flowers in his mother's garden released a perfume that came waft-
ing through the open window, and I breathed it in dreamily. I had so much
to tell my best friend.

It had been almost six years since I'd first met Vin on Joyce Larson's
stoop. She was a button-cute blonde from our seventh-grade class whose
father, as it turned out, kept her under tight wraps, so she was completely
unavailable to either of us. But we had laughed at the idea of ourselves as
Bluto and Popeye, then had quickly forgotten about her, keen to the potential of our own friendship.

Vin and I were now members of an informal club that pretty much ran
Calhoun High School. I was the editor of the newspaper and chairman of
the district's Student Involvement Committee, a transparent attempt by
the administration to get us to vent rather than demonstrate. Vin was
president of the Calhoun Choir, one of the best high school chorales in the
nation and the school's most prestigious organization. Ben Cohen ran
Pacer, the yearbook, and all three of us, along with Feldo, had been active
in the drama club and many other activities. Almost nothing of signifi-
cance happened at Calhoun—or in my life—without their involvement.

It was fitting that Ben had touched off my Southern adventure by waving *The Yazooan* in my face. He and I had been inspiring craziness in each
other for years, since we'd met at a party at the end of ninth grade and had
spontaneously begun talking like stage Indians and swigging pop from
"whiskey" bottles:

"Ugh! You know, me like-um way you hold your firewater. You want-um form tribe? Go forth and multiply?"

"Ugh! Multiply-um sound good, Ben. But we need-um squaws, no?"

"Ugh! You right! How we get-um squaws? Got-um any ideas?"

That night we founded the Tribe, agreeing that he would be chief and I secretary of tribal affairs and sole member. Of course we had to have a pagan deity to worship, and his name was revealed to us a few months later in tenth grade, when our social studies teacher, Mr. Kurth, gave us a difficult exam he called the "crux" test.

Within days we were staging sacrifices to our great hairy god, our friends looking on in awed twos and threes as we danced and chanted around small pyres of charcoal, leaves and twigs in Ben's backyard.

"CRUX!" Ben would cry, halting in place and supplicating the heavens as I circled the fire chanting "HEE yay yah, hah, HEE yay yah, hah."

"CRUX! This be-um the chief of your Tribe! Hear-um your Tribe, o great hairy god!"

This was my signal to halt as well and howl the antiphon:

"UGH! Hear-um your Tribe, o mighty Crux!"

Handsome, good-natured and dutiful Fred Thaler, Ben's friend since infancy, would stand on the periphery of the sacred circle, part of him wanting to join us and part of him holding back, out of either native good sense or fear that the neighbors might call his parents. Ronnie Bauch, a cantor's son and accomplished violinist who practiced for five hours a day but was otherwise normal, had pretty much the same reaction, as did Jerry, a funny but diffident kid who was on track to becoming class valedictorian until he fell in with us.

Ben would issue pronouncements from Crux like Moses from the mountain, and his prime commandment, Ben said, was that we should find squaws and produce additions to the Tribe. For our part, we frankly admitted that we needed some divine assistance in this pursuit and often reminded our god that he would get more sacrificial ham bones if we could father some papooses to help with the hunt. But although the girls found our tribal shtick cute, it wasn't quite enough to move them to multiply with us. Horny as we were in those days, we would have killed for a kiss and gladly died for a feel.

Ben really wanted to be the all-American boy and have a dog, which his father forbade, and not cello lessons, which his mother encouraged. For me, the product of a decidedly goyish, middle-middle-class family that was but once removed from the Queens of Archie Bunker, it was exhilarating to find that he was a manic soul brother.

Toward the end of tenth grade we recruited Dave Feldman, who definitely was not a squaw but who had no qualms about dancing and howling with us. We gave him the title of tribal apprentice so he wouldn't get too uppity and try to take over the franchise. A devoted reader of Tolkien's Hobbit tales, he sometimes called himself Feldo Baggins.

Until twelfth grade, we were also tight with Wayne Walcoff, an extravagant, impulsive kid with whom I felt an instant bond because he, too, was fatherless—his dad had died when Wayne was about twelve. We called him "The Wack" because of his wild, Byronic ardor—the way he would fall head over heels for a girl and sing "ain't no mountain high enough, ain't no river wide enough" as if he really meant it. Soon after I met him, I adopted his over-the-top romantic style as my own.

Vin had never attended our sacrifices or hung out much with the other guys before tenth grade, but he and I remained friends, and gradually he joined our group, which became my surrogate family. They taught me how to live without fighting and confrontation, how to treat other people well and engender their affection in turn, how to grow up. I loved them all, although I would sooner have died than say so. I also was proud of the fact that I, with my spotty academic and disciplinary records, had become their peer.

Lost in reverie, I hadn't noticed Vin's return; now he was standing next to me and offering pretzels and a soft drink. "Where were you, Durst?" he said, grinning. "Way down South in the land of cotton?"

"Oh, yeah," I said. "Good times there are not forgotten. Not by me, anyway. It's too bad you couldn't have come, man. It was totally amazing."

He laughed. He'd had no desire to go to Mississippi, but he did envy me my adventure. "So what's next? Are you going to drive down there again? Or are we going to get a chance to view your delectable Southern belles here?"

I told him I thought the next moves would be Ruth's and Alice's; they were already working on their parents to let them visit Merrick, and since their school year ended a lot earlier than ours, they could theoretically come up by the beginning of June, less than two months away. I sighed; that seemed like an eternity. Vin gave me a wry smile and a pat on the shoulder. "You'll survive, man."

The Innocent Seductress

In the weeks that followed, the prospect of Alice nearly drove me crazy. I knew the odds against me were great. Sustaining a relationship with someone who lived even fifty miles away would have been difficult, but I had ventured halfway across a continent to find my sweetheart. And I couldn't quite believe that a creature as desirable as Alice could return or even begin to understand the attraction I felt for her.

My main weapon was letters, and I began inundating her with them as soon as I got back to Merrick. But I wasn't interested in the usual pen-pal scribblings; I knew she and I were far apart not only geographically but in almost every way, and I began a furious campaign to update her politically and socially, to bring her into the late sixties. Her racial views were already very progressive for a Southerner, but they weren't my main concern.

I knew she would allow me to kiss her; she already had. But what else might she allow? As I had told Ruth in more than one letter (and now told Alice as well, although it must have shocked her deeply), I didn't think there was anything wrong with two adults, as I considered us to be, deciding to get it on. But I knew it would be a long time before she agreed.

There also was a part of me that prized Alice specifically for her innocence, that was strongly attracted to it. Deep down, I sensed I needed a fresh start, a new lease on virtue that only a girl like Alice could give me. So, while I never missed an opportunity to let my male peers—and even some females—know just how incredibly experienced I was, I never told Alice. I knew it would make her afraid of me. I was, however, ardent in extolling the joys of the flesh in the abstract.

Some of the sexual laissez-faire in my letters came of the free-love vapors emanating from such countercultural milestones as the Summer of Love in San Francisco and *Oh! Calcutta* and *Hair* on the New York stage, but a good deal of it had seeped into my mind from *Playboy*. A candy-store owner—fighting the good fight for free speech, no doubt—had been selling it to me since I was fifteen.

Although virginity was still the norm among high school girls then, I assumed we would leave cloying bourgeois morality behind once we got to college, and I saw it as my mission to prepare Alice for the inevitable liberation. But Alice, a born debater, answered my letters point for point, zestfully debunking the carnal rhapsodies inspired by those centerfolds. She attended the Methodist church every Sunday, and she believed her pastor when he said that sex outside of marriage must always be a shabby abomination. But at the end of each letter she would sweetly apologize for skewering my ideas, afraid I might not write back. It was a vexing, if touching, one-two punch.

She was a bit distant and correct with me in her first letters—confining them mostly to discussions of the touchy "situation" at school in Yazoo, especially the aftereffects of my two-day incursion with Jerry and Feldo. We had, she said in her first letter, brought about a profound change among her friends. No longer would they be content merely to sputter about the mishandling of integration, or about the paucity of the school's academic offerings. Now they knew they could speak up and make a difference. This was all very flattering, of course, but what I really wanted was some evidence that the honeysuckle kiss on our date hadn't been a fluke.

Toward the end of one of her first letters, she said I was "sweet." But did she, could she, return my passion? I constantly imagined us making out, rolling in wild transports of ardor on my bed—everything, in fact, but the act of love itself. Even in my dreams I never went that far.

But I did bombard her, like Alvie Singer and Annie Hall, with things to read—Robert Ardrey's *African Genesis,* which I felt offered the key insight that human behavior is based on animal instincts; articles about the war, politics and popular culture; liberationist rock lyrics. Willie Morris later would write, in *Yazoo,* his book about the integration crisis in 1970, that Alice DeCell was perhaps the only white student at YHS who had a copy of *Soul on Ice*—and had read it. What he didn't know was that I had badgered her relentlessly to do so.

When Bob Dylan's groundbreaking "Lay Lady Lay" came out, I sent her a copy, explaining that although I didn't expect her to take the title literally, the song expressed some of my deepest feelings toward her. She thanked me for the gift, but the tone of her next letter was several degrees cooler, as if to warn me not to get any ideas about "big brass beds." She and Ruth didn't cancel their plans to visit, however, and my keen anticipation in the days before their arrival was almost more than I could bear.

worlds

collide

leaving on a jet plane

"Get down here, young lady," my father's voice growled at me through the intercom over my bed. I reluctantly put down the letter I was writing Jeff, bemoaning what seemed inevitable: Alice and I would not be going to New York that summer. It had been a long six weeks of lobbying, and I still hadn't gotten permission, much less a plane ticket. I stopped in the bathroom to blow my nose and wipe my eyes, then headed downstairs.

Daddy sat in his easy chair, and I glowered at him.

"What have you been doing up there all this time?"

"I don't see how that's any of your business."

"A little girl who wants her parents to pay for an expensive trip to New York shouldn't be so impertinent." I looked closely at him. Through the cigarette smoke that curled around his head in lazy swirls, I thought I saw a twinkle in his eye.

"What do you mean?"

My mother had come into the den and was standing to one side. Her look of disapproval gave me more hope than I'd had in weeks. Daddy handed me a slim box. "This is from your mother and me, a graduation present."

With trembling hands I pulled off the wrappings. It was a plane ticket.

"I'm going to New York?"

He smiled and nodded. I gave him a long hug. My mother grudgingly accepted a kiss on the cheek. Then she said, "This isn't permission to run wild, you know. Alice DeCell is going with you and her mother has worked out all the travel plans."

We would stay with Marilyn Mauler, the girl Alice had met at camp in Andover, for five days, then fly on to Boston to tour Wellesley, something the DeCells thought would be useful in Alice's college search. It was all handed to me as a neatly packaged fait accompli.

During the flight I read the *New York Times* for the first time, and was disappointed when I didn't find any mention of my Merrick friends or any of the places they had told me about. The details of Paul McCartney's recent marriage to Linda Eastman held my attention, though, even while we were circling Kennedy. Alice, who'd been up all night at the annual Midnight-'til-Dawn Dance, was sound asleep beside me for most of the trip. I prodded her awake just as we began our descent.

"Can you see the Empire State Building?" she asked me, rubbing sleep from her eyes.

"What does it look like?"

She leaned over me and surveyed the city, which was laid out below us like a child's toy set. Glints of bright sunlight reflected off the water, and tiny boats left triangles of white foam in their wake. "Thayut's eee-it!" she finally cried out, and I jostled her out of the way so I could see King Kong's hangout before it disappeared under the plane's wing.

From where I was listening in the upstairs hallway of the Maulers' home, I could hear Jeff and Alice's excited voices. Alice's was high and slightly hysterical, Jeff's deep and filled with joy at being by the side of his Southern belle again. My eyes teared up as I stood there and remembered how I'd felt the first time I heard his voice on the phone, and all the dreams I'd built around him.

"You'd better hurry," Marilyn said as she ran down the stairs. Jeff had brought dates for us, too. But I suddenly felt nervous and shy. Returning to the bedroom, I removed all my makeup and started over, conscious of the minutes ticking by on Marilyn's little bedside clock.

"Ruth," Alice called up the stairs, "hurry up!"

I brushed my long brown hair one more time and sighed.

"You remember how tall I am, don't you?" I'd asked Jeff earlier when he'd phoned to tell us the evening's agenda.

"Oh, yeah. Don't worry about that," he'd said, laughing. "Who knows better than I do?"

But I wasn't reassured and I dreaded the now-familiar expression of a boy who didn't want to crane his neck all night. When I finally steeled myself to walk downstairs, there was a gaggle of people in the entranceway—Mr. and Mrs. Mauler, Marilyn, who was a dark-eyed beauty, Alice, with Jeff's arm around her, and Phil Marzullo, Marilyn's date. My heart lurched. There wasn't anyone for me.

Jeff immediately left Alice's side and swept me into a tight hug. He was slightly overwrought with being master of ceremonies for the evening, but I thought he looked pretty satisfied with how he had worked things out. "Mike McCourt—your date—is on his way in," Jeff said. Then he whispered, "Don't worry. He's tall."

As Alice filled Jeff in on our itinerary, I watched the door. In a moment I was looking up into friendly blue eyes that sparked with intelligence. Mike was tall and wiry and wore tight jeans with a plaid shirt. His bright red hair fell in thick waves well below his ears, and he kept it under control with a patterned headband. I gripped the newel post to steady myself. He was a hippie—my parents' worst nightmare.

Jeff came over to introduce us, and Mike stroked his full beard as he sized me up.

"Hello," he said after a dramatic pause.

"Hi," I mumbled noncommittally. Then I blurted out, "I've never seen a beard before."

"And I've never heard an accent like that before." Then, outrageously, he took my hand as we walked out the door. Before we drove away from the curb, I was snuggled up under his arm in the backseat of Jeff's car, sharing tender, silly and impetuous thoughts I'd stored for years, keeping them, it seemed, just for this boy, who listened and laughed with me and nestled me close to him. In Queens, we parked the car and took a subway connection into Manhattan.

The evening unfolded around me—melodic at times, crashing with sounds and sights at others, the first movement in a four-day performance that I would always remember as perfection.

New York City. The city of cities. The train, with its bright lights and plastic seats; the passengers—strange, scared-looking people, clutching bags and parcels and holding on to stainless steel poles; Mike's eyes and passionate words, shouted over the din of the subway—it would all be mine forever after that night.

"Are you a racist?" Mike asked me.

I swore I was not.

"Don't you have black servants?"

"Yes, but we treat them like members of the family."

"That's only an excuse to pay them less than a white person. What *do* you pay them?"

"We pay Rita twenty-one dollars a week." I felt compelled to be truthful.

"Twenty-one dollars a week?" He looked flabbergasted, and I regretted my honesty.

"She gets to take food home, and we give her clothes—our old clothes—too," I stammered.

"What does she do for twenty-one dollars?"

"Oh, she cleans the house, and does the laundry. She cooks dinner every day. But Momma does the shopping," I said, feeling defensive. "She gets Sundays off."

"Can she read and write?"

"Yes, but when we first moved back to Yazoo City we had the same maid Momma did when she was a child, and *she* never learned to read or write. We read her anything she needed to know about. She signed her name with an 'X.' But Kay was old. She grew up before black people were allowed to go to school, I guess."

He looked away and said, "Good God."

"Everyone should be educated," I said. "I really believe that. I'm not a racist."

I could see I had offended him. "Just as long as the blacks don't start thinking they're as good as white people, I don't see any harm in letting them take time off from picking cotton to go to school once or twice a week." My sarcasm made him laugh, and I changed the subject. We talked about his classes. He was a junior honors student at Calhoun High School, but was considering switching out of college preparatory courses into the shop curriculum. I couldn't believe this. What did he plan to do, work in a gas station?

"I need the skills—for the revolutionary underground," he said.

"What revolution?"

"Against the war, the establishment, the pigs. Not a revolution with guns, though. More like Gandhi, or Martin Luther King. With passive resistance."

I struggled to pull together the little bit I knew about Gandhi, and to see King as a hero for me, not just for black people. All I came up with was an emaciated guy in a loincloth and the sad faces of the black students who, with their parents anxiously trailing on the sidewalks, had marched by the high school in Yazoo City the day after King's assassination, unaware that armed white deputies were stalking them from the bushes. "Gandhi, he was that Indian guy, right?"

Mike's eyes shone with a messianic fervor. "I've got a lot to teach you."

He pulled me to him and kissed me for a long time. The lights blinked on and off, the train rumbled beneath us, and my brain spun trying to take it all in. I was happy to be kissed, though, and found it much more fun than dissecting my racial ignorance. But I had seen myself through his eyes, and my disaffection with my Mississippi heritage deepened.

When the subway went through Harlem, Jeff made Alice promise to keep her mouth shut and her Southern accent under wraps. She and I were ignorant of any potential danger—I'd never heard of Harlem—but the others were watchful and alert, tense even, and at one point Mike told me I'd better take off my diamond ring, which I did. I realized then that this was as much of an adventure for these Long Island teenagers as it was for Alice and me. I looked at Mike to make sure everything was okay, and he squeezed my hand reassuringly. Then we rode in silence into Manhattan.

Our destination was the Kip's Bay Theater, where *Monterey Pop* was showing. We were a long way from the theater and no one seemed exactly sure how to get there. But we set out in a state of high excitement anyway. Mike and I ran ahead. He was pointing out the eye-popping array of jewelry in the store windows, saying, "Can you believe this decadence? People are starving, and they put this junk on display."

As I looked around, I had to admit that the filth in the streets, and the ragged appearance of some of our fellow pedestrians, was shocking.

"We'll change all of that," Mike said ferociously, "after the revolution."

Then he pulled me into a doorway and we kissed, my arms stretched high around his neck, our long, thin bodies a perfect fit. It was a giddy jaunt for me, with the lights of Manhattan overhead, cabs and buses hooting and tooting all around us, and the knowledge that somewhere behind me was Jeff, my friend, who had made all of this possible. Occasionally he called something out to us like "Rockefeller Center is over there," or "You turn here to get to Macy's."

We arrived at Kip's Bay just as the show was starting. The cost of admission was breathtaking—ten dollars a couple. I would have offered to help pay, but felt it would be impolite. After all, I was the girl, and girls didn't pay. It was one of those things I had learned at my mother's knee. "It's a man's world," she often said. "Let *him* pay for it."

Watching Jimi Hendrix sexually assault and smash his guitar in *Monterey Pop* made me fidget in my seat. I was embarrassed to see it in mixed company, and amazed that no parental censor was turning off the projector and sending us home. But when I looked around the packed theater, I realized that something deliciously different was afoot. *We're all teenagers here,* I thought. *And we're in control.*

When Janis Joplin came on the screen, I hugged Mike with excitement. I wanted to be her, belting out songs, slugging whiskey straight from the bottle, awash in adoration. Mike sang the lyrics to "Me and Bobby McGee" in my ear and we swayed back and forth, our arms wrapped tightly around each other. At the end of the film, we stood with the rest of the audience, stamped our feet, shouted and called out, "Right on!" with one fist raised and clenched, the other hand lifted in the "V" of peace.

As we left the theater, Mike said, "Hey, Jeff, we'll see you guys at the station. We're going to the Rainbow Room."

"Yeah man, sure." Jeff laughed skeptically. "Have fun."

I thought the Rainbow Room must be a political hangout for hippies, and breathlessly ran beside Mike to Rockefeller Center. He led me to the elevator.

"These are mighty rich hippies," I said as we rode to the top floor.

"What are you talking about?"

"I don't know. I don't know what I'm talking about." We started laughing, and I was on the verge of hysteria when the doors opened.

"Wow," I said.

"Far out," Mike said. "Far fucking out."

I gripped his hand and we stepped into the lobby and stood there uncertainly, looking at the cosmopolitan patrons in the dimly lit dining room. Piano music tinkled through the murmur of conversations. Silverware clinked against china and ripples of discreet laughter washed over us.

As we gawked, the maître d' walked over. He scrutinized us for a long moment. "Can I help you?"

"I want the best table you have," Mike said. "We're going to have drinks."

"And I suppose you're eighteen?"

"Of course," Mike responded. I was agog at his bold-faced lie—I was seventeen and *he* was only sixteen—but I kept my mouth shut.

"I see," the maître d' said, looking as if he did see, and know, everything. "Well, sir, our best table is taken, but I can seat you right here."

He ushered us to a tiny table just inside the door, so that later we could claim, barely, that we had been to the Rainbow Room. Then he snapped his fingers at a passing waiter. "These are my personal guests," he said. "Please take care of them."

Mike ordered tequila sunrises for us both. We sat there, holding hands across the table, watching the glitterati of New York City pass by. When our drinks arrived, Mike raised his glass and said in a husky voice, "To Ruth, my Southern belle."

We saw Dave in school on Monday, but we never did spend any time with Jerry. He would take me to task for that in a letter he sent later in the summer. "I think we were robbed," he wrote. "No one got to see you."

But of course that was impossible at the time, because we were—Mike and I, Jeff and Alice—completely enthralled with each other. Alice and I used the Maulers' home as a way station, leaving the first thing in the morning when Jeff came to pick us up, and returning in the wee hours to catch a few hours' sleep. I don't think we ever ate a meal with them, or had a conversation. It was a shameful way for two well-bred Southern girls to act.

Reality Shifts

When we went to Jones Beach on the second day it was cold and windy, and Mike and I took shelter in a phone booth outside the bathhouse. Wind beat at our ankles from under the glass sides, and my summery dress flapped around me. Then Mike pulled me close and I forgot about being cold. Streetlights came on, the sound of the surf picked up, but we were oblivious to time's passing.

We finally stopped kissing and Mike leaned back against the sides of the booth, gripping both of my hands and blowing on them to warm them. "I can't believe I'm falling in love with *you*."

The words arrived one at a time, buffeted between gusts of wind, and it took me a minute to piece them together. When I understood what he'd said, my limbs went liquid. "Why not?" I yelled back, widening my eyes as innocently as I could.

"Well, look who you are, and who I am. We're so different." He pulled me to him.

"What do you mean?" I gasped at the end of another long kiss.

"Well, admit it—you're a racist bigot. And I'm just the opposite."

"I told you, I'm not a racist—or a bigot."

"Oh yeah, then would you still like me if I was black?"

"That's not a fair question." I tried to turn my back on him, but got stuck halfway around and had to turn back to face him. "Have you ever dated a black girl?"

"No."

"Then how are you different from me?"

"Because I would date a black girl, if I knew one. No question about it."

We were face to face, belly to belly, screaming to be heard over the wind, and as our debate progressed we both got angrier and angrier. I was relieved when Alice and Jeff tapped on the glass door. "Let's go!"

It was hard getting the phone booth's door open, since neither of us wanted to give way to the other, but finally we tumbled out and I huffed away, determined to get to the car first. I was furious. But I knew, in my heart, that I wouldn't date a black man, and by that definition I was a racist. It made me even angrier to know Mike was right. Then I felt his hand on my arm and stopped walking.

"I'm sorry," he said. "I can get intense, but I don't really mean anything by it." I saw Jeff and Alice leaning against the car, talking. They looked lost in another world, so Mike and I walked across a grassy area and lay down to look at the stars. Away from the beach, the wind was gone and it didn't feel so cold.

"I'm sorry, too," I said finally. "I guess you're right. I am a bigot, but I can change, can't I?"

He didn't answer, just laid his body on mine and made me forget about everything but our two selves. We all spent the rest of that night in the car at Salisbury Park, flushed with love, not giving a thought to the Maulers or what they might think of us. But every so often Alice said "Stop" to Jeff, and I'd say "No," to Mike, too. We gave them good reason to recall that we were conservative Southern girls, saving ourselves for marriage, and they proved that even Yankees could be gallant. Not a single button was breached during that long and frustrating night.

I looked for Mike as Jeff parked his car in the lot at Calhoun High. He'd promised to wait for me by the back door, but since I woke up every morning in Merrick believing I'd dreamed the whole thing, it wouldn't have surprised me to discover he didn't exist. Then he was there. Opening the car door, holding me in his arms, taking my hand and leading me into the school.

Alice and I had dressed carefully that morning. We wanted to make our guys proud. But the hose, skirts and blouses we wore couldn't have been more wrong. Our Yankee counterparts had on pants! I was thunderstruck. They wore bell-bottoms with raveled hems and flowers embroidered onto the pockets. No one had on any makeup.

As we walked through the halls I felt like a pariah, awash in wave after wave of curious looks. But Jeff and Mike didn't seem to notice. They stayed by our sides and showed us off as though we were prizes they had won.

Jeff had arranged for me to sit in on an anthropology class, and we went there first. Then he introduced me to the teacher, Mr. Hall, and left with Mike and Alice. I took a seat at the back of the room and listened to a rather lackluster discussion on what causes cultural evolution. Though I was stifling yawns at first—it had been a late night, after all—I pricked up my ears when one student said that given enough time, human beings could control evolution through selective intervention, Nazi style. She hastened to add she didn't recommend it.

"What about God?" I asked.

The teacher turned toward me with a happy glint in his eye. "Yes, what about God? Does anyone have anything to say about that?"

One young man raised his hand. "Assuming there is a God, which is a big assumption"—he looked at me and raised a knowing eyebrow—"you'd have to prove He really gives a damn about people, before you count Him as an evolutionary influence."

"Miss Tuttle," the teacher said, "is that what you had in mind?"

Later, when I told this story at a Sunday night church service in Yazoo City, ladies in the congregation cried and the men looked stern. But I was in a bully pulpit that night, back among the devout, and at the time it happened, I was just trying to offer another viewpoint, not win souls.

"No, that's not what I had in mind," I said to the class. "The Bible is the word of God, the literal word of God, and it says that God created the world. And he created Adam and Eve and gave them a place to live. That's a pretty strong influence on cultural evolution, I would say." I didn't think I was delivering a unique argument—just basic Christian theology. But when I looked around the classroom I saw wide eyes, gaping mouths and pale faces. Even a few angry looks.

The teacher said, "Does anyone want to respond?" and almost every arm shot up, along with a welling tide of voices. I was heartily glad to walk out of that classroom when the bell rang, and to find Jeff waiting for me with Alice.

"What did you do?" he said, having already been confronted by several of his classmates.

"Nothing, really. I just talked about Adam and Eve, how God created the world. You know—all that."

"You didn't!" he said, and took my arm to propel me down the hall like a recalcitrant child. "Wait until Mike hears about this."

That day, for the first time, I walked around a high school—not my own, but a real school nonetheless—holding a boy's hand. Mike carried the books Jeff had lent me and bought my lunch. Then we sat in languorous repose on the grass in the courtyard, eating our sandwiches, basking in the pleasure of being together, and chatting with our friends. It was everything my heart desired.

Mike and I walked into a large, bright room filled with children in wheelchairs. When they saw him, the children, whose bodies were twisted and contorted, started calling to him: "My! My!" Some of them waved their arms or nodded their heads to get his attention. He spoke to each one, tousling their hair, squeezing their palsied hands, and introducing me all around. I watched in wonder as he lifted a small boy from his wheelchair, tenderly rearranged his spasmed limbs and then gently belted him back into the chair. We finished our walk through the room by the side of a bright-eyed youngster named Frank. His dark hair fell in an unruly mop into his eyes. "Frank, this is Ruth," Mike said.

It took Frank a long time to put his halting response together. "Is she your girlfriend?"

"Yeah, she is."

"No, she's *my* girlfriend," Frank shouted gleefully, enjoying the banter. "She's pretty."

Mike said, "You'll have to fight me for her!" We all laughed. I stayed with Frank while Mike went to help with some of the other children. I saw a chessboard and chess pieces in a bag draped over the arm of Frank's wheelchair and asked, doubtfully, if he could play.

"Better than you, I bet," he said with a grin.

That turned out to be the case, even though I thought I was a pretty good chess player. But maybe my mind wasn't completely on the game, because I was fascinated with watching Mike. I'd never known a guy with such a heart, who had already learned to take the measure of his convictions—and everyone else's as well. I felt lucky to have met him, and for the first time realized how hard it was going to be to leave him the next day. But I was already planning ways we could get together again, especially after I was at Mary Baldwin and on my own. That was, after all, only three months off.

We left the cerebral palsy center, where he volunteered several times a week, late that afternoon, and went to Mike's home. It was an older craftsman-style house with dark woodwork and a large screened porch. While his mother did the ironing—something I'd never seen my own mother do—he and I sat on the porch and played the Peter, Paul and Mary hit "Leaving on a Jet Plane" again and again.

"*Will* you wait for me?" he asked me once.

"Yes, you know I will." And I would have. To prove it, I held him, like the song says, as though I'd never let him go. We could hardly speak as the impending catastrophe of separation pressed in on us.

Temporary Insanity

When it was time for Alice and me to go back to the Maulers' that night, the gloom in the car was almost unbearable. Surely this wasn't the end? We had to have more time. The four of us plotted almost until dawn. Then, satisfied that we'd have at least one more morning, we said good night.

Alice and I were dressed and packed by six. We had a quiet breakfast with the Maulers, all of whom looked a little done in by our visit. "I hope we haven't been too much trouble," Alice said.

They didn't try to deny the obvious, but wished us a safe trip home. A few minutes later Mr. Mauler went to work and Mrs. Mauler drove Marilyn to school. Alice and I were left alone with Marilyn's older sister Denise, who was going to drive us to the airport. It was essential to the plan that we make her our ally, but what her parents had tried to hide, she expressed openly with angry looks and sarcastic remarks. Though I felt it was a hopeless cause, I began to tell her what we wanted to do. At first she listened tight-lipped, but when Alice and I both broke into tears, she got up and brought us a box of tissues. "Please, Denise," I sobbed as I took one. "Please help us see our loves again."

She crumbled and agreed to pick Jeff and Mike up so they could go with us to the airport. When we stopped in front of Jeff's house, he appeared instantly, and nonchalantly got into the car. "Where's the other one?" Denise asked.

"He had to take a test. He'll be waiting outside school," I told her, and she drove on to Calhoun. But as we approached the building, Mike came crawling out of some bushes, waving his arms, and Denise slammed on her brakes. She wouldn't go any farther.

"This is probably illegal."

But Mike was already scrambling in, yelling, "You'd better get out of here fast!"

Looking both furious and scared, Denise gave the car too much gas, and it screeched away from the corner. We chortled over our coup, patting Denise's shoulders to make her feel part of the group, but she drove without speaking. Then the airport came into view and we all fell silent. Mike and I gripped each other's hands.

"Make this quick," Denise said.

"Denise, this means so much to us," I wheedled. "I know you're upset, but we're really grateful to you. Please don't be mad."

"I'm just going to make sure you get checked in, then I'm leaving." She gave me a no-nonsense look.

We all went into the airport together. But when we stopped at the Delta ticket counter, none of us was in a hurry to get in line. Mike and I were holding on to each other, making wild promises about love that wouldn't end and distances that didn't matter. My whole world was compressed into a glowing circle that stopped about two inches from his face.

Denise checked the luggage and got our tickets stamped. When everything was taken care of, she handed us our boarding passes and said, "Now get going. It's the last gate on that end."

Mike and I looked at each other with dawning horror. "This isn't the end," he said. "I promise." Then, "Hell, I'm going with you to the gate."

Denise knew she was beat. "I'll be waiting in the car," she said and turned to go. But Alice and I ran after her and hugged her tightly. The last time I saw her, she was standing by the ticket counter, tearfully waving good-bye. I think she forgave us in the end.

We walked as slowly as possible down a glassed-in linoleum hallway, heading toward the gate in a kind of slow-motion frenzy. Mike and I were deep in the midst of a new game plan. "Let's get married," he said. "Right now."

"Here?" I said weakly, and wondered why it didn't sound crazy. *Maybe,* I thought, *I've lost my mind,* which of course was what had happened. It was the state that lawyers try to describe to juries: temporary insanity, which, I can attest, is brought on by emotional excess. Getting married sounded like just the right thing to do.

"All we need is a priest, or a minister, or a justice of the peace," Mike said. "There's got to be one in the airport." He ran off to find out.

"What's he doing?" Jeff asked.

"He's looking for a priest, I think. We're going to get married."

"What will your parents say?" Alice quavered. Her eyes were as big as her face.

"Don't you need banns or something?" Jeff asked, rubbing his chin speculatively.

We three stood together, waiting for Mike to return. Then Jeff said, "How about it, Alice? Want to have a double wedding?"

Alice nodded yes, then Mike was back. He had found a priest, but of course there was no hope for a wedding. "We're both underage," he said. Tears stood in his blue eyes, and I finally let my own well up. We began sobbing, holding each other, and continuing to make promises. A flight attendant came over to us. "You've got to hurry."

I ran through the door with Alice behind me. We stumbled up the steps to the plane and burst into the cabin with a gush of renewed emotion, causing everyone on board to look up in alarm. The attendant tried to calm us. "Please take your seats. I'll get you some water." We huddled in our seats and as the big plane began to roll, I turned for one more look out the window. Suddenly, the terminal door flew open and Jeff and Mike ran onto the runway, an official in hot pursuit. Alice and I pounded on the window and I screamed, "Stop the plane! They're coming with us!" Passengers craned their necks to see what was happening. But the boys were soon apprehended. As the plane took off, Alice and I cried uncontrollably.

One man in a dark business suit called for the attendant and told her to bring us some brandy. "I can't serve them liquor. They're minors," she said.

"Then bring it to me," he growled at her.

When she brought it, he handed Alice and me each a glass of B&B. After three sips I was sound asleep, and didn't awake until we had landed in Boston.

15. Jeff

whistling dixie

Mike and I were silent during the ride home from Kennedy, two shell-shocked soldiers of love on the way to the rear. The emotional wind had been knocked out of us, yet the morning's afterglow lingered as well. After dashing onto the runway, we had been waylaid and led off, like overwrought fans at a rock concert, by security guards. They were understanding souls, luckily, and let us go with a warning. I'm sure they were laughing as Mike and I wandered off toward the parking lot.

We got out of Denise Mauler's car at Mike's house, neither of us remembering to thank her for dropping us off or for becoming our reluctant accomplice. For a while we just sat on the couch on Mike's porch, shaking our heads and starting to say things, but not getting very far. "You know, I really love that girl," he'd say, smiling through unfocused eyes, and I'd sigh, shake my head yes and say, "Yeah, I know what you mean. I've never loved anyone else like this."

"Yeah," Mike would reply.

After an hour or two of this, I got up, silently patted Mike on the shoulder and went home. It was a long walk, but that was fine because I needed time to assimilate the incredibly good news and the devastatingly bad news: She loved me, but she'd had to go. Still, the more I thought about what had happened during those four days—and the more that surreal half hour at the airport receded into history—the happier I became.

She had been willing to get married that morning; only our age had stopped us. But that had been okay, because as wild as our emotions had gotten, I had known, deep down, that marriage wasn't a real option. But she'd agreed to the *idea* of getting married. She'd shown that she loved me as I loved her, and the world had become a perfect place.

Over the next few days a raft of letters sallied back and forth, most of hers written in various airports from Boston to Jackson. Before this, she'd never used the word "love" in her letters, but now she used it liberally while noting that it was inadequate to express how she felt about what we'd shared. Her letters were all the confirmation I could have asked for. I sent her my silver ID ring, and my heart soared when she said she'd wear it every day.

That summer of 1969—my personal summer of love—also held the fantastic moment when science surpassed fiction and mankind visited the moon. I was working at the deli that hot July night, but of course there were no customers in the store when the lunar module landed and Neil Armstrong took his giant step. There was, however, a tiny black-and-white TV in the back room, and my coworkers and I, three gangly boys in white shirts and aprons, watched the grainy images from Tranquillity Base in a haze of glory.

I called Yazoo City while the broadcast was still on, pumping quarters into the pay phone in a frenzy. "Alice—did you see them walking on the moon?"

"Jeff—how sweet of you to call! Yes, we saw everything. Wasn't it amazing?"

Whatever happened that summer, trivial or epoch-making, I had to call or write her, or both. The financial burden was heavy, given that I was making two dollars an hour. My monthly phone bills averaged about forty dollars, but that didn't seem too much to pay for having her breathless drawl piped directly into my ear.

But when I told her, a few days later, that I could come down at the end of that month, the line seemed to develop some static. Although I'd already arranged to take a week off from work, I didn't get an immediate okay. Then she wrote that her parents had stalled inexplicably for several days and finally said that a visit would be "inconvenient." Not being familiar with Southern protocol, I didn't realize this meant "over our dead bodies."

"I can switch weeks," I told Alice, "but you've got to get me a definite date so I can schedule it." Finally, it seemed that the first week in August would be okay, so I rescheduled my week off. But a few days later she called to say that her parents had invoked the "i" word again. I tried to arrange something with Ruth, but her parents also declined to invite me.

I still had to take off the time I'd scheduled at the deli, and I couldn't afford to lose the wages, so I got a hack license and drove a Merrick cab for a week, seething with improbable schemes and dreaming of Alice nonstop. As the prospect of seeing her grew and then faded like a mirage, my longing boiled over. On the phone, I joked that I planned to "molest" her as soon as I saw her at the Jackson airport and that her parents were probably delaying my visit so they could find her a chastity belt. She laughed, but I could hear a chill creep into her voice.

Meanwhile, her parents had intercepted a particularly overwrought letter and drawn the understandable conclusion that I was after Alice's virtue rather than her love. And Alice said she found something "different" in my letters. I started to panic, and since I could no longer call or write her at home, I wrote to her in care of Ruth.

July 31, 1969

My Dearest Alice:

I've been waiting for your letter for three days now, but nothing has come. . . .

I hope you understand . . . it's NOT all sex with me. When I think of you, I don't just think of having sex with you. I DON'T. How can I make you see how I feel???

Alice, I realize that we come from very different backgrounds, environments, etc. Therefore of course our ideas are bound to be different on some things . . . you believe very strongly in your own moral code when it comes to sex. I believe differently, BUT—I love you, and so I try to understand. I know how you feel about it, and I know that you feel very strongly about it. HOW can you believe that I'd even WANT to attack and destroy all you believe in just for a few moments of my own pleasure? How can you even think that?

. . . Ruth said that one thing that really bugged you a lot was what I said about sleeping around with everyone at Oswego. Dammit, Alice—I was trying to tell you that no matter WHAT happens, no one is likely to replace you in my mind. You had asked me not to find another girlfriend—I was TRYING to tell you, in my own roundabout way, that I wouldn't. I DON'T really expect to sleep with every girl I see at Oswego—I was only trying to let you know that even though I'll have to go out with the girls up there (you don't expect me not to go out with other girls until I see you again, do you? If you don't want me to, I won't) and even if I DO sleep with someone up there, it really won't matter where you're concerned. You're the one I love. No other girl could possibly make me love her the way you do.

Another thing—when I tell you that I've been "good," and that I haven't gone out with other girls since you left, I say it because it means that other girls just haven't interested me enough to go out with them. . . . It DOES NOT mean that I'm saving every last bit of sexual energy and virility for the "big push" when I get down to Mississippi. God, I still don't know how you ever got that idea. You'll always be safe with me, doll. Don't you believe that?

The letter went on in that vein for page after anguished page—eight in all. The real problem was not the loose remarks I'd made, but our irreconcilable ideas about sex. I had agreed to abide by her rules when we were together, but if we were going to be separated for a long time, I wanted her permission to practice my own code.

This may have looked like a "have your cake and eat it" policy to her, but to me, lying would have been the real crime. And maybe that candor, along with my vows of undying devotion, turned the tide. On my birthday, a few days later, I received an India-print bedspread from Alice and Ruth, along with a hilarious telegram, which I took as proof that the big "misunderstanding" had been cleared up. But her parents still weren't cooperating.

It seemed the South had set up a blockade. But I, in the finest rebel tradition, would try to run it.

your roots are showing

Momma carefully maneuvered our new powder blue Cadillac into a space at the post office, but I couldn't wait for her to come to a complete stop before I leaped out and ran inside the building. I spun the combination lock on our box, as I had several times each day that week, and eagerly peered inside. Mike had promised me a letter by now.

Amid the piles of bills and circulars, I spied a thin envelope with a New York imprint. At last! I left the box hanging open and went to stand by a window to read the letter. The summer sun was hot on my hands as I ripped open the envelope. It contained a two-page poem, written in a tortured hand with many scratched-out words and a few tear stains that Mike had circled and labeled "teardrops" to make sure I didn't miss them.

His poetic metaphors were deep and murky, and I couldn't find much in them that I understood. He did, however, communicate one happy, if stark, image of our roots growing together to create a flourishing hybrid. But this offspring was a mysterious mutated creature, and I assumed that was how Mike pictured our feelings for each other. It wasn't exactly the variety of passion I'd hoped for, but I left the post office dizzy with joy anyway.

On paper I plied every wile I could. I rehashed our few days together in New York, dwelling lyrically on what might have been if we'd had more time. I pointed out that I would be on my own in a mere three months, much closer to Merrick, and able to drive up for long weekends. He replied that three months seemed an eternity, and it might be better to live life in the present. While I burrowed deeper into the fantasy of our lifelong commitment, he pointed out all our differences.

His pragmatism only spurred me on. I offered to pay for his plane ticket if he would just come visit me in August. But travel to Mississippi seemed to offend his social conscience, so I jokingly pointed out that I was only one girl and, as much as I'd like to, I couldn't clean up Mississippi's act by August.

Two weeks later he wrote me back, three paragraphs of excited plans to spend the rest of the summer working with VISTA in Kentucky. The only crumb he threw to my heart was the "Love, Mike" at the end. I began a blistering literary assault. I can only imagine his dismay as my letters arrived two or three a day, doomed Confederate soldiers refusing to accept defeat, fighting for the survival of my futile cause. He stonewalled me. Then one day it came to me with a little "ping" of awareness—he'd lost interest. For the first time since those perfect days in Merrick, I felt alone.

My heart breaking, I composed a last letter to him and ended it with: "There seems to be no other choice for us but to place our relationship in memory." Then I mailed it and expected to hear no more from him. But he had already written, and I got his letter the next day. Once again he discussed roots, underlining the word three times. He urged me to accept the inevitable and admit that our roots were too deep, and too different, to ever intermingle. "I couldn't in good conscience have a girlfriend who won't date a black man," he said. Then he wished me well, said he would remember me fondly and signed the letter "Your Brother, Mike."

I walked to the cemetery that day, trying to understand how so thrilling an adventure had ended as a social debate rather than a love story. I finally found all the fault in myself, and came to believe it was my culture, my education and my upbringing that were to blame. I sat under the cedar tree by the witch's grave and wrote a note to myself: "Only two more months and I can leave Yazoo, leave Mississippi, too. Not that I hate it that much, but I feel like I've learned everything my mind can accept from Mississippi . . . and now I'm ready to take on things from other places. This summer is only a kind of breathing space, a time when I can look back and plan, as much as possible, what I want from the future. Right now, all I know is that I want to discover people as unique personalities instead of stereotypes."

While the Dew Is Still on the Roses

Though the loss of Mike was a sorrow, I mostly remember my last innocent summer as an idyll of cloistered contemplation. I found solace and comfort in my old church, with its familiar Gothic turrets and stained glass windows, and spent many peaceful hours alongside Reverend Jorgenson, helping him organize that summer's Bible school.

He was a solemn Midwestern presbyter, tall and white-haired, whose sermons were exercises in precise theology rather than inspiration. He seemed the most solid and dependable man in the world to me, and proved to be so. An Old World gentleman who believed that everyone, especially himself, should keep the Commandments, he was unfailingly dignified and circumspect. He had a slight lisp that I found endearing, and I cherished the quiet conversations we had in the sunny office where I worked. There, after we'd chatted about crafts for Bible school and inventoried the church's supply of wheat paste, I told him the story of my journey to New York, and of my broken heart. He listened quietly, then took my hand into his large, warm grip and said, "God works in mysterious ways, Ruth. Someday, after the pain is gone, you might find some hidden blessings." Then, in a gruff voice, he said, "You have an honest heart. It won't lead you astray, and it's not broken."

Suddenly, I knew he was right.

Every afternoon, after I waved good-bye to the children then cleaned up the remnants of cookies and Kool-Aid in the fellowship hall, I would go across the street to Ricks Library and read until closing time at one of the long mahogany tables. The librarians—Mary Louise Williams and Zell Huxtable—prepared a list of reading materials for me, and would greet me as I walked in with, "*Black Like Me* came in yesterday. I put it away for you." Or, "Another volume of Dostoevsky is here." I never questioned the strange mix of philosophies. It was all equally foreign, and I pictured the real world as a neatly arranged structure built on great minds. *Somehow*, I thought, *if I read enough, it will make sense to me, too.*

One day Mrs. Williams led me upstairs to the storage room. There I found a private wonderland of seemingly ancient tomes, stored for decades, uncategorized, and lusciously appealing. She revealed the room to me as if it was a treasure, her eyes shining, her hands—crippled with rheumatoid arthritis—stroking each book lovingly. I browsed indiscriminately among Kant, Jane Austen and Chekhov. I shared her joy in them, sitting in dust-filled sunlight among the stacks.

In the evenings I mostly wrote letters to Jeff.

Dear Jeff,

I just got back the pictures that I took in Merrick. I thought you might like this one of Alice. . . .

A lot's been happening here this summer. There's a boycott by the blacks that is slowly shutting down the stores. But the whites are getting their pound of flesh, too. The blacks have lost a recreation center and a prospective shoe factory, which was to be 100% black-owned and -operated. A black housing project has been cancelled. The NAACP has announced that Yazoo needs to have a fire built under it and people say the KKK is getting ready to fight fire with fire. I think this town is heading for destruction. I just don't want to go with it.

I read **Soul on Ice.** *It was enlightening, interesting, but a little bit too bitter to be taken seriously. E. Cleaver gives the* *impression that he typifies the black race, which might be true, but is unlikely.*

Please write me a friendly letter and let's not discuss Alice or Mike. I doubt that they'd appreciate it. It feels good to be writing you again. Really good. Like breathing fresh air after a day in a smokehouse. I never thanked you for showing Alice and me such a good time in Merrick. I don't even remember telling you good-bye. So, good-bye, thanks for the wonderful time—and hello again.

He wrote back almost immediately. The sight of his handwriting on the envelope made my heart leap, as it always would.

I was a bit worried about you—I hope your stay in the "smokehouse" didn't do any lingering harm. What can I say? I felt really bad about it, but you knew Mike was a strange guy.

Thanks for the picture of Alice. It is now my official inspiration.

I really couldn't believe what you said about Cleaver's book . . . anyone who reads **Soul on Ice** *and comes out underestimating the blacks' bitterness has missed the point. Really, Ruth—I'm not trying to be sarcastic or superior or anything, but I honestly think you missed the point. E.C. is only one man, but think of what E.C. symbolizes. You can't think of your maid or some of the more docile blacks in Yazoo when you think of "blacks." Cleaver is the new symbol. Make no mistake about it, either—that's extremely dangerous for any white in this world to do.*

The day before Jeff's birthday, Alice and I made a secret visit to the local Western Union office. Using some of the Yiddish vocabulary we'd learned in Merrick, we sent this telegram: "Happy Birthday schmackel. Our souls are on ice. The South shall rise again. Peace Brother Love." If we'd waited a few days we could have delivered it in person, because Jeff had decided to fly to Yazoo whether he had an invitation or not.

17. *Jeff*

desperadoes

When I finally made my way back to Yazoo City in early August, the first person I saw was Ruth. We hugged, a tight, heartfelt, been-through-it-all embrace that seemed to sum up our brief but extremely eventful relationship. We'd known each other for only six months, but we'd already been on an emotional roller coaster that made us feel like old war buddies.

She stepped back and smiled, and I smiled, too, flicking away the embarrassing moisture that had formed in the corners of my eyes. I was glad that she didn't seem to be holding me in any way accountable for the debacle with Mike, which I felt guilty about. Of course, I knew I wasn't responsible for Mike's feelings, and I could look Ruth in the eyes and tell her, if she ever asked, that I had done my best to argue Mike back into her arms. Still, I thought I hadn't been as good a friend in her hour of need as I might have been. I was simply too caught up in my Alice obsession to extend much support to Ruth.

She had put on a brave front whenever the subject of Mike came up in our calls and letters. But I'd been able to read between the lines and listen between the words and I knew she'd been deeply hurt. Now, though, it was Ruth who was surveying me as if I'd just walked away from a car wreck.

I had flown from New York to Jackson without a parental visa from Yazoo City, trusting that Alice and Ruth would be at the airport when I arrived. But neither one was there. Alice had been placed under house arrest, and Ruth's parents had forbidden her to get involved. In desperation I had called Kenny Waldrop, the boyfriend of June Langston, Alice's best friend. I'd met this mop-haired, good-natured kid in April, when we'd chatted about rock music and compared notes on the bands we'd been in. He had invited me to look him up if I ever needed anything in Yazoo City, and I'd brought his phone number with me just in case. Luckily for me, he and his family came through in a way that gave me a new appreciation of Southern hospitality.

Now I was at their house, being treated like visiting royalty rather than the lovesick desperado I really was.

Ruth stood in front of me, searching in her purse for a note from Alice, and a shadow crossed her eyes when she handed it to me. The note, written in obvious distress, said that Alice's parents were so upset by my arrival that they'd forbidden her to leave the house while I was in town. But, she'd added at the end, she would always love me, no matter what.

Ruth waited as I read. "Well," she said when I finished, "you're here, and you have a place to stay. There's still hope." Then she left, squeezing my hand and saying she would see me later.

I pondered my next move as I washed up before joining the Waldrops for supper. There had been one ray of hope in Alice's note: Although she had been forbidden to leave her house, her parents apparently hadn't banned visitors. I asked Kenny and June to drive me to Alice's that night after supper and accompany me inside. I would ask Ruth to come, too, to defuse any potential confrontation.

I was on my guard as I sauntered toward the DeCells' door an hour or so later. Would I get a kiss from Alice, or would I have to settle for a handshake? Would her parents turn me back at the door, like some underage kid at a gin mill? *Hell, no!* I thought grimly.

After knocking, we three nonchalantly walked in. Alice, looking devastating in jeans and a simple blouse, greeted us alone, so we were free to steal a brief but sweetly urgent kiss. And I was heartened to see that she was wearing my ring on a chain about her neck. She took my hand and held it tightly until we entered the den, where her parents sat stiffly. They did, however, rise to greet me.

Glad there hadn't been a scene, I made jokes and small talk. After a while, Ruth arrived and Kenny and June left, saying they'd be back to pick me up later. Alice's parents seemed determined to sit with us at first, but as time went on they relaxed their vigil, spelling each other and finally leaving us three alone. Nor did they return after Ruth left, so that by the end of the evening Alice and I even managed to cuddle a few times.

For the rest of the week I more or less planted myself in the middle of the DeCells' household, which wasn't as awkward as it sounds. Alice's parents seemed to accept the arrangement, apparently because they felt her honor was safe within the familial walls. They were almost friendly toward me after a few days, although they didn't immediately rescind Alice's arrest. The afternoon before I was to leave, we were writing a silly letter to Feldo and Jerry between kisses in the den when we were interrupted by a fidgeting Brister. At first we glared at him, because Mrs. D. had been sending him to haunt us periodically that afternoon. But he looked slyly at his sister and said: "Momma's got something to tell you, Alice."

She followed Brister out of the room and came back a few moments later. "Momma says, since it's your last day here, we can go horseback riding for one hour." She paused to give this incredible news time to sink in.

Then, with a demure smile, she added: "Alone." Like Adam and Eve in reverse, we fled our state of shame and stepped out into a sunlit paradise.

The DeCell property included some hilly, wooded acreage with a small pond behind the house. We rode off together on Alice's horse—a perfect arrangement, since it gave me an excuse to keep my arms around her slender waist. After a while, we came to rest by the pond.

While katydids chirped and buzzards wheeled in the sultry Mississippi afternoon, we shared an hour of loving softness and warmth. There was no insult to chastity or even any thought of it—we just held on to each other as tightly as we could. But soon enough the relentless minutes resumed their march, the sun settled lower in the hazy sky and it was time to go back. I didn't realize it then, but I had experienced the high point of my youth. Afterward, nothing would ever seem quite as good, as pure, as sweet.

That night, Ruth came over to the DeCells' house and found me with my arm around Alice, holding forth like a favored son-in-law. But later, when it was almost time for me to go, Alice and I just weren't ready to part with each other. Gradually, a plot took shape: I would recruit Kenny, my Sancho Panza, and come for Alice at dawn. She would leave a note for her parents saying she'd gone to Jackson to shop with Ruth, whom we would meet at the Waldrops' house. Ruth would drive us to the airport and stay in Jackson, having told her parents she'd be with Alice.

But Alice would fly to New York with me, and we'd spend as much time as we could together before she got on another plane to head back to Jackson. Ruth would be waiting at the airport so they could return to Yazoo together, shopping bags in hand, in time for supper. Alice went to her room to count up her "Merrick fund," then we called Delta and made Alice's reservation. We would have another day together, and that was all we asked.

The plan's chief flaw, aside from its flagrant implausibility, was that it called for early-morning maneuvers after a late night of scheming. I was supposed to set things in motion by about 4:30 A.M., but Alice and I were having a hard time letting go of each other at 12:30 that same morning. I finally did return to Kenny's house for a few hours of fitful sleep, but I awoke from a vivid dream that something had gone wrong—as it had, because the clock read 5:30. I had to call Alice to tell her we were running late, and the whole escapade began to unravel.

By the time Kenny and I finally arrived, her parents were up. She couldn't leave through the front door, so she went out her bedroom window. But Mrs. DeCell stormed out of the house and intercepted Alice on the lawn near her room. The loud voices from that side of the house told us that the jig was up, and Kenny—who didn't want to tangle with Mrs. DeCell—sounded the retreat.

We roared back to his house, where we met Ruth and told her about the debacle. Then Ruth and Kenny drove off—Kenny to make himself scarce and Ruth to see if there was any way she could help Alice. I stayed at the Waldrops' house, waiting by the phone and feeling miserable and guilty.

Finally, Ruth came back. She had phoned Alice and found out that Mrs. DeCell had gotten wind of the plot by listening on another extension when I'd called early that morning. "They were screaming at each other while we talked," Ruth said. "Mrs. DeCell wants Alice to give up your ring, but Alice won't do it." I had heard enough; I told Ruth I was going to call Alice. "I wouldn't if I were you," Ruth warned. "Her mother sounds really mad."

But as soon as she left, the phone rang. It was Alice. Sounding hurt and beleaguered, she said she needed help, and I told her I'd be there as soon as I could.

I asked Mrs. Waldrop, who seemed to be a sympathizer, for a ride to the DeCells' house, and she dropped me off at the foot of their driveway. She asked if I wanted her to wait, but I said no; I envisioned myself comforting Alice and trying to explain things to her parents all afternoon. I walked past Alice's yellow Firebird, which was parked near the garage, and up to the front door.

The house was strangely quiet, and the door was standing open. I knocked a few times but got no answer, so I walked in—just in time to hear the sounds of an argument. "You give me that ring right now, young lady. *Give it to me!*"

"No—it's mine! I won't give it up unless he says he wants it back."

"You'll give it to me right now!"

Then Alice burst into the living room with her mother in hot pursuit. Alice's eyes met mine for a split second, but her mother grabbed her from behind and whirled her around so forcefully that Alice cried out. Mrs. De-Cell grabbed my ring out of Alice's hand and pushed her back into her room; then she came flying toward me.

"This is yours," she snapped, practically throwing the ring at me as she hustled me out the door. "Alice won't be needing it anymore. You just get yourself in that car," she said, motioning toward the Firebird and radiating anger from every pore. I was too stunned to say what I'd come to say: that we hadn't planned to do anything terrible, and that we would have asked permission if we'd had any hope of receiving it.

In a moment I was seated in the front seat of Alice's car, not more than a foot from fury incarnate. Mrs. DeCell threw the Firebird into gear and took off at breakneck speed, seldom taking her blazing eyes off mine. I heard a scathing litany of my faults and one compliment during that brief but unforgettable drive. My taste in girlfriends, she noted tartly, was impeccable. But it was too bad my father had been away at sea during my upbringing, and that I'd apparently been too much for my mother to handle, because I was out of control and irresponsible, the kind of young man who could only mean trouble for an innocent like her daughter.

I felt deeply offended, although I never got in a word in my own defense. Who was she to be critiquing my upbringing, and why did she presume that I—who adored her daughter—would be bad for Alice? Of course, I was indeed out of control and far less mature than I realized.

I spent the rest of my time in Yazoo City trying to comprehend how the sweetest day of my life had somehow, in less than twenty-four hours, become the most painful. Worst of all—even worse than knowing that Alice was beyond my help—was the certainty that we wouldn't be allowed to see each other again. Ruth tried to console me, but we both knew my case was hopeless.

South of Woodstock

I brooded, alone in my tragic world, all the way from Jackson to La Guardia. But when Feldo bounded up to me at the gate, I knew I was home. He picked me up in a bone-crushing embrace and then walked away with my bag under one arm and me under the other. I threatened to knee him in the crotch if he didn't put me down, which he promptly did. He was vastly pleased with his little jape, but he narrowed his eyes when he saw I wasn't smiling.

"Ugh," said Feldo. "Tribe look-um heap whaled out. What happen-um in land of Yazoo?"

"Ugh," I replied halfheartedly. "Tribe get-um whaled big-time, Turd-nose. *Big* time. Squaw love me. Mother of squaw hate-um my guts. Heap hairy mess."

Feldo listened attentively as I told him the story of my week in Yazoo City, his mobile features registering shock, glee, joy, surprise and despair. When I finished, he commiserated awhile and then changed the subject, chattering about the plans he and Mona had made for the few weeks until he left for college. But I listened with only half an ear, my thoughts stuck somewhere between that perfect hour at the pond and the hellish ride with Harriet DeCell.

The radio was on, and the deejay was speaking in awed tones about a concert that had drawn hundreds of thousands of young people that day to a farm in a tiny upstate hamlet called Bethel—a concert that would come to be known as Woodstock. Feldo reminded me that his parents had some property near there, and he said his father had been thinking of going up to keep it from being trashed. But then the Thruway had been closed, for the first time in its history. No one could go up now.

I had planned to go to Woodstock with some friends, but I'd backed out when I realized I'd have to work the weekend I got back from Mississippi. *Oh, well,* I thought ruefully as Feldo careened the Devilbug around the tight curve of the parkway ramp in Merrick, *I've already had my own celebration.* But while I'd found love in that little town very far south of Woodstock, I hadn't found peace.

September 1, 1969

Dear Soul-Sister Ruth:

Ruth, I am (if you will please excuse the expression) really fucked up something fierce. . . . I'm wandering around in a daze, and I haven't heard from Alice in a week. I'm going to go insane if I don't tell someone how I feel.

I've written her four times since Tuesday, and the first one had two pages on why she had to keep writing to me. Also I told her to try to be at someone else's house on Sunday night so she could call me collect—I figured we could talk about seeing each other again without worrying about her mother listening in. But she didn't call. I don't know what to do.

Please tell A.D. I love her very much no matter what happens.

September 4, 1969

Dear Jeff,

I've done your bidding and scoped Alice out. She didn't get to call you Sunday because she couldn't spend the night out. My account of your trauma and never-ending love brought tears to her eyes. She's extremely repentant, but meant no harm in waiting so long to write. You should have a letter by now.

Take it easy. Don't be so strung out. Jeff, as wonderful and necessary as it is, love (between man & woman) is not enough to build a life on. It can be the impetus, the food, the greatest joy of life, the greatest moment of life. But it is NOT life. There are so many more things, different kinds of love, different kinds of fulfillment. Don't tune these out!

September 9, 1969

Dearest Ruth,

You are the only person in the world who can put my mind at rest about Alice. Not even Alice can do that, really. Thanks.

> *Please write as much as you can when you get to college.*
> *If you see Al before you go, tell her I love her. I know that*
> *you'll know what I mean when I say that I love you, too, very*
> *much.*

Soon after I got home from Yazoo, I returned early from the beach one day and found my mother reading one of Alice's letters, which prompted a bitter argument. She said she had decided to read them because she was worried I might do something I'd regret for the rest of my life.

That night I called Alice, who was at a friend's house, and told her what my mother had done. She said her parents had done the same thing. We marveled at what we considered their callous disregard for our privacy and vowed we would never do anything of the kind when we had children.

Of course, Alice's parents had every right to take steps to protect her. But although they had read what I was writing to Alice, they didn't see her replies. And that was too bad, because her staunch defenses of traditional morality were exactly what they'd sent her to Sunday school to learn.

If they had ever asked me to state my intentions toward their daughter, I would have told them that I loved her deeply, and that I could well imagine us marrying—perhaps after finishing college. And I would have assured them that neither she nor they had anything to fear from me. Even in my dreams, I would have said, I'd never done anything that my sweet Dixie darling wouldn't allow.

18. Ruth

calm between storms

Jeff's departure was like a magician disappearing behind a puff of smoke. One minute he was churning away in our midst, creating shock waves of dissension, then in the next—all was calm. But it was a superficial calm, the kind that keeps parents happy in the illusion of control over their children, while these same children spin quiet, audacious strategies of escape into their own destinies.

I had watched Jeff wooing and winning the girl of his dreams, and my affection had grown for this impulsive boy who paid such a steep price in the end. I felt selfishly fortunate that he and I had chosen friendship over romance, for we were able to remain linked to each other. But the shared pain of our lost loves would twine through our letters for a quarter of a century, the ghostly echoing of a desperate, youthful gamble that had come up snake eyes for us both.

For myself, I retreated from the debacle and began the final task of my childhood: getting ready for college. Overstuffed trunks and suitcases were sent ahead to Staunton, Virginia, the makings of my future life folded around a few remnants of the old. But most of my scribblings, scrapbooks and memorabilia I left at home—love letters never sent to boys who never asked me out; notes passed back and forth among Lea Huxtable, Sue Ross, Patty Woodell, Debbie Hill and me. I smiled as I reread some of them, mentally patting my own silly self on the head with grown-up indulgence.

"He smiled at me in the hall after third period!" I had written to Lea in the ninth grade. "You should wait in the same place tomorrow," she wrote back.

There was one, hastily scrawled in red ink on a brown envelope, from Debbie: "A bunch of hoods (Pam was the main one) shoved me into a locker and told me to tell you you'd better get those Yankee boys out of here. I'm scared!"

And a note from Patty that had almost broken my heart in the tenth grade: "Amzi asked me out. Do you mind?"

"You have to tell me everything," I wrote back.

There were spiral-bound notebooks with wear-blighted covers elaborately decorated by bowers of hand-drawn hearts and daisies entwined around boys' names: Amzi, Danny, Jimmy, Byron, Jeffrey Paul Durstewitz. In some cases I had added a "Mrs." in front of the names. I spent days sorting and filing these remains of childhood and adolescence into cardboard boxes. On top of each in black Magic Marker I wrote "Personal and Confidential. Stay Out. Ruth's Property."

There were only two things I didn't leave behind. The first was a pile of typed letters with small handwritten notes attached that I'd found in Aunt Ruth's files. I packed these, I think, as a talisman, realizing in some prescient way that I would need reminders of who I was in the years to come, and of the eccentric old lady who had once made me feel safe.

May 31, 1958

Claim Agent
Illinois Central Railroad
Dear Sir:
Henry Lee of RFD 3 had a hog weight 150 pounds killed by your train. You sent him a blank claim check which he filled and returned to you, placing a value of $20 as he wanted quick payment but felt his hog was worth more. Your man came and got the hog and buried him at Cell Cessna's place. Please issue the check for $20 as this has been placed in my hands for collection.

Yours truly,
Ruth Campbell

September 5, 1958

Henry Lee,
You have not lived up to our deal. You got the $20. I now need you to pick my cotton.

Ruth Campbell
Attorney at Law

Saturday, September 27, 1958

Dear Miss Ruth Campbell Attorney at Law,
This come to acknowledge your letter has reach me the message was the truth. I am wrong. Monday morning shall find me in your field to do all I can while God stilleds the

rain. The table of my heart is a prayer book to God as the days past by to let your cotton make an ample supply and give me strength enough to gather it and I shall keep the faith. Miss Ruth you has brought me through the valleys of death.

Henry Lee

The other was a packet of Jeff's letters, loosely tied together by a pink hair ribbon and an old Howdy Doody barrette. I had grown to need them close to me, to be thumbed and peeked into, like picture windows with a view of innocence. So I kept them, and all their brothers that continued to come, time and again, as I moved on through life. I never doubted that Jeff was saving my letters, too.

Leaving Home

August 5, 1969

Dear Ruth,
    I will warn you that Mary Baldwin is filled with many "Southern Conservatives" who hate beards and boys with long hair and blue jeans, etc. . . . but there are also girls you can have long, interesting talks with . . . I don't mean to scare you but MB is not very Northern—but I think you'll like it in spite of that. As for the boys, there are plenty. University of Virginia is mostly boys, Washington and Lee (boys), VMI (military boys). There will be a mixer the first Saturday . . . with boys from all of these colleges. . . .

Your "Big Sister" Bitsy Harper

After I got this note, I had second thoughts about Mary Baldwin, which had appealed to the romantic, feminine ideals I'd nurtured through countless readings of *Gone With the Wind*. I had envisioned myself as a willful heroine in an architecturally significant setting. Now, when it was too late to change my mind, I wished I had considered other options.
    Then, one early morning in September, my parents and I drove down the alley behind our old house, headed for Virginia, where I hoped I would finally be free to move beyond Mississippi's legacies. I wanted, that morning, to enjoy the feel of old shackles dropping away, and of my sweet, sweet imagined future. But instead I found myself fighting back tears as the red-

shingled house vanished from sight. I stared at the back of my mother's head, and I wanted to call her Mommy just one more time and to wind one of her blond curls around my finger. I didn't feel like a woman that morning, sitting groggy-eyed in the backseat of the big Cadillac. I felt, for one last, incandescent moment, like a little girl, grateful for my parents' warm attentions.

We drove past the country club, beginning to thread our way between infinite Delta and cresty white clouds to Memphis. Sprinklers on the golf course sent arcs of watery diamonds high into the air, where they were turned into rainbows by the sun.

a

brave

new

world

19. Jeff

wizards of oz

September 16, 1969

Dearest Ruth,

Well, here I am at Oswego. I've been going out of my mind with the freshman orientation crap—this is really the first opportunity I've had to write.

Did Alice say anything after that phone call on Friday? I wish to hell she would write. She said she would that day, but I haven't gotten anything so far. If you write to Alice, tell her not to worry because I haven't seen anybody on this campus to equal her—really (and don't imply that I've been looking, either).

I would have been far happier at Oswego State that fall if I'd never met Alice. At the very least, I would have been much less confused.

Most of the confusion arose from the fact that while I was still very much in love with Alice, I also was aching to join the sexual free-for-all that had become, along with drugs, rock 'n' roll and opposition to the Vietnam War, one of the Boomers' hallmarks. I saw nothing contradictory about telling Alice that I would love only her even if I went to bed with other women. Love and sex were two separate things in my mind, and to link them was to surrender to the very absurdities we were trying to overthrow. I knew Alice didn't accept this reasoning, but I rejected the obvious corollary that we would therefore have to break up.

I also had an attitude problem about attending Oswego. It had been lowest on my preferred list of colleges, but Harpur College, the undergraduate school of the State University of New York at Binghamton, and Stony Brook—my first and second choices—hadn't taken me. This really rankled, since most of my old friends were going to Ivys and Little Ivys.

Vin had made the situation much more tolerable by volunteering to go to Oswego with me even though he'd been accepted at Harpur. He never really explained his choice, but at the time I felt no need to look a gift horse in the mouth. Perhaps he wanted the security of having a friend with him in a new environment, or perhaps he thought I needed that security. The truth was, neither of us was as cocksure as we acted. Whatever the reason, I was secretly very grateful to him for sharing my academic exile.

But on the hot, hazy September afternoon my parents delivered me and my belongings to the door of Seneca Hall, the decision to go to Oz didn't seem like such a bad one. The dorm, a concrete high-rise set no more than two hundred yards from Lake Ontario, was a beehive of swarming frosh, their parents and siblings and yellow-jacketed orientation leaders. It was quite a scene, and I was impressed with the campus. Coming from seagirt Long Island, I found it comforting to be able to look out my dorm window across a limitless expanse of blue water.

Alice had written that my head would be turned by other girls as soon as I set foot on the Oswego campus, and she had been right. I felt like the proverbial rooster in a henhouse that day as I watched dozens of beauties move into Cayuga Hall, right across from my dorm. I knew full well that many of the girls receiving parting lectures from their parents were about to throw their rules—including those involving chastity—to the playful lakeshore breezes.

I would have traded all the beauties of Oz for the news that Alice was moving into Cayuga Hall or coming to visit me, but I knew that wasn't to be. So I mourned and moped, dreaming of my Sunshine Supergirl and gnashing my teeth when I wasn't ogling some smashing coed.

September 22, 1969

Dearest Ruthie,

*Still no epistle from the golden Miss DeCell. It practically drove me insane last week, but I'm adjusting to it now—i.e., I've found someone else to while away my waking hours with. The only trouble is, Alice still manages to wreck things for me because I can't get really turned on about this other girl. I'll be making out with her and thinking of Alice, and you **know** where that's at.*

*Don't misinterpret, though—I still love Alice very much, and I'm definitely not looking for another girl to take her place. But I can't help but feel that she couldn't possibly give a damn about me when she doesn't write—it almost seems as if she's telling me she **wants** me to find someone else. And that really bothers me. When you write to her again, **tell** her—maybe she'll believe it from you.*

It was a frustrating life, but cheap relief—in the form of beer—was always available. You could drown your sorrows for as little as fifteen cents a glass in some townie joints. Or pay two or three bucks to get into a beer blast on campus, then spend the rest of the night trying to swill your money's worth out of plastic cups.

We freshmen drank with a kind of frenzy, trying to be grown up, trying to get loose enough to pick up girls, trying to forget that earning below a 2.0 grade point average might mean a trip to Vietnam. But beer wasn't the only chemical distraction available.

Vin and I had our first close encounter with the drug culture soon after we arrived on campus. A sophomore named Dave, who'd gone to Calhoun, showed up just as we were unloading Vin's stuff, and Mr. Vito took a picture of the three of us mugging in front of the dorm. Dave helped carry some of Vin's gear up to our room on the seventh floor, then said he would return after Vin had settled in. An hour later there was a knock on our door. Dave came in, a knowing smile playing about his lips. "Want to get stoned?"

"Um . . . right now?" I asked.

"Sure. Why not?"

"Well, we . . ."

"You're afraid of getting caught, right?"

I nodded.

"No problem." Dave grabbed the towels Vin and I had neatly draped over our racks and stuffed them under the door. Then he went to the window. "We'll smoke over here—the smell will go out the window instead of toward the door."

Vin—who'd told me he'd done grass with some older guys over the summer—was cool when Dave produced a plastic bag of small, dark dried leaves and some rolling papers. I, however, was rattled. I'd never tried pot or any other drug, and I was keenly aware that getting caught smoking a joint could mean expulsion from school and even jail time. But if Vin wasn't going to chicken out, neither was I.

Dave started to roll joints while I put a Jefferson Airplane album on the stereo. He kept up a constant patter of dope talk as he worked, while Vin nodded knowingly. Finally, Dave handed Vin a joint and lit a match. Smoke wafted around Vin's head as an odd, somewhat cloying smell filled the room. Dave didn't partake, but he kept the joint moving between me and Vin. The stuff tasted terrible, and I was having a hard time controlling my coughing. Vin, who had smoked cigarettes for years, wasn't coughing, but he also didn't seem to be getting high. Dave kept prodding him:

"Can't you feel it? It's great shit, isn't it? Aren't you getting a buzz yet?"

I wasn't feeling anything but bronchial discomfort, but I kept quiet. I figured the stuff probably just didn't work well your first time. Vin, however, finally seemed to be getting off.

"Yeah," he said with a beatific smile. "Yeah, I'm starting to feel it. It's good stuff—real good." Dave was cackling now and encouraging us to smoke more, although he still hadn't touched the joints himself. After twenty minutes I had a headache and a sore throat. But Vin said: "This is really good shit, Dave."

"Yeah," he replied with a malignant grin. "It's great, isn't it—great *tea!*"

With that, he dumped the remaining contents of the bag on Vin's bed and reached into his pocket. Pulling out about a dozen Tetley tea-bag labels, he threw them in the air like confetti and guffawed. "You guys have been smoking *tea,* not pot. I'm sure you're getting a great high off that Tetley, Vin!"

Then he pulled the towels out from under the door and left, hooting. Vin and I looked at each other, mortified. I hurriedly closed the door, but I knew better than to say anything as Vin angrily brushed the tea leaves off his bed.

"Asshole," he yelled at the door. *"You're an asshole!"*

Within a few months, we would become regular weekend tokers. But not with Dave.

Vin's parents and younger sister, Dolores, who were staying in town, came back to the dorm that first evening and invited us out to dinner with them. But we had other plans, and Mr. V. knew exactly what they were. "Ah, forget it, Antoinette," he said. "These two don't want to go out with us tonight—they want to eat with the guys."

Mrs. Vito turned to us in mock horror. "What? You're turning down restaurant food?"

Putting my hand on her arm, I assured her it would be different if she were doing the cooking. That got a laugh, but tears came to her eyes as she turned to leave. She knew her boy was fast becoming a man and that this was the beginning of the end of their close-knit family life. Shaking her head and clucking, she gave us both kisses and hugs, and then, overcome, let Dolores lead her toward the elevator.

Mr. V.—a boilermaker by trade—gave me, then Vin, his usual bone-crushing embrace. He was getting misty, too, and his nose was turning red as he held Vin by the shoulders and looked him in the eyes. "Hey, Enzo—you do a good job on your studies and take care of your friend here, you hear me?"

"I will, Dad."

"Good. You know, your mother and I are very proud of you." He was choked up for a moment. "You *know* that, don't you?" Vin, who was the first in his family to attend college, knew it very well. He nodded, and then Mr. Vito looked from him to me. "I want you two to watch out for each other. Remember that—always take care of your best friend." Then he tore himself away and strode off down the hall.

Vin and I stood there for a moment or two just inside our room and let our new reality sink in. Slowly, we turned to each other, big grins on our faces, and gave each other high fives.

After supper, we sauntered down to the South Lounge for our first floor meeting. The orientation leaders, two frat brothers named Sean Connaught and Roger House, looked at us with the blasé disgust of drill sergeants inspecting raw recruits. And in fact Seneca Hall's Seventh Sons, as we would come to call ourselves, were a spectacularly motley crew.

The lake sparkled behind the huge picture window in the waning daylight, and finally House cleared his throat. "Okay, you guys, listen up. Classes start at eight, and you only get three cuts before they flunk you. So don't be an idiot—stay away from eight o'clock classes." This drew a polite chuckle, because most of us were used to being in school by eight o'clock. But none of us was used to playing cards till three and four in the morning the night before, high on grass and beer, and eight o'clock classes were to take a terrible toll on those who ignored House's advice.

Connaught got up at one point to emphasize that the main thing about the rules was not to be dumb enough to get caught breaking them. "For instance," he said, "you're not allowed to have any ass in your room overnight, and you're supposed to leave your door open a crack at all times when you've got some in there."

"Right," House chimed in, *"open a crack."*

"So close the door and tell her to keep quiet while you're boffing her," Connaught said. There was knowing laughter all around.

"Sounds like a few of you may not be virgins," House said, a sarcastic smile spreading across his heavy features. "Well, if any of you think you've got what it takes, you can come with me and Sean tonight on the Bridge Street run."

Someone boomed out: "How much pussy on the Bridge Street run?"

"More than enough for YOU, pal," said Connaught, who now took over with the air of a practiced orator. "When you leave this dorm tonight, I want you to be thinking about PUSSY—sweet, tender, young pussy, all of it just dying for you. I mean, if you can't score here, boys, you're just pathetic."

He looked to House for support, but House was fairly squeaking with mirth and could only manage a nod.

"In fact," said Connaught, an Elmer Gantry of poontang building to his crescendo, "if you can't score here, you'll probably NEVER score! And if you can't score, WHAT GOOD ARE YOU?"

Caught up in the spirit, most of us were laughing, shouting and stomping. Connaught and House began to exit, struggling to keep their composure. Just before they got to the double doors that led to the elevators, House tossed over his shoulder:

"Do Bridge Street with us tonight, and we'll just see if you've got what it takes to be an Oswego State man."

I was laughing and cheering like the rest, but inwardly I felt a bit of resentment. Of course it would be wonderful to get laid on one's first night of college, but was it really considered mandatory?

Although Nixon had been president for less than ten months in October of 1969, another ten thousand American soldiers had been killed in Vietnam during that time. His public approval rating for the conduct of the war was high—71 percent—but he was still anathema to the peace movement.

My own position on the war was somewhat schizoid, although it made sense to me then. I knew guys who had gone into the service right after high school, and I knew they weren't the murderers or warmongers of radical cant. So I opposed the war as a big mistake, but not the American soldiers fighting it. In fact, I considered them victims of the war rather than perpetrators, and I hated the thought that they might feel that the peace demonstrations were directed against them. I was also aware that opposing the war made the enemy—which I considered to be North Vietnam—stronger. But I felt it still had to be done.

On the day of the massive moratorium against the war in mid-October of 1969, Vin and I joined thousands of other students and professors who marched the mile or so from the campus to the post office, which housed the draft board. The mood was somber and righteous, if a bit self-conscious. For the most part, the citizens of Oswego simply stared at us as we brought their small city to a standstill. Some had lost sons and brothers in Vietnam, and although I didn't see any overt hostility, there wasn't much support, either.

There were three other historical mileposts around that time: In early September Ho Chi Minh, the tenacious old Vietnamese nationalist and Communist, died at the age of 79 and a computer network that would eventually become the Internet was born; and in November the slaughter of innocents at My Lai—the obscene underbelly of the war—was acknowledged through indictments against Lieutenant Calley and Captain Medina. But these events passed largely unnoticed amid the feverish tapping of kegs and parting of legs at Oswego.

Vin and I began to think about transferring to Harpur early on. We both wanted to prove ourselves at a more challenging school, and our Calhoun classmate Sue Ball, who had gone there, told us it had a good choir, a really tough academic environment and a drugs-and-freak rather than suds-and-Greek culture. We loved our brother Seventh Sons, but they held academic virtues in such low esteem that the floor's cumulative average stood at about 1.2 at the end of the first semester.

Sunday, October 12

Dear Ruthie,
 I am really really screwed up. I could take not being able to make it with the girls here and getting bombed all the time if only Alice would write. But she doesn't, and that makes me feel like the biggest idiot in the world.

By late November, I hadn't had a letter from Alice in two months, and the few times we'd spoken on the phone, she'd sounded as distant as she was. Her parents had put tremendous pressure on her to drop me, and in the end she'd given way. The realization that I'd lost her sent me into a tailspin of drinking, moping and commiserating with other guys who were having similar troubles. It got so bad that even Vin lost patience with me, urging that I either shut up about Alice or "go down there and try to get her back." But that was out of the question.

My one consolation was that I knew she was planning to attend Wellesley College, near Boston, the following fall. When she did, I would try to get her back. In the meantime, I kept up my written conversation with Ruth at the rate of about one letter per week. Foolish and feckless as I was, at least I had enough sense to know what a precious thing her friendship was.

20. Ruth

ivory towers

My college career began decorously, with a series of afternoon teas. I found myself becoming intimate with Earl Grey at the home of Mary Baldwin's president and at several freshman orientations. Just when I was beginning to think I couldn't drink another drop, I pulled an invitation out of my mailbox from a distant relation, Miss Francis Ralston, to visit her Civil War—era cottage on the north edge of campus. She was in her mid-eighties and had gone to school at Mary Baldwin—then Mary Baldwin Seminary—with my great-aunts Ruth and Fanny in the 1890s, and I knew her only from a photo in an old yearbook, a winsome Gay Nineties girl in corset and bouffant hairdo.

When I met her the next afternoon, I found a sweet-faced old lady in flowered gingham who walked with a silver-tipped cane. We sat in her sunny parlor on velvet chairs, balancing tiny demitasses of tea and eating cucumber-and-butter sandwiches with the crusts cut off. The visit, despite my bad attitude, was enjoyable—a gossipy chat about our relations—but it made me realize that Mary Baldwin was closer in its philosophy to the nineteenth century than the second half of the twentieth.

"You girls are so independent these days," Cousin Francis said. "When Fanny and I were in school, we were chaperoned every time we left our dormitory. We were never alone with a young man, not for an instant."

I had to grimace, because her assessment of my independence was far more liberal than the reality. As I learned from Jeff, coed dormitories were springing up all over the country, and my peers were positively gorging themselves on free love and anarchy. But we Mary Baldwin girls were dutifully signing in and out of tightly regulated dormitories under the watchful eyes of housemothers.

Dating cubicles lined the main parlor of my dorm and a starchy middle-aged woman made both the girls and their dates sign in, and then monitored each visit.

I recall an uncomfortable gold satin sofa and trying to sneak a few kisses with a handsome VMI cadet. But the matron was on patrol, peering into each cubicle as she passed. When she saw something amiss—a skirt hiked up too high, a blouse pulled askew—she would clear her throat, tap her watch and say, "*Miss* Tuttle, the *time*."

In the midst of all this propriety, more stringent than I had ever endured at home, I seethed. I wanted to participate in the raucous political life of my peers, and I wanted to find a boyfriend. It seemed neither would be possible at Mary Baldwin.

In October, a group of girls circulated handbills in the elegant dining hall just before lunch, announcing the formation of a committee to support the National Moratorium Day against the Vietnam War, October 15. Students at more than five hundred colleges and universities were participating. When the meeting was called to order by the student body president, Janie, about twenty of us were gathered. Janie briefly explained the moratorium, prefacing her remarks with the statement that she was not in favor of it. Before anyone else could start a discussion, she put a proposal on the table. "Instead of marching, or joining the moratorium, why don't we have a seminar on Vietnam, what the issues are, and what the history is? And a prayer vigil?"

Another girl, Paula, rose up in outrage. "The whole world is watching. We can't cop out and say we're 'studying the issues.' I demand action. Now."

In 1969 there were over 540,000 American men and women in action in Vietnam. Nixon had taken office in 1968 with a promise that he had a "secret plan" and that the war would end with "peace and honor," yet it seemed to get larger every day. In October of 1969 he said in the *New York Times*, "Under no circumstances will I be affected by the Vietnam Moratorium." There is "nothing new that we can learn from demonstrations. . . . I must consider the consequences of each proposed course of action—Others can say of Vietnam 'Get out now,' they can ignore the consequences. . . . I can only conclude that history would rightly condemn a president who took such a course. . . . To allow government policy to be made in the streets would destroy the Democratic process."

Yet his very mention of the Moratorium lent it credence, and it seemed to challenge us genteel Mary Baldwin girls to pay better attention to the distant, powerful rallying of the antiwar movement. We formed ranks behind Paula.

A motion was made that we march through downtown Staunton, and it was carried by a small margin. But Janie spoke up again. "I think a march will offend a lot of our students. Can't we offer an alternative, so the rest of us can still support our boys in Vietnam?"

So we voted to also hold a twenty-four-hour prayer vigil in the college chapel, in which at least one girl at a time would always be praying. I put my name at the top of the list of marchers. It didn't matter that I had no understanding of the war. I still remembered the vet I'd met in Yazoo and the horror I'd seen in his eyes. Anything that could do that to a person had to be bad.

But I was still only seventeen and used to getting my parents' permission for everything. So, even as I inwardly raged against supervision, I wrote them a letter and told them I wanted to march, but would respect their wishes. In a melodramatic gesture, I offered to change my name if they asked me to do it. My mother's reply was scathing.

> We don't want you to change your name, but we do want you to think before you get involved in movements. All it takes to march is two legs and no brains. President Nixon is already well aware of how the people feel about the war and he is doing all he can to end it. At this time he needs your support, not your heckling. You would spend your time to better advantage packing "ditty bags" for the boys in Vietnam. . . . Keeping their morale up is far more important than marching around with a sign.
>
> Ruth, you are a beautiful, charming, intelligent young lady of whom we are very proud. We are struggling to place you in surroundings where you can use your capacities to the fullest. Unfortunately, you seem to have fallen in with a radical minority who can only lead you to unhappiness.
>
> I thought after the last visit Jeff made to Mississippi your eyes would be open. . . . Jeff is as radical as they come, so please discourage his calls. You have a marvelous opportunity to meet boys and girls of your social and intellectual level. If you seek those people you will find life can be fun, happy and meaningful and not full of problems, crises, etc.
>
> Ruth, if you persist in leaning toward radicals and leftists we will bring you back to Mississippi and put you in a college where we can have more control over your actions. I hate having to write this letter, but we love you dearly and I have to fight for your happiness.

My father wrote also, and systematically listed the pros of marching (standing up for my principles) and cons (having my picture taken by the FBI as a Communist), then summed up with: "Think this thing through, but if you decide to march anyway, here's a contribution to the cause." He enclosed a check for fifty dollars, which I donated to the National Mobilization Committee to End the War in Vietnam. Shocked at this breach in my parents' habitually united front, I resolved to march.

My mother persisted, though, and finally extracted a promise from me to stay out of it. Bitter, I joined the prayer vigil and wrote a short letter to a soldier from a list Janie posted in the chapel. I remember that I tried, very politely, to tell him he had made a big mistake by going to Vietnam. He soon wrote me back.

> *Dear Ruth,*
>
> *I hope the fact that I answered your letter doesn't shock you too much. . . . I felt that if you could take the time to write to a guy over here, the least I could do is to write back and tell you your time wasn't wasted.*
>
> *I guess I better tell you a little about myself. My name is Mike. . . . I'm presently in the Air Force and serving my year at Ton Son Nhut Air Base just outside of Saigon. I guess you could say that I really have it pretty good over here. I live in a barracks with 54 other guys and work in an air-conditioned building. I'm what is known as a photo interpreter. . . . What I do is look at film that reconnaissance aircraft fly. . . . A plane goes up and flies over an assigned target and after . . . the film is brought to me and I plot it and look at it to see if I can find anything that might mean the VC are in the area. In all I look at about 1500 ft. of film a day. . . . We work 12 hours a day and get one day a week off. . . . This is my 10th month here so I'll be going home on the 25th of January. I sure miss home and things like bathtubs. . . . All we have here is showers and most of the time all that comes out is cold water.*
>
> *You asked if I liked the place where I'm at. Well, I'm sorry to say I hate it. Every day is exactly like the one before, which in a way is good because it makes time pass faster.*

I was disappointed in the letter. I didn't think this guy was very enlightened, or sensitive, to be complaining about no bathtubs when thousands of people were dying in the war he reconnoitered. I had no concept of denial and its survival benefits. Disgusted, I put him and Vietnam out of my mind. If it didn't bother him, and he was right in the middle of the fray, why should it bother me? For a few weeks after that I tended to more intellectual pursuits, discovering Mary Baldwin's well-deserved reputation for academic excellence. But then I began a series of off-campus escapades that brought me in contact with others of my "social and intellectual level" that my mother had wished me to meet. I wrote Jeff about what happened next.

Dear Jeff,

Picture this: I'm all dressed up along with twenty other girls, walking up a grassy hill to a fraternity house. Suddenly, at least sixty boys come running out onto the porch and down the hill. They all have beer and cigarettes in their hands, but their clothes are ragged, wet and stuck to their drunken bodies. They stink. They scream. They herd us girls like cattle into the house where beer is an inch thick on the floors. Everywhere I look, boys are spitting and dumping beer on each other. Really a filthy scene.

I stood in a little hallway and tried to keep out of the beer throwing, until a boy asked me to dance. After a while I went with him to the basement for another beer. There were a dozen or so boys in there and they started pouring pitchers of beer on me. It was barbaric. Drenched, I went to his room to dry off and put on some of his clothes. That's when it happened. He attacked me. You wouldn't believe some of the things he tried—even padlocked the door. Finally, I got him to let me out and the last thing I heard was, "Well baby, if that's what you want—keep it."

I cried all the way back to school. Now, if you know why I get into messes like that, tell me. I'd love to do something about it.

Dear Ruth,

My God, your letter really amazes me. Actually, to be honest, it hurt me to see you getting so completely messed up. Well, you have asked me what I think.

Ruth, you shouldn't have been in that position to begin with. I mean, I know it's a girl's school and girls can get just as horny as guys and you must need a release by the end of the week. Still, when you saw grown-up men behaving like orangutans—immersing each other in brew and vomit (which was probably there even if you didn't see it)—you should have known. What I'm trying to say is that a girl like you has much better things to do than to go to drunken UVa frat orgy parties. I think just about anything should be better than a scene like that. The thing is, Ruth, you have a hang-up. You like the idea that you're attractive and that you can "get" boys,

*but that's all you want to do. I mean, after casually going
to the guy's room to change your clothes, what did you expect? He had you pegged for a definite swinger. You acted
the part.* **What** *did you expect??? Honestly, I think I'd be jus-
tified in saying that you led him on. You gave him encouragement. You were just very lucky that he stopped short of raping
you. O.K., enough analysis and lecture. Just be more careful
in the future, huh Ruthie? (So Uncle Jeff doesn't have to
worry.)*

Maybe Jeff was trying to fix me up with someone more suitable, because
his friend Vinny also wrote to me. Some days, when I was sure I had ir-
retrievably buried myself in another Southern backwater, Vin's salacious,
tongue-in-cheek letters were the only things that kept me optimistic. I
started posting them on my bulletin board next to his longhaired hippie
photo, and they became a kind of magnet for other girls, too. I used to find
my dorm mates, gape-mouthed with astonishment, reading them.

"Is what he says true?" they would ask me. I'd just put on my poker
face and nod.

My dearest girl,

*My heart grieves at the thought of your unhappiness and
maladjusted life at Mary Baldwin. . . . somewhere in the
course of my perusals through numerous volumes of informa-
tive materials (often known as pretentious bullshit), I came
across the very name Mary Baldwin. It seems she led the life
of an ever-ready harlot who would declare bed-sheets and
perfumes as business expenses on her tax forms. Intrigued, I
ventured on to find that her parents, who were cultured, fine,
upstanding white Anglo-Saxon Protestants (BEES) were
shamed by their daughter's behavior and ostracized from the
community.*

*They took up roots and, along with a fantastic sum of
money they had amassed from stocks in the slavery market,
moved to an isolated town called Staunton. There, they decided to correct the injustice done to their name by opening
an institution . . . dedicated to the cause of chastity and pu-
rity for all women. So you see, my child of beauty and loveli-
ness, YOU ARE PAYING FOR THE SINS OF MARY
BALDWIN.*

*Take care my flower of fragrance and God's speed till you
reach my bed and your eternal pillow.*

I responded in kind.

> *I lie alone at night in a burning sweat, but girlish modesty prevents me from attributing it to my passion for you rather than a faulty air conditioner.*

"Stop taunting Vin," Jeff pleaded after a while. "He's becoming impossible to live with."

21. *Jeff*

you say you want a revolution

On the evening of May 6, 1970, Mother Nature put on one of the most stunning aerial shows I'd ever seen at Oswego, and I had perhaps the best seat in the house. The sunsets on Lake Ontario were famous; they'd even been featured in a *National Geographic* article a few years before. But the writer hadn't mentioned Oswego's dirty little secret—the gorgeous colors were partly due to the pollution spewing constantly from Huey, Dewey, Louie and Frank, the four stacks that jutted up from Niagara Mohawk's gigantic coal-burning power station.

Perched as I was atop the ten-story administration building, my legs dangling out over the abyss, I was too enthralled with the show to think about pollution. A vault of baby blue arched directly above my head, while washes of pink, heliotrope and violet painted the majestically swirling clouds to the west. If I thought at all of the smoke that turned the waning light to Technicolor, it may have been with some satisfaction; the tense tableau unfolding far below me would surely mark the beginning of the end of war, poverty, racism, pollution—all of humanity's bad dreams.

The breeze was soft and playful, but I leaned back, away from the edge, and gripped the low parapet behind me. I was taking no chances on being wafted to my death. The grim policemen in the quad below seemed like so many Lilliputians now, made puny by perspective and the awesome spectacle overhead. I looked again at the salmon skies, and a serene, sitar-inflected hymn from the Moody Blues' *In Search of the Lost Chord* began to sound in my head. I sang quietly to the breeze:

The rain is on the roof; hurry high, butterfly.
As clouds roll past my head—I know why the skies all cry.
Om. Heaven.
The Earth turns slowly round; can you hear the distant sound?
It's with us every day—can you hear what it says?
Om. Heaven.

How many times had I listened to that song, stoned into a state of bliss, in my room back at the dorm? It had soothed my grief at losing Alice, but it seemed that I had never really understood it until now. I sat there, more than one hundred feet off the ground, chanting until the lake extinguished the setting sun and the breeze, suddenly cooler, kicked up. It was time to come down out of my private paradise, but come down to what? Would I ever resume life as a student? The seizure of the administration building was now in its sixth or seventh hour, and the answer to that question was still unclear.

The day had begun normally enough, given that it was two days after four student demonstrators were shot dead by National Guardsmen at Kent State. A group of us from Seneca Hall's seventh floor had awakened to a call to arms from the campus radio station. "There'll be some intense doings on campus today," the deejay had said. "Eat hearty, because you'll need the *breakfast of champions* to get through it."

It may have been code or it may have been a bit of whimsy on the part of a stoned kid sitting bleary-eyed behind a mike. In any case, our group had a leisurely breakfast over which we tried to figure out what the strikers at Oz and nationwide would do next and how the power structure—the college administration and the Nixon administration—would answer it. Could we, in concert with our alienated peers throughout the land, raise enough hell to make Nixon pull out of Cambodia?

From the dining hall we'd gone back to Seneca 7 and duly brushed our teeth—we were still the children of the bourgeoisie, after all—before heading across campus. The brief trek to the student union had become a morning ritual since the beginning of the strike, and the building itself had become an antiwar theme park. We signed petitions, wrote letters to Congress and talked to the hitchhiking heralds who daily brought news of organizing, demonstrations, moratoria and marches. Reminders of Kent State were everywhere.

We were dressed in the ragtag uniform of the antiwarrior: faded, patched and/or embroidered bell-bottom jeans; fatigue shirts and jackets and tie-dyed T-shirts. A wooden peace symbol hung from a leather thong around my neck; one of us wore psychedelic sneakers while another sported an old bowler hat. None of us had gotten a haircut in ages, and nearly all were sprouting facial hair. A few of us almost certainly were high.

We loped across the campus in good spirits; classes had been canceled indefinitely, and no one thought the administration would have the balls to flunk the whole student body. For many strikers, however, such a reprisal would have amounted to an express ticket to 'Nam.

I don't know when we first noticed the mass of students surging toward Culkin Hall, popularly known as the Power Tower, or if we noticed it at all before we became part of it. The quad next to the union was full of milling people, and the column that headed toward the nearby administration building seemed to just swell out of it. We suddenly found ourselves borne along, in a tightly pressed mass, across the quad and up the cement steps to the Power Tower's heavy glass doors.

A few frustrated-looking cops stood outside with rifles held athwart their bodies; tense and quiet, they were doubtless under orders to avoid a situation resembling what had happened at Kent State. They may have been waiting for reinforcements before making their move, but that day—with eruptions on so many state and private campuses—reinforcements would have been hard to come by.

The door in front of me yawned open and I was swept in; then, abruptly, it closed right behind me, practically in Vin's face. I was on the inside, and Vin, who'd been only a step behind me, was on the outside with the others. There was no time to marvel at this odd dealing of fate, however, because things suddenly got intense. Several club-carrying members of the black student union were running chains through the handles on the doors and connecting them with padlocks. It was clear that they were playing the revolution game for keeps.

Their leader, an angry-looking young man who'd been arrested a month earlier on a weapons charge, faced us with his back to the glass doors. "Any of you pussy motherfuckers want to get out," he snarled, "you better get out now, because we're takin' over this building in the name of the brothers who've died in this racist war. See those pigs out there? They're ready to kill us, and they'll be killin' your white asses, too, if you get in the way, so you better be ready to die here if you're gonna stay!"

No one wanted to be branded a pussy motherfucker, so no one moved. The black students faced the cops through the door, parting only for a stream of deans, provosts, secretaries, typists and computer operators who filed out of the elevators and up to the main doors like refugees from a war zone. The blacks sullenly opened the chains long enough to let them out; then the waiting began.

The students outside shouted encouragement and gave us the peace sign or clenched fist, and we occupiers, about one hundred strong, dispersed inside the building. Some lit joints, some set about "liberating" various pieces of office equipment and personal property, and others, thinking it was required in such situations, attempted to trash the place. One student tried to kick down a massive oak door before giving up, somewhat sheepishly, to find an easier target for his wrath. Another student walked around with a portable electric typewriter under his khaki jacket.

I had no stomach for the standoff in the lobby, and headed upstairs to where the campus nerve center had been, only an hour or so earlier. Now, instead of administrators filling out forms and secretaries making copies, the scions of the middle class were gamboling—tearing up papers, making photocopies of their naked butts, placing long-distance calls and in general having a ball. In the office of the dean of students dope smoke filled the air and antiwar slogans were being scrawled on the walls. Some of the liberators rummaged about for their own academic records or those of their friends; others called their girlfriends.

At one point, the phone on Dean Houghton's desk rang; startled, a longhaired kid picked it up and said, "Yeah?" Thinking it might be the "pigs" with an ultimatum, the revelers hushed. Soon, though, the kid was smiling. "Far out," he said several times. "Great! Hey, who's . . ." Just then all the lights and phones went off, disconnected from outside. The kid put down the dean's phone. "Shit," he said, "they must've cut us off."

"Who was it?" someone asked.

"It was the kids at Oneonta," he answered with a beatific grin. "They were calling from *their* power tower."

Soon a delectable rumor began to circulate: Upstairs, in President Perdue's office, dope was being smoked—*with Perdue's own pipes.* I made my way there and found, seated and standing around the president's desk, a group of kids loading grass into the pipes from a circular rack and toking up. I joined in as cannabis smoke filled the room. Perdue, who claimed to oppose the war but was viewed by the students as a temporizer, may well have resented this illegal use of his property, but the pipes probably would have been stolen as souvenirs if they hadn't been ritually defiled. The idea was to force him to smoke dope along with us because, as everyone knew, once you "freaked out," you couldn't fail to see the light about the war.

As the stalemate wore on, the building began to seem more like a prison than a playground. At one point during the afternoon a huge box of sandwiches had been sent over from the union and allowed into the building, a gesture of goodwill that boded we knew not what. Had the cafeteria staff, as was rumored, sent the food over in a show of solidarity, or had the students milling around the building been responsible? No one knew, but it seemed encouraging that the cops had let it pass. But when I reluctantly came down from my aerie on the roof at nightfall, I discovered that there had been no negotiations with the cops or the administration.

Someone tuned a portable radio to the campus station, which was carrying a live session of the faculty senate. Most of the professoriat had met to decide our fate, among other things, and the debate raged back and forth: Putting aside its overwhelming sympathy toward the antiwar movement, could the faculty condone this kind of affront to order? And what about the senior class? The strike and takeover had jeopardized its graduation.

We in the building alternately cheered and booed as various professors, some of whom had been grading our papers only a few days before, spoke on one side or the other. Finally the faculty approved a generous settlement, which included full amnesty for those of us in the Power Tower. I relayed the terms to Ruth in a letter a few days later:

1. A telegram will be sent to Nixon deploring the war in Vietnam and Cambodia, and another one sent to protest the suppression of dissent (i.e. Bobby Seale, although they didn't mention him specifically).
2. Regular academic procedure will be suspended in favor of holding workshops and relevant classes to discuss and take action on current issues.
3. A provisional, temporary grading system was established in deference to those participating in the strike.

What I didn't mention was how good the night air smelled when they opened the doors and let us out without taking names. We'd been extremely lucky, and we knew it.

Most students juggled the grading options to their own advantage, as I also noted in my letter, and none more than I. Not only had I been let off the hook for any civil or criminal liability, I also got to take my grades as they stood going into the strike week. I'd been working on five A's but had been falling steadily behind as the weather got nicer and the tempo of antiwar activity picked up. Ultimately, courtesy of Kent State and a forbearing faculty, I finished the second semester with a 4.0.

As if that wasn't enough to ask of the revolution, I also had nearly a month with nothing much to do and a room to myself. Vin, who took his antiwar duties more seriously than I, and who perhaps felt the need to make up for missing the Power Tower coup, went hitching to campuses all over the state, attending rallies and spreading the word of David Dellinger, a member of the Chicago Seven who'd spoken at Oswego.

But I felt more of a need to enjoy life after my harrowing day in Culkin Hall. I found a girl to help me while away my leisure hours and joined my few remaining floormates in turning Seneca Hall into a kind of residential country club.

22. Ruth

as radical as they come

In the spring of 1970, Nixon's military "incursion" into Cambodia radicalized millions of students who, like me, had been desperately trying to straddle the fence or forget the whole thing. After Kent State and Jackson State, there could be no doubt: The United States was losing its moral right to call itself a free country.

While Mary Baldwin was an island of calm in the sea of student protest, off campus I was increasingly aware of the quickening political undertow. I saw my peers clotted together by their sense of rightness. The angry, stern and even scared faces of May 1970 were far different from the blissed-out flower children of Woodstock the summer before. At times I was sure our generation would bring not just the Vietnam War but *all* wars to an end. And I would for a day or two identify with the antiwar movement and with its fervent masses, and adore them, aching to be one of them. Then I'd think that perhaps they were muddying the waters, impeding Nixon and Kissinger in their effort to end the war. *If those people would hush up,* I'd think, *the whole mess could be dealt with. Let the government do its job.*

I personally didn't have any answers. No one did, except to "get out now." But most Americans couldn't imagine losing a war. The entire American system seemed to be tottering. My head pounded with frustration when I watched Nixon on television after Kent State. He was lame, lame, lame. *And wrong,* I thought. But it was easier to just let him be the daddy. I wanted desperately to ignore my doubts, to have some fun and quit taking things so seriously. On one of those days I wrote Jeff to advise him of what I thought was my final decision about the war.

May 10, 1970

Dear Jeff,
    Hey man, what's happening? I've got so much work to do, but I've decided to forget it all and just have a good time, end [the semester] with a resounding clash of social cymbals.
    I almost ended up in Washington at the rallies yesterday.

But I made a decision not to go, and now I have to tell you why. I'm extremely IN FAVOR of Nixon's policies. I think he's a sincere man who is keeping his promise to get us out of Vietnam by forcing North Vietnam to negotiate. Cambodia seems to be the logical way to exert necessary pressure, cripple NV supply lines, win and leave. This seems the fastest way. I HATE Benjamin Spock!

I was at UVa Friday. There were "strike rallies," "violence drives," general chaos, and what seemed like a costume ball of outlandish outfits. The girls were disgusting, padding along behind their "men" with headbands on, but no opinion lodged in their heads. It's all a big game at UVa to get out of school early or go to DC and egg Tricky Dick.

I remember putting the letter in its envelope with relief. I was out of the fray. I knew it wouldn't please Jeff, who had always prided himself on bringing me along politically. But it pleased me at that moment. One of my roommates, Debbie Ellswood, was going to transfer with me to the University of Tennessee, and we were considering joining a sorority. I already had an invitation to be a "little sister" for a fraternity. But then I got Jeff's reply and those plans began to seem frivolous.

May 13, 1970

Dearest of Ruthies,

I underwent a minor spiritual catharsis when I saw that red-stamped letter with the flowery handwriting on the outside. I had been considering calling up the Staunton police and asking them if you were being held incommunicado or something.

Things have been going at a really wild pace around here. Much confusion of sentiments, much debate and argumentation. Anyway, from your letter it looks as though you and I have jumped in opposite directions, which kind of surprised me because I thought that if you did jump, you'd jump to the other side.

The basic issue is this: Is war sanctionable in any case? As a good Christian, I think your answer should be NO. I've read all about the strategy behind the Cambodian thing and it's fairly obvious that it was more or less a necessary tactical and strategic move which might very well go toward ending the war sooner. On the other hand it might prove to be a tactical disaster which will get us involved in Cambodia for

*years. All of that is irrelevant, however; the real truth is that
hatred has never been effectively dealt with by war. War has
never solved anything, and it leaves behind the seeds of future conflict. I'm speaking on very good authority: history.*

*I don't believe in war or killing for any reason, simply be-
cause I don't think that any human doctrine or ideology is
worth the price of life, even if it's the plant life . . . (good old
chemical defoliants). I think we Americans have been fed the
most incredible bullshit imaginable. "Free enterprise," "de-
mocracy," "Yankee know-how," and "America, America God
shed His grace on thee," have all become rather sick jokes in
the face of racism and the systematic destruction of the environment. This country is among the most fucked-up in the
world, and the sooner more of us realize that, the sooner we
can get to work on improving it. Nixon is not the man, and
Agnew is a preposterous anachronism. Don't ask me who the
man is, but he's got to be found soon.*

*Well, love, I hope you're not mad or disgusted with me,
but that's the way I feel. I still love you and respect you and I
hope it's mutual. OK?*

The letter went on for twelve pages, and I was greatly influenced by what I
saw as Jeff's superior grasp of the issues. What had seemed to me like an
inscrutable tangle of history, emotion, murder and secrets, was evidently a
coherent worldview for Jeff.

It didn't occur to me, in the midst of one of America's most painful historical reckonings, that no one—not even Nixon, who later complained
about being ignored or kept in the dark by his military commanders—knew
what was happening. I fiercely believed that I could make sense of it all
with a few days of book learning, and went to the library.

Only seven months before, my mother had called Jeff "as radical as
they come." I had thought she was probably right; I just didn't know then
how I felt about that. But by May of 1970 I had decided that radicalism
was called for. And, as she had feared, I knew it was Jeff's words that led
me to that conclusion. But I never suspected that I would soon be walking
a political edge far to the left of my "radical" New York friend.

Still, as a child of the South who grew up disturbed by its unresolved
anger, hatred and societal rifts, a break with all I'd been taught was probably inevitable anyway, and Jeff, my Northern icon who had become so dear,
can't be held responsible for most of what followed.

23. Jeff

the numbers game

The heady months of revolution and reveling at Oz were over in June of 1970, and Vin and I found ourselves back on Long Island trying to make money to pay the next year's tuition bills.

Attempting to follow the path Ben Cohen and Fred Thaler had taken to riches the summer before, we partnered on an ice cream route. We rented an aged pickup truck with a Bungalow Bar ice cream box on the back and steered it on daily rounds, earning about seventy-five dollars a week each—not nearly as much as we'd hoped to make, but not awful. We hippie-dippie ice cream men also made quite a few friends on that route, some of whom occasionally paid us in substances other than cash.

It was a carefree time, except that I had the draft hanging over my head. Since Harpur wouldn't let me transfer credits for a first-semester course in which I'd pulled a D, I wouldn't be a bona fide sophomore next semester, which meant the draft board could come after me. I worried about the situation until I had a visit one day from Mitch Kupperman, a friend from Seneca 7 who had tracked me down on my route. When I got out of the truck, he seemed startled.

"Jeff," he said, "you'd better eat more ice cream. You look like a skeleton." I never kept track of my weight and hadn't been aware of how many meals I was skipping in my zeal to maximize sales. I told him I thought I was at my normal weight—about 125—but he shook his head.

"No way. You're under one-fifteen. At your height, if you lose a couple more pounds, you're 4-F."

I made a point of stepping on the scale that night. Mitch, who'd been a wrestler in high school and was a keen judge of human poundage, had been right—I was down to 114. Far from being alarmed, I was ecstatic.

Vin and I felt guilty, in that summer after the first Earth Day, about the clouds of black smoke our truck spewed out. We hated the idea of poisoning our customers and told the wholesaler, a bald Jewish leprechaun named Marty Hershkowitz ("Hershkowitz," he'd grin, "rhymes with Durshkowitz"), that we simply wouldn't drive it if it wasn't fixed. He pointed out that we'd miss the July 4 holiday, the busiest ice cream weekend of the year. Determined to stop fouling the air, we okayed the repair anyway and the engine was taken out. But one of the other drivers loaded the truck's box with product and towed it back and forth to Salisbury Park, where he proceeded to sell out twice and make a fortune.

"It's all right, Durst," Vin said after Marty broke the news about how much our environmentalism had cost us. "We did the right thing."

July 15th, 1970 (happy belated Bastille Day . . .)

My Dearest Ruth—

Your comments in relation to my becoming a fiendish user of "the weed with roots in hell" were appreciated because I know that you're not just trying to be self-righteous . . . but honestly, Ruthie, there's **no** *cause for alarm.*

I've come to the definite conclusion that the human brain is a gift much too valuable to be constantly bombarded and saturated with foreign chemicals. The thing is, I always have very good highs—I've never taken anything stronger than very strong hash, but still I almost always "trip" on grass, so I don't need anything stronger. In other words I don't want to get any "higher" than I've been, for fear of hitting the ground really hard. Being very stoned is an entirely different dimension, Ruth . . . you really should try it just to educate yourself.

I just had a big talk with Mike McCourt about college, protest, politics, religion, violence vs. pacifism (he's now a violent pacifist, more or less). He doesn't really know what he's going to do after this summer (he's working at the cerebral palsy center) besides that he's going to apply for a conscientious objector card and maybe go out West for a while.

Love, Jeff

P.S. Please don't leave **this** *letter around your house, because if I ever do get down to Y.C. again, I don't want* **your** *parents hating me, too.*

At the end of that summer Ben, Jerry, Feldo, Vin, Fred and I got together with Ronnie Bauch in his basement for a coming-of-age ritual. We all, except Ron, either had already turned nineteen in 1970 or were about to, and that meant that the draft lottery—"Death Lotto," as someone called it—applied to us. The annual call-up then was about 250,000 men; the first third picked by the lottery were, we thought, virtually certain to be called, the next third were borderline cases and the last third were home free. The year before, at Oswego, I'd watched a lot of sophomores wash out of school on a tide of beer after they received high numbers in December. Nationwide, ROTC programs—which gave their members deferments— lost participants and schools saw a sudden dip in enrollment as newly emancipated students dropped out.

That evening in Ron's basement began in high spirits; we had bought a watermelon, put a hole in one end and filled it with vodka. Then we sat down to slurp alcoholic melon and watch our birthdays come up. The melon tasted terrible—Ron, who ultimately became a gourmet chef as well as a concert violinist, opined later that we probably should have used rum and sugar rather than vodka—but we amused ourselves singing Country Joe and the Fish's "I Feel Like I'm Fixin' To Die Rag" while waiting for the drawing:

> And it's one, two, three
> what are we fightin' for?
> don't ask me, I don't give a damn—
> next stop is Vietnam
> And it's five, six, seven open up the pearly gates
> I ain't got time to wonder why—whoopee!—we're all gonna die.

We also talked about Mrs. Stoloff, who had been our social studies teacher in eighth grade and a staunch supporter of the domino theory. Ben said it was too bad her number wouldn't be coming up in the lottery.

Jerry's birthday was the first of the group's to be drawn, and it was low—below twenty. The bantering and horseplay stopped suddenly as the smile on Jerry's face froze. Ronnie, trying to make the best of a bad situation, made a comic speech and handed Jerry his prize for first place: a Vietnamese cookbook.

Vin's number also was very low, and he felt his fate was sealed. I drew a borderline number—101—while Fred and Feldo got numbers in the 200s. Ben's luck was best; he drew something in the mid-300s, which meant he wouldn't have to worry about the draft again. By the end of the next semester, he'd departed Colgate and begun the rootless life that eventually would lead to an ice-cream-and-crepes stand in Burlington, Vermont.

Vin and Jerry heard of a deal later that year that turned the lottery into something resembling Russian roulette. You could, it was said, give up your deferment and declare yourself available for the draft in December. If you weren't called up by the end of the year, you were out of the draft for good—no matter what your number was. They agonized about it over Thanksgiving vacation, but ultimately decided it would be worth the risk to get out from under the shadow of those low numbers. So they entered into a kind of suicide pact and went, arm in arm, to the draft board on the first of December to give up their deferments.

Luckily for them, the military had already filled its manpower needs for 1970, and they weren't called.

24. Ruth

the white house affair

September 1, 1970

Dear Jeff,

I don't know if there's such a thing as a mental explosion, but I'm having one. For the first time I really believe blacks are equal to whites. Black or white—no difference as far as human value goes.

As for sex, drugs, my total outlook on humanity—all different like you wouldn't believe. The general enthusiasm for life that I have now is something I never expected.

When we stumbled upon each other 18 months ago we were both kind of watching for an experience to happen. It did and wow did we ever need it. The other people were like fringes, the beach where the waves hit.

Forget George Wallace. He was the representative of what has already been changed. Between us there just isn't the gap of Mississippi and New York anymore. That has become irrelevant.

"What are you doing, now?" my father yelled up the stairs at me.

Exasperated, I threw my pen down and yelled back, "Writing a letter. Do you mind?"

It had been a summer of conflict with him, and I was sick of being home. He had dogged my steps for three months, trying to put the wildcat back in its sack, and I'd had to claw my way out again and again. But he never gave up, and until the day I left for Knoxville, he and I met daily with bared teeth.

But for my mother it had been a summer of deep satisfaction, because, in her words, I'd finally "bloomed."

"Our family is known for late bloomers," she'd told me. And evidently it was true. Planters' sons, Ole Miss SAEs, a few unknown secret admirers and even some itinerant students from Boston had been calling me all summer. I'd attained belledom at last.

Now I'd been in the backseat of too many Bubbas' Caddies and hot rods and seen the Delta from Yazoo to Memphis by moonlight. I'd sipped bourbon and fought the battle for my virginity for three months. But none of my beaux had appealed to me, and I was ready to take my suddenly killer pheromones to Knoxville, Tennessee, where I was sure I'd find a willing Volunteer with the right combination of sex appeal, charisma and intellect.

The University of Tennessee, which had over twenty thousand students on its Knoxville campus in 1970, seemed at first glance to be everything I was looking for: It was diverse, coed and had a recent history of activism. Except for the Panhellenic Building, it didn't even feel "Southern." Unlike Jeff, I hadn't given a thought to academic merit, and neither had my parents, as they had made clear that spring when I told them I had applied to Radcliffe and thought I would be accepted.

"And who's going to pay for *that,* I wonder?" my mother had responded. "Ole Miss is good enough." I began to look at other options. In the end we reached a compromise based on geography. UT was halfway between Staunton and Yazoo City: closer to home, but still beyond their immediate reach. And once I got there, I thought I had made a very good bargain.

As Debbie and I lounged on the grass outside Sophronia Strong Hall and watched the traffic flow by on Cumberland Avenue and Seventeenth Street, we were hugely excited. It was good to be back together again. We sat catching up on our various summer adventures and greeting the too-cool-to-be-true hippies who sauntered by, raising their fingers in the "V" sign of peace and stepping carefully around broken places in the sidewalk. Bare feet weren't made for traversing the inner-city student ghetto, but the times dictated a certain loyalty to one's creed regardless of personal discomfort.

The ghetto began just behind Strong Hall, ten square city blocks of formerly genteel turn-of-the-century and Depression-era homes now fallen into graceless squalor. They were inhabited by a mishmash of foreign graduate students living twenty or thirty to a single-family residence that had been subdivided into tiny apartments; undergraduates with their new cars and Greek letters adorning the fronts of the better buildings; and owner-occupants who ranged from longtime residents to blue-collar families just out of the Smoky Mountains, often barely literate and clinging tightly to their high-country values. As hippie politicos moved in and turned the old houses into communal experiments, a dangerous cross-cultural brew was created.

We had already heard the story about the "best" commune in the area—known locally as the White House—just up the street, next door to Epworth Church. It was inhabited by none other than one of the Knoxville twenty-two, Carroll Bible.

On January 15, 1970, twenty-five hundred UT students had assembled in front of the administration building to watch the outcome of a challenge: Peter Kami, a gentle Brazilian student with soft honey-brown curls and a slender body who was called "Peter Commie" by the hippie community, had challenged the newly appointed president of the university, Edward Boling, to hand-to-hand combat, "a symbol" of the aggressive way Boling had been selected without student involvement. Sitting on the shoulders of another student, Peter shook his fist at the building and called for Boling to come forth. The challenge drew scattered laughs and then a roar from the crowd, which began to press against the doors. Some newspaper accounts said that Carroll was one of the leaders, encouraging students to enter the building. Chancellor Charles Weaver called in the Knoxville police, who confronted the crowd in full riot gear—helmets, billy clubs, gas masks and shields.

"I'm afraid," Peter was heard to say, "but I'm not going to back down." The panicked students fought back with slushy snowballs. At the end of the five-hour melee, twenty-two students had been arrested, six injured. Carroll and Peter were charged with inciting to riot and both faced the possibility of five to ten years in federal prison if convicted.

I'd been shown some back issues of the UT *Daily Beacon* where Carroll, wearing a full-length striped caftan, his long blond hair and beard spilling over its V-neck, was pictured standing on a car and holding up a sign at another demonstration in May of 1970, against Nixon's attendance at a Billy Graham Crusade at UT's Neyland Stadium. Earlier, he had been chased and assaulted by a Vietnam vet at the corner of Fifteenth and Clinch Streets. Perhaps it had hardened his resolve, because in the photo his young eyes were wide and unflinching, staring directly into the camera's lens. The sign said "Let my people go." He radiated fanaticism. He was arrested a few hours later and became known as a leader of another band of student radicals, the "Nixon 6." NBC News ran four minutes of coverage of the demonstration and in September of 1970 when I arrived at UT, *Esquire* magazine had just published a six-page exposé on Knoxville student radicals and the Graham Crusade. More than anything, I wanted to meet Carroll.

I soon had my chance.

His girlfriend, Lori, lived across the hall from Debbie and me, but only to keep up appearances for her mother, she said. She really lived with Carroll at the White House.

On my second morning at UT, I returned from the bookstore to find her digging in my clothes closet while Debbie watched skeptically from the bed.

"She wouldn't leave," Debbie whispered when I looked a question at her.

In a few minutes, Lori burrowed her way out and said, "This is perfect!" holding up my black cashmere pullover like a trophy.

"Hey, you can't have that," I said.

Unperturbed, Lori clutched it to her chest, rubbing its softness against her face, and said, "Carroll will just love this on me."

"You mean they wear cashmere at the commune?" Debbie asked sarcastically. I laughed, but Lori missed the joke.

She danced down the hall and back, doing a kind of artistic striptease. On her the sweater was transformed from the basic black staple of my wardrobe into a sexual instrument. Her braless breasts quivered like high-strung racehorses lightly saddled with cashmere. Before I could stop her she had vanished into her room and wouldn't come out. She eventually slipped a note under the door: "I'm only borrowing it."

The next day I received another note. It said, *"Come to the White House. Lori."* I got directions and set out, curious to see a communal Camelot and glad to have an invitation from the person I thought was its Guinevere.

It was a warm September afternoon, and the traffic along Seventeenth Street was heavy, spraying the noxious fumes of pre–catalytic converter days and making me surprisingly homesick for Mary Baldwin's traffic-free campus. But I trudged up the hill, tripping occasionally over my too-long bell-bottoms with their frayed hems. I had taken special care to choose an appropriate ensemble: sandals, bell-bottoms, a fringed vest and a plain white T-shirt. My hair fell straight to the center of my back.

The house was a white Victorian with a columned porch. Paint peeled underfoot as I walked up to the door, which stood open.

"Welcome, friend," a slow-talking man said from his place at a long table that stretched the length of the house's former parlor. He tipped back in his chair and slowly looked me up and down. The room was full of other women, and I felt like a piece of fruit as he mentally fondled me, comparing me, it seemed, to my sister plums for ripeness.

"Hello," I said to him. "I'm looking for Lori."

One of the women was pounding on a mound of bread dough in the center of the table. One large breast made a voluptuous escape through the overlarge armhole of her sleeveless granny dress and she hitched it back into place before looking up at me.

"I'm Puddin'," the man said to me, his voice slow and lazy. Two of the women set a plate of food in front of him. He hunched over it and began to eat.

"Little Flower," the young woman shaping bread dough said to a girl on the other side of the room, "if you burn the vegetables again, we can't afford to get any more. Go check on them."

Little Flower, a childlike waif in a flowered smock with dull blond hair and bare feet, turned from a dreamy reverie at the window and looked around the room. I thought she must be mentally deficient, because her expression was blank and her eyes unfocused. She raised an arm in front of her face and began to spin around the room, singing a tune of her own concocting.

"Is Lori here?" I tried again.

"Probably," Puddin' said, and without looking up from his dish he slid his hand down my back, capturing me by the waist and pulling me up next to him. "Why do you want her, sister?"

I stood like a statue, my heart fluttering. Was there a sexual toll to pay for admittance to the White House? "I have an invitation," I said, holding up the note.

The woman at the end of the table snorted. I didn't move. Finally someone said, "Lori's where she always is, with Carroll, waiting on a free meal." She pointed toward the stairs.

I pulled free of Puddin', who said, "Maybe we can ball later?" Speechless, I backed into the wall, tripped on my bell-bottoms and finally ran upstairs, my face flushing. "Peace, sister," he called after me.

Upstairs was a collection of rooms with mattresses on the floor, India-print wall hangings and remnants of past meals decaying in the corners. The sun poured in and street noises came through the open windows. It was stifling.

I found Lori sprawled across one of the mattresses with a tall, gaunt man who bore a striking resemblance to the portrait of Jesus that had hung over my grandmother's bed. I envied Lori her closeness with this hero of the Knoxville underground. The fact that he could be facing a jail term made him seem even more romantic. I would have been surprised to know then that Carroll was desperately trying to make sense of it all, just like me. The messianic part was accurate, though, for he had done a missionary stint in Brazil not long before. The harem I'd seen downstairs belonged to Puddin', who was also rumored to be a narc.

Carroll put his arm over his face when he saw me and turned toward the wall, causing Lori to slide onto the floor. "Hey, stop that," she said, looking up to see me in the doorway.

She jumped up and quickly pushed me into the hall. "Carroll's so tired. He just finished a double all-nighter. You really shouldn't disturb us now."

"But you asked me to come," I said. "Do you have my sweater?"

Lori indignantly puffed herself up. "I gave it to one of the sisters. You've got plenty more."

"I only loaned it to you."

"Lori," Carroll groaned in the background.

"I can't talk now. Can't you see that?" She whirled back into the bedroom. There was no door, so I stood there for a minute watching her drape herself into submission at the foot of the mattress, murmuring apologies and endearments as she stroked Carroll's legs.

Aware I'd been put in my place for my attachment to property in the face of such angst, I went downstairs, where Puddin' was still sitting at the table. The women—except for Little Flower, who was curled up fetal style in the corner, waving her fingers in front of her face—were blaming each other for the vegetables that had burned and were filling the room with black smoke. Puddin' said, "You chicks are bumming me out. I'm splittin'."

I hurried to get out the front door before he could join me.

Walking back to the dorm, I mulled over what I had just seen. I felt a great experiment was languishing in inept hands. Surely I could do better. At least I had seen the revolution, though. Wasn't this why I had left the protected world of Mary Baldwin? Wasn't this what I was looking for? A world with no rules, no restrictions, no judgments?

One True Love

That night was warm and starlit. Debbie and I sat on the lawn outside Strong Hall again, and conversation became disjointed and difficult. She ruminated about joining a sorority, and I talked about communes. After only a week, we had already begun to grow apart, and in the days to come, we would each feel betrayed by the other. By Christmas she would decide to room with someone else.

But that night I was still trying to win her over to my viewpoint. "Why would you want to live like that?" she asked me.

"It's an experiment. They believe in something. They're not worrying about their nails and what sorority they're gonna pledge. They're real."

"Your parents would die," Debbie said.

"I don't care. They'd just have to get over it."

"But those people believe in free love. You'd have to sleep with all the guys, wouldn't you?"

"They don't seem to have any real rules. And I know I'm a better cook than those girls. Maybe they'd let me run the kitchen."

"Yeah," Debbie said. "I guess food's as important as sex."

"How would you know?" I laughed.

"No one had on a bra?"

"Of course not. That's an invention of men to imprison women. Our bodies should be as free as our minds."

"I don't see you going without one."

"Oh yeah, watch." I unhooked my bra, pulled it through the armhole of my T-shirt and flung it onto the sidewalk.

It fell almost at the feet of a longhaired freak. He was muscular and dark and wore a headband over his curly shoulder-length hair. I had waved to him the night before and twice that night. In fact, it seemed like he was passing by every few minutes. "Hey man, what's happening?" he called to us. Then he stooped and picked up my bra, holding it aloft by one strap.

I was struck mute, but Debbie snatched it out of his hand, then stuffed it into her jeans pocket.

"Can I sit with you chicks?" he asked.

"Sure." My blood raced.

"Peace, sisters. I'm Bobby." While he and Debbie chatted, I studied Bobby's face. It was rugged with high cheekbones, dark eyes and a sensuous mouth. But some other, intangible characteristic, a charming accessibility, made conversation with him feel like physical intimacy. I wanted to curl up in his lap like a cat.

I think Debbie stayed for a while, but I don't really remember. It seemed Bobby and I were alone from the beginning. He pressed his face into my hair, pulled me next to him and shut out the world for me. I was amazed and flattered. We started walking, hand in hand, dodging traffic, and letting the streetlights change from green to red to green while we kissed each other breathless.

He gave me a campus tour, pointing out where the "pigs" had attacked unarmed students with truncheons, and the riot that had ensued in front of the student union. "I wish I had been there," I said.

"It was heavy," he said.

But he took pains to point out his own commitment to peace and love, punctuating his visionary dreamings with lips and hands that opened my mind as they caressed my body. That it was only hours since I had first met him didn't concern me. My body knew him, and for the time being that was enough.

He told me he was thinking of moving to Canada to avoid being drafted, and I thought he was brave and principled, more courageous than I could ever be. That he might have to flee the country made him irresistibly sexy.

When I asked if he had a girlfriend, he looked into my eyes and said, "I don't have a girlfriend, but I'd sure like one. Only she'd have to be very, very special."

My stomach flipped over, and his arms got tighter around me. My one true love, at last. I was sure. We got back to the dorm at sunrise. I heard a whisper in the depths of my brain, that I was supposed to start classes that morning. But I wasn't listening. I was numbed with emotion, thrilling with love, desperately unhappy to be leaving Bobby until that night.

"You are going to spend the night with me tonight, aren't you?" Bobby said as we stood by the doorway.

"I'm a virgin," I answered, searching his face for a reaction.

His eyes lit up. "I've never had a virgin before," he said. "It'll be great! Don't worry. I'll take care of everything." We spent another hour, sheltering in the bushes from sleepy students on their way to early classes, pressed together in frustrated erotic frenzy until we had to quit from total exhaustion.

Debbie was angry with me for staying out all night, and when I told her my plans for the evening, she screamed: "You only met him ten hours ago. You don't know this guy from Adam! Why him?"

I could only say I just knew he was the one. We had a lot in common.

"Like?"

"Our politics."

"What politics? You just got politics yesterday. You don't know what your politics are, for God's sake."

"I'm against the war," I countered. "I know that."

"No, this isn't about politics, and having stuff in common, this is about being horny. Just admit it. He's a knockout, and you've got the hots for him."

"I've had the hots for lots of guys," I said. "Bobby is more than that."

"You mean you think you're in love with him?" Her voice was becoming shrill with disbelief.

"Maybe I am. Don't you believe in love at first sight?"

"Just think about it a little longer, that's all," she said. Then she rushed off to her first class.

I cut classes and went to bed, hugging a pillow next to my churning stomach and daydreaming, because I couldn't sleep. As the hours went by, Debbie came in and out, giving an exasperated sigh each time she saw me pretending to sleep.

Bobby called our room just before dark. "Are you ready?" he asked. I'd been ready for two hours.

As I came around the corner of the stairs into the lobby, Bobby stepped out from a shadow and wrapped his arms around me. Then he pulled me outside and into the bushes. Soon we were rolling on the ground in a pile of dried leaves and branches as he said between kisses, "Hello, hello, hello, my little virgin."

We walked seven blocks to the Highland Avenue house where he was staying, taking over four hours to get there because of frequent amorous interludes. Like the White House, it was a communal arrangement. When my eyes adjusted to the dark, I saw a scattering of mattresses around the large main room. Male and female bodies lay entwined in various intimate positions, but no one moved. They all seemed to be asleep or otherwise out of it.

Bobby had indeed "taken care of everything." We had an entire full-size mattress to ourselves, though it butted right next to another one with four people on it.

Though we had spent our whole twenty-four-hour relationship working up to it, the actual denouement took only a few minutes. I was expecting something akin to the heights of ecstasy described in the few bodice rippers I had read. What those heights consisted of, I didn't know, because "orgasm" was a word I'd never heard or seen, and the experience hadn't been described to me by my friends. They were as innocent as I. So I wasn't expecting orgasm. But I was expecting the indefinable, the unknown, the thrilling, the tender and the life-bonding experience I knew must accompany an act that seemed to me at the moment it happened to be an unholy mess.

I lay very still until morning, stricken into sleeplessness by the enormity of what I had lost and the puniness of what I had gained. My one true love was sleeping soundly next to me, adding his slow breathing to the symphony of other sleepers in the room. Maybe the first time was always a downer, I thought. Surely it got better with practice? I knew from what Bobby had told me that he had ample experience, though, so I felt the fault must be with me.

Just as the sun was beginning to make the room hot, Bobby woke up and snuggled next to me. "Hey babe, that was great," he said. "You *are* on the Pill, aren't you?"

"No," I said. Bobby sat up.

"You'd better take a bath, wash out your insides and all."

I was already miserable, believing that our night together had been as awful for him as for me, and I didn't want to give him something to hold against me, so I did take a bath. But like many of my friends, I believed pregnancy couldn't happen the first time you had sex. Ann Landers would set us all straight on that.

Bobby and I agreed to get together that evening and I walked back to my dorm. But life's lessons were far more interesting to me that day than academia, so I cut all my classes again and went to the library. *The Joy of Sex* told me everything I needed to know, and as I had suspected, I had indeed been shortchanged the night before. Armed with a more complete concept of foreplay, I felt sure that all could be made right that evening.

But he didn't show up, and the next day I went to the Highland Street address to find him. He was just getting out of a car with three pretty girls. When he saw me he spoke to one of them, making her giggle. She went into the house with the rest of the group.

"Sorry I couldn't make it last night," he said. "I was wiped out from the night before."

That sounded reasonable, so I smiled at him.

"Deflowering virgins is hard work," he teased me. "Took me a while to recover. Come on, let me walk you back to your dorm." He took my arm and gave me a lingering kiss.

As we walked, I tried several times to bring up what I still thought of as "our" dismal experience, but he always countered with "It was great, wasn't it?" or "I'll never forget it."

When we got to the dorm he took my face in his hands and looked earnestly into my eyes for a long time. "Thank you," Bobby said slowly. "Thank you." He drew the words out as though I didn't understand English. But I did, and in this case what he was saying was "Good-bye."

I wanted to say, "Will I see you again?" but didn't, knowing I'd cry if I had to ask that. He jauntily walked away. "See you around," I called after him, feigning nonchalance. He looked back and flashed me a peace sign.

From then on I watched for him every time I went out, and ran into him once at the student post office. Again he told me—deeply, soulfully—how grateful he was for our night together.

Finally, about six weeks later, I got a note from him. "I'm leaving for Canada. Please come to the house tonight." My heart leaped and broke all at once, for the note seemed to say that, when it came time to go, I was the one he wanted to be with. Yet, I would have to tell him good-bye.

When I got there, I saw candles flickering in the windows, and at least ten girls were milling around in the yard. Everyone was crying or talking quietly in groups. I walked into the house in a state of wonder, not knowing what was happening until I saw Bobby sitting in a chair against the far wall. Dozens of girls stood in line, or sat at his feet, passing candles from hand to hand, watching him. There was a murmured incantation in the room: "Bobby's going. Bobby's going." I saw a few girls from my dorm who waved at me and smiled tearfully. "Isn't it awful?" one of them said, holding me in a tight embrace while she sobbed. "We're losing Bobby."

"What are all these girls doing here?" I asked.

"We all loved him," she sobbed.

"You mean we all slept with him."

"Yeah, I guess so," she said, but reverently.

I looked over their heads at Bobby. Young women approached him quietly, walking in single file. He whispered to and hugged each one—holding and touching her tenderly—before she silently carried her candle to sit with the others around the edge of the room. It was like going up to the rail for Holy Communion, followed by a few moments of quiet meditation.

I realized that I had been seduced by a hippie Don Juan, and as Bobby received the blessings of his assembled minions, I stood at the back of the room in the shadows and watched until he finally saw me. I wanted desperately to flip him the finger, something I had never done before and couldn't do even then. But when he smiled and nodded at me, then gestured for me to come forward, I pointedly turned and walked out. I couldn't stand another thank-you.

25. Jeff

seeking alice, finding ruth

I called Alice soon after I transferred to Harpur in the fall of 1970, but our brief conversation wasn't very auspicious. I'd gotten her number at Wellesley College from my faithful agent, Ruth, and was hoping to renew my claim in person before she was scooped up by some swaggering Harvard man with a Dixie drawl.

Alice sounded distracted and far from thrilled to hear from me, but she was too much the well-bred Southern girl to turn me down flat. She warned me, though, that her course load was heavy and that she might not have much time to talk. It would be our first meeting in over a year, and I had no idea what to expect.

My disappointing new roommate, the King, a small-time hood and Elvis wanna-be who'd left a good deal of his mind on the other side of the acid rainbow, kept up a typically doltish patter as he flogged his Super Beetle down the highway, trying to impress the two freshman girls who were riding with us. I tuned him out as much as I could, the engine noise whirring me back to the magical journey in Feldo's pinstriped Bug.

The young man who'd set off for Mississippi with his two friends had been brash, focused and fundamentally optimistic in a way that now seemed quaint, almost pathetic. He'd been master of his small suburban world and more than ready to burst free of it, but now, just over eighteen months later, he was an uneasy rider on the storm of change that had swept the nation and transformed his own life.

The times had become very weird indeed by September of 1970. The nation was in the midst of repudiating the heavy commitments its leaders had made, mostly in secret, to South Vietnam and Southeast Asia, and thousands of American families were attending government-paid burials each month as Nixon and his advisers searched for the exit. It would be a few more years before they found it, and societal pressures in the meantime were turning the Boomers and their parents into combatants in ways that went far beyond normal generational conflict.

"Gotta get down to it, soldiers are cutting us down. Should have been done long ago," sang Crosby, Stills, Nash and Young in "Ohio," which had come to supplant "Woodstock" as our generation's anthem. But get down to what? Out-and-out war with society, as the Weathermen and Black Panthers demanded? Secession to communes in the hinterlands? The days following Kent State had marked the high-water mark of youthful rebellion, and now, as the tide receded, we all struggled to find our places in the new order.

Drugs, meanwhile, had become so pervasive that door-to-door salesmen plied their wares openly in Harpur's dorms. Grass, hash, uppers, downers and psychedelics of varying strengths were all to be had from little brown bags on easy terms, no questions asked. This open flouting of the drug laws would have been unthinkable at Oswego only a year before. But with growing drug use came growing risk, as we were reminded when Janis Joplin, Jimi Hendrix and other rock icons died of overdoses that fall.

I was smoking highly psychedelic Jamaican weed at the time, but only on weekends. Having made it into a good school at last, I had no intention of getting lousy grades. Still, taking a weekend out to reestablish contact with Alice was at the top of my priority list.

The King drove the girls to their beaux' colleges when we got to Boston, then headed to Boston College, where he had arranged for us to crash. The next morning he drove me out to Wellesley, and I told him I would call "if" I needed a ride back to Boston.

The Wellesley campus, with its tall shade trees, limpid pond, manicured lawns and scaled-down Westminster Abbey of a campus chapel, was clearly one of those places where the nation's elite sent their children to learn how to run the country—or to marry those who would. I felt more than a little twinge of class envy as I navigated the parklike grounds to Alice's dorm. Harpur might be among the toughest colleges in the nation, but its state-issue sheepskin would never rival the old-money cachet of places like this. For the first time, I began to wonder: *Did Alice's parents really chase me off because my family couldn't afford a college like this?*

Such thoughts gave way to a vague disorientation at the idea of seeing her in this Yankee bastion so far from cotton, kudzu and magnolias. Still, I was awash in hope as I dialed her number from the walnut-paneled lobby of her dorm. I wanted to throw my arms around her and tell her personally, for the first time since that awful day in Yazoo City, that I still loved her and was sorry she'd suffered so much.

In a few moments a door opened at the end of a short corridor, and suddenly she was standing in front of me, a half-smile playing across her luscious lips. But her clothes—faded jeans and an old sweatshirt—sent a clear message that she didn't consider this a date. As if to reinforce the point, her hair looked as if it had been styled by a hurricane, with honey-blond wisps sticking out here and there. My dismay must have been apparent, but she made no attempt to explain. Her smile faded and she looked away.

"Alice," I finally stammered, "I can't believe it. Is it really you?"

She said nothing and avoided my eyes. I tried to ignore her clothes and hair—she was still ten times prettier than most girls, after all—and get her to focus on us.

"You know, I've really missed you a lot." She didn't answer, but looked quickly at the wall clock. "I mean, I really loved you. You know that, don't you?" I tried to make eye contact, but she kept avoiding my gaze.

"Well, that was a long time ago. We were both a lot younger then, I guess."

"But we loved each other—I know you loved me. I still have your letters." I waited for her to say that she still had mine, too, but instead she looked at me wonderingly and said, "You do? Whyever would you keep *them*?"

I could see this was going nowhere. Whoever she was now, she clearly was *not* the girl I'd steamed up the windows of my car with or the girl who had let me listen to her heartbeat behind a dune at Jones Beach. After a few more fumbling sallies on my part, she sighed and said, "Well, I've really got to go. I've got a test coming up in Philosophy 101, and I'm way behind in my reading. I'm trying to make all A's this semester."

I smiled in spite of myself when she said "myke ow-wool ayes," her lush accent reminding me of those brief, wonderful days when everything she said seemed to carry an invitation to sweep her into my arms. I had imagined that we might kiss again at the end of this meeting, even if only briefly, but her demeanor told me there was no chance of that.

"Alice," I tried once more, "do you really have to go so soon? Can't we take a walk or go over to the union for coffee or something? I've come a long way to see you, you know."

"I know you have. And it was very sweet of you to come. But I've got to go. Maybe we can get together some other time. 'Bye." She reached for my hand and shook it quickly, and her eyes met mine for a split second. There was nothing in them for me. I wanted to reach out and stop her, but I didn't dare.

She turned away and left without a backward glance.

I wandered away from the dorm in a daze, oblivious to the sunny campus scene. I'd been her first love, and we'd exchanged a hundred or so letters in a brief span of months. Yet it was as if that magnificent girl—the heart-stopping beauty who'd braved her mother's fury to be with me just one more day—had been replaced by an alien.

I called the King, who smirked as I climbed into his car. "No nookie, huh?" he asked as he gunned us into traffic. Desperate to share my feelings with someone—even him—I started to tell him all about Alice. But he soon grew impatient. "Ah, forget about her, man. I'm pretty sure we can get laid tonight if we play our cards right. My friend knows these chicks at

BU, see, and he says they're really hot. . . ." I tuned him out as we drove back to Boston. He would never understand my feelings for Alice. And neither, I was beginning to think, would I.

The King was about 95 percent bullshit, but we did manage to insinuate ourselves into Charlesgate, a girls' dorm at BU, and I did end up meeting a cute freshman from Pennsylvania named Liza. She and I went for a romantic walk in the fog rolling off the Charles late that night, and while we were making out in a doorway I felt a tap on my shoulder. Standing behind me was a grinning gnome of a hippie with a flower in his hand. "Here, man," he said, as he handed it to us. "Peace."

The next day the hippie, whose name was Lenny, happened by Liza's room just as I was getting ready to leave. We thanked him again for the flower, but he had yet another gift.

"You want a credit card number?" he asked us. "Free long distance, man."

I was skeptical—credit cards hadn't yet permeated every level of society down to grade school students—although I'd heard of cards that allowed you to charge calls to an account. I hesitated, but Liza said, "Sure—how does it work?"

"Just use this, man," said Lenny, handing her a piece of paper with a number scrawled on it. She made copies for both of us.

"You just go to a phone booth and tell the operator you want to make a credit card call, man," Lenny said, grinning. "You give them this number, then you tell them the number you want to call. That's it. Talk as long as you want."

"But who pays?" I asked. I was on a very tight budget.

"What do you care, man? It won't be you. It's probably some pig—a businessman or someone like that. He probably won't even notice. And if he complains, the phone company will have to eat it."

With that, Lenny laughed and walked away. "Free long distance, man," he called over his shoulder. "Now you two can keep in touch."

Even at my most countercultural, I wouldn't have dreamed of taking money out of someone's pocket or bank account. But the idea that monolithic Ma Bell would end up footing the bill for my calls seemed perfectly acceptable. It wasn't stealing, exactly. It was a blow against "Amerika."

Liza and I didn't use the number much, but Ruth and I did. The first time I called, she was a bit surprised. I'd been penniless since leaving Merrick, and it wasn't like me to gab for hours. But she didn't mind conspiring with me after I told her about the card. "I'm sure Ma Bell would be glad of the good use we're putting this number to," she laughed, "if she only knew."

I told Ruth about my deeply disappointing meeting with Alice and asked her if she had any advice.

"You've got to move on, Jeff," Ruth sighed with just a hint of exasperation. "What's past is past. I'd rather hear about Liza."

I felt I could reach out and touch Ruth with the phone card whenever I pleased, and its liberal use that semester helped forge even stronger bonds between us. But I got an unpleasant surprise when Ma Bell tried to reach out and touch *me* for the bill. An investigator had called Ruth at UT and asked if she knew anyone in Binghamton. She said she didn't.

The next time I called, Ruth warned me the jig was up. "Better quit calling on the credit card, Jeff. They're on to you. You'd better call anyone else you've been talking to on that card, too, and warn them not to give you away."

A little later I found out how much money Ruth had saved me. I'd passed the number along to Vin, whose girlfriend's mother identified him as the frequent caller from Binghamton. Her honesty ended up costing him five hundred dollars.

Before the phone company closed them down, though, those chats with Ruth were a lifeline. We traded stories about our romantic escapades, and she told me about a guy she'd met named Bobby. He was very special, she confided, and she loved him more than anyone she'd known since Mike McCourt. But she wasn't on the Pill, and she feared he might have gotten her pregnant.

I listened as she expressed her deepest fears, inwardly cursing that her first lovemaking had brought her so much anxiety and so little joy. She hardly knew what an abortion was, let alone how to get one in pre-*Roe* Tennessee. I told her I would help in any way possible if it came to that, but I didn't think it would.

"Ruth," I said, speaking from my vast store of sexual experience, "girls sometimes miss their periods for no reason. That's probably what happened with you, so don't worry about it."

"I don't know, Jeff. I sure hope you're right."

In that case, luckily, I was.

Another thing I shared with Ruth was my growing disillusionment with Harpur, which struck me as more of a concentration camp than a college. Although Vin was there, too, he and I were taking a much-needed vacation from each other after our yearlong cohabitation at Oz. We lived at opposite ends of the Harpur campus and rarely saw each other.

That left me reliant on the King for companionship, which meant that I found myself hitchhiking the hundred or so miles to Oz regularly on weekends, sometimes with Vin but mostly alone. Our old comrades on

Seneca 7—those who had managed to survive our riotous freshman year—had booked the floor again and had formed a rollicking community along with the girls who now shared the floor with them. Within weeks, several had coupled off and moved in together, switching rooms in a way that left a second-semester opening for me.

I knew I'd be giving up all pretensions to academic glory by returning to Oz, but there would be a major compensation: I could rejoin the ragged little band Vin and I had formed freshman year with a floormate, Big Jim Guldenstern, and three local guys. The band had added a chick singer, too, and rumor had it that she was gorgeous.

26. Ruth

oh where have you been, billy boy?

November 17, 1970

Dear Jeffrey, my own neglected one—

I send my love in hopes it will warm your displeasure. For many long days and nights my own desires have been denied fulfillment until now, when at long last I can beseech your forgiveness and try to make amends.

My life seems to be flowing along, making new convolutions and turns every day. Sometimes I almost lose touch with it. I have no control. Really weird . . .

Jeff, if I could I'd become a nun or something else to remove me from the male half of the world. Here I am— Christian, practically fundamentalist, hating drugs—and I've begun a serious relationship with a socialist, acid freak, all religions are equally relevant, anthropology major. How did this happen?

"You're a selfish cretin. You're too slop-brained with all your theories to re- member a simple obligation," I cried out. It was somewhat like scolding a well-meaning child and Bill looked bitterly wronged. I dragged him into the parking lot outside the Yardarm, a local hangout, and continued to work myself into a louder and louder protest at the way he had cavalierly left me waiting for him all evening. Now it was past midnight. He danced away from me like Muhammad Ali, grinning as if I was putting on an en- tertaining show. Car lights from the highway arched over our heads.

The Yardarm was located on the dark fringe of the student ghetto, jammed up against rundown houses and I-40. Though many of its patrons were medical and graduate students, it was also a favorite hangout of hard- edged mountain boys, taking refuge from the twin cudgels of poverty and isolation. The place had seen better times, and I rarely went there.

I had given up my tirade, and was standing in furious silence, when I felt hands on my shoulders, then others on each arm. I tried to yank away from them, but they held tight, and I looked around to see four grinning, mostly toothless thugs, one with a drawn switchblade. The blur of rage that had grown like a cloud around my head vanished, and I noticed how forsaken this place was. The horror of an impending, life-altering trauma landed on me like a gut punch.

"This girl don't want you around, Bub," the guy with the knife said to Bill. "Why don't you go inside? We'll take care of her."

I froze as he stroked my hair, keeping a fair-sized hunk of it in his fist. Four men, one with a knife, against a drunk academic—though he was a large one—seemed like insurmountable odds. But then I saw Bill take a step back and crouch, dropping his head between his bent knees—like a dog familiar with abuse, trying to deflect a blow.

My tormentors relaxed, and one of them laughed a little. "Get on out of here, now. We ain't gonna hurt you," he said to Bill's bent head.

Bill extended his hands upward before our faces in supplication. They hung there, as though a lofty puppet master had hoisted them just so and kept them suspended from invisible strands. The gesture was eerie. Then, like a banshee, he rose screaming to his full six feet, two inches and leapt forward. Even I fell back in terror. The thugs fled for their lives, but not before the leader threw his knife at Bill. It came end over end through the air, its handle striking Bill's chest, and he caught it in one hand before it hit the ground.

Bill did a fiendish dance, laughing and cackling with triumph. Then he swooped me up and we cavorted across the parking lot. Safety felt inebriating.

When we went back inside the Yardarm, I sat with Bill at a table in the corner, my rage giving way to awe and gratitude. A group of his friends had gathered around us to hear the tale when Bill spotted the owner of the knife leaning against the bar. He got up and walked toward him. People grew quiet.

"Hey, man, let me buy you a beer," Bill said, his hand extended in conciliation.

"Bill," I called out, "come back." He didn't even look at me.

He laid the knife on the scarred pine bar and cheerily locked eyes with its owner. The young man, sweating and bug-eyed, snatched up his weapon. "Get away from me! Get away—away!" he screamed, throwing wild punches and stumbling over his own feet.

As people fell back, making way for the screamer to get by, he cried a warning: "He's some kinda demon!" His buddies crowded around him, and they rushed out the door together, a tangled knot of scared and smutty humanity. For the first time, Bill looked ruffled. "I just offered him a beer," he said.

I had met Bill about a month after Bobby left Knoxville, following a performance by the great balladeer of the antiwar movement, Phil Ochs, outside the student union. I saw Lori and Carroll sitting in front of the large crowd, waiting on the great man to come out. Suddenly Ochs appeared, walking nonchalantly out the front door and stopping to stand on the front steps. Spontaneous applause sputtered from the audience. Softly, he began to make a matter-of-fact statement about that day's death tally in Vietnam.

"Twelve Americans and two hundred Vietnamese died today in the rice paddies of 'Nam." He paused and looked hopefully at the crowd. But it was hot, and no one seemed to want to hear another antiwar message. A restless murmuring rose up.

"A year ago you were all in the streets, fighting to stop the war. Right there, on Cumberland Avenue. Today, no one's interested anymore?" A white-haired minister, Baxton Bryant, took the microphone. "If there was any respect for the Constitution," he said, "a tender person like Peter Kami would be here tonight instead of in a cell in the workhouse. If you want to get arrested, test the First Amendment."

I glanced at Carroll, a local boy, who would show up for his own trial twelve days later, clean-shaven and freshly shorn of his long hair, wearing a sport coat and tie with his white-haired, corsage-wearing momma on his arm. Instead of the two years in the workhouse Peter ultimately received, Carroll was found guilty of obstructing the entrance to the administration building and fined $150. I recognized Southern justice in those sentences— the wink at the homegrown and the slap at the outside agitator.

Then Ochs came back to the microphone.

"Play a song!" a boy yelled out.

Ochs paused and seemed to lose heart. I thought he was going to turn around and leave. But instead, he reached around the door for his guitar and began to play "Okie from Muskokie," "Joe Hill" and "A Small Circle of Friends." Then he launched into "I Ain't Marching Anymore," his raspy voice wavering between anger and despair. Tears glistened in his eyes. A few people in the crowd called out, "Right on, brother," and he picked up steam, finally grinding the lyrics to a halt with a raucous blast of chords. He knew then, I think, that the movement had passed its zenith, that the world was already beginning to move on. But he never grew beyond his passionate political nature, and continued to be a crusader for peace, finally ending up in South Africa where he was mugged. The beating badly damaged his vocal cords, and ended his career. He went to live with his sister, Sonny, in Far Rockaway, New York. On April 9, 1976, he hung himself in her home.

While the dissonant chords still vibrated, Ochs turned and walked back into the union. The crowd began to wander off, but I stood awhile, deeply moved. Soon, only myself and a tall, handsome man were left. He was crying openly and shooting his fist into the air in support. He looked very strange to me, out of character with the hippiefied fashions of the day and older than his twenty years. This guy wore a natty blue blazer with gold buttons, and a white turtleneck that accented the classic lines of his face. His beard was neatly trimmed, as was his mustache, and his hair, though not short, was combed. Under his left arm he carried a book called *Yąnomamö, the Fierce People.*

I watched him for a while, liking the intensity in his face and the way he stopped occasionally to jot something down in a notebook, stroking his beard and muttering under his breath. He left alone, walking quickly past my dormitory toward Epworth Church.

Over the next few weeks I took note of his comings and goings and began to wait by my window in the afternoons when he usually passed by the dorm. Debbie had started teasing me about my "mystery man," though she admitted he was a real looker—and seemed prosperous and intellectual, too.

Then one day as I was working on a German translation, Diana, a new friend, came bursting into the room. "Are you still mooning after that guy?"

I nodded.

"I met him in the cafeteria," she said.

I screamed.

She had told him about me and he was standing outside, waiting to meet me at that very moment. With my hair quickly braided into two long plaits, I nervously followed Diana downstairs.

"Bill, meet Ruth. And Ruth, this is Bill. He's a real brain . . . and a hunk." Diana giggled, and Bill rather formally extended his hand. I saw that his eyes were a greenish hazel color and seemed focused not on me—but on some internal world of his own. I shook hands with him. Then I couldn't think of anything to say except, "Why are the Yąnomamö 'the fierce people'?"

"Oh, you know that tribe," he said matter-of-factly. Then he launched into a lengthy regurgitation of the book I'd seen him with a few weeks before, lapsing occasionally into Portuguese, which he'd learned when his family lived in Brazil. Since I knew nothing about the subject, and couldn't understand most of what Bill said, I contented myself with watching his handsome face. He seemed satisfied to be the only one talking.

I grew bored with the Yąnomamö, and interrupted him. "What do you think about Vietnam?"

His eyes popped and he shot his fist into the air. "Get out. Get out now," he growled through clenched teeth. I laughed and danced along in front of him, and it didn't take much prodding to extract his activist vitae from him. It began with his arrest for arson at Neyland Stadium.

"I'd climbed to the top of the stadium with another guy and a chick to watch the sun come up," he told me, "and suddenly the cops were all over us."

He laughed out loud. "I was carrying a lighter and a pack of cigarettes and they hauled my ass in for arson."

"That's pretty ridiculous."

"Yeah, well, they're pigs, you know." His face grew somber. "They had to let me go for lack of evidence, but they got their pound of flesh anyway."

I waited for him to continue, the stream of words coming a little slower now. We found a place to sit on the wall by Strong Hall. "When the ROTC building was firebombed in May 1970, the FBI broke into my apartment before dawn and beat me up with flashlights, trying to get me to tell them who did it. Three big guys with these long black flashlights, you know?"

"Did you tell them?"

"I didn't know who did it." He glowered at me. "But if I had, I would have let them kill me first."

I believed him.

That evening we drove to the mountains in a borrowed car and, though Bill told me I wasn't his type—he was a breast man—he persisted in showing up regularly at my dorm. I began to think, for the first time in my life, that I had a steady boyfriend. His absentmindedness often left me stranded, eating or watching a movie alone, but nothing could have convinced me he wasn't the man for me.

Lucy in the Sky with Diamonds

"How about taking a trip with me?" Bill asked a few days after we met.

"Where?"

"Here, Ruthie," Bill said, tapping his head and smiling broadly. "Here— and everywhere."

I'd never even smoked a cigarette, I had no experience with drugs of any kind and three beers were about my limit when it came to alcohol—they didn't make me drunk, they put me to sleep. But Bill was determined to show me the mind-expanding effects of LSD, and I wanted to please him.

By midnight we were hitchhiking to Sevierville, carrying two sleeping bags I'd borrowed from a suitemate, a bag of hot dogs and a couple of cans of beans. Bill had also brought his copy of Alan Watts's *The Way of Zen*. We got to Clingmans Dome in the Great Smoky Mountains National Park just before daybreak and hiked down a hillside into the woods. The bathhouse and the Appalachian Trail were only a hundred yards behind us.

As the sun rose, busloads of tourists began pulling into the parking lot and people swarmed down the trail to use the facilities. Though I felt a bit silly, sitting as we were in meditation position with our backs to all the activity, watching the sun move higher, I tried to listen as Bill read passages from his book.

"The true Self is non-Self," he read, "since any attempt to conceive the Self, believe in the Self, or seek for the Self immediately thrusts it away."

"That's it," Bill said. "LSD blasts through Self. It's the road to dharma."

"So you say, but what if it's bad acid? What if it's poison or something?"

"No, this is great stuff," Bill said. "If we take it now, we'll just be peaking when the sun's setting." He put a small square of colored paper in my hand.

"I don't think I want to do this."

"Just suck on it," he said, ignoring me. "Then chew it up and swallow it."

"This is windowpane acid?" I held it up to the light. It looked harmless, like a piece of colored construction paper.

Still ignoring me, Bill popped the square into his mouth and calmly chewed on it. Then he picked up the book again. He seemed so peaceful, tugging on his mustache and reading. I heard children and their parents calling to each other behind us. The weather was gorgeous, the temperature mild, and I lay back in the fallen leaves. Ignoring my thumping heart, I put the windowpane in my mouth.

Ten minutes later the trees began to shimmer unnaturally, as though a gale, not an autumn breeze, was blowing. Colors started melting from them. Endless colors. And when I turned to Bill, I saw him gaping in wonder.

"This is good shit," he said, the words trailing into broken chimes of sound around me. I looked at him, uncomprehending, piecing together what he'd said. Perhaps an hour later, or maybe it was only a moment, I responded. "I'm scared."

Bill stood up and began stomping through the leaves, quoting passages from his book, gesturing and whirling as he revealed point after immutable point from its pages.

I sat as still as death, because I was afraid to move. Afraid that if I did, the earth would tilt and throw me off. I tried to say the Lord's Prayer, but the words evoked images in my brain that seemed to morph out of tree limbs and clouds. "Give us this day" set off a kaleidoscope of sunsets and sunrises, a spinning turbine of days passing in front of my eyes. I spent the afternoon hardly aware of Bill as I inventoried the contents of my brain, now separated into many parts. I focused on trying to meld them together again, chasing stray bits of thoughts and images and retrieving them like playful puppies, only to watch others scamper off. It created a mounting sense of anxiety. The Self I had sought to lose remained intact, and she was worried.

As the sun set, the air grew cold, and my teeth were aching with it. I ran my tongue over them and remembered a painful childhood accident, when I'd been thrown over the handlebars of a bicycle and knocked out my front teeth. *Don't think about that,* I warned myself, but the pain grew anyway and I began rocking back and forth, moaning.

"Ruthie!" I heard Bill yelling. He was sitting next to me, his arms wrapped tightly around me. I didn't know how long he'd been there. "You're tripping out on something, but nothing's wrong. You're fine. Everything's fine!"

"I am?" I asked him, wonderingly. And instantly everything *was* fine. It was incredibly fine, and I was transported with giddiness and relief. The colors of the sunset sparkled around me like jewels.

"I'm going to build a fire," Bill said.

"Yes, a fire. A fire. We need a fire." I began laughing hysterically.

Bill was thrashing about in the underbrush, looking for wood, when I saw him shrink. He became an elf, with long pointed ears and little red hands. But, incredibly, this tiny elf was picking up whole trees and cracking them like twigs and stacking them in front of me for a fire. I drew back, thinking the fire would be too big and consume everything.

Then the scene returned to normal, and Bill was sitting before a pitiful pile of twigs, trying to get them to burn. But something was wrong. I blinked hard and concentrated, trying to figure out what it was that had gone wrong.

It was raining. Bill began to tear up his book, laying page after page on the pile and lighting it.

I couldn't remember when it had become night, but when I looked around me it was dark. We seemed to be engulfed in a dripping black cloud, and the film of moisture was beginning to freeze. Then I saw that all the pages of Bill's book were gone. Only the cover remained, and now he laid it on the pile of twigs. "Please, God," I prayed, "let it burn." But Bill snorted with disgust as his last match blew out. "Just get in your bag," he told me. "Try to keep warm."

But I wanted heat and light, not a wet sleeping bag, and I tried to focus all my will on the damp sticks, talking out loud and begging them to burn. The next thing I remember is a roaring fire and Bill scrambling from his bag to get more wood to keep it going. I have no idea what started it, but that night I told Bill it must have been God. "And Alan Watts," he retorted.

After smashing a can open with a rock, we ate cold beans and uncooked hot dogs and tried to sleep. But I became violently ill. The combination of LSD, the amphetamine some chemical engineer had laced it with, and crummy food kept me awake all night. When the sun was up, I climbed out of my bag to wake Bill. He lay with a dusting of snow on his mustache, sleeping like a baby.

I sat on a rock and watched him sleep, listening to little forest creatures rustling in the fallen leaves. *This is my guy,* I thought. And I felt very protective of his rest. When he awoke a few minutes later, he pulled me down next to him and we made love for the first time, there in the snow.

Christmas Scenes

Bill was tall and charismatic, intense and opinionated. I thought he was going to lead me into a world of political power, potent ideals and righteous activism. But even if he'd suddenly become a banker, nothing could have shaken my faith in our future together. I'd grown addicted to his passionate attentions. It felt like love. I believed it was.

In December, Bill drove to Mississippi to meet my family, bringing along his favorite sidekick, Marty.

When I'd described Bill to my family, I had touched lightly on the fact that he was Catholic. But laid it on thick about his father's important job with Union Carbide, their lovely home in Clinton, Tennessee and the fact that Bill was a "genius." My parents were nervously optimistic about meeting him and we had delayed Christmas dinner in anticipation of his arrival. When we heard the car pull into the alley, my whole family tumbled out the back door into the eighty-degree sunshine of a Mississippi Christmas Day.

Bill's plan was to spend a few hours with my family and then take me to New Orleans. There we would, in his words, "drink from the twin titties of Timothy Leary and Bacchus." But I disliked Marty, who seemed to always come around with drugs and the problems they created, and I wanted to send him on his way while I paraded Bill in Yazoo for a few days. (I'd already shown his picture to Sue, and her response—"How'd *you* get *him*?"— had made me want to rub it in a little.)

As we all walked into the house, I held Bill back and whispered, "Is Marty tripping?"

"Yeah. We got some good acid."

"But you're not, are you?"

He just cackled gleefully. He was tripping his brains out.

I joined Momma and Rita in the kitchen to help with the meal, and Momma said, "He's a mighty attractive boy, but his friend seems strange."

"I know. I hope he leaves soon," I said. Then we carried the turkey out, along with bourbon sweet potatoes and marshmallows, broccoli and rice casserole, cornbread dressing, tomato aspic and homemade rolls. I could hear my youngest sister, Margie, playing in the den with her Christmas toys. My father had given Bill and Marty potent eggnogs and taken them into the living room, where Marty gazed in stoned awe at the Christmas tree lights, his eggnog dribbling onto the carpet, and Bill paced like a cat, smoking and taking big drafts of his drink. My father watched silently. Bill was deeply ensconced in the role of "gentleman caller."

"Sir," he was saying, "I find your daughter to be a veritable flower of Southern womanhood. She brings to mind the sweet smell of magnolia blossoms, the ripeness of a piece of fruit, the voluptuous pleasure of a—" I interrupted him. My father's free hand was clenched into a tight fist, his face reddening.

"Dinner's ready," I said, taking Bill's arm and steering him into the dining room. He sat down next to my father's seat at the head of the table, and Margie rushed to get the seat next to Bill. I sat across from him on my father's other side, too far away to quiet him with a kick if things got out of hand.

While Daddy said the blessing, I watched Marty, who had taken the chair next to my mother. He had a coarse way of speaking, and I saw now that either his manners matched his vocabulary or the drug had obscured reality. Oblivious to the praying, Marty was scooping up peas and rice with his fingers and shoving them into his mouth, making satisfied sucking sounds with each bite.

As soon as he said "Amen," my father asked Bill, "Son, what are ya'll on?"

With a stupid grin—his version of a Southern yokel, I think—Bill replied, "Well, raht naow Ah'm on a mahty fine chair, suh."

My mother looked scared and said, "Now, Doug . . ."

They locked eyes. There was a long, seething look from my father as he struggled to regain his composure. I felt the edges of that look when it whiplashed down the table.

"Bill," my mother said, "Ruth tells us you're studying anthropology. What kind of job can an anthropologist get?"

Bill, miraculously, stayed on the subject for a few minutes, and even managed to converse politely with my father about Margaret Mead, but then the subject turned to capitalist economics. "Colonialism and neocolonialism have almost destroyed the indigenous peoples of the world," Bill opined.

With one of his more charming smiles, Daddy said, "Son, you're gonna have to speak a little plainer here. I'm just an old boy from Texas, and I don't know what most of those words mean."

It was like an invitation to Bill, especially with the added goads of a potent hallucinogen and a Christmas eggnog. He got on a verbal soapbox, explaining colonialism, comparing it to socialism and communism, veering into *Das Kapital* and Trotsky's Fourth International movement. Finally, he punched his fist into the air and began singing a bastardized rendition of

"The International," the anthem of the Communist Party of the Soviet Union.

"A-RISE! You PRIS'ners of star-VA-A-tion," he sang, as Margie, wide-eyed, ate a bite of sweet potato off his plate. He got louder. *" 'Tis the FI-NAL CON-FLICT!"* and stood up, directing his performance to the chandelier. Its crystal prisms began gently tinkling back and forth. *"The IN-ter-NA-tion-al U-U-NION will BE the HU-man RACE—"*

I had wadded my linen napkin around one hand so tightly that it felt like a tourniquet, and I used that hand to shield my face when my father slammed his fist onto the table. Peas and rice flew through the air. Water glasses turned over. His loaded plate tipped into his lap. Bill, stopped in mid-finale, looked at me as if for an explanation. My father leaned forward and screamed at my mother, "I won't stand for this!" Then he stalked off. We heard the back door slam.

The silence of the dining room was disturbed only by the sound of tires squealing as Daddy took off up Lintonia Avenue. Bill cleared his throat. "Well, anyway, right on, man. Whatever. Let's eat."

My mother looked at him, her eyes tearing with shock. Then she turned and called into the kitchen, "Rita, we have a mess out here."

27. *Jeff*

return to oz

It seemed like a hundred degrees below zero on the January night in 1971 when I returned to Oswego, but it couldn't have been much worse than minus fifteen or twenty, since my eyeballs didn't freeze in their sockets as I schlepped my gear into Seneca Hall. I'd had an eyeball freeze once on a cross-campus jaunt freshman year, so I knew what it felt like.

As bleak as it was, though, coming back to Oswego felt like a home-coming. There was nothing particularly homey about the gray concrete pile I was moving into, but I knew my old buddies on Seneca 7 would welcome me back with open arms, their friendship providing a much-needed antidote to the alienation of my Harpur months. And I knew I'd soon be playing with my band again. One of the first things I did after getting settled in was to ask Big Jim when the next practice was scheduled.

"Hold your horses, Durst," he said with a big grin that said he'd read me like a book. "There'll be plenty of time for you to meet Miss Teri."

I'd first seen her, a tiny brunette with a smile that could warm the Os-wego winter, at a gig back in the fall. It had been very clear that the band had improved greatly over the summer, but Teri herself had seemed a good enough reason to return.

Jim had told me then how she had stopped in at a practice session one day. She'd bopped and grooved to the music and seemed very interested in the proceedings, and when one of the guys jokingly asked her if she knew "White Rabbit," she'd grabbed a microphone and worked through it with them as if she'd been performing her whole life. The impromptu audition had been a smash, and they'd signed her up on the spot. Besides having a strong, clear voice and perfect pitch, she read music and was an excellent dancer. Even more important, as far as I was concerned, was that she didn't have a boyfriend.

I might have come back even if Teri hadn't been in the band. Vin and I had formed a band in high school, and I'd been bitterly disappointed when it broke up, after hundreds of hours of practice, just as it was beginning to gain momentum. The Cream of Creation, the group we'd formed freshman year, had been an excellent vehicle for making a little pocket money, meeting chicks and having a good time, but Vin and I had known early on that we would be leaving, and that had put a damper on it. I'd sung a few sets with some musicians at Harpur, but nothing had jelled. Now, however, I was stepping back into a band—which I somewhat brashly renamed The Second Coming—that really seemed poised to take off.

I bought a set of conga drums and timbales soon after I got back to Oz, providing the Latin accents that the band's dynamite Santana medley— "Oye Como Va," "Black Magic Woman" and "Soul Sacrifice"—had been lacking. Now, with a guitar, organ, bass and drums and three singers, we were prepared to tackle virtually anything in the rock repertoire. And Jim, who'd had classical training, was writing original songs as well. Within a few months we had worked up covers of thirty to forty album cuts, along with a few Top 40 hits. By March, when I finally got around to writing to Ruth, we were ready to start accepting gigs.

March 14, 1971

Dearest Ruth—

*Well . . . how do I start **this** off? I wouldn't blame you if you cut me off your list of "live" correspondents. How are we ever going to become a part of each other's lives again? Two summers ago I had visions of us as old friends at 30, 50, 75, 90 . . . and here we are at 19, little more than memories for each other. And the memories are getting indistinct already. Just try to remember that day we first "whaled" into Yazoo, try to remember that night in New York City with Alice and Mike, Jimi Hendrix burning and assaulting his guitar, all of us blowing our minds on Ravi Shankar, and you and Mike excitedly trying to convince us that you had actually had drinks in the **Rainbow Room**! Ruth, sometimes I can't see how people can disbelieve in reincarnation when it's so plain that even two years ago was a different life.*

Our lives had begun to diverge sharply by this point, but I wasn't really worried about losing touch with her. Our shared adventure had forged what I considered unbreakable, if somewhat mystical, bonds.

I began my campaign to woo and win Teri, who lived just down the hall from me, almost immediately. I heard early on that she had had a somewhat feckless suitor during the first semester, but he had dropped out of school. The bass player in our band, Dave Brown, also had his eye on her, but she hadn't reciprocated. The field seemed to be wide open.

In addition to her wholesome natural beauty, I was attracted to her cheerful disposition. She was a bright and serious student, but uncomplicated and sweet in a way that made her easy to be with. She was completely honest, although she didn't often volunteer her personal thoughts. She was also, as I would soon discover, almost completely innocent. She had never had a boyfriend in high school and had only dated a few times freshman year. It seemed almost miraculous that fate had handed me, once again, a clear shot at a gorgeous but unspoiled girl.

Before we could get serious, though, I had to administer a litmus test, telling her all about Ruth and Alice and my deep Mississippi connection. I wasn't trying to scare her off, but I knew there could be no future for us if she couldn't accept the fact that I'd had other girlfriends and that Ruth was one female friend who would remain very important to me.

She listened, her eyes widening, as I told her of my great adventure. She'd had a sheltered and conventional suburban upbringing, and there was nothing analogous in her own past. It was my favorite role: mentor to a stunning ingenue. In talking to her, though, I found I often had to avert my eyes. She was so beautiful it was distracting.

Her delectable lips pursed a bit when I told her about the blond siren of Yazoo, but I hastily added that I considered our relationship over, although I didn't realize how long it would take for me to accept that completely. She took my word for it, though, and told me she had no problems with my staying friends with Ruth. In fact, she said, she hoped she would get a chance to meet her someday.

28. Ruth

every little girl's dream come true

April 12, 1971

Dear Jeff,

Bill and I are getting married. What a stiff, playlike word that sounds like: married. I can't believe it. Love is a strange thing. If I didn't love Bill this would be the last thing I'd want. But even though I see, and feel, the constriction of my freedom, I'm constantly reinforcing love. I mean, I want to marry Bill, but sometimes this twang springs up and I feel nineteen, nostalgic, and bound.

Jeff, I don't want us to stop writing or caring about each other because of Bill. That would be too sad. Please come see me. You can meet Bill and we can get to know each other again. I hope I'm not being sticky or sadly sentimental when I say there's a lonely throb when I think about you. The problem is that my funds are all marked for necessities, like food and a roof. If not, I swear I'd clean out my bank account and fly to Oswego. But here I am, existing on love with an unpredictable, absentminded genius. Somehow, I don't believe Bill and I will slip into the usual marital rut . . . still, for now, I am grounded and penniless.

Bill proposed to me after his parents used their key to get into his apartment and found us in bed together. It had been a hot day, and sheets as well as clothes lay on the floor. In fact, the only thing covering me when I finally saw them standing in the doorway was Bill. Bill raised up and looked over his shoulder at his parents. For a moment we all stared at each other in astonishment. Then I made a dash for the bathroom, Bill's mom began to cry and his dad started yelling. While I searched the dismal bathroom in vain for clothing, or even a towel, I heard mention of the Pope and mortal sin, followed by a long silence. Bill tapped on the door and said, "Come on out. My parents want to talk to both of us."

But I didn't have anything to put on—except maybe the shower curtain—and I had to poke my head out the door to ask for my clothes. That evoked a loud snort and more sobbing from Bill's father and mother. In a minute Bill tossed a sour-smelling bathing suit top and my India-print skirt through the door. "Not this!" I hissed at him, but he'd already gone.

Looking like a soiled Carmen Miranda (all I needed was a bowl of fruit on my head), I emerged to find Bill's mother reading out loud from a *Redbook* magazine she'd gotten from their car about the pitfalls of "trial marriages." Her foot rested daintily on my panties, which lay on the floor in front of her. Bill senior stood behind her chair, his jaw set and arms folded like Patton facing his troops.

I, of course, was easily shamed, and hid my face in my hands during their tirade. When they asked me if I was proud of myself, I shook my head "no," and after they left, I said to Bill, "Your mother's right. It is a sin. We should stop seeing each other."

Then we cried and said good-bye forever. But the next day I found a note from Bill in my mailbox, asking me to stop by his apartment. When I got there he was starry-eyed. "I've been doing a lot of thinking," he said, pulling me down beside him on the bed. "Will you marry me?"

"Yes. Yes. Yes," I said again and again as we kissed and hugged and giggled together like the children we were.

Momma and I began to plan the wedding, one that every little girl dreams of: an elaborate affair involving hundreds of invitations, a floor-length satin gown and a flowing Spanish mantilla. There were many gifts from family and friends on both sides of the union. From Bill's side we got linens, appliances and cash, which Bill's parents expropriated and stashed away for "the future." From my side we got silver, china and crystal. The pomp and circumstance, showers and shopping, soon overwhelmed my tenuous grasp of reality, which was that Bill and I were penniless and possessed only one ambition for our future together: to march, march, march into political activism. I never stopped to wonder how sterling silver place settings would fit into that.

> May 1, 1971
>
> *Dear Jeff,*
>   *I hope you can come to my wedding. The date is June 12. I just think this wedding is going to generate so much love. . . . It makes me feel humble to think I have such a good friend. That's a marriage of a different kind, but still it is a marriage—a union of faithfulness and acceptance.*
>   *Of course, maybe I have ulterior motives for clinging to*

you. . . . After all, I expect to be able to call on the writer of
the book of the century, on the most relaxed terms, and to
publish in my memoirs a total collection of said author's let-
ters to me. Your glory will be my bath in its reflection.

Jeff didn't acknowledge my impending nuptials. I told myself he was, in some secret way, jealous. Or perhaps he was offended because I hadn't consulted him. But my father wasn't so closemouthed.

During the rehearsal dinner he had been fractious and confrontational with me, asking me with a sneer what it felt like to be "living on love." I held Bill's hand hard and looked my father in the eye when I said, "Haven't you heard? Money can't buy love."

After we got home that night, he finally started to vent, only it was my sister, Patty, who caught the brunt of it. I heard her running up the stairs, screaming over her shoulder at him, and Daddy, taking two steps at a time, caught her on the landing. By the time I got up there, he and Patty seemed to be doing a wrathful dance, punctuated by screams and slaps.

"You're nothing but a drill sergeant," I yelled at my father, pulling him off her and giving Patty the chance she needed to escape into her room. "You know why I'm getting married?" I shrieked into his face. "To get away from you."

For a moment he stood there looking at me, gaping with astonishment. Then he turned and walked heavily back down the stairs. Tears sprang to my eyes at the sight of his stooped shoulders. And pity, perhaps remorse that I had hurt him, made them flow. But there was also triumph, and only after he'd gone out of the house, a bottle of bourbon in his hand, did I leave the stairwell.

"Go after him," my mother beseeched me. I refused. That night I listened to her pacing downstairs, dialing the phone, looking for him, and I wondered if he would really stand us up in front of the whole town on my wedding day. Years later, he told me he was halfway to Memphis that night before the booze took the edge off his hurt and he could face the wedding. Then he turned around and came home. I heard the back door slam just as Patty and I were attaching the lace mantilla to its headpiece. She and Margie flitted around me in their pumpkin-colored bridesmaid dresses. We put flowers in their hair and sneaked some makeup onto Margie's eleven-year-old face. The room was filled with our giggles and the rustling of long skirts on cypress floors.

When I got downstairs Daddy was lying on his side in bed with his back to the door. I sat down in my wedding dress and laid my hand on his shoulder. He didn't move or look at me. I thought he was adrift in self-pity, but it could also have been a hangover from his night on the road with Jack Daniel's. I said, "I guess there're a lot of bad things between us, and I've gotten out of the habit of keeping my thoughts to myself. But there's a lot of good, too, isn't there? Can't we try to focus on that, at least today?" He didn't answer me, and I left the room. But when it was time to go, Daddy walked out in his tuxedo and we drove to the church in silence.

As we waited outside the sanctuary for the first strains of "The Wedding March," he took my hand in his. I felt him trembling. "Darling, it's still not too late," he said. "You can blame me. Tell everyone I *made* you do it. Let's just call it off."

"No way," I was saying as Mrs. Sigrest finished singing a transcendent "Lord's Prayer" and the organ sounded its joyful call. The doors opened and we walked to the altar, to Bill, standing with his father in front of Reverend Jorgenson.

When Mr. Jorgenson got to the passage that asks, "Who gives this woman to be married to this man?" my father said, "Her mother and I do." I guess he couldn't bring himself to take sole responsibility.

29. *Jeff*

somebody to love

When Ruth wrote to invite me to her wedding, it was as if she'd said, "I'm about to go to Outer Mongolia and live in a yurt, and I want you to come to the *bon voyage* party and sip yak tea." I was dead set against the marriage—not because I had anything against Bill or because I foresaw insurmountable obstacles to a successful union, but because it seemed almost a betrayal of our generation. Who, in the brave, new post-Woodstock world we were struggling to build, needed a license? It just wasn't *cool* to get married.

But while I'd challenged Ruth's cautious politics head-on the year before, I felt tongue-tied now. I hadn't met Bill, although I accepted her portrait of him as really far out, the kind of guy I saw when I looked in the mirror. But if that was so, this wedding didn't make sense. Why would he want to get married? And how could I tell Ruth that there must be something wrong with him if he did? I was more than a little disappointed in her, and I almost told her so. But my letters ended up in the trash can. She was still a Southern girl, and I didn't want to provoke an open break.

On the actual day of her wedding, my band was playing at Buckland's, the biggest college bar in Oz, and I didn't give Ruth a thought. The Second Coming was attracting all the adulation the six of us could handle, and we were earning the astronomical sum of six hundred dollars, plus free food and drinks, for three gigs a week.

By day, I was a horseman and trail guide at Fallbrook, Oswego State's riding academy, where I also received free lessons in dressage and jumping and even got to play polo once or twice. By night I was Jumpin' Jack Flash, local rock star. And at all times I had my lovely lady, Teri, by my side.

But the foundations of this dream summer were threatened early on, when her parents called to say they were coming up to visit on a work night. Not knowing what else to do with them, she swallowed hard and invited them to hear the band.

Teri's father was a manager at a big drug company, and her mother worked in a middle-school library. That night, alone in their pressed sports attire amid the red-eyed and tie-dyed throng, they looked like the deeply put-out parents in a Robert Altman movie. I found their obvious discomfort comical and never even considered the idea that they might become my in-laws one day.

Teri sang her Grace Slick tributes, "White Rabbit" and "Somebody to Love," as her parents stared at us with stoney faces. But they had also brought Teri's younger sister, Julie, who was snapping her fingers and bopping in her seat. She could hardly believe that Teri, who'd left home with a few albums of show tunes in her trunk, had emerged as a rock diva singing lyrics like "One pill makes you larger, and the other makes you small, and the ones that mother gives you don't do anything at all."

By our first break, it was clear that Teri's parents weren't going to become rock fans. And it suddenly dawned on me that everything I took for granted—Teri's loving companionship, the band, the money I needed for next semester—was in grave jeopardy. What if they ordered her home? That prospect wiped the smart-ass grin off my face.

I sat at their table during the break and made respectful conversation, trying to decipher how this game of generational chicken would go. But their replies, which were almost inaudible anyway over the loud jukebox, gave no hint of what they might do. Finally I got a chance to speak to Teri privately.

"What are you going to do if they tell you to quit the band?" I hissed.

"Don't worry about it," she said coolly. "They won't. Look at my sister."

Julie was bursting with pride, alternately smiling and plying Teri with questions about the band. No parent wants to alienate all their children at once, so Teri—and my own enviable lifestyle—was safe.

Our love life had blossomed by then, but she was a virgin when I met her and wanted to stay one until she was sure about me. So she kept putting me off, and I began to despair of ever doing the thing we were constantly singing about. One sunny day, however, she called with an announcement.

"I've made an appointment at the Planned Parenthood clinic in Syracuse, and I need a ride down and back."

At first it didn't click. *Parenthood?* I thought. *What's that got to do with us?* Then it hit me: the Pill! The grin never left my face as I drove the forty miles to Syracuse. These pills, unlike the ones mother gave you, had a very definite payoff.

Teri had eschewed her freaky band garb for a prim dress, as if she were going to open a bank account rather than stock up on the tiny one-a-day bullets of the sexual revolution. We didn't discuss the purpose of our journey on the way; we talked about what songs the band might tackle (would "Ohio" be too much of a downer for kids who mostly wanted to dance?) and how our classes had gone. Then we were in front of the clinic, whose doors seemed like portals to a world of feminine mysteries.

"I should be about forty-five minutes," she said. "You can hang out on Marshall for a while if you want." Marshall, near the Syracuse University campus, was full of head shops and record stores. "Okay, babe," I said, grinning. I was prepared to follow virtually any suggestion of hers at this point.

She gave me a foxy little smile and a quick kiss with only the slightest hint of "later" in it. Then she got out of the car, her minidress riding high up her thighs as she swiveled, and walked purposefully to the office door. I felt not only love and desire but great admiration as I watched her go. She had shown pluck, which I'd always loved in women. And I was thankful that she had chosen me, in her nineteen-year-old wisdom, for her loving gift—without requiring a vow of marriage. And, not least, I was grateful that it was she, and not I, who had to step inside that clinic.

On the way home I flogged my car, a black 1960 Falcon my grandfather had given me, until the tiny straight six whined its disapproval.

"Why are you driving so fast?" Teri asked. "You'll get a ticket." Thereafter I kept a sharp eye out for the Man, but I also kept the gas pedal down.

That afternoon, after some initial fumbling on my part, we reached the heights of sensual love together, neither of us realizing what a rare thing a dual climax could be. A small, enchanting spot appeared on my saffron-colored sheet.

"Look at that," I said, "the red badge of bliss." She laughed.

I wanted to admire it for a while, maybe even frame it for posterity. But she, always practical, had other ideas. "We've got to get it out right away," she said, "or it'll set."

Normally she would have called her mother at such a time for up-to-the-minute technical advice, but that didn't seem appropriate. So she took it to the bathroom and bombarded it with cold water. The little crimson emblem of innocence lost—and trust granted and knowledge gained—soon vanished. But it remains in my memory.

That summer I roomed with our ace guitarist, Ted Gerdes, in a walk-up in the student ghetto called "The Garden, Home for Wayward Vegetables." Teri lived directly overhead with a girlfriend, but she often stayed with me. Ted's girlfriend attended most of the band's gigs, after which she'd come back to our room. We four laughed at least as much as we lusted once the lights went out.

One night, just as things on both sides of the room were heating up, Ted said, "Gentlemen, start your engines."

Teri replied: "First one finished is a rotten egg."

When I turned twenty that summer, she organized a surprise party at Buckland's and baked a huge chocolate cake. Someone took a picture of us with it, both looking flushed and happy and impossibly young. It was a literal and figurative high point. Never again would I experience such an idyll: the band, the sun-dappled days at Fallbrook, my sweet lady in the first blush of love.

The Second Coming got semi-big in the Oswego area, with smoke-blowing agents and self-deluding promoters dangling deals in front of us almost weekly. We were constantly negotiating and fending off rivals, but nothing came of it all, and the band broke up after about a year.

I missed the rock 'n' roll life after it was gone, but I knew The Second Coming had been a lark, not a career. Twenty years later, Teri and I would sing a few blasts from the past with Big Jim and his band at a party celebrating his belated graduation from college, and the pure electric rush of performing came back as our peers danced and smiled and clapped. Being Jumpin' Jack Flash really was a gas, gas, gas while it lasted.

It occurred to me, early in the first semester of my senior year, that I was likely to survive graduation and that I'd probably need to make some plans for supporting myself afterward. I looked around at my professor friends— among them Campbell Black, a prodigious writer who helped me get started in that trade—and decided that academia, a kind of paid intellectual adolescence, was just the thing for me. But by May of 1973 American involvement in the war was winding down, and my draft number was high enough to keep me out of it. *What's the rush to go to grad school?* I asked myself. The real world beckoned.

30. *Ruth*

chaos

October 10, 1972

Dear Jeff,

*It is all a matter of conjecture for me to assemble the new
Jeffrey. There were wisps and wafts of you in your letter and
only a small part was recognizable to me. It seems like you
have changed (as of course I knew we both would), but long
hair and a beard don't hide much. Outward rudiments of appearance fade and disappear with acquaintance. Anyway, I'm
sure it is much easier for me to picture you as a single,
freaky, intelligent student than it is for you to picture me
amid the trappings of holy matrimony—since I can only seldom adjust myself to it!*

My marriage was a shock to me. Not because it committed me to a life of
conformity and fidelity, but because it did not.

Bill and I came home to our apartment in Knoxville after a five-day
honeymoon in an airless five-dollar-a-day cabin at Pawleys Island, South
Carolina. We were sunburned and hungry, having run out of money about
two days before. So when we walked into our kitchen and found it full of
food, it was a pleasant surprise. Bill's mom and her sister had scrubbed the
grungy old place from top to bottom and then left a week's worth of gro-
ceries for us.

We were both enrolled in summer school, and the next morning we got
up early. I told Bill I'd cook that night, and he said he'd be home about six,
then we went our separate ways. After classes I spent the rest of the day in
the kitchen, making a big Southern supper. By seven I was sitting alone
with a platter of fried chicken and a bowl of mashed potatoes, wondering if
I should call the police. We didn't have a phone—it was too expensive—so
I set out to look for him, reasonably certain he had just lost track of time. I
walked all over the campus and checked out his regular hangouts, but no
one had seen him. At last I gave up and went home. It was 2 A.M.

My head ached, and the clammy mashed potatoes in their blue bowl on the kitchen table made my stomach churn. I drank a glass of water in front of the kitchen sink and wondered what I should do. I had already used a pay phone to contact all of the hospitals in Knoxville, checking with their emergency rooms, and knew that no one matching Bill's description had been brought in. Ditto for the highway patrol, where a kindhearted young man had told me not to worry, everything would be fine. I decided to take a bath.

I dozed off in the tub, which was a long, claw-footed monster, a remnant of the apartment's more affluent past. It sat next to a towering window, which looked out on the side yard. There was no blind on the window—another luxury we couldn't afford. About 3 A.M., I jerked awake, feeling uncomfortably cool in the tepid water, but also tickled into wakefulness by a sixth sense. Something wasn't right. Sitting up in the tub, I felt compelled to turn and look out the window. There, in ghostly illumination from the light in the alleyway, was a man's face. Right next to the glass. Watching me. I froze in terror, and he, instead of ducking or running away when he knew I had seen him, opened his mouth and extended his tongue, his eyes wide and voracious to see my reaction.

Panicked, I jumped from the tub, turned off the light, and stood for many minutes in the dark, waiting for him to leave. He peered hopefully through the old, wavy windowpanes for a while, then I saw him turn and struggle back through the overgrown shrubbery. I wrapped myself in my robe and went to sit in a broken-down easy chair in the bedroom, away from the window. At 8 A.M. Bill was standing by the chair, tousling my hair, and saying, "Wake up, sleepyhead."

I bolted up. "Where have you been?" I sobbed and yelled at once.

He looked startled, but said in an offhand way, "I met this girl. I couldn't help it. We really hit it off. She had tits out to here."

Shock hit me like physical pain. I think I staggered a little, because Bill reached out to steady me.

"Hey," he said, "I didn't say I was in love with her. It's just sex. Besides, once she found out I was married, she dumped me." With that he fished his wedding band out of his pocket and put it back on.

I didn't take it quietly, the end of our marital idyll, which had lasted only six days. But what had I expected? It was the height of the sexual revolution, and open marriage was a societal experiment among our peers. Wife-swapping, swap meets, communal marriages, all of these things were becoming commonplace. I was so busy buying into the thrills that I had been blinded to the spills. My attitude was akin to that of affluent parents who aggressively call for harsher jail time for drug pushers, until their own golden-haired boy turns out to be one of them.

I cried harder, and Bill, not even trying to defend himself, shrugged it off. He told me I was an albatross. "This is a drag," he finally said, and walked out.

I sat all day, looking at the remains of dinner, the daisy placemats with matching napkins, the pottery dishes with matching salt and pepper shakers. What had I been doing? But I saw no way out. Marriage was a lifetime commitment, I thought, and since I had chosen to be married at a time when everyone else was gleefully experimenting with other options, it was just too bad for me. I'd have to learn how to be married in a new way, in a way Ward and June Cleaver never dreamed of. So I began to carve out a marital lifestyle, an attempt to separate love from fidelity, commitment from passing flings. The full burden of marriage fell on me that day with an awakening horror. But I could adapt. I never once considered leaving, or filing for divorce or calling my mother. I had no girlfriends who would understand. I didn't tell anyone. It was the life I'd chosen, and I'd make it work.

I asked Bill not to sleep around anymore, admitting that I wasn't the progressive thinker he was. It was like exposing a disgusting personal habit to admit that, but I wanted to be honest. He responded by telling me he loved me deeply, and would never love another woman in the same way, and though he couldn't promise, he would try to be monogamous. But it was ultimately beyond his ability.

In the months and years to come, I was repeatedly thrown free of my resolve to adapt, during other long nights of not knowing where Bill was, or days when I'd walk in and hear the panicked sounds of some unknown woman rushing around as she exited through the back of the apartment. Once I found a terrified girl in the hall closet, who darted out when I opened the door to hang up my jacket; even six years later, when I came home early for lunch, I was greeted by a blur of naked bodies running from our bedroom. But always, after hours of my anguished histrionics, and after finally extracting another useless promise to "try" from Bill—who once described himself as "a kid in a poontang candy shop"—I'd force myself to keep going. We would have a few days or weeks of marital calm, then another crisis.

I tried to be as casually smorgasbordian as he was about sexual encounters, and might have gotten more into it if that had made him jealous, but he was completely laissez-faire. I never doubted he loved me, in the way he understood love, and he was a delightful companion: warmhearted and generous, always bringing in stray cats and dogs and people and offering assistance. Stimulating conversation was never lacking in our home. We had fun, and laughed, and toughed out the more mundane discomforts of poverty with a companionable stoicism. But in the end I knew it was my loyalty to him that kept us together. His infidelity couldn't drive us apart as long as I held fast, because I never feared he would leave me for another woman. I worried more often that he might simply get on a train and become some sort of political hobo.

Any relationships I had with other men never involved sharing of the least portion of my soul. But I wasn't often tempted. I remember thinking during those dark years that men didn't look at me anymore, perhaps because I circumscribed myself so tightly with rage. Peter Kami, the much persecuted Brazilian student who was still fighting for his freedom in appeal after appeal, found his way through that pain one night, and gave me a little courage. Bill and I and a friend, who had dropped acid, were on the way from our newly rented house in the country to the Yardarm. The friend was acting scary, screaming and crawling around on the outside of our Ford Pinto, and had almost fallen off on the Alcoa Highway. As we drove down Laurel Avenue, I was pleading with Bill.

"Get him inside, Bill. He's going to get killed."

"Leave him alone, Ruthie. You're turning into some kind of old grandma, aren't you?" He tapped on the windshield where the young man was licking the glass in front of our faces, and grinned out at him. The night had already been long and loud, with drugs and booze in abundance. I deeply regretted allowing them to drag me into the car for this outing.

"Stop! Let me out."

"Here? It's after midnight. How are you gonna get home?"

"I don't care," I yelled. "Let me out."

The car stopped and I stumbled onto the sidewalk. They drove off. For a few minutes I stood there crying softly to myself, then I heard someone move behind me. It was Peter. He was sitting on the stoop of his boarding house, petting his St. Bernard dog, Boname.

When I turned, he asked, "Can I help?"

His overlarge, horn-rimmed glasses glinted under the streetlight and his soft curly hair glowed. He looked like a bespectacled angel.

He took me inside to his tiny room, with its single hotplate and narrow mattress thrown on the floor under the front window. We sat and talked most of the night, and he told me the story of his own recently ended marriage, and how it had broken his heart. He seemed a tragic man to me that night, a tender person, as Rev. Bryant had said two years before. Just before sunrise we lay down together, and made love, a soft healing interlude between two people who were cast adrift in a strange land. When I awoke, Peter was making coffee for us on his hotplate, and apologized for taking advantage of me. I smiled at the courtliness of it, there in the midst of the sexual revolution where "do your own thing" was the norm.

"It's against my ethics. You're a married woman," he said, adding wistfully, "unfortunately."

It was the sanest thing I'd heard in a long time. I went back to Bill determined to face life with the same gentle acceptance and moral outlook as Peter, while he fought his personal demons and the Knoxville courts. His goal beyond that was to bring St. Bernards, renowned for their peace-loving temperament, into as many lives as possible. If he realized that goal, it must have been in Sweden, because I've heard that he was ultimately granted asylum there, an enemy of the people of the United States.

My college education occurred around the edges of this personal holocaust. I went to classes and made decent grades, but only because I dropped all the challenging courses. I left English and literature behind and switched to the fine arts curriculum. I began to spend all my time in drawing and painting classes, awash in swirling colors or bold black lines, emoting more than feeling. When I tried to write, even letters, an excruciating internal dialogue ensued. But painting numbed the pain. So I painted.

On weekends Bill and I went to his parents' house in Clinton to do our laundry. His mother taught me how to fold a man's shirt with tissue as if it had come from a commercial cleaner's, and how to iron. I enjoyed those Saturday afternoons of organizing our domestic world into neat piles, a contrast to my chaotic life.

The Knoxville counterculture was in a meltdown of decadence and drugs. Living among its human dregs was like trying to avoid slaughter at a stockyard; there were burned-out carcasses everywhere. That these people were only in their late teens and early twenties made it more horrifying. For three weeks a friend of Bill's lived in our back bedroom with his cat, neither of them coming out even to heed nature's call. The only sounds were an occasional shouted "All is vanity saith the Lord!" I put meals outside the door, and they disappeared, but the dishes never came back. I woke one morning to find the friend and his cat gone, and the room filled with excrement and dirty dishes.

When I called home, some of this Kafkaesque world must have filtered through, because my mother developed a recurring litany of advice: "Quit looking for the dark side of life. You're young. Enjoy yourself. Be happy." But I was immersed in hippie gothic and incapable of knowing what "happy" was. I had rejected everything that could have given me a comparison by which to measure. It was the downside of living a revolution. You don't know how it's going until it's too late to change course, but by then you're being drawn and quartered.

I struggled for normality.

We were invited to dinner one night with another married couple, Deana and Osman, a talented painter, and I spent the afternoon preparing a green bean casserole to take with us. We arrived to find Deana sitting in the dark. A single candle stood on a table that took up most of one room in their two-room apartment. She didn't look at us when we came in, but continued to stare warily into the corner of the room. She was a renowned beauty on campus, an escapee from the Panhellenic set. Her eyes were a beautiful deep gray color, and her hair was thick and luxuriant, hanging to her waist. Breast milk stained the front of her peasant blouse. I looked into the corner and saw Osman, holding their newborn baby, dangling a square of bright pink paper over its open mouth. It was a familiar object— a piece of windowpane acid torn from a sheet that had been circulating for a few days.

Bill and I both yelled at the same time, "Don't do that!"

Deana, seizing the moment, ran around the table and snatched the baby away, then disappeared with it into the next room. Bill said, "Hey man, are you crazy?" But I knew he was. This was the man who had dropped sixteen hits of LSD, burned his art, set his apartment building on fire and run cackling through the flames. He was seen, but no one identified him to the police and he was never arrested. Since then, Crazy Osman had become an icon of the student ghetto.

While Deana was pregnant, she and Osman had tripped constantly. There was widespread astonishment when the infant arrived in apparent good health with all its parts. We were all expecting a monster. Osman viewed his child as proof that the Establishment had been trying to brainwash everyone with false information about the damaging effects of LSD.

We never had dinner that night, but Bill and I stayed for a while talking to Osman. What he had tried to do would be called child abuse today, a felony. Then, he felt like a proper papa, giving his child a helping hand into nirvana. His particular take on hallucinogens was straight from Timothy Leary. Osman, who was twenty-four, was one of the original flower children. He started using LSD to expand his mind, accelerate into a higher consciousness and sidestep the plodding banality of earthbound mortals. LSD for him was never a recreational drug but a spiritual aid. But by 1972, Osman's idealistic tripping friends were disillusioned, sure that by then they should have been levitating at will. Some of them gave up searching for enlightenment with drugs, and turned to religious fanaticism or political radicalism. Yogis, born-again Christians and Marxist-Leninist philosophers began to be commonplace on campus, each taking their little piece of the countercultural pie. But most students simply left it all behind and got back to their studies.

Later, Deana fled with the baby to her parents' home in Florida. Though Osman followed them and promised to go straight, he eventually came back to Knoxville alone and, a friend told me, killed himself by driving his motorcycle at full throttle into a brick wall. But another friend is just as sure that he is now living quietly in the mountains, and that the guy who died on the motorcycle was a disturbed Vietnam vet—a big, handsome guy we had once befriended.

31. R u t h

activists

The highway into Miami was jammed, and Bill and I had no choice but to go with the traffic. When most of the vehicles exited, we followed the crowd to Miami's Flamingo Park, where thousands of hippies, Yippies, Black Panthers, gay/lesbian coalition members, Vietnam Veterans Against the War, Students for a Democratic Society (SDS) and dozens of one-issue splinter groups from the countercultural revolution were gathering.

It was August 1972, the Republican National Convention, where Richard Nixon was about to be nominated for his second term. Bill and I spoke derisively to each other of the Young Republicans who claimed to represent our generation. We had come to show the world that even as the movement waned, it was still a force to be reckoned with. When Tricky Dick celebrated his nomination, we would crash the party.

The park teemed with bearded, braless and penniless young people. There were a few smatterings of organization: flyers tacked to trees showing the location of the convention center, a table set up under a tree where you could get materials to hand out about the continuing war in Vietnam. But no one had organized toilets, showers, food or water. For those basic necessities we were all dependent on the city of Miami—which hadn't planned to give a free-for-all that week.

Two days before, Bill had brought a flyer home. "Ten Days to Change the World," it had said. The Youth International Party (Yippies) was organizing a demonstration to protest Nixon's nomination.

"Let's go," Bill had said, carefully tacking the flyer to the wall by our kitchen table.

"Okay," I'd replied.

An hour after reading it, we were on the road, twenty-five dollars in my purse, a tent and sleeping bags in the trunk. Thirty hours after that we'd arrived.

While I set up our tent, Bill went to scope things out. We both wanted to know when the demonstrations were scheduled and what the plan was. But when he came back, Bill said, "No one knows anything. There's not really a plan."

"Then what are all these people doing here?" I asked. I couldn't believe that thousands of students had, like us, just picked up on the spur of the moment and driven to Miami. But as they continued to pour into the park, it became apparent that was exactly what had happened.

There were only rumors of organized activities. For the most part people spent their time lounging in the hot Miami sun. Half-clad children ran from one drugged-out campsite to another. I awoke one night with a cherubic two-year-old curled up next to me. A kitten was in her arms. The next morning I found the baby's mother, stoned and unconcerned, sitting under a tree. "Far out," she murmured when I returned her daughter, who was already tugging her mother's breast into the open. She wanted breakfast.

As a political event, our trip to Miami was turning out badly. I spent most of my time miserably trying to prepare food on one of the park's public grills, and listening to high-flown schemes about how to derail Nixon's nomination. But the real source of my misery was more personal. The temperature was in the nineties, and I hadn't been able to bathe since we left Knoxville, four days earlier. Though Bill had enjoyed several showers in the men's bathhouse, the women's facilities were out of commission. I had even stood in line at the only working pay phone in the park to call the city and point out the problem. But, except for infuriating the woman who took my call, it got no response. Finally, I reached the breaking point and told Bill we'd have to leave if I couldn't take a shower. We had absolutely no money for a motel room, and I was ready to make a run for it back to Knoxville.

"Don't be such a prude," he said to me. "Just come with me to the men's shower." I had been agonizing about this and, when I realized there really wasn't any other way, I agreed. But on the way over, I spoke with other women and asked them to join me, thinking it would be a lot easier if we went in together and "liberated" the men's bathhouse. By the time we got there, there were ten or so women with us, carrying towels.

Bill went into the bathhouse to pave the way for our entrance. A security guard ushered him out.

"Girls, girls, girls," the man said. "This is the *men's* shower. You ladies should just disperse." He sounded like a peeved older brother.

Most of our group turned to go, but Bill said to them, "Come on! The guys know you're coming. It's okay!" They stopped and looked at me.

"Are you going in?" a small brunette in a makeshift sari asked me. Her young son stood by her side.

Though I had no taste for exhibitionism, I was determined to take a shower. I could hear the water running not twenty feet away from me. "Yes," I said, but still no one moved.

The security guard snickered and trudged back into the bathhouse, speaking into his walkie-talkie. The sight of his khaki-clad shoulders infuriated me. Why didn't he set up a schedule for this bathhouse? It seemed ridiculously stupid, and I took Bill's hand and walked into the concrete-block building. The other women stayed outside in mute sisterhood, waiting to see what happened.

When my eyes had adjusted to the dark interior of the building, I saw I was standing in a sort of locker room. The bathing area was through another doorway. It was a large, concrete-block room with a row of shower-heads along one wall. The security guard lounged confidently on a bench in the locker room. When he saw me standing in the doorway he said, "Well, only one taker?" With Bill holding a towel for me, I got undressed and wrapped myself in it. He preceded me into the shower room. "Hey, guys, this is my wife. Make room."

Eight pairs of eyes, among other things, turned toward me as I walked in and dropped my towel. I tried to project an air of business as usual by immediately immersing myself in a stream of hot water. It felt wonderful. The guys had given me a showerhead all to myself and they clustered in groups under the others. Soon I had my hair lathered and was feeling pretty good about everything. But then I noticed that the guard had insinuated himself into the room and was standing bug-eyed, sweat and steam rolling down his face as he leered at me.

Bill said, "What are you looking at?" in a loud voice. Everyone turned toward the man. Almost in unison, the other guys joined Bill in standing between me and the guard. Their arms crossed, faces set, they became silent sentinels while I showered—a line of backs and butts, black, brown and white; muscular, fat and skinny; shielding me from the big-bellied guard.

With my towel wrapped securely around me, I squeezed through the line, said, "Thanks, guys," and went with Bill back into the dressing room. By now the other women had come in and were standing huddled in the doorway. When they saw me come out, flushed with hot water and triumph, they cheered.

The shower was liberated once and for all as the women disrobed and went in, and the guard ran panting from the building, his walkie-talkie bouncing against his leg. It turned out to be the most significant contribution I ever made to the movement. Word spread through the park, and dozens of other women soon crowded into the bathhouse, along with their children and mates, and for a time it was quite the place to be in Miami.

When we got back to our tent, there was a note from one of our neighbors: "The Yippies are organizing a march. Meet us at the literature table."

By 1972, the Youth International Party—founded by Jerry Rubin and Abbie Hoffman, among others, at a 1968 New Year's Eve party—had thrown money at stockbrokers from the balcony of the New York Stock Exchange, attempted to levitate the Pentagon, burned money, poured soot on Con Edison officials, organized "free stores" where shoplifting was the only means of exchange, held smoke-ins to legalize pot, and ran a pig named Pigasus for president.

Bill and I, who were earnest ideologues compared to the headline-grabbing Yippies, let their enthusiasm carry us along anyway. With a handful of them "yip, yip, yip" -ing and twirling like drum majorettes at our head, about fifty of us marched to the convention center. We were joined by an SDS women's contingent. The sun was high and hot, and the streets were deserted, traffic blocked off by grim-faced policemen. The SDS women ran to the front of our group and began to chant "Equal pay for equal work. Smash male chauvinism." They smashed the windows of two stores that advertised pornography with bricks and rocks. I stumbled through broken glass, wondering why the police, who stood at every intersection holding back traffic, were letting it happen. I thought they must be afraid of us, or in sympathy with us, and yelled louder, holding Bill's hand as we surged on to the Convention Center. I never thought they were just biding their time.

When we got there, delegates were flowing in and out of the building, but the broad avenue out front was almost empty. We began milling around in the street, shaking some "Stop the War" placards and chanting antiwar slogans for about twenty minutes. It was so hot the asphalt was beginning to melt, and I began to think of returning to Flamingo Park. Then I noticed that two of the SDS women were pointing at the red, white and blue banners that draped the light poles along the street. Another chant rose up and the women pulled their blouses off, taunting a line of policemen who had quietly come to stand along the curb. Their bare breasts blazed white in the sun, jiggling like so much warm Jell-O, as they strutted and shimmied their way through the crowd calling, "Come here Piggy, Piggy, Piggy."

Then one woman, breasts bobbing, was hoisted onto the shoulders of another. She stretched to grab a piece of the banner and, just as she got a good hold on it, she slipped off her friend's shoulders. They fell in a heap on the asphalt, with the banner trailing down around them.

We were all so busy watching this that no one noticed a paddy wagon and a bus coming down the boulevard, led by a large phalanx of policemen armed with shields and billy clubs, until a loudspeaker blared out, "Step into the middle of the street. You are under arrest. Do not resist arrest."

The riot squad surrounded us almost immediately, and I felt panic start to rise in my throat. Then some coolheaded individual in our group started shouting, "Kneel down. Link arms. Keep your heads down. Make them carry you off."

We all did this. But the stream of Republicans and innocent bystanders who had stopped to watch were pressed into our midst by the ever-advancing police line. Everyone, whether kneeling, standing on the sidewalk or just wandering by, was arrested. The two shirtless women shrieked and kicked at the policemen as they were hoisted over our heads into a vehicle.

As the men were loaded into the bus, the women were hustled into the paddy wagon and taken to the city jail to await arraignment.

I sat on one of the benches inside the paddy wagon and surveyed my fellow prisoners. It was a largely tie-dyed bunch, all dressed alike in frayed jeans and T-shirts, or India-print blouses—except for the woman sitting next to me. She was neatly dressed in a blue linen skirt and white blouse, with a patent leather purse clutched in her well-manicured hand, a Young Republican in the flesh. I spoke to her.

"This is a mess, isn't it?" I said.

Her blue eyes welled with tears. "I'm supposed to meet my husband for lunch. He's going to be so worried."

Jennifer, who introduced herself as a Canadian-American, had the ride of her life that day. One of the bare-breasted women pulled a body-painting kit from a large macrame bag, and we watched as six other women joined her in stripping naked and painting themselves from head to toe with peace signs and flowers. They wadded their clothes up, crammed them under one of the benches and chanted "so-o-e-e piggy" all the way to jail.

When the door to the windowless van was opened, eight naked women jumped out, yelling "Catch, Pigs!" as they sailed through the air. Jennifer and I got off last, and found a mostly embarrassed, tittering group of policemen, and two policewomen, waiting to take us inside.

We were led into the building. I heard Jennifer parroting again and again, "I'm a Republican. I'm voting for Nixon." The others were chanting, "Where are our men? Where are our men? Where are our men?"

They put us all in the same room and stationed a grim-faced matron outside the door in the hallway. One of the naked women, who was looking a little sobered by the situation, asked the matron for her clothes, and after thirty minutes or so, all the clothes were brought in. By that time the women had tried to wash off the body paint in a cold-water shower in the corner of the room. But they had only made things worse. Now they stood dripping with color and water, trying to rub the paint off each other with their bare hands.

When one of them asked for towels, the matron laughed and said, "Honey, this ain't no hotel." Paint clung to the roots of their dripping hair and eyebrows, was embedded in their nostrils and ears and was soon smeared all over their clothes.

I watched all of this from a far corner with Jennifer, nursing a strong sense of self-preservation as I took in the heavy wire mesh that covered two tiny windows, the bare bulbs overhead and toilets with no stalls. The large room was a God-awful yellow—even the ceilings, benches and concrete floors were yellow—and I began to feel claustrophobic. I thought longingly of my tent at the park and stood up to try and look out one of the high windows. A few hours later, when we were called to the courtroom, I was sitting quietly, staring at my feet and wondering what would become of me.

Public defenders were assigned to us. Mine was a fresh-faced young Hispanic man. "Let me do the talking," he said. "You could be charged with inciting to riot and unlawful assembly, maybe resisting arrest." I quaked. The still-soggy women to my right were looking downcast and repentant, and when the judge flicked his gaze over them, I saw his lip curl with distaste. Jennifer's name was called first.

After only a few minutes of quiet consultation at the bench, the judge said, "Young lady, I apologize to you for the people of Miami. You are free to go." On her way out, Jennifer stopped to hug me, a gesture that could only help my case, I thought. "I'll be waiting outside for you with a cab," she whispered. I nodded but—though I was appalled at my SDS sisters, who I thought had acted like idiots—I couldn't help noticing Jennifer's self-satisfied smirk as she turned to walk away. No matter how stupidly my cohorts had behaved, I still wasn't a Republican.

When my turn came at the bench, the judge seemed to have already decided to focus the wrath of the law on the SDS women. He released me on my own recognizance, with a warning to stay out of trouble. I practically sprinted up the aisle. While signing papers for the clerk, I watched the judge decide the fate of the trembling young woman who had been sitting next to me. Even though she cried, and pleaded, and apologized, he was unmoved. When I turned to leave, he was threatening to withhold bail.

That night I stayed in the tent alone. There were rumors that the men had been taken to a penitentiary. That they were being tortured by the CIA. That drugs had been found, and they were all busted. That they could be sent to prison for thirty years. I huddled in my sleeping bag and feared the worst. At daybreak, I got into our battered Pinto and drove to the jail. After a morning of fruitless questioning of police clerks, I finally heard—from another woman who was looking for her boyfriend—that the men were being released back at the park. She rode with me, and we arrived just in time to see a bus pull up and begin to disgorge the disheveled men.

Bill emerged beaming. He and his fellow prisoners were chanting and punching their fists into the air in an orgy of mutual admiration as they traipsed down the bus's steps. When he saw me, he said, "Ruthie, it was great! We stayed up all night planning how we were going to sneak a message out to the press. We were going to tear the place up! Then this morning they just loaded us all in the bus and brought us back here."

That afternoon we went to the first organized rally of the week. A soundstage was set up in front of the convention center, and thousands of people filled the streets. But I'd had enough. After the Black Panthers spoke, I succeeded in getting Bill to leave.

I graduated that March. At the ceremony I was an anonymous cap and gown bobbing in a sea of fellow graduates. I had done nothing to distinguish myself academically, and I felt fortunate to have come through with a 3.25 average and a diploma. I was jubilant, and eager to get out of Knoxville.

On an impulse, Bill and I packed and left that very night for Yazoo City, where we would get jobs for the summer before going to California in August. We wanted to check out Berkeley. Or we might drive on to the University of Wisconsin. Maybe we would go to graduate school. Maybe we would fall into a political milieu. Maybe we would just see what was out there.

As we hurriedly packed and hauled trash to the curb, throwing away anything we didn't need for a nomad's life, I found Jeff's letters bundled into a shoe box on a shelf in the pantry. "Those can go," Bill said, holding out a trash bag.

"Hell no, they can't," I snapped at him. He looked surprised, but didn't say any more before he turned to carry another box down the stairs. Though I didn't know then what I wanted from my life, or how to get it, I knew I had to stay in touch with Jeff.

making

our

way

32. *Jeff*

career blazers

In January of 1974, I moved into the very funky apartment Ben and Jerry were renting at 216 East Tenth Street in New York. It was a ratty fifth-floor walk-up in a rundown building between First and Second Avenues, and although it was already cramped with just the two of them in it, Ben and Jerry had let me and Vin know that they—and Ben's huge dog, Malcolm—needed roommates to share the two-hundred-dollar-a-month rent. Vin moved in about a month after I did.

The East Village in those days had been hippified but not gentrified, and decay was everywhere you looked. The filthy and unsafe streets, the dirty air and the constant feeling of being hemmed in by buildings and noise made life there a daily crisis of the spirit. But living at home was impossible, and the price was right.

Ben, ever the entrepreneur, was running Ben's Pots and Jewelry out of the apartment, along with a pottery-wheel delivery service. He hawked his inventive but ponderous clayware and free-form jewelry at crafts fairs, and he was taking courses at the New School and elsewhere. He worked full-time as a clerk in the pediatric emergency ward at Bellevue, and he had applied for a staff job at the Settlement House, a haven for disturbed kids. (He didn't get it because his personality test had revealed a deep-seated problem with authority.) He also drove a cab weekend nights and taught crafts in a Settlement House program.

Jerry had graduated with good, but not great, grades from Oberlin's premed program, and his first round of medical school applications had failed. He was licking his psychic wounds at the time and working as an assistant at a lab across from Bellevue Hospital while he got a second batch of applications together.

Malcolm—intelligent, brave and responsible, at least when there wasn't a bitch in heat around—was my main companion before Vin arrived. We all came to love him during those gritty days, not only because he was a colossus among dogs and a great friend but because he gave us a kind of access to the frenetic Ben.

February 26, 1974

Dear Ruth:

A bona fide Gothamite must not only shed his sensibilities, he or she must soon begin to grow a particularly horny and impenetrable shell, an armored carapace, which, as I have only recently come to understand, is what Brooks Brothers, Bond Street, A. Sulka and the like actually sell. What look like merely fashionable or traditional suits of clothes are in fact subtly wrought suits of mail, each houndstooth pattern a link, each expensive tie a gorget, each component designed expressly to shield one from the outrageous slings and arrows of those farther along in the power hierarchy.

The above urban Gothic realization occurred to me yesterday as I sat, inwardly seething, waiting for some gimlet-eyed female executioner to come out and lay the bad news on me about my chances of getting a job with her company, G. P. Putnam's, as a reader of raw manuscripts. I had been kept waiting in an overlit, barren anteroom for the better part of 45 minutes, had walked 18 blocks in a wet snowstorm, and was sure that I must look like some unrepentant Visigoth, because I had butchered my face with a new but cheap razor blade.

I should explain that during my first two weeks here, I was bounced like a human shuttlecock between employment agencies and their steely-eyed opposite numbers, personnel directors. More than once I lost a job because I am not a well-trained secretary and cannot type a mistake-free 60 w.p.m.; other times the restless movement of my fingers has betrayed me ("he'll get bored with this and quit in no time"); still other times the reasons for my rejection were not disclosed. In general, I'm feeling less than charitable toward the whole fucked-up system.

I didn't get hired at Putnam's, and they didn't even let me know if the anonymous book I'd read, and panned, belonged to a nobody or some famous author. Disgusted and discouraged, I soldiered on, determined to find my niche. The fact that the New York job market was glutted with people just like me, and that the economy had a bad case of "stagflation" that would send the stock market into its worst tailspin since the Depression, meant nothing to me. I figured there had to be something in the teeming city for a reasonably apt lad willing to work for carfare.

After weeks of getting nowhere—and watching my tiny bank account dwindle—I made an appointment with the Career Blazers personnel agency. It seemed a natural choice, because it not only lined up interviews, it also placed its clients in temporary jobs, so they could eat and pay the rent while waiting for their big break.

The first thing the agency did was to evaluate my résumé, a painful process since I had almost no relevant job experience. It seemed the only overtly salable skill I'd gotten out of four years of high school and four years of college was typing.

I typed mailing labels for weeks at a West Side packaging company that was struggling to find its way out of the nineteenth century, and at the posh Park Avenue offices of a big charity. I also got assigned to the profit-planning department of McGraw-Hill, a publisher I'd peppered with résumés. Now I found myself, through placement as a temporary typist, deep in its control center.

McGraw-Hill published a huge line of trade and specialty mags with titles like *Avionics Week,* and my clerical duties offered a view of just how lucrative an editorial job could be. It seemed that the top editors not only made grand salaries, but also got percentages of their magazines' rich ad revenues. I racked my brain for a way to break into this business.

One of the executives I worked for gave me a few assignments that stretched the clerk-typist definition a bit, and she took some time to talk to me about my background, which I embroidered freely, and my goals. One day she asked me point-blank: "What in the world are you doing in this department as a typist? Why don't you apply to our editorial intern program?"

I laughed and told her I'd been applying to it steadily for weeks.

"Don't worry," she smiled, patting me on the hand. "I'll see if I can get you in. You're really wasting your talent here." She gave me a big smile and the thumbs-up sign before heading back to her office. *This must be the point in the musical when the hero bursts into song,* I thought. The next day I went to work with a grin on my face, expecting to see a letter inviting me to join McGraw-Hill's junior bullpen. But there was nothing on my desk but a pile of typing, and no sign of my mentor. After an hour or so, she approached with an apologetic look on her face.

"I'm sorry, Jeff. I told them about you, but I couldn't get you into the program. They said if you were black, or a woman—or especially a black or Hispanic woman—they'd sign you right up. But for now, they're just not admitting white males. I'm really sorry." Then she hurried off.

Given my later career in newspapers, it's reasonable to think I could have made a substantial amount of money at McGraw-Hill if I'd been admitted to the training program. But in 1974 my consciousness of lost opportunity wasn't nearly as acute as it would become later, after many golden chances had slipped away. I shrugged the whole thing off, and told the story to cynical laughter at the apartment that night. It didn't occur to any of us that I should call a lawyer.

On days when I wasn't working, life revolved around walking Malcolm, sending out résumés and earnest-sounding cover letters, taking tests for government jobs I didn't really want and roaming the city, wondering why it all seemed such a drag.

I'd been through the educational mill and generally done what was expected of me, and now—where was the reward? The job market appeared closed, yet the counterculture seemed more and more irrelevant. The antiwar movement had been marginalized by its own successes and by Nixon's ongoing demise, which was coming at the hands of the establishment rather than radicals. The movement's foot soldiers, the students of 1967 to 1973, had either joined the establishment themselves or succumbed to the drug culture or the paranoid appeal of gurus and false messiahs.

When I looked up the word "anomie," which Ruth had used in one of her letters, I discovered it was exactly what I was feeling then: "lack of purpose, identity, or ethical values in a person or in a society; disorganization, rootlessness, etc." But although Ruth had named the malady correctly, I didn't buy Bill's radical cure. Having listened to Lennon rather than Lenin, I'd been well warned against people prating about revolution and waving little red books.

Going off to college in 1969, I'd been sure that my peers and I would soon produce a profoundly better world. In 1972 that had still seemed possible, and I'd gone to the polls to cast my vote for George McGovern in a last gasp of youthful optimism. By 1974, however, it was clear that the Age of Aquarius would not arrive anytime soon. We had failed to beat the system, and now it mocked our halfhearted efforts to join it.

Jerry, for instance, had taken a course at Oberlin called Carnival Techniques. It would prove valuable four years later, when he and Ben opened their ice cream store and needed to attract and entertain crowds, but in 1974 the medical schools weren't impressed. Vin had put together his own major at Harpur, which he'd called Philosophy of Education. In the do-your-own-thing spirit of the times, Harpur had obligingly given him a degree that allowed him to call himself a philosopher. But schools weren't hiring philosophers of education; they were hiring certified teachers when they were hiring at all.

Our opposition to the long and bloody war had given our various rebellions a righteous sheen, but the war was largely over for the United States, and the sheen was off rebellion. Most days, given the choice of joining a protest at Washington Square, amid the druggies and panhandlers, or trying to get a job, I chose the latter.

As part of that quest, I'd buy the *Times* nearly every day, along with the *Village Voice* when I had extra change in my pocket. I found that I no longer identified with much of its radical cheek, but it, too, had job ads. Another paper we got—only because it was so often left on our doorstep—was *New Solidarity*. I remember reading it from cover to cover one sunny afternoon, shaking my head in wonder: Every article, at some point, linked Nelson A. Rockefeller—good ol' Rocky, vice president, longtime governor of New York and husband of "Happy" Murphy—with a heinous crime against humanity. It seemed that Rocky, who'd spent his entire adult life under the scrutiny of the toughest journalists in the country, secretly was exterminating people on a grand scale, in our own country as well as in the Third World. I wrote mockingly of *New Solidarity* in a letter to Ruth, but didn't receive an immediate response.

There would be other interviews and tests by the time I left East Tenth Street in early April of 1974, but none of them seemed likely to pan out. So I accepted a job selling ads for the *Pulaski Democrat,* a small Oswego County weekly owned by Ted Gerdes's father.

My roomies and I had been too caught up in our private rat races to give each other much support, and three months in Manhattan had proved to me that I was not, at heart, a cosmopolite. I longed to get back to greener precincts, and I had plenty of friends in Oz. Economically, I wasn't giving up much; my 1974 tax return shows that I earned $686.57 in my nearly three months of working for Career Blazers.

So I got my car out of storage in my parents' backyard, loaded it with my few belongings at East Tenth Street and said some brief good-byes before heading north. Ben wasn't there, but his proxy, Malcolm, looked concerned and whined a bit as he gave me his paw to shake. Jerry wished me luck and so did Vin, who was glad to be getting my bedroom, but who also—as I could see in his eyes—envied my escape.

33. *Ruth*

high finance

Bill and I were exhausted after three days of steady driving through the Sierra Nevada mountains and the Nebraska flatlands. But I didn't want to use any of our remaining cash for a motel. At about 2 A.M., we parked in a dark construction site on the western side of Madison, Wisconsin, and went to sleep.

It was mid-September, 1973, and we'd been traveling and living out of our car for six weeks. But we'd had a good time; Bill had surfed; I had read. And now we were ready to settle down somewhere.

We picked Madison one day while we were lying on San Clemente Beach. Bill, who had been reading *Rolling Stone*, laid it down and said, "Let's go to Madison, Ruthie. It's got an active student movement, probably better than Berkeley. Things are dead there."

I quickly agreed. It was where I had wanted to go from the beginning. While our brief stay on the Berkeley campus had been pleasant, something about the gorgeous setting, beautiful architecture and magnificent weather had awakened my liberal guilt. Even if the entire student movement had splintered into self-interested enclaves, I didn't think living in splendid exile was appropriate, at least not until the Vietnam War was over. I pictured Madison as an arctic wasteland, sure to be as dark and brooding as my own political beliefs. I didn't know that it had just been named, for the umpteenth time, America's most livable city. Or that University of Wisconsin was every bit as beautiful as Berkeley.

In Reno we stopped for gas, and as I stood in line to pay I noticed a row of slot machines by the door. I thought, *Why not?* and began feeding the one-armed bandit the four quarters I had in my pocket. I did say a silent prayer before I put the first one in, and by the third one I was whispering, "Please, God," under my breath. Then I pulled the handle for the fourth time and watched in amazement as three cherries lined up in the window. For an instant nothing happened, then I heard the wonderful chink, chink, chink of a hundred dollars in quarters as they fell into the tray and overflowed onto the floor.

Several excited bystanders helped me collect my winnings in a paper sack, which I took back to the car before Bill returned from the men's room. I hid the sack behind the seat so he wouldn't ask about it. Though I was bursting to tell him about the miraculous shower of quarters, I knew this was our nest egg and I didn't want to spend any of it.

When we awoke in the car that first morning in Wisconsin, Bill was eager to go to the student union at the university to "shoot the breeze." As it turned out, the union wasn't a bad place to be when you had a limited budget, a raging hunger and the need for a bathroom. The cafeteria provided a seventy-five-cent breakfast special, including coffee, and there were several fine bathrooms just up the hall. I took a change of clothes into one and washed my hair in the sink. No one seemed to mind.

When I came out, I was wearing a conservative jumper with a white blouse and a pair of Mary Janes. I had dried my hair with the hot-air blower on the wall and pulled it back to one side with a barrette. This respectable appearance was part of my plan for using the one-hundred-dollar windfall waiting in the car.

I found Bill deeply absorbed in a theoretical discussion with a group of students on the expansive patio outside the cafeteria. It faced Madison's beautiful Lake Mendota and was encircled with a low stone wall and tall trees. A kayaker was busily flipping his craft so that he was submerged and then corkscrewing it upright again. Groups of students and faculty lounged at the tables on the terrace, enjoying their coffee, flipping through books. The breeze coming off the lake was light and flirtatious, and I felt the same.

All in all I was quite impressed with Madison. The dark stone buildings and low northern light gave the campus the sober persona I'd been looking for, and I was optimistic and full of energy, ready to get our domestic life under way. I told Bill I had some things to do—he never asked what they were—and that I'd be back before dark to pick him up. Then I gave him a dollar for coffee and cigarettes and left. I had a simple plan. First I needed more money, then I needed an apartment with lights and hot water.

I began making the rounds of area banks, applying for credit cards and using them to get cash advances. By giving the name of the president of Delta National Bank in Yazoo City, Miller Holmes, as a reference, I made it a smooth process. Computers were still a rarity, and the tellers simply left their windows for a few minutes and made the call. By two o'clock I had the $100 I had started with, $250 on deposit in two local banks and $550 in unused credit on two Visa cards.

Flushed with the success of my financial ventures, I quickly found a one-bedroom apartment and signed the lease. Finally, I was away from home, from parental pocketbooks, from academic expectations and white Southern agendas. Yet, rebellion was not really on my mind as I looked around our new home.

The apartment was beautiful, with a view of a verdant marsh, blue-green shag carpet, floor-length draperies and a kitchen full of brand-new built-in appliances. I spread our sleeping bags on the floor of the bedroom. Our clothes fit easily into one end of the closet, and our two towels hung in the bathroom like refugees, still carrying the smells of California beaches and Nevada desert. Then something unexpected welled up in me. Tears. I brushed them away. "How bourgeois," I said under my breath. But I felt so happy.

I went to find Bill, who was holding forth amid a clutter of cigarette butts and coffee cups in the union. He was on his feet, loudly extolling the virtues of Trotsky over Stalin to a group of students, so caught up in rhetoric that he seemed to have trouble remembering my name.

"Oh, Ruthie," he said finally, holding a book out to me. "We're just getting down to the nitty-gritty. Look at this."

It was Trotsky's *Diary in Exile, 1935.* "Does it have any pictures?" I asked, smiling. One of the guys at the table laughed, but Bill looked embarrassed. Humor, as I should have known by then, is not part of the repertoire of a fanatic when he is courting potential converts.

But I was beginning to feel the day's stress in my tensed shoulders. "Come on, Bill. Let's go."

He lit a cigarette and took a long drag, squinting through the smoke at me. "Where are we going?"

"Home," I said.

"Home? What are you talking about?"

"It's a surprise."

Reluctantly Bill gave the book back to its owner and stuffed his Camels into his pocket. Then we walked to the car hand in hand.

When I opened the door to the apartment, he was flabbergasted. "Where did you get the money?" Bill asked, and I tried to explain. But his eyes glazed over at the details, and he wandered into the bathroom before I could finish. "Well, whatever," he said. "It's a nifty pad."

The next morning Bill went to the graduate studies building and around lunchtime he returned with good news. He had cornered three members of the history graduate program committee who were willing to interview him for admission.

January 5, 1974

Dear Jeff,

Not the least of my surprises this Christmas was your card. I'd thought we would never communicate again. I don't have any idea what you are doing now. I'm sure you have suffered and grown as much as I have, trying to find a place somewhere.

Here in Madison, we are experiencing the throes of anomie. It's very difficult, even in supposedly "radical" Madison, to find friends who bear up under political scrutiny. For Bill everyday life is inseparable from future goals.

I laugh at myself when I remember the sermon on Christianity I delivered to you after I received your first letter, but I feel like crying, too, because it was easy for me to believe in then and now I can't believe in much of anything. . . . What about God? It was so easy to be a Christian, Jeff, because it felt so right and pure. Now it feels foolish, but something in the back of my mind refuses to dive into the depths of chaos with nothing to believe in but the words of other men.

Who is Karl Marx, or Sigmund Freud, or Kurt Vonnegut? What makes them truth tellers? Scientific method, or is it just another scheme with which to deceive oneself into believing in one's own rightness?

Jeff, I know you are caught up in the throes of responsibility and lost youth or whatever, but couldn't you manage to forestall all that for a while and come visit us? I'd like to do some assessing of where things have gone, from where and to where and for what reasons. . . .

I was so happy to receive your card, like a friendly hand reaching me. Now that we're up here in the Yankee North, can you come see us?

I was working as a graphic designer with the American Society of Agronomy, a publishing company, and Bill had been accepted into graduate school. He also received a grant that included tuition and living expenses. It seemed the harder I looked for a cause to foment revolution, the better life got. Occasionally, even Bill succumbed to our burgeoning bourgeois blessings.

When I came home from my first day at work, he had met me at the door with a wide grin on his face. "Sit down, Ruthie," he said, propelling me to the sofa we had bought at the St. Vincent DePaul shop. I sat and watched him dance across the room, cavorting like a circus clown, until he pulled a giant wad of bills from his pocket. Then I jumped up and tried to snatch them from his hand.

"They gave you the whole thing at once?" I screamed. He threw the money into the air—nine hundred dollars in one-dollar bills, his grant. We danced around the room, catching it in our mouths as it floated to the floor, and shrieking with the joy of it all.

34. Jeff

kate o'malley

April 11, 1974

Hell-o Dursht—
    Everybody is güd. Ben just returned from Saratoga proba-
bly still not aware that you are not here. Jerry asks, "Where
the hell is Durstewitz?" Malcolm had the loose shits for a
while but he's OK now.
    >Beware of returning themes you once thought dead and
gone.<
    Take care—say hello to Ted.

DO IT, DON'T DOUBT IT—
Vince

Vin's note, sent about a week after I moved from Tenth Street, included an
ad he'd clipped from the *New York Times*: Oswego State was looking for a
community relations director. I considered applying for the job—I thought
I could maybe even have a few strings pulled for me in the Power Tower I'd
helped occupy four years before—but in the end I didn't pursue it. I had
enlisted in the good fight for Ted's father, John B. Gerdes, a tall, driven
man who had gone into hock up to his eyeballs to buy a little weekly newspaper in Pulaski several years before. John had a sense of mission about
community journalism—you put out the best product you could because
people depended on you, and you pulled no punches and played no fa-
vorites even though there's no place to hide in a small town.

But his uncompromising nature had gotten him into serious trouble.
He'd offended a neighboring publisher with political aspirations through
an impolitic editorial, and now he was fighting for his life as his nemesis
flooded Pulaski and its environs with a free newspaper that purported
to be—but wasn't—every bit as good as the paid-circulation *Democrat*. I
wasn't making much money—two dollars an hour plus free gas for my
car—and was finding it tough to sell ads to rural Oswego County's bone-
cautious and somewhat polarized merchants. But I liked the job anyway,
because it gave me a sense of having joined a crusade for what was good

and right, even if only on a minor and local scale. Maybe I couldn't transform the world, but I could help save the *Pulaski Democrat*.

It also allowed me to reestablish ties with my old friend and roomie,
Ted, who was finishing up his senior year at Oz when I got back to town.
He would soon join the fray, distributing a summer supplement to the cot-
tagers on the shores of Lake Ontario while I tried to fill it with ads and
even a piece of writing or two. It would turn out to be a hopeless battle,
but we would have given it our all even if we had known the outcome.

Teri, meanwhile, had found herself a job in the fashion industry in
New York, and we had dated a few times while I still lived at East Tenth
Street. If we had graduated from college in 1963 or 1983, or if I'd been a
more stable and mature young man, I probably would have asked her to
marry me after we graduated, and we might have been sharing an apartment in New York by 1974. But although I was no longer opposed to the
concept of marriage, I wasn't ready to commit myself to a monogamous
relationship—especially one enforceable by contract. And she, to her credit,
decided she had better things to do than wait for me to come around.

Vin was all aflame with his plans to visit Birgit Höllbrugge, a pretty,
English-speaking fräulein he'd met while we were painting houses in Oz
the summer before. It had been a case of love at first sight, and he was determined to see where this liaison—as impractical, in its way, as mine with
Alice had been—would lead him.

Ben and Jerry remained in New York after I left, but both were looking
for a way out of the city. Ben found himself traveling up the Hudson many
a weekend to visit his college girlfriend in gracious old Saratoga Springs,
and Jerry often went along. Later, Jerry's girlfriend would move to North
Carolina and take him with her. Fred was well on his way to becoming Dr.
Thaler at this time, and Ron was getting involved with some concert musicians who felt they didn't really need a conductor. (The difference between
a bull and an orchestra, he confided in me, was that the bull had its horns
in front and its ass in the rear.) They would eventually achieve world re-
nown as the Orpheus Chamber Orchestra.

All that was missing for me in that spring of 1974 was romance, and
one night, at a bar in downtown Oswego, I found it in the person of Kate
Anne O'Malley.

Kate was a classic Irish beauty from the Boston area—auburn-haired,
with an engaging Kennedyesque smile and a form that evoked the buxom
hills of the Old Sod itself. She'd come to Oz to get a master's degree in English after two years of teaching elementary school, and when I met her
she was just regaining her emotional stability after a disastrous affair with
a married man.

The chemistry was right that night, and it didn't take us long to start
living together. She seemed to have everything I was looking for in a

woman, and within a few weeks it felt as if we'd been waiting all our lives to find each other. We couldn't bear to be separated on workdays, so when the *Democrat* had a temporary opening for a door-to-door canvasser, I put Kate up for the job. Soon she was handing out sample copies and urging Pulaskians to start or renew their subscriptions to the *Democrat*. And many did, since the smiling Kate was not easy to resist.

When I wasn't on my sales rounds or lunching with Kate or Ted, I was usually at the table of John and his crusty buddy, Floyd Nolan. Floyd was a local businessman who had made himself a modest fortune—or at least acted as if he had—and who liked to flaunt the fact that he didn't have to kiss anyone's butt. His "screw 'em all" bravado appealed to me, but beneath it I heard the voice of a man who cared deeply about his community and was genuinely appalled at the bumbling that passed for state and federal policies toward it.

He and John would play a daily fanfare for the small businessman, the self-starter who got out of bed early in the morning and made things happen, turning nothing into something with a little money and a lot of grit. I knew this was the kind of thing that intellectuals condescendingly referred to as "Babbittry," and I'd had a professor at Oz who had called people like John and Floyd "pigs." But I couldn't see anything piggish about them. For a young man trying to get a fix on how things worked and why they sometimes didn't, their cantankerous duet was like a lunchtime seminar. There was something in the intensity of these two men—one who had carved out a secure niche for himself and his family and one who was locked in a desperate battle to survive—that made a deep impression on me.

Kate and I passed an idyll in each other's company that summer, enjoying ourselves at the beach and in the mountains and making love, it seemed, whenever no one was looking. But after a few months of bliss, an issue surfaced. Kate was twenty-five, two years older than I, and she wanted not only love, but commitment, marriage and a baby before too long. I was ready for love—especially the unreserved way Kate gave it—but not for the rest, and I told her so. She was willing to let the matter ride for a while, but I'd been given fair notice that she would eventually expect me to graduate from lover to mate.

Toward the end of that summer, John Gerdes called me into his office in the ancient *Democrat* building and regretfully told me he would have to let me go. I knew this was coming; Ted had graduated, and, now that his seasonal circulation job was over, there simply would be no room on the payroll for the two of us. I knew Ted had the greater stake in the paper's success, and I also knew that ad sales wasn't really my thing. I wanted to sell ideas—to write—but the *Democrat* already had a dedicated editor/reporter. So I listened stoically, confident that John wouldn't let me down flat.

Twirling his cigar and giving me the peculiar grimace that passed for a smile, he told me he had called his friend Vince Caravan in Fulton, a small city about ten miles south of Oswego, who published a fat little weekly tabloid and who was looking for a utility man for sales, circulation, reporting, editing, what have you. "Vince is all right," John growled. "He'll treat you well. And," he added with a grin, "he's got the dough to pay you."

There were two catches, however: I would still have to interview for the job, and it wouldn't be open for another month or so. But that was fine with me; I knew John's recommendation would carry a lot of weight, and I was looking forward to taking a month off. Jerry had given me a copy of Jack Kerouac's *On the Road* the year before, and ever since I'd read it, I'd been hot to make tracks across the U.S.A. So was Kate, and she had a brand-new car to boot.

When I contacted Ruth and told her we were planning to put Madison on our itinerary, she sounded thrilled—even relieved, somehow. "It'll be so good to see you again, Jeff. It's been *how* long?" It actually had been five years—an unimaginable stretch of time for young people. "I'm looking forward to meeting Kate," she said. "She sounds like a really great lady. And," she added, "you and Bill will finally get a chance to meet each other."

35.   R u t h

worlds collide, again

My life in Madison was schizophrenic, torn as I was between Marx and Gimbel's, revolution and interior decorating, anguish and complacent domesticity. Some days I gratefully laid the activist's banner down. But Bill was always there to pick it up again, steadily looking for a new movement.

By spring, he was presenting another political option to me: Communism. "If someone could show me how to move it out of the conceptual realm of Marx and into the real world," I'd say to him, "maybe I'd be more enthusiastic."

The truth was, his politics were beginning to bore me. I would listen to his polemics, but realize after a few minutes that my mind had wandered. Then, on the Sunday before Jeff and Kate arrived, he finally captured my full attention. "I'm moving to Milwaukee," he said.

My heart fluttered with anxiety. Was this an ultimatum? Would he go without me?

But I was impatient with the timing of this confrontation. It was nine o'clock, and I wanted to watch *Upstairs, Downstairs,* the British soap opera that had become like electronic laudanum, injected weekly into my confusing life. At least the characters seemed to know their places in the world. I drew closer to the TV.

"What's in Milwaukee?" I asked, arranging a bed of cushions on the floor.

Bill began to pace. The "da-ta-da-ta-da" of "Rondeau" by Mouret, the *Masterpiece Theatre* theme, filled the edges of my mind while he gestured and talked, his voice rising when needed to overwhelm the television. "We've been wasting our time looking for political consciousness in Madison. I think it's time to get serious—I'm joining the National Caucus of Labor Committees. No matter what you decide to do, I'm joining."

"But Bill," I said, looking for a chink in the armor of his resolve, "my job's here, and we've made friends. Besides, I thought you had decided the Labor Committees was a bunch of crisis-mongering extremists? I thought you couldn't stomach their views on Stalin?"

"I'm willing to withhold judgment for a while about that. Besides,

LaRouche is a Trotskyite, and that's where it's at for me." He went on to paraphrase Lenin as saying that in times of revolution it was more important to knock heads than to cradle them.

I watched Rose carrying her tea tray into the Bellamys' drawing room, and wished I didn't have to think about Stalin right then. I sighed and turned off the set. It was getting more and more difficult to keep my safe philosophical perch, from which I could comfortably survey Bill's political forays as though they were merely an afternoon's entertainment.

I had created an alternative Bill, my Billy, whom I deeply loved for his ability to engage me intellectually and for the affectionate patter we exchanged as we moved around our cozy apartment. Still, when I was presented with the entire package of "Bill-ness," I felt threatened and unsure about what I was doing with him. But after struggling for so long to keep our marriage together, I pricked up my ears when he said that the NCLC had strict moral requirements: no drinking, no drugs and no frivolous sexual involvements. So, the next day I went with him to an NCLC meeting.

"Stop thinking about your mother," someone yelled. "You don't need mother's magic." The thin, bearded man writhing on the floor nodded his head and struggled to breathe. His face was becoming blue. In 1974, many people thought asthma was psychosomatic, and I figured this man was trying to overcome a neurosis, though it seemed an extreme cure. But I became really alarmed when he began to lose consciousness.

A plump, blond woman was telling me that she was on her way to MIT, armed with several awards and grants for her unique mathematical theories and also with her fanatic devotion to the Labor Committees. I put my hand on her arm to get her to stop talking. "He's going to die," I protested.

She turned around to look and, almost reluctantly, said, "I'll call an ambulance." I was relieved to hear sirens even before she hung up—the hospital was right across the street.

Arlen, a tall, balding intellectual who seemed to be the leader of NCLC's Madison cadre, knelt on the floor and held the man's head. "You know asthma is a mother-induced illness, don't you? You know that. We've discussed it."

The man could no longer nod. His chest rattled, and I saw bubbles of foam beginning to come from his mouth. Arlen turned to the rest of us and said, "He'll be fine. Really. He's been doing a lot better lately, and it's just going to take some time before he becomes a fully realized human being. It's hard work." The group nodded sympathetically. Then three paramedics burst into the room and began to revive the man. After a hypodermic and some oxygen, he was breathing again.

"I'm sorry," he mumbled as he was carried to the ambulance.

I turned a horrified face to the MIT woman. "What was that all about?"

"He'll be fine," she consoled me. "It's been a long time since he needed medical care. It's just a little setback. Eventually he won't have asthma anymore." She looked totally convinced of what she'd just said. Evidently NCLC members believed they could fight disease and human frailty as well as change the face of American politics, and they were already practicing psychology on the membership. Why had this well-educated, highly intelligent woman joined what I had thought was an insignificant fringe organization? Was there more to it than I saw?

I let her put an arm around my waist as we walked to some chairs in the back of the room. She knelt on the floor beside me and said, "You really love your husband, don't you?"

"Yes."

"I loved mine, too. But sometimes *real* human beings have to make hard choices. I had to divorce my husband."

"Why?"

"He wouldn't join the Labor Committees. Even after he heard Lyndon LaRouche speak in New York last spring—wait until *you* hear him, he's a genius—he wouldn't let go of his fears. I had to move on."

"Like Bill will, you mean? If *I* don't join?"

She crooked an eyebrow, a knowing "what else could he do?" look. Then she said, "But that's not what has to happen. You can *both* be in the vanguard of a new American renaissance."

We seemed to be making quantum leaps, from this bare, basement meeting room to a renaissance. From divorce to a vanguard. My head was spinning. She went on, "There's only one thing stopping you from joining him."

"What's that?"

"You have to forget mother's homeside magic. Forget Reverend Jorgenson. Forget—"

"Hey, how do you know about him?"

"Bill and I had a long talk yesterday. I understand you were a big Christian—once."

I looked over her shoulder at Bill, who was watching us. He looked happier than I had seen him in months. He smiled at me.

"What do you mean by renaissance?" I asked the woman.

By the time Jeff and Kate arrived, I was beginning to digest the Labor Committees' essence. I was finding some of it delightful, like Beethoven's "Ode to Joy," the NCLC's theme song. The political and economic theory I mostly dismissed, but I found it easy to revile consumer-oriented "Amerika" and to float above the humdrum of nine-to-five life. I was a dreamer, susceptible to the influence of people who hailed from the cream of academia. The NCLC spoon-fed all of it to me in prodigious quantities.

Still, I wasn't ready to quit my job and move to Milwaukee to become a full-time organizer. It was my only effective argument—how would we live? But soon even that argument became moot.

My employer (a former military man reputed to pick his secretaries by their bra size), while introducing the women on his professional staff at an annual meeting, described us as "the most gorgeous girls" he'd ever been privileged to employ. We "gorgeous girls" were then invited to parade across the stage to prove his point. It was a humiliating spectacle.

I quit on feminist principle—though no one else did—and sued for unemployment compensation. I won the case after my former boss got on the witness stand and offended the female judge by saying he didn't understand what was wrong with his behavior. The verdict was later overturned and I had to repay the money I'd collected, but that didn't happen until two years later. Slowly, all the obstacles to joining the NCLC began to vanish.

When Jeff and Kate arrived, I rushed out to the parking lot to meet them, with Bill following close behind. Kate got out of the car first. She was a gorgeous young woman, with a figure that struck envy in my heart, and I quickly glanced at Bill, whose eyes were popping out. Then Jeff was there beside me—not the boy of my memories, but a handsome, self-assured man with long hair and sideburns. My face burned with pleasure. We hugged for a long time.

"You're still taller than me," he said.

"Oh Jeff, just let it go," I laughed.

"But, you know, I still wonder. Which one of us led the other one on?"

"What are you talking about?" Kate asked. I let the subject drop and led them into our apartment. Bill brought up the rear with their bags.

That first night, Jeff and I relived our Yazoo-Merrick adventures, laughing until we cried over our hapless attempt at matrimony in the airport. Every so often one of us would look over at Bill, who was reading, or Kate, who had dozed off on the sofa. But mostly we reveled in our time with each other and didn't try to include them. Later, behind our closed bedroom door, Bill heaped scorn on me for my lapse into "burgher fantasies with a political lightweight." And the next morning, though they were civil to each other, I could see that Jeff wasn't enamored of Bill, either. Things weren't going well.

Jeff and I didn't have a chance to discuss it, though, because he had to have emergency dental surgery that afternoon. For three more days he lay on our couch, drifting in and out of a drugged sleep. As Kate nursed him, I cooked soups to tempt his appetite. By the time Jeff was back on his feet, it was the last day of their visit.

That night, we went to see *The Battleship Potemkin,* the classic Soviet-era film about a 1905 naval uprising. Its idealistic Communist message seemed to push both men over the edge. When Bill said it was a great movie, Jeff replied that it was "a great piece of propaganda." By the time we got home, Bill had let loose with a mind-numbing torrent of statistics about Soviet steel production under Stalin. Jeff called the statistics immoral justifications of genocide, punctuating points by pounding his fist on the kitchen counter. I knew Bill was using Jeff as a devil's advocate, because this was precisely the issue he had been grappling with lately. But they both seemed to be trying to inflame rather than elucidate. I was angry with Jeff for getting sucked into Bill's tirade, and angry with Bill for launching it. I wanted someone to reach a reasoned conclusion, the answer to my own doubts. But instead they were indulging in useless political one-upsmanship. When Kate slipped off to bed around midnight, I did, too, though it was several hours before I fell asleep. And Bill and Jeff kept right on arguing.

Saying good-bye to Jeff the next morning felt final, though he smiled and hugged me and promised to write again soon. But the look in his eyes told me all I needed to know: He was appalled, confused and upset by what he'd seen. I had no idea what he stood for, and it was a time when I thought everyone should stand for *something.* He seemed to me the epitome of a complacent ex-activist as he slid into the shiny new car and continued his leisurely cross-country trip with his hot girlfriend. I didn't know the car was Kate's, or that he was between jobs, or that he and Kate would return home to a subsistence lifestyle that made mine look positively middle-class.

I hardened my heart against him and turned to Bill, who seemed in comparison like a noble crusader. We went back into our apartment arm in arm, and a week later I joined the NCLC with him.

36. *Jeff*

on the road

When Kate and I entered Ruth's apartment, the first thing we saw was a garish early Soviet-era poster of Lenin. You couldn't miss it, since it was directly opposite the door. I thought to myself: *My God, Ruth really has become a Communist.* Other than the face of Lenin, though, there was almost nothing in the apartment inconsistent with a tidy middle-class existence. It struck me during our visit that while Bill might be a fervent Marxist, Ruth's heart really wasn't into it.

Our few days in Madison were spent in the shadow of two imperatives: my dental emergency and Bill's need to administer an ideological litmus test. The pall from our "kitchen debate"—a comical echo of Nixon and Khrushchev, if anyone had noticed—kept things pretty subdued on the morning we left. I felt a bit silly for having gone at it hammer and tongs the night before, although I'm sure I would have started the battle right back up again at the drop of a steel-production statistic. But the looks on Ruth's and Kate's faces made it clear that another round was the last thing they wanted to see, so Bill and I kept things low-key.

I was afraid that the argument would put a strain on my and Ruth's friendship, since I had clearly revealed myself as an enemy in Bill's eyes. Still, I was confident that it would survive. I had no idea to what lengths she would go to preserve her marriage, but nothing could have shaken my belief in our special bond.

Of more immediate concern as we drove away from Madison was the somewhat frosty atmosphere in the car. Kate told me that she had felt very hurt that first night when Ruth and I had ignored her and Bill to delve into our youthful adventures. She had been tempted to leave the next morning without me, she said.

I tried to explain to her the inexplicable—the mystical, irresistible force that had brought Ruth and me together in the first place, and its continuing effects. We hadn't seen each other in so long, I told Kate, that being together had overwhelmed us. But my communion with Ruth hadn't been meant to shut her out, I assured her, adding that she meant more to me than I could say.

That unfroze her heart, and late that night, in a motel room some-where in Minnesota, she made it abundantly clear that all was forgiven. The next night, as we hurtled west across the pitch-dark plains of Ne-braska, I realized with a kind of weak-kneed rush that I really did treasure this wonderful lady who had cared for me so selflessly in Madison, and that I should tell her so, which I did. She was driving, and when she leaned over to give me a passionate kiss, her hand on my thigh, we almost went off the road. Confessing love was at once liberating and frightening, as if I'd drained the moat around my castle and lowered the drawbridge. I'd given someone the run of my heart at last, but could I keep the commit-ment up and the drawbridge down? I was at last ready to try.

We stopped to visit Feldo and his girlfriend, Mona Bernstein, in San Francisco, but they had just rented a huge Victorian on spec and were frantic to find paying sublessees before the next month's rent came due. Their financial obligations—which constituted a real crisis, Feldo gravely informed me—meant they were wrapped up in placing ads, working the phone and interviewing possible housemates while we were there. We made the best of our visit anyway, going up to the Napa Valley for a some-what pixilated tour of the wineries and noshing and buying souvenirs at Fisherman's Wharf. Feldo and Mona took us out for dinner on our last night in town, and we tried not to gawk as several gay couples made out in the dark anteroom of a pizza restaurant—something we'd never seen in Oswego.

The rest of the trip was a series of snapshots, some preserved on film and some in the crystal-clear/soft-focus medium of memory: Kate, smiling in the brittle light of early morning, with the cozy little log cabin we'd rented just outside Yellowstone behind her; me sitting, like the Cheshire Cat, suspended off the ground on a tree limb in San Francisco's Golden Gate Park; the two of us gasping for breath in the waiting room of a Dodge dealership in L.A., breathing literary laughing gas from Woody Allen's *Without Feathers* while Kate's car was being serviced; a skunk with tail up-raised, its business end pointed directly at my face, at our campsite just south of the Grand Canyon; Kate perched on the canyon's rim, her own fresh-faced radiance rivaling the glories of nature.

We slept most of the day we got back, but then reality hit with a thud. I had borrowed from Kate, my mother and my brother for expenses during the trip, and I was even in hock to the kindly dentist Ruth had set me up with in Madison, who had agreed to remove two wisdom teeth, with local anesthesia, for sixty dollars, with only thirty dollars down.

I set off for my job interview in Fulton, about a fifteen-minute drive south along the Oswego River, on a windy, overcast day soon after return-ing home. There was no trace of snow in Oz when I left—as there shouldn't have been, given that it was only the tenth of October. In Fulton, however, a freakish lake-effect storm had dumped more than a foot of snow, snapping trees and cutting power. My doughty '67 Beetle was indifferent to slick roads, and I was able to thread my way past downed limbs to the *Oswego Valley News* on time, if just barely. But when I entered its cold, dark building—which the paper shared with a gas station in those days—the receptionist told me Mr. Caravan would be delayed. I fidgeted for the better part of an hour, thinking that I could hardly have picked a worse day to apply for a job and wishing I'd brought my camera so that I could at least get some shots of the storm damage while I waited.

Vince Caravan probably thought I was a very determined—or very desperate—job seeker to have shown up on such a day. In any case, he hired me for an amount that came out, after taxes, to ninety-five dollars a week—a big raise from the *Democrat*. Still, that odd number bugged me. I took my first check in to his office the day I got it and pointed out that if he would just toss another few dollars into the pot, I could take home an even hundred. He stared at me at first; then he smiled and said, "I like even numbers, too. A hundred it is."

friendly fire

When I joined the Labor Committees, I wrote Jeff a letter that inflicted a grievous wound to our friendship, and for years afterward I thought it had been fatal. Later, when things became clearer to me, I felt riven with shock and shame at my wrongheadedness.

January 13, 1975

Dear Jeff,

Much has changed since your visit and I hesitate to unfold it within the limited scope of a letter but it must be attempted if we hope to continue to communicate. There are innumerable reasons to recoil in dismay from reality. However, Bill and I have ruthlessly confronted those reasons and found them less than human, if not totally insane. Throughout our lives, Jeff, we have been surrounded with fantasy—TV, mother's homeside magic, Vietnam and its deluded antiwar "revolutionaries," the myth of success, etc.—and we have responded with neurotic insanity, feverishly constructing more fantasy, performing propitiatory rituals to dead pasts. Now the fantasies are melting away.

This letter is VERITABLY IMPOSSIBLE for me to write, so big is the gulf between yourself (who can write impassively of Rockefeller and William F. Buckley) and myself (who is pouring my intellect, creativity, time, energy, probably my life's blood into the battle for humanity against the bestialized filth of those men and their following). Have you read about TRIAGE as suggested by Rocky's Trilateral Commission? If so, how can you possibly tolerate it and call yourself human? Examine fusion power, negentropy, Descartes, Spinoza, Einstein, Feuerbach, Marx, Luxemburg, Hegel, Oparin, Vernadsky—in essence break out of the controlled environment spawned by "higher education" and begin your education anew.

Bill and I have embarked on the excruciating task of finding the real world and we are tempted to backslide daily, but the realization of the discovery of self-conscious mentation of the type experienced by Descartes, "I think therefore I am," and the responsibility it carries of negentropic growth constantly compels us to tear out the demons of our education. I.e., we are confronting the "giggling, nervous infants of bourgeois fear" which grip and strangle the minds of most of our acquaintances, our families, our friends—and we are becoming members of a new species, equipped to make the conceptual leap which is absolutely necessary if the human race is to survive an impending ecological holocaust.

Political, economic, psychological, personal, moral, scientific, artistic levels—all the pursuits of mankind—must be conceptually raised to the next level of human progress. We are in the process of an intellectual renaissance, Jeff, and it is very real. I would be less than equal to the demands of a truly creative friendship if I didn't joyfully bring it within the grasp of your mind.

I've enclosed several clippings which I hope you will read. They're from **New Solidarity**—*you know, the paper you used to laugh at? We are planning to leave Madison and will be organizing full-time with the Labor Committees in Milwaukee and Chicago. I quit my job in November and have since been making the intellectual leaps necessary to maintain the integrity of my decision to be a world historical being rather than Ruth Tuttle of Yazoo City. I am beginning to locate myself by my mental coordinates rather than geographically. Within me exists not only the experiences of 23 years, but also an intensifying sensuous grasp of the geometry of the universe and the laws and forms I am capable of imposing on it.*

Of all my friends, you are the one I know best intellectually. We have shared our minds much more than our experiences and for this reason, I am convinced that you have the intellectual integrity to grapple with your bourgeois persona and fear and to discover your humanity, your pride. This will be very straining to our relationship because it calls for an honesty not accepted in polite society and is certainly far removed from the magnanimous apathy of the counterculture many of our peers have opted for.

So, there you have an infinitesimal glance into the burgeoning currents of my life. Jeff, I feel like every human being can potentially feel. I feel like God.

The week after I mailed this letter, Bill and I moved to Milwaukee. With the Labor Committees' help, I came to believe that my passion for eclectic thinkers, historical drama and storytelling was a symptom of a fatal flaw: At twenty-four, I was too intellectually soft.

I developed deep friendships with some of the NCLC members, a sense of camaraderie and a fascination with the mores and inhabitants of America's industrialized heartland. There were some days when I might have believed I was happy. On the streets outside grocery stores, in airports, in Sears parking lots, I learned to hawk the NCLC's publications, shouting out the daily headlines: "Only two more weeks until nuclear holocaust." "Only one more week . . ." "Only three more days . . ." When it didn't happen we deliriously proclaimed the news: "NCLC averts nuclear holocaust!"

We sold enough *New Solidarity* newspapers, we thought, to build the organization's international network of telex communications—state-of-the-art for the times. Some members of the group were privileged children of wealthy families, and their trust funds also helped pay for an expansive Virginia farm and mansion for Lyndon LaRouche, as well as for the much-touted technology.

Bill and I lived better than most of the membership, in a cold upstairs apartment in the inner city, all my sixty dollars a week in unemployment compensation would allow. We rose each morning at 6:30, attended a briefing, set out for a day of selling newspapers, then returned to headquarters to count money, be debriefed and have evening "classes" before we went home about eleven o'clock to fall into bed.

Some weekends we would go to Chicago or New York to hear the doctrine of LaRouche, who would speak for hours on Germanic philosophers, musical counterpoint, art and nuclear fusion power without once consulting a note. His lieutenants would usually rise to brief us all on the constant threat of assassination he lived under, and to solicit emergency funds to pay for security.

According to Dennis King, in his book *Lyndon LaRouche, and the New American Fascism,* LaRouche foresaw a society in which he would be the ultimate dictator and would be able to exercise "total control over the individual's innermost thoughts." The entire story of LaRouche's flawed genius is told in detail by Mr. King. My experience with him is limited to a nine-month period in 1974–75 when I was a local organizer. This was the time when the organization was being whipped into shape financially. Using the telex system, the national committee inundated media and key political contacts around the world with updates on our rallying cry: Nelson Rockefeller's conspiracy against mankind through the evil Trilateral Commission. It also began the more lucrative activity of soliciting loans that were never repaid. They were called campaign donations under the guise of the formation of a new national political party, the U.S. Labor Party, which began fielding candidates in elections across the country. LaRouche himself ran for president in 1976 as a Labor Party candidate, and in Democratic primaries from 1980 to 1996. In 1988 he was indicted for defrauding lenders of more than $30 million. He was convicted the same year of fraud and conspiracy. On his Web site résumé, he had also claimed that in 1982–83 he participated in exploratory talks with the then Soviet government, which led to Reagan's Strategic Defense Initiative.

The political philosophy feeding LaRouche's party in 1974 was deemed "beyond Marxism." Mastery of it was a requisite of membership. Among other things, we were told that the black community was a CIA target and blacks were being manipulated within their CIA-controlled ghetto cultures. Jazz was defined as brainwashing. The final logic of this scenario was that black inner city youth—who had obviously succumbed to their CIA masters—could be addressed as "nigger."

"What are you people, fascists?" Bill interjected when we were told this at a briefing. Others in our group quickly backed him up. There was nervous laughter.

"Why don't we just call ourselves the Ku Klux Klan?" I asked. More laughter.

The speaker merely smiled and switched to a discussion of Beethoven.

We would have been shocked to know that the NCLC was, according to King, in very amicable discussions with members of the KKK. I was worried about being affiliated with a Communist organization, when the NCLC was even then moving far to the right. Beyond Marxism indeed.

Bill and I spent countless hours reading and studying, getting a better education in Western philosophy and politics than we had gotten at UT. But that benefit was far outweighed by the brutalized and controlled nature of our day-to-day lives. Even as we were verbally flogged each day to use creative thinking to achieve "humanistic relevance" in the world, the reality was that we and our comrades spent most of our time in dehumanizing and mind-deadening activity, hawking newspapers to blue-collar workers.

38. Jeff

wreckage

From late 1974 to mid-1976, I worked my way up the ladder, such as it was, at the *Oswego Valley News*: delivering papers and operating the clackety old Addressograph machine in the early days; taking pictures of kids' birthday parties and the ever-popular reunion shots (once I captured five generations of daughters on film); editing the gobs of community news that came in over the transom every week (no occurrence in Fulton was beneath our notice); covering school boards and town boards; reporting on the proceedings of the Oswego County legislature; and writing editorials and a regular political column. I did everything but assign others, since there was no one under me.

Photos from those days show a young man with merry eyes, loud clothes and a cocky smile, his arm around this striking redhead or that zaftig blonde. Life for me was about to become just the sort of sexual playground Ruth had so often caught Bill veering into, with the exception that I'd neither pledged nor contracted my fidelity.

Things had started to go sour with Kate not long after our epiphany on the plains of Nebraska. Within a week or two of my starting work, the *Valley News* hired a heart-stopping blonde, just out of high school, to set type and lay out pages. With her flawless features, glorious hair and svelte figure, she was a miraculous freak of nature. Although she was engaged, I found it nearly impossible to keep my eyes off her. One day, Kate picked me up for lunch, and when we got back to the paper, we pulled up next to the blonde. She got out of her car and walked the ten feet or so to the door, waving to me discreetly—we were coworkers, after all—and giving us a shyly dazzling smile before vanishing into the building.

Kate's eyes drilled into mine and wiped the appreciative grin off my face. *"Who,"* she demanded, "was *that*?"

I told her there was nothing between us, which was true—the blonde had been ignoring my overtures. But I was meeting a lot of new women then, and some of them were not indifferent to me. By the end of that year, I told Kate I needed "more freedom." She was clearly hurt, but instead of crying, she promptly moved out. She told me that if I could see others, so could she, and that upset me. We dated for a while longer, but the glow of that Nebraska night—the first time I'd accepted the idea of a mature commitment to a woman—had faded.

We went our separate ways for Thanksgiving that year—she to Quincy and I to Merrick, where I would see Vin for the first time in about four months. He'd come back from Germany, having finally admitted to himself that he couldn't stay in a country where he couldn't express himself adequately, his lover's support and help with the language notwithstanding. When I saw him at his house, we hugged for a long time before talking. I didn't say it, but I was very relieved he'd come home.

When I got Ruth's "I feel like God" letter a few months later, I recoiled from it as if from an unexpected slap to the face. I reread it perhaps half a dozen times, desperately searching for some link to the person she had been, some clue as to how I might be able to restart our conversation. But I found none. For the second time in my life I'd been rocked to my foundations by a letter from Ruth, but this one, unlike her response to my first letter back in 1969, seemed to contain no invitation to keep the dialogue going. The sensitive, intelligent Ruth I'd known was gone, replaced by a cant-spewing fanatic. Cults by then had become a major societal concern, and it seemed clear to me that Ruth and Bill had joined some kind of a political cult. But I was in no position to "deprogram" her, so I regretfully put her letter away, trusting that her extraordinary mind would eventually bring her back to her senses. And that she would get back in touch with me when it did.

Ben, meanwhile, had taken a job at Highland Community School in tiny Paradox, a flyspeck of a settlement in the wild Adirondacks. He was teaching disturbed children what he had learned: how to turn their anger and frustration into art. He had a girlfriend there, along with his now free-ranging dog, Malcolm, who needed a place as big as the north woods to roam. But Malcolm's advent at Highland coincided with the suspicious disappearance of several chickens, and he was banished from the school. When I heard the story of how Ben had kept his listeners rapt during his masterful but ultimately unsuccessful defense of Malcolm, it was easy to picture it. Ben had played the lawyer, Alfieri, in our high school production of Arthur Miller's *A View from the Bridge,* and he'd been waiting ever since to do a courtroom scene. As for Malcolm, he eventually went to live with Fred Thaler, who didn't keep chickens.

We old friends from Merrick gathered at Highland one summer afternoon in 1975—the Paradox Summit, I called it. We had beards then, and a lot more hair in general. The photo shows me in a characteristic pose—leaning against Vin. He's sitting on the roof of his old blue Renault, Pepe LePew, which I'd named after he told me that it stank as a car, but women thought it was cute. Ben is behind the wheel, waving, and Fred sits on the roof with his legs draped over the shoulders of a grinning Jerry. We were twenty-four, and the living was easy. Looking at this picture always makes me smile, but it also makes me sad. None of us could have predicted how drastically our lives were about to change, and how soon.

Within three years, Ben and Jerry started a little shop that would lead them to riches and fame but consume them in a way that the two carefree young men in that photo couldn't have imagined. The seeds of it had always been in Ben, of course; it was no accident that we'd named him chief of the Tribe in high school.

Movie-star handsome, Fred could have been a Don Juan but was ever the most sensitive and responsible of us. He would get married the next year to his beautiful betrothed, Alalia Kempner, the first of us to take the plunge.

Jerry had always been diffident and self-effacing, and what little ego he had took a drubbing when he failed twice to get into medical school. But none of that shows in the picture. A good sport, steady, tolerant and sensible, he would later characterize his main contribution to Ben & Jerry's, typically of him, in the negative.

"You know how they say these great guys always surround themselves with yes men, Dursht? Well, I was Ben's no man. He'd get an idea, and I'd say no. Then he'd come back with another idea, and I'd say no again. It kept me sane and the business solvent."

Two faces are missing from the group portrait—Ron, who was playing summers at the Aspen Music Festival back then, and Feldo, who'd begun his career as David Harp, blues-harmonica and meditation guru to the Bay Area. Later, he would move east and rejoin the group. Ron, disciplined and musically gifted, had always been Mr. Know-it-all, and we tolerated his airs with reasonably good humor. Later, to our horror, we realized he really did know it all, or at least most of it.

In the picture, I had a stalk of hay sticking out from what Vin called my "Mona Durst" smile and was playing my traditional role: jester, gadfly, skeptic, chronicler and idea man who was always trying to hand his inspirations off to someone else—usually Fred or Jerry or Vin—to actualize.

Vin was dressed incongruously in a black shirt and dark jeans, his smiling face masked by a heavy beard and stark shadow as he leaned against Pepe's windshield. There were so many Vins: the brooding philosopher, the charismatic storyteller, the suave Latin lover, the paragon of practicality who once told me he'd bought Pepe mainly because it had four doors. ("A car's got to have ease of access, Durst—it's the first thing I look for.") He was the uncomplicated Vin who just plain loved to sing, preferably in harmony with others, and the calculating Vin who, at the height of the gas crisis, considered selling his little car for double what he'd paid for it. "I'll just put a sign on it," he said. "FOR SALE—call in your bid at 1-800-38MPG."

Even then, when the picture was taken, Vin was prone to terrible headaches. But none of us gave them a second thought.

One morning in March of 1975, Kate set out for Syracuse on business. She didn't get far. A mile or two south of Oswego on Route 57, her little import hit an ice patch just as she was reaching highway speed and slid into the path of an oncoming Buick. Her seat belt kept her alive, but it didn't keep her face from hitting the steering wheel with tremendous force.

I got a phone call later that day, after coming home from an early shift at the paper. They'd been trying to call me for hours, the woman at the hospital said. Kate, in her few moments of consciousness, had kept repeating, over and over: "Call Jeff, call Jeff, I want Jeff here." Finally, they'd gotten my name from another friend who'd heard about the accident on the radio. "We called as soon as we got your number," the woman said. "We're not sure she's going to make it, but she sure wants to see you."

They were wheeling her from the OR to the acute-care section of Oswego Hospital just as I burst through the door, numb with shock.

The Kate I saw in the wheelchair at that moment looked almost inhuman, with her hair tied back, bandages everywhere and tubes growing out of her like weird appendages. There was nothing recognizable of her face except her eyes, and in them I saw terror, pain and, finally, a flicker of hope when she saw me. Then they wheeled her away.

I stayed in the waiting room and in the corridor outside for what seemed an eternity, pacing, sitting, standing, pacing, repeating a kind of prayer out loud over and over: "Save Kate, make her well again, make her all right." It was something I'd learned from a Buddhist author when I was a teenager—formulate a simple prayer or mantra, focus all your will on it, envision it happening and repeat the words out loud to give them more force. In my mind, I saw her as she had been, and as I hoped she would be: the lovely young woman with whom I'd shared life, the sweet joys of the flesh and an all-too-brief touching of the soul.

Eventually, whether my prayers had anything to do with it or not, she did recover. That alone, her doctor told me, was a miracle. "When they first brought her in here," he said, "we thought she was a goner for sure." They were surprised when she was still alive after twenty-four hours, and they were amazed at her strong recovery. She looked ravaged when they finally allowed me in to see her, but I held her hand, kissed her brow and told her I would be there for her, and that she would be okay.

And I was there nearly every day for weeks, watching with growing satisfaction as she progressed from battered invalid to halting walker to almost-good-as-new young woman. But her face would not be the same again. Luckily there was a very good reconstructive specialist at Oswego Hospital, and Kate was still a very attractive woman when the surgeons finished. But she was not the blooming Irish rose she had been.

She was so vulnerable then, so needy, that she mistook my very real concern for a rebirth of love, and I had to tell her, when I thought she was strong enough to bear it, that although I still held her very, very dear and would do everything I could to get her back on her feet, I didn't love her in that way anymore. She cried then, perhaps mourning her lost beauty and the power it once had over me. But I told her, near tears myself, that that wasn't it.

What *was* it? That question racked my soul for a long time after that terrible winter's day. I had indeed loved her, and love had died, well before the accident. A false friend of hers had told her I would surely take her back, love her again after the crash, because I owed her nothing less. But I knew Kate herself didn't really believe that. She wanted my love, but not pity disguised as love.

On a bitterly cold and blustery day about a week after the crash I went, at her parents' behest, to check the wrecked car for any personal items that might still be in it. But nothing of a personal nature remained except her blood, which had splashed liberally over the front seat, the dashboard and the floor. It was strange, trying to pry open the glove compartment in that twisted hulk of a car—a car I had practically lived in for a month and associated with so many fond memories.

After that day, I often found myself imagining what the crash must have been like, feeling Kate's terror constrict my own gut as its inevitability became clear. I'd had nothing to do with the wrecking of her car or her beauty, but I was afraid I'd wrecked her heart and maybe her life. I wished, time after time, that I could have loved her again, as she had wanted. But I couldn't. We stayed in touch for a few years, then faded from each other's lives.

39.   R u t h

epiphany

A dazed housewife, who had come to the door in her robe and slippers, handed me a quarter and took a copy of *New Solidarity*. Then we heard a commotion across the street.

"Get out of here, you motherfucking bitch!"

I turned to see what was happening. My customer quickly closed her door.

A woman in a soiled cotton nightgown was punching my friend Lorice, who was on her knees, frantically trying to pick up her bundles of papers.

"I'm leaving. I'm leaving," she kept saying. But the woman seemed to be oblivious. She began slapping at Lorice's head and shouting inchoate curses.

Lorice pulled her black beret down over her ears and tried to cover her head with her arms, but as she cowered, the woman leaped forward. Lorice fell down the porch steps under the impact, with the harridan clinging to her. Foam flew from the woman's lips and her nightgown tore away as they rolled together in the grass.

The woman's body was hard and black, and her grip on Lorice was predatory, the black widow suffocating her prey. I tasted bile in my throat as I watched.

Bill, Rodney, Lorice and I had been ringing doorbells in midtown Milwaukee for hours, and though we hadn't sold many papers, this was the first time we'd been assaulted for trying. What I was seeing was almost too brutal to believe. *She's going to* kill *her,* I thought.

I threw down my bundles and ran across the street toward the struggling women just as Lorice broke free and began to stumble away, blood flowing down both sides of her face.

At the sight of the blood, adrenaline pumped through me and I began waving my arms over my head as I ran, yelling at the woman to "get back in your house," to "shut the fuck up," to "watch out," though for what I didn't know. But I was gratified to see a look of incredible, unreasonable fear come over her face, and she scurried back toward her house, screaming curses at us.

Lorice had quit running and was sitting on the sidewalk by the woman's front steps, crying and moaning. When I reached her, I knelt down and tried to figure out where the blood was coming from. She hadn't been cut. Her head wasn't smashed open. Finally I saw several oozing scalp wounds where her hair had been ripped out by the roots, skin and all. Knobby blue bruises were beginning to rise on her face and shoulders.

I looked around for Bill and Rodney. They stood a few houses up, watching like stunned statuary. "Bill," I yelled, "go get the car."

Then I hauled Lorice up and dragged her down the sidewalk. Fear-sweat made my grip on her bare arm slippery and out of the corner of my eye I saw the madwoman coming toward us again.

"Run, Lorice. Run!" I screamed. She tried, but her legs kept buckling and she started babbling in terror. The woman quickly reached us, shoved me to one side and grabbed Lorice's dark hair, dragging her back up the front walk. Lorice writhed and struggled, and in a few seconds the woman fell backward with another bloody hank of hair in her hands. But Lorice was free. She half-crawled, half-ran toward me. Together, we stumbled across the street.

I grabbed a tree limb that was lying in the gutter and Lorice crouched on the ground behind me. But the woman began to retreat to her house, yelling, "You goddamn whitey devils. You come back up on my porch, you be dead. You be burning in hell."

After she went inside—it was probably only a minute since the attack had begun—I looked around for Bill and the car. I saw Rodney running up the street in the opposite direction from us and noticed, oddly, that one of his shoes had a hole in the sole. I didn't see Bill.

Lorice was saying, "Let's get out of here," her mouth so swollen she could hardly speak. We started limping up the block toward the car, both of us looking back fearfully, expecting any minute to be broadsided. Copies of *New Solidarity* were blowing around our feet. Lorice's shoulders trembled under my supporting arm, and I was afraid she was going into shock. I wrapped my sweater around her.

"How bad is it?" she asked me, patting at her hair and desperately feeling the torn patches. Her fingers came away covered with blood, and when she saw it she uttered a cry so bereft and lost that my heart lurched. I wiped it off her hand as best I could with the tail of my shirt, but we kept walking. When we got to the car, Bill came stumbling out of the bushes, sliding on his butt down a small incline in his haste.

"Where were you?" I screamed, and then surprised myself by bursting into tears.

"God, Lorice," Bill said, looking at her bloodied face and head. Lorice tried to cover her head with my sweater, saying, "Don't look at me. Don't look at me."

Just then, a police car pulled up, with an ambulance right behind. Bill had run to a pay phone and called them. Lorice was trundled into the ambulance, and I got in with her. Bill followed in the car.

At the hospital, Bill called the Milwaukee local of the NCLC and told them what had happened. I wasn't surprised at the response. "They said we shouldn't hang around here. They want us back out in the street, selling. Just tell Lorice to call when she's done and someone'll come get her." I left the message with a nurse, and we went to a nearby supermarket where we managed to sell almost fifty copies of *New Solidarity* by nightfall. I used some of the money to buy two bratwursts and some doughnuts, something I didn't have any qualms about. I thought of it as my commission.

When we got back to Arlen's apartment, our headquarters, in an old German blue-collar section of Milwaukee, Lorice had just returned. She sat at the kitchen table and was being debriefed by phone, telling someone at the Chicago local about the attack. To hide the bandages, she had stylishly wrapped her head with a black kerchief. She took long drags from a cigarette while she listened to the debriefer.

"No, we didn't tell anyone we were going to that neighborhood," she was saying, and Bill and I nodded in affirmation. "Yeah, Rodney's a new recruit. But I don't think . . ." She listened a few minutes. "There was nothing I could do. I know it was my responsibility . . ." Finally, she sighed and handed me the phone. I saw her walk wearily into the front room to join the rest of the group as Arlen read them the latest briefing updates, giving everyone their evening fix of information from the National Committees.

I told my version of the incident to the man on the phone, adding, "At the hospital the police told me the woman is known in the neighborhood as mentally ill. She's always hallucinating about the devil, and today she was tripping her brains out, too. They were trying to contact a family member to get her committed."

"And you believed them?"

"Well, yeah," I said. "You don't?"

"Look at the facts: The working class is being systematically destroyed by Rocky's Trilateral Commission. There's a psychological holocaust going on out there. This is the direct result of Nelson Rockefeller's interference in our daily organizing. If you do your job better, the workers won't be destroyed like this."

"So it's my fault?"

"Let's go over the story again, only this time I want you to tell me more about what Rodney was doing."

"Look, he was ringing doorbells, just like the rest of us. That's all."

About ten people were gathered in the next room. Some of them were talking. Others sat quietly, slumped in their chairs. What I saw when I looked through the kitchen door was a group of demoralized, drifting souls. We had become dumb animals with gaunt faces and dark-rimmed eyes, members of the same soul-starved family. There was only one person who seemed to be untouched by Labor Committee angst, a genial black youth named Teddy.

I caught his eye and he came into the kitchen. While I talked on the phone, he stood behind me and rubbed my shoulders. I think he knew what I meant when I hung up the phone and said, "I'm going home now."

"Yep, I'm about done with this scene, too," he replied. Teddy's roots ran deep into the heart of the South, to a sharecropper's shack in Louisiana. The NCLC was a lark for him—a strange outing with the white folks he had met during the first week after he'd migrated north to Milwaukee, looking for work. Thanks to the help of his uncle, he'd found it at A.O. Smith, and that's where we met.

I was assigned to bring him along. I would meet him at A.O. Smith during the morning shift change and hand him some copies of *New Solidarity*. Within twenty minutes all his buddies would buy us out, the younger ones ribbing Teddy about his "white piece," the older ones delivering advice with their twenty-five cents: "Boy, you bes' be lookin' after yo' momma, 'stead of hustlin' this garbage." Almost without exception they'd then toss the paper into the trash cans next to the ramp. Teddy and I just laughed it off. The rest of the afternoon we'd hang out in a coffee shop, laughing—and sometimes crying—as we shared life stories. I loved the sound of his gentle Southern voice, though the tales he told me were often sad. For the first time I realized what life was like behind the spare, bare boards of those shacks I used to pass all-unaware in my yellow Camaro convertible.

Not long after I met Teddy, the United States pulled out of Saigon, leaving it to the Vietcong. It was Teddy who burst into Arlen's living room—where I was dutifully listening to Lorice's presentation on the life of Rosa Luxemburg—shouting, "It's over! The Vietnam War is *over*." He turned on the TV set and we all gathered round.

As the panic of the evacuation of Saigon unfolded on the television, he and I stood next to each other. He put his arm around my shoulder, and I put mine around his waist. We watched a frantic American help a Vietnamese woman climb the ladder into a helicopter that hovered atop the CIA station chief's house. Then it took off. The fear and panic of the Vietnamese who were left behind was awful to see.

I tried to feel victorious. *This is what we all wanted,* I thought. Instead I felt sad. I glanced up at Teddy. He was crying. "This is still America," he said to me.

The day Lorice was attacked was my last in the NCLC. I told Bill that I was quitting. He would have to make up his own mind. I hugged Teddy and left that dour apartment for the last time.

I remember how good it felt to go out and close the door, and how fearful I was that someone might try to stop me. Arlen did call after me, but I just kept on walking and he eventually went back inside. The air was cold and bracing. Snow was mounded along the roadways. The world seemed big and new, and my heart lifted as I walked on. When I neared a neighborhood bar, I went inside for a beer, and drank several, while two kindly grandfathers explained the corrosive evils of road salt to me.

40. *Jeff*

a political man

Nineteen seventy-six dawned with the feel of a new beginning, a watershed year. It was America's bicentennial and a presidential year to boot, and there was a sense that the nation had finally come out of the long, dark tunnels of Vietnam and Watergate.

At some point early that year, I began to have the persistent feeling that I was spinning my wheels. Working for the *Valley News* wasn't as much fun as it had been, especially since I'd been forced, for logistical reasons, to farm out my plum assignment—covering the county legislature— to a part-time reporter. The money was okay—Vince Caravan was paying me two hundred dollars a week by this time, a sum that had caused another publisher to question his sanity. But I was beginning to think about moving on, perhaps to the daily in Oswego or even to the Syracuse newspapers.

Then, in April or May, just as I was saying my good-byes at County Hall, I got a call from Norma Bartle, a legislator I knew better than most because her district was within our circulation area. She told me she was putting together a team to help her run for Congress and wanted me to join.

The very audacity of the idea appealed to me. Norma was a female Democrat in perhaps the most Republican and conservative area of the state, and she was unknown outside of Oswego County. Even there she wasn't exactly a household name—she'd only been representing the tiny town of Minetto for two years. The Thirtieth District also presented a logistical nightmare. It was comprised of seven large but sparsely populated counties that spanned the northern cap of New York State from Oswego to Lake Champlain and had no population hub or districtwide media.

On the other hand, she was bright, energetic, articulate and gutsy. And, at forty-seven, she'd been around the track a few times and had made a lot of contacts. Her husband, Fred, who would act as campaign director, was a political science professor at Oswego State who at one time had written speeches for Adlai Stevenson and John Kennedy. He, too, had some good contacts—among them Daniel Patrick Moynihan, who would be leaving his post as U.S. representative to the United Nations and mounting a run for the U.S. Senate that year. Aside from all that, Norma had verve and the ability to laugh at herself—tremendous assets, in my book.

And her opponent, Robert McEwen, though an entrenched incumbent, was hardly a fireball. In fact, he had cruised to victory every two years without leaving much of a trace. But his margins had been declining steeply over the last two elections. Unemployment in the north country was high—17 percent—even though the rest of the country was perking up economically. As a Democrat, Norma could claim that she would be a member of a powerful majority if elected—someone who could help the district with jobs programs in those pre-Reagan days.

All in all, '76—with its feeling of change in the air and a strong challenge to Jerry Ford being mounted by a moderate "New South" Democrat named Jimmy Carter—seemed like an excellent time to oust the incumbent. And it seemed Norma could do it if anyone could.

She assured me the campaign would be professionally run and reasonably well funded; in fact, she had just gotten back from a campaign school run by the Democratic Party. If I signed on as her press secretary, she told me, I would be paid my present salary until the election, and if she won I would have a fair shot at the same job in her Washington office.

Washington! That was the magic word for me. It was, with the possible exception of New York, the most influential city in the world, and it was said to be a hell of a lot easier to live in. I was no longer a McGovern liberal, but neither was Norma—although I knew McEwen would try to paint her as one. I wasn't a gung-ho Democrat either, but I was leaning toward Carter, based on his "zero-base budget" proposal and other ideas that made him sound fiscally responsible. I also knew I couldn't vote for his opponent—the man who'd pardoned Nixon.

Washington. I turned the word over in my mind, imagining bill signings in the Rose Garden and comely aides and interns sharing my bed in a paneled Georgetown flat. I gave notice at the *Valley News* the next day.

After coming back from Germany, Vin had moved to Brookline, Massachusetts, and taken a job home-tutoring truants in inner-city Boston. He liked helping ghetto kids, but it was stressful. He'd done a similar job in New York after I moved back to Oz, and he'd written me about it from East Tenth Street:

> *Haven't been mugged yet, but sometimes I feel it's coming*
> *right around the corner, and the hairs on the back of my neck*

*rise to attention (so as to support my head as it goes whipping
around, no doubt). I meet some crazies every day, but none
crazier than those right here in my own backyard. I've gotten into pantomiming deafness when approached for spare
coins or else looking them straight in the eyes then letting
go with a verse of Bach's Easter cantata or other songs in
German while salivating. Even degenerates know when they're
beaten.*

At one point in 1975 Vin had written from Brookline: "Ah, the big times
here in Bosstown are, I fear, too much for a stalemated twenty-three-year-
old rookie kid." But he was surviving—even thriving—in the metropolis,
living only a block or so from where the young JFK had gone forth to conquer the world. We old friends from Merrick consulted with and referred
to each other constantly, forming a young-boy network that doubled as a
safety net. As Vin put it in reference to a disastrous meeting between a lady
friend and Fred:

> *They did not get along A-TALL.*
> *Well, it's surely easier to lose a lover than to even con-
> sider losing one of youse guys. I don't want to lose any of you
> to women, not just yet. Jerry says there is a proposal on the
> floor, to be delivered to each of us by the U.S. Postal Service,
> for a trip in January. He says all he needs is 10 minutes' no-
> tice and he's gone. It'll take me 15 and I'll be there, too.
> What about you?*

It was a dilemma we all faced: make a break for freedom with the boys as
Jack Kerouac had done, or settle down with the good women who were, by
and large, impatient to turn us into husbands and dads. Except for Fred,
we all bolted and ran.

As for me, I'd swooped down between Sweet Petite—the most delectable nineteen-year-old in the universe—and her fiancé, a construction
worker whose fooling around had alienated her. He arrived at my apartment one day, ostensibly to thrash me, but his own sins had demoralized
him, as it turned out, and he ended up confessing them and then leaving
in some confusion after I offered him a beer.

A typical day for me that summer was to stroll over to Bartle headquarters, a block from home, at eight or nine in the morning, write a
speech or a press release or two, have a leisurely lunch and afternoon de-
light with Petite then return to HQ until five or six, when I'd head to one
of the better gin mills on Bridge Street for supper.

Meanwhile, the campaign had attracted national attention, because it looked like the Republicans could lose a "safe" seat. At the very least, they had been put on notice that their boy faced a real fight this time. Money was coming in steadily, if not torrentially, the unions were pitching in with phone banks and volunteers and press coverage was becoming increasingly frequent and respectful. With Ford in trouble and the Democrats anticipating major gains in Congress, I could well imagine leaving for Washington in January.

I went to visit Vin one weekend early that summer and had an odd experience. He'd given me instructions to find his house in Brookline, but I got lost and had to call for help. He said he'd drive Pepe out to meet me and then guide me back. As I followed him through the narrow, congested streets near his home, however, he suddenly pulled over and stopped. But he was still partially blocking traffic, and the notoriously impatient Beantown drivers behind us began honking away. I pulled over, too, and trotted to his car. I found him leaning against the wheel, his eyes shut tightly and his jaw clenched. He said he was okay, except that he'd had a sudden, blinding headache. It would pass in a moment or two, he told me, and then we could get going.

I grilled him when we got to his flat, but he shrugged. "I dunno, Durst. I just keep getting these godawful headaches, and the doctors don't seem to know what's wrong. One of them says it's stress from my crazy job—I had a knife and a gun pulled on me just last week—and another one says he thinks I may have epilepsy. So he's giving me an antiseizure drug, but it doesn't seem to be doing much good."

I was concerned—especially at the mention of epilepsy—but he seemed fine for the rest of the weekend. Before leaving I urged him to look for a new job, but I lost track of his situation when I returned to Oz.

The campaign gathered momentum as summer faded into fall, and the atmosphere at Bartle HQ became more intense. It had always been an uphill battle for Norma, but Moynihan did a tour of the district with her, raising a lot of money and getting her a lot of press. McEwen actually seemed to be running scared, calling in "his friend" the president to campaign for him twice.

But we were laboring under some big disadvantages. For one thing, we had no money for polling and didn't really know how to shape and target our message for maximum effect. For another, our opponent was safely on the "right" side of a very sensitive issue in that district—abortion—and generally wasn't being asked the tough questions Norma was facing.

The district's populace was descended mainly from flinty Yankees and Scotch-Irish immigrants who had settled in upstate New York after the Revolutionary War. But it also contained a large dollop of French

Canadian Catholics, who tended to vote Democratic but were generally right-to-life. In the days before "wedge" issues had been scientifically honed to split voting blocs—and at a time when the *Roe v. Wade* debate was still fresh in people's minds—abortion was our third rail.

Norma, a mother herself, gave heartfelt speeches about it:

"I've seen mothers so poor that they couldn't afford to feed the several children they already had, and were desperate when they found themselves pregnant again," she'd say if pressed, as she frequently was. "It's just not right that women of means, who *could afford* another child, can fly off to some expensive clinic to have an abortion while impoverished women can't have the same procedure in order to help protect and nourish the children they already have."

My own feelings about abortion were unsettled then, as they are now. I knew that women needed access to safe abortions at certain times; on the other hand, to make abortion a "right," with the inevitable implication of government subsidies, seemed to be going too far. One thing was clear then and still is: A fetus will almost certainly become a person unless it is aborted.

The politically expedient course would have been to avoid the issue, but Norma met it head on whenever it was raised. It was my job to frame the very careful words she would issue to the media on this subject, and although she was comfortable with our position, I wasn't sure I was. But what *was* the best solution? Whatever it was, I didn't think we had it. Why, then, I asked myself, did we deserve the voters' support? The bicentennial celebrations that summer—the tall ships, the fireworks, the reenactments and commentaries on the American experiment—made this question all the more relevant. Were we enhancing the Founders' work or degrading it? It's a measure of what an amateur I was that the question really mattered to me.

My education in practical politics had come mainly at County Hall, where I'd watched the majority grind the pitiful Democrats under heel time and again, giving appointments to faithful tithers and doling out fat contracts. Everyone seemed to have a script, and when the play-acting was done, the victors unerringly scooped up the spoils. The people's interests often seemed to come last.

Could I say for sure that the Republic would be better off with us in McEwen's place? I wasn't 100 percent certain I could, but the devil of politics is that winning tends to become the only thing that matters. Power and money were in play, and the politicos expected us to get a job done: help their side and hurt their enemies. This game, I was increasingly coming to realize, wasn't for me. And I wasn't at all sure that even the best-intentioned people in Washington really could solve the problems of people in places like Oswego, Carthage and Plattsburgh.

But what was the alternative? If Norma lost, the district and the nation would get another two years of a nonentity who had left almost no trace in Washington for all his time there, and I'd be out a job. That thought made me buckle down hard.

It seemed we could win, but the signs and portents were hard to read. The party sachems were flustered, for instance, when Jimmy Carter's interview appeared in *Playboy* that October, and although the campaign staff snickered at the idea that the steamy picture on the cover (and the confession of "lust in my heart" inside) might hurt our own candidate, our laughter rang hollow.

It was raining on election eve, which we found bleakly hopeful because we felt our supporters were more likely to brave the weather. As I drove back into town after taking a friend to vote, I passed Oswego State's Power Tower, which loomed up to probe the dark skies. Seeing it always made me recall that apocalyptic night of the takeover in 1970 and wonder what had happened to us, the tie-dyed usurpers who had filed out past the grim state troopers.

In the wake of our coup I'd flaunted my radical bona fides, even though my own participation had been purely accidental. As the marijuana smoke gradually cleared, I realized that my radicalism was topical, a response to the threat of being dragged off to kill or die in a war that already seemed pointless by 1969. But I'd since come to see that although the people who'd led the antiwar movement were generally right about the war, that didn't make them right about everything else.

I drove on through the sodden town, and soon I was standing in the faded dining room of the Pontiac Hotel, a drink in my hand. As I watched the numbers pile up against us, I tried to remind myself that it had always been a long shot. But the debacle was galling. Though Norma ran ahead of both Carter and Moynihan in the Thirtieth District, in the end we lost by more than twenty thousand votes. She conceded with a feisty smile and tears in her eyes.

We were all a bit numb when we shook hands and embraced later that night. "You take care of yourself, Jeff," Norma said. "And keep in touch!" Then, worried at how shattered I was, she hugged me again. Caring and thorough as ever, she had checked to make sure that the paid staffers would qualify for unemployment benefits. She told me to make sure and apply the next day. "And thanks again, Jeff," she said. "You did a great job."

I smiled weakly, squeezed her arm and hurried toward the door, eager to put the lights and noise and smoke of the suffocating room behind me. On the way out I met a friend, a local newspaper editor, who shook my hand and said: "Tough luck, Jeff. But you gave it all you had."

"Yeah," I mumbled, "I guess so." Had it really been a matter of luck? Or had we been kidding ourselves all along? And had I really given it my best shot? In his column the next day, my friend would write about an encounter with the human side of politics: a gritty but humbled candidate, a young aide's face "dazed with defeat."

41.   *Ruth*

the scent of magnolias

Daddy covered my hand where it lay on the hospital sheet. His face was sad and he turned away after a moment to blow his nose. Bill sat morosely in a corner of the room. I had just gotten off the phone with Momma, who said she would be over in the morning to take me home. But in my drugged presurgery state, I was sure everyone was making too big a fuss.

Women had babies all the time. Doctors could work miracles, I believed, and all this hysteria about miscarriage was just a dramatic punctuation to the inevitable happy ending. Later tonight I would wake up after the D&C and learn everything was fine.

I was worried, but not about losing the baby. My real concern was that they'd tell me I had to stay in bed until the baby came—how would we pay our bills? As the nurse bustled into the room with a gurney and two aides, I told myself that we'd make do somehow. If we had to, we'd move back in with my parents.

These worrisome thoughts flew around my brain like bats in a darkening cave, then were extinguished by the full force of the anesthesia. "Everything's going to be fine," I heard a kindly voice say.

Bill had left the NCLC soon after I had. He never said his decision had anything to do with my defection, and I don't think it did. For him, it had been a matter of right thinking. He had exploded one day during a briefing, ranting and raving to the handful of people in Arlen's kitchen, laying out a chronicle of Stalin's excesses, much as Jeff had once done in *our* kitchen. He had been summarily dismissed from the organization.

We hung around Milwaukee for a few weeks, and when I was offered a job as creative director at the National Audubon Society's publishing office, I accepted it on the spot. But as I brushed snow from the windshield of our Mazda and told myself I'd just plucked a career plum hard on the heels of utter devastation, I couldn't shake the feeling—the compulsion, really—that I had to go home to Mississippi.

Later, as I stood in our tiny bedroom and told Bill about it, a chasm seemed to open between us. He lay in bed, where he had been for the past three days, morose and depressed, a man without a cause. He said nothing to my news, rolling over and pulling the blanket up to his chin. I quit talking, abruptly forgetting my bright-feathered career prospects.

"Let's go home," I said.

"When?"

He might just as easily have asked "Where?" because of course we had no home. But without further discussion, I called Atlas Van Lines and arranged to be moved to Yazoo City within the week. To pay for this extravagance, I sold my only asset, some stock my mother and I had researched together years before and she had purchased for me through her broker. Mother's magic indeed.

Bill and I arrived in Yazoo City just ahead of the moving truck. Momma and Margie burst onto the porch to greet us, and I found myself running up the front steps. As the movers went in with our ragtag furnishings, I wandered the big rooms in numbed ecstasy, touching my great-grandmother's demitasse cups, opening Empire-style cupboards, hugging our dog Mr. Ginger, who, at twelve, could barely walk.

"Remember me, old fella?" I cooed into his ear. An excess of drool and the steady thumping of his tail let me know he did.

Bill fussed around the boxes, making sure his books had arrived in good shape, but I couldn't bear to look at the material remains of our former life. I was in full retreat from it. For the next two weeks I mostly stayed asleep in my old bedroom or read, curled in a gold brocade wing chair, getting up only for meals and solitary walks to the cemetery. I reread *Little Women* for the third time, and *Jane Eyre* and *The Magic Mountain*. Nothing contemporary felt sane enough.

No one pressed me for details about our plans. If they had, I would have blinked uncomprehendingly. How could I look beyond this wonderful safe place? But one evening before supper, Daddy handed Bill a beer and said, "Son, I've got a job for you."

He offered him a job as night watchman at a government housing project, one of several he oversaw in Jackson, an overt act of nepotism. But also a great kindness. Bill jumped at the chance. It was the perfect job for him, a place where he could escape into his own fantasy world in the solitude of night. He spent most of his time lying on a pallet in the guardroom, reading with a flashlight, glad to be out of my ancestors' shadows.

But waking up every day to the scent of magnolias worked like a tonic on me, and the fearful emptiness that had set in after I left the NCLC began to abate. One morning I turned over in bed and looked out the window to see a dogwood blooming and cars moving sedately up Lintonia Avenue. The wind blew, thrashing the big cedar tree for a few minutes, then settling to a murmur. I could smell coffee and bacon, and heard Rita and

Momma outside in the hall, ruminating over the condition of the twenty-year-old vacuum cleaner. Joy flooded over me like a warm bath. I lay in bed listening to the rain begin to come down, and wind rattling the old, wavy windows. I curled my toes with pleasure. Then I started crying, wrapped in my covers and in my long-ago forgotten life, under my great-grandfather's high-pitched roof. The room where he had died was where I would learn to live again.

I held Bill close when he crawled in beside me late that night, and we talked for the first time about restarting our life. A few weeks later we signed a lease for a tiny white frame house on Alabama Avenue in Jackson, forty miles away. The trees around it were towering oaks, and the yard was almost an acre. A little screened porch ran down one side.

I got a job at Jackson Printing Company doing typesetting and paste-up. It was the first place I applied, and the job definitely didn't have a career track. But it was only a few blocks from our house, and I looked forward to being able to walk to work. Each morning, weather permitting, I strolled down tree-lined streets, getting to know the neighborhood dogs and cats and thinking of nothing more pressing than what I would have for lunch that day.

The next year was, for me, the happiest of our marriage. We put in a large garden with some help from the grizzled old man who lived next door. Gardening, it seemed, was his life. He gave us some of his precious compost and showed us how to work it in with a tiller. Sometimes in the evenings he would come outside and lean over the fence, pointing out potential trouble spots in our garden. He showed me how to properly hold a hoe, a lesson he'd learned while chopping cotton in his youth. Soon he and I were comparing calluses and hoeing side by side.

By early summer the okra, lima beans, snap beans and tomatoes were crying to be canned or frozen or eaten right away, and we were hard pressed to harvest and preserve them all. We gave our neighbor much of it to sell at the farmers' market on Woodrow Wilson Avenue, splitting the profits with him, and the little bit of pocket change came in handy.

But one evening, as the smell of grilling chicken wafted through the head-high okra plants, I keeled over and threw up. After stumbling into the house and falling into an almost comatose state for twelve hours, I dragged myself to see my gynecologist. I vaguely remembered missing a period.

After the exam Dr. Odom said, "You're pregnant, about six weeks."

When I told Bill that night, he just stared at me. "What?" he finally said. I patiently told him the due date, seven and a half months away.

"Oh, well, we have lots of time," he mumbled, as he grabbed a book and bolted outside to read.

My mother and I began a week-long shopping spree that started at Winnie's maternity shop in Westland Plaza and ended with a seamstress in Yazoo City. I could hardly wait the two weeks it took for her to finish my clothes, my waistline was expanding so quickly.

But as the pregnancy progressed, the optimism of those first weeks faded. Many mornings I could hardly drag myself from bed to bath to work because of unrelenting nausea. The smell of printer's ink and darkroom chemicals destroyed what small appetite I had, and soon I was losing weight instead of gaining it. Gloria, my workmate, a beautiful, warm woman in her midthirties with three children of her own, encouraged me, assuring me the discomfort would pass. We would sit in the back of the shop eating lunch, swapping pregnancy stories and tales of clueless husbands. I was part of a women's club at last, sharing secrets of maternity and bodily mysteries that grew more uncomfortable each day.

About the end of the third month, I thought the baby moved. It felt like nothing more than an internal hiccup, but the next morning there was a lot of blood, and I drove in a panic to Dr. Odom's office.

After a brief exam, he looked at me gravely. "This could be the beginnings of a spontaneous abortion," he said. "I want you to stay in bed, move around as little as possible, and let's try to hold on to this baby." He offered some consolation. "Generally, at this stage of pregnancy, if something goes wrong it's nature's way of taking over. These things happen for a reason."

A few days later, the incessant nausea ended. My mood lifted, and I felt hungry. Bill bustled around in the kitchen and brought me a heaping plate of scrambled eggs, grits and toast. I ate and savored every bite, thinking I'd turned a corner and everything would be fine. Bill sat in his Naugahyde recliner across the room and said for the first time that he was looking forward to being a daddy. While he was describing how he planned to have our child surfing by age three, I felt a hard pinch in my womb and looked down to see blood everywhere. We hurried to the emergency room.

When I woke up from the anesthesia that night, I heard "D&C," then fell back into unconsciousness.

I was back at work in about three days, but things had changed. The walk up Culbertson Street wasn't so charming anymore. The companionable chatter during lunch was boring. The okra in the garden grew long, and dried out, and unpicked tomatoes rotted on the vine.

One night I came home from work to find Bill camped out in the living room with a dirty man who smelled of wine and sweat. The stench was overpowering. While Bill held forth for hours about race, labor unions, the legacy of Vietnam and the evils of capitalism, the man obliviously swilled from a bottle of cheap wine. When I got up the next morning he was curled on the floor by the couch in a pool of his own vomit.

I went into the kitchen and called the Salvation Army. They put me in touch with a Catholic organization that could give the man food and shelter. I gave Bill the address and made him promise to take care of it. Then I left for work, let down by the return of behavior that reminded me of our first months of marriage.

"Hey darlin', it's Daddy. Can you have dinner with me tonight?"

"Why? What's up?"

"We might have something to celebrate."

I told him I'd meet him right after work and hung up the phone. He and my mother were getting a divorce and I was having a hard time accepting a footloose father who was dating women my age. Still, he had been in such a good mood on the phone, I thought it might be a good time to ask for his help finding another job. I wanted something more challenging than typesetting.

But it turned out to be an evening of awkward conversation and long silences, and I gave up my plan to ask for his help. Then, after dinner, he finally told me his good news.

We were in his car on the way back to my house. Daddy coddled a bourbon and water as he drove, giving me a mellow summation of his life. When the downtown skyline came into view, black against a bright orange sunset, he pointed to it and said, "See that? That's my canvas. If we can keep the race thing from tearing this city apart—if we can learn to work together—there's nothing standing in the way of progress." I listened for a while longer as he went on about his job as director of the Jackson Redevelopment Authority and all the plans his office had for the city. Then he turned to me. "Let's rap," he said.

I bugged my eyes at him. "Oh, Daddy."

"Isn't that what you kids call it? Rapping? I want to talk to you. Hell, I want you to talk to me."

"What about?"

"I know of a good job opportunity for you. I want you to at least consider it."

"Okay," I said.

"Okay?" He smiled. As he aged, he was beginning to look more like Anthony Quinn than Clark Gable, but his dimpled grin was still charming. "Darlin', you always surprise me. I was ready for a fight."

Two days later I interviewed for, and got, a job as exhibitions preparator for the fledgling Mississippi Museum of Art. But Daddy had done more than finagle a good job for me. He had put events into motion that would separate Bill and me forever.

"Can you help me with this?" I turned from the frame I was mending and looked into Randy's kind blue eyes. Our gaze held for a long moment, then he said, "Do I know you?"

I think there was a bright light around him. I certainly remember it that way. But perhaps that is only an illusion. Still, more than twenty years have passed since that day, more than enough time to debunk all my first romanticized impressions of him, yet they persist. They must be the real thing.

Randy was the artist son of the Yazoo City librarian, Mary Louise Williams, who had befriended me in the summer of 1969. He stood before me now, a bemused smile crooking his mustache to one side, and held the hand I had placed, almost unconsciously, in his. "Yes. I'm Ruth Tuttle. From Yazoo City." I could tell he still didn't recognize me.

"Randy Williams. I'm here to hang my exhibition?"

"I know. I'm here to help you do it."

I wasn't surprised he didn't remember me. We had never spoken before. In the tiny world of Yazoo City, Randy's world had been even smaller than most.

When I first saw him, I was wrestling with horror-filled impressions of Yazoo City, just after we moved there in 1963. I found myself sitting in classrooms with dirty, barefoot children and listening to teachers who pronounced Thailand "Thigh-land." And who taught history as the product of mere malicious murmurings from "outsiders." What was I going to do?

Filled with self-pity, I had been wandering alone one day during recess when Randy, a young god of the playground, had streaked in front of me, followed by Allen Roark, his partner in mischief. I had stood the whole period and watched them, Randy's blond hair curling, outgrowing the crew cut of the times, his wide mouth open and innocent, his tight, athletic body leaping and twisting. For that fifteen-minute recess, I secretly shared his hard-driven glee.

But he moved on to high school while I stayed in junior high, and a car wreck a year later left him with a serious head injury. It changed him from a fun-filled child into a reclusive youth. The next time I encountered him he was in a basement filled with pot smoke, his face scarred with more than time's passing, though he was still a handsome boy. My friend, Debbie Hill, had a crush on him, and I went along for moral support. But he ignored us both.

Now, in 1977, I was happy to see that a twinkle had returned to his eyes. And I responded to the golden child I could see once again in their depths.

I helped him unload his Datsun truck, and by late afternoon we were standing together in a roomful of ethereal paintings of clouds and softly iridescent Smoky Mountains, feeling strangely unwilling to say good-bye. But I had a husband waiting, and I regretfully went home.

Though Randy returned to his solitary mountain cabin in Tennessee later that week, he would never again be far from my thoughts. I wasn't surprised when he was hired as an instructor in the museum's art school and moved back to Mississippi. I helped him get the job.

Inspired by his work, I started painting again, which was a big yawn for Bill. But by then, his activities were boring for me, too. He seemed little changed from the man I had met five years before in Knoxville, and his politics had begun to seem ridiculous.

"The world is moving on," I said, "and you're wasting your life. When are you going to *do* something?" Bill turned his back to me.

"I gave up all my friends for your ideals," I said. "I ran Jeff off, and I'll probably never hear from him again. I gave up way too much for a bunch of bunk."

"I don't see how you can regret losing the friendship of a bourgeois slave like Jeff. He's a fascist," Bill spat out. This anger had begun to creep into many of our conversations, and I was glad when he found a like-minded group of friends that included a gay former Black Panther and a Midwestern Jewish political science professor at Tougaloo College. As long as he left me to my own pastimes, I left him to his.

The headlights moving down Robinson Road played over the hood of Randy's truck. It was 2 A.M., and he was driving me home after another long day and night at the museum. But I never minded the long hours or hard work. They gave me a reason to be with Randy.

In the eight months since his return to Mississippi, he had become the love of my life. We had spent countless hours choosing color swatches and toting paint buckets, climbing ladders and sharing late suppers of fast food and bad wine. Our talk was never-ending—we had so many things in common. I had never known another human being who seemed so much a part of me, and for the first time I found myself thinking my life was fun.

When we pulled up in front of the home Bill and I had bought in West Jackson, I lifted Randy's hand to my lips. He laid it, briefly, against my cheek. We had been affectionate with each other from the beginning.

Then I got out of the truck and let myself into my dark house. Empty beer cans were scattered around the couch, and ashtrays overflowed with butts. I picked everything up and wiped the kitchen counters before going into the bedroom. Bill lay asleep, evidently unaware of the emotional tsunami building in the heart of his life. I stood over him and looked dis-passionately at his face, realizing for the first time that I didn't love him anymore.

It is horrifically scary to contemplate pulling your life apart, and I had fought hard for this difficult marriage, believing that one day it would be everything I wanted. But now I knew the difference between true compati-bility and my years-long struggle to transform almost all of my beliefs. Shocked by these thoughts, I huddled in the bathroom and cried—long, strangled sobs that rose up from deep grieving.

I was surprised when Bill came in, sleepy-eyed and concerned. He held me and rocked me back and forth like a child, patting my hair and saying I was exhausted from overwork. I swallowed the words I'd been pre-pared to say to end our marriage, and it would be many more months be-fore I could tell him the truth.

In some ways he had begun to make a life in Jackson, though he chafed at its isolation from the "mainstream," as he called the rest of the world. He was working at a daycare center in a black church on Gallatin Street and had discovered a wonderful talent and enjoyment in tending young children. His imaginative game-playing and love of books had helped bring some of these underprivileged little ones up to their grade levels. They went on to kindergarten with a more promising future than they might have had without Bill. He was like a pied piper to those chil-dren, who adored him. Many days I would arrive at the church to pick him up and watch as a bevy of mobile babies trailed after him. He would pat and pull them into a giggling, squirming mass, then direct them back into the redbrick building, sprinting for the gate before they reemerged.

But there was no future for him there. Already, the harried program coordinator had told him of impending cutbacks and begged him to work full-time for half-time pay. Bill had agreed, but it was discouraging. He be-gan to dredge up an old dream.

Since I'd first known him, he had talked of eventually living in Portu-gal so he could use the language he'd learned in Brazil, and perhaps get a job teaching over there. Now, after a recent socialist revolution in Portu-gal, he was keen to go.

I surprised him. I said I thought we should go as soon as possible, pro-vided we could sell our house to raise the money. I thought I owed it to him to get away from Randy, to give the marriage one last try. Secretly, I believed our house wouldn't bring enough to finance the trip. I was wrong. Six days later we sold it without a realtor for our asking price.

We began to sell everything we had except our clothes, books and art-work. Bill ordered a custom-made surfboard—the beaches of Portugal were legendary. I ordered an easel made of hollowcore steel bars that stood over seven feet tall.

Randy was going to keep our dog, Louie, then ship him to Portugal after we got settled. On my last day in Jackson, I drove out to Randy's house
to drop off Louie. He had rented a sharecropper's house in rural Madison
County. For the past six months, it had been our haven from the world. I'd
helped him scrub the bare board floors and whitewash the wooden walls.
Together, we had made the white muslin curtains that fluttered at the windows. A potbellied stove stood in the main room with a comfortable overstuffed sofa and a rocking chair next to it. The coffee table was made out
of a piece of a pecan tree that had died in my mother's yard. His studio,
with its smell of turpentine and oil paint, took up over half of the house.

It was a shrine to self-sufficiency, simplicity and beauty. I loved to sit
in front of the woodstove with a cup of hot coffee while he rocked in companionable silence next to me and we contemplated the next stage of the
renovation of the house, or whether he'd put too much blue in a painting.

This will be the last time, I thought, *that I'll be here.* We stood together
on the porch and he tried to cheer me up, telling me I would have an incredible adventure and that he had finally ordered a telephone, "for trans-
Atlantic calls only." He hugged me, and I left. But once the house was out
of sight, I had to pull over. I couldn't see through my tears to drive.

The next morning—a cool, sunny November morning in 1978—I woke up
once again in my bedroom in Yazoo City. Daddy had said his good-byes the
night before and then gone home to his new wife in Jackson. My brother
and sisters were at school. Only Momma was there to see us off.

She walked us to the front door. "Well, Mom," Bill said as he hugged
her, "this is good-bye."

She pulled me close against her breast and I hugged her tight, my head
resting on top of her blond curls. We both started crying. "Write me," she
said, her voice thick with tears, then she pushed me away and turned
quickly back into the house. The door closed. I stood on the porch for a
moment, thinking I might not go after all. But Bill reached over and took
my hand, and we left.

42. Jeff

unfinished business

The night my Washington fantasy got buried in a landslide, I went home and found myself drinking alone in my apartment. My friend and roommate, Jim Post, had moved out, and since I hadn't asked Sweet Petite to share election night with me, she'd made other plans. I myself hadn't made any plans beyond election day, but I knew one thing for sure: I wanted to break out of Oz and make a new beginning. But first, I had some unfinished business to pursue.

I had started thinking about Alice again that fall, and her face would haunt me at odd times. A Southern dateline in a newspaper, the Virginia accent of a campaign worker, a TV report on the rise of Jimmy Carter and the New South—each brought visions of Alice. And of Ruth, because the two were almost inseparable in my mind. Of the two, I felt Ruth was even less accessible.

But Ruth had told me, the last time we'd seen each other, that she'd heard Alice was still single. Even though that had been two years ago, the idea began to prey on me that maybe she was still waiting for that certain someone, and that I might be him. She'd been my first love, and I thought maybe she'd ruined me for anyone else. *Maybe,* I thought, *I've ruined her for anyone else, too.*

A few days after the election, I pulled out my battered old phone book from high school and looked up her number. I picked up the phone but quickly put it down again. I realized I might get Harriet or Herman rather than Alice, and they might hang up or start yelling at me. Even if I got one of her siblings, he or she might sound the alarm.

Then I smiled, amazed at how sensitive I still was about the disaster in Yazoo. We were adults now, and I had a perfect right to call her. Still, my hand was shaking when I dialed the old familiar number, and my pulse picked up. Then I heard her voice, just as I'd remembered it, and found myself stammering: "Alice, it's Jeff. Remember? Jeff Durstewitz. I hope you haven't forgotten me after all these years."

She laughed—a winsome, breathy sound redolent of honeysuckle and magnolia that took me right back to 1969. "Of course not, Jeff—I've thought about you many times. I'm so glad you called. How are you?"

We didn't have much of a chance to talk, because I'd caught her going out the door on her way to a job interview. But she sounded genuinely pleased to hear from me, and I managed to find out that she wasn't seeing anyone special, which seemed like more than a coincidence.

I decided to buy a Rail Pass—two weeks of unlimited travel for about $150. The Southern Crescent, I noted as I browsed through the Amtrak brochure, ran from New Orleans to Atlanta—and right through Mississippi. I called Feldo in San Francisco and Jerry in North Carolina and told them to expect me. Then I wrote Alice a long, heartfelt letter.

Could it be, I wrote, that both of us were still unattached because we were the missing pieces to each other's puzzles? Couldn't we try, as adults, to build on what we'd felt as kids? I told her I was planning to travel through Mississippi on my way to Atlanta, and that I would jump the train and find my way to her if she would only say the word. Her reply came about a week later.

It was the gentlest letting-down I'd ever had, and as I reread it again and again, touched by her kindness and intelligence, the old feelings started bubbling up. She'd been careful not to give her impulsive ex-beau too much encouragement, but she said she loved me like a brother, and I knew brotherly love could sometimes be changed to the kind I was looking for.

In another part of her letter she told me she was taking a teaching job in Kosciusko, Mississippi, where she would try to introduce high-schoolers to the wonders of English literature. I had to smile at the idea of adolescent boys trying to focus on Shakespeare with Miss DeCell standing before them. But the important thing was, she would be on her own in a matter of days.

Before I left, I called Alice at her new home and asked her to reconsider. "I just want to see you again," I said, the words tumbling out. "It's been six years since the last time, and who knows how long it will be after this? I'm just asking for an hour or two with you. It would be the high point of the whole trip for me."

She paused, and something in that pause sank my hopes. Then she said she wanted me to know that although there would always be a special place in her heart for me, a visit wouldn't be a good idea. "We just weren't meant for each other, Jeff. And there's no sense trying to ignore that."

I argued for a while, but I didn't have the stomach to go toe to toe with Alice's practical side. And this time, I couldn't imagine showing up at her door uninvited. I hung up and resolved to put her out of my mind. A few weeks later, though, as I clattered through Mississippi on the Southern Crescent and wondered what it might have been like to see Alice again, regret settled over me like a cloud.

·   ·   ·

"Just picture Fred in that chair, Durst, rocking on his front porch with his kids in his lap. And every time he rocks back and forth, he'll think of . . ." Vin stopped in midsentence and I looked up at him. It was my first inkling of disaster. Sweet Petite had come with us to my parents' vacation home in the Adirondacks, and I was stoking the wood stove in the kitchen while Vin held forth on a joyful yet delicate matter: Fred was about to get married, and we needed to find a group gift that would neither embarrass nor bankrupt us. Vin was lobbying hard for a rocking chair.

As I watched, his smile faded, and he blinked once or twice. He looked anxious and confused for half a minute. Then he closed his eyes, slowly shook his head and said: " 'Scuse me, folks. That just happens sometimes."

I was too shocked to respond, and as his rocking-chair spiel gradually regained momentum I watched him closely, looking for clues. But there were none—he just went back to being his funny, utterly charming self. Later that day, while Vin and Petite chatted, I brooded, remembering the blackout I'd seen months before in Brookline.

I had been concerned about him during that Boston visit, but now I felt something like panic. Later that night, lying next to Petite in bed, I was still dazed from what I'd seen earlier that day and what it might mean. I hadn't tried to explain my feelings about Vin to her, but I think she understood them all the same, because that night she invited me into her arms and gave me a gift of pure amnesia and release.

Soon after that, Petite got tired of waiting for me to realize what a fine woman she was and left me. But I'll never forget her exquisitely kind, loving gesture.

Vin's situation caught up with me again a week or two before Thanksgiving as I sat in the sunny living room of Jerry's apartment in Chapel Hill. He'd gone there to work as a lab technician while his lady, Elizabeth, got an advanced degree in psychology. The phone rang, and Elizabeth and I kept chatting as Jerry got up to answer it. When he came back, he looked stricken.

"That was Fred," he said, turning to stare out the window. "Vin's in the hospital with a brain tumor, and the Vito family wants us to meet them in Boston."

Within twenty-four hours we were all together at Beth Israel Hospital, where we found out that a new diagnostic tool, just installed at the hospital—the CAT scan—had turned up a many-tendriled mass the size of a lemon. Vin was under heavy sedation, so we left the hospital to join his family at the home of Mark and Anne Berman, old friends who had offered their house as an operations center.

Fred, who was finishing medical school at Brown, was acting as liaison with the medical establishment. After talking on the phone with Vin's doctors, he broke the grim news at the Bermans' kitchen table.

"There's really nothing that can be done for Vin because the tumor is pretty advanced . . . and because its star shape basically makes it inoperable," he said in an even, steady voice. "Radiation might slow the tumor's progress," he added, "but Vin's suffering will probably be unbearable. So the best we can hope for, realistically . . . is a speedy end."

Appalled at the script fate had handed him, Fred had spoken the last part very softly. Vin's sister, Dolores, and I had been reassuring each other just before he spoke. We knew Fred had been consulting with Vin's doctors, and we had expected him to give us a plan—which treatment would cure Vin the fastest and how we could help. I saw incomprehension in her eyes as she looked at me.

"What did he say?"

Vin's parents, shutting it all out to preserve their sanity, went on discussing insurance issues, moving Vin to New York, the logistics of fighting a medical siege. Fred closed his eyes. It had cost him tremendously to say his piece, and he wasn't going to repeat it.

"Jeff!" I heard Dolores' voice over the confused murmur as if in a dream. "What did Fred say? Tell me he didn't say what I think he said, Jeff. Tell me!"

Medical science underestimated Vin's sheer vitality. He fought the cancer to a standstill over the next six months, suffering greatly as Fred had predicted. By the end of his radiation treatments he'd lost his hair and so much weight that he looked like a prisoner of war. Perhaps even worse, for someone who had always been so self-directed, was that he found himself the ward of an impersonal medical system. Fighting for your dignity while you fought for your life was, he told me, a deeply humiliating and frustrating experience.

I moved back to my parents' house at the end of 1976 to be near Vin, hitting the bricks to find a job in New York once again and accompanying him to his radiation treatments when I could. All of us old friends chipped in to buy him a guitar that Christmas, and his halting efforts to play it gave us hope.

I was too wrapped up in Vin's crisis to give much thought to my own life, but below the surface, fundamental changes were under way. Gone was the reckless kid who'd invaded Mississippi on the strength of a few forbidden letters and breathless phone calls, and who had left a top college for a rock band and a pretty face. Gone was the young man who had traded a job for a shaky political bet. Even the avid rake was beginning to feel some of the pain he'd left in his path.

Now, late at night, when I needed someone to talk with and ease my anguish and confusion, I had no one. I began to see how young lives start to get old, how the pristine optimism of youth becomes the pained caution of middle age. It finally occurred to me that if I wanted a woman I could depend on, I would have to become dependable myself. And that I could grow old before I found everything I wanted in one package—the package I thought I'd stumbled upon as a boy in 1969.

I found myself calling Teri. She had been close to Vin since college, and she wanted to know all about his situation and help if she could. But while she couldn't do much for Vin, she was able to help me.

She was still working in New York and living with her parents in nearby Rockland County, and she was between beaux just then. She and I found that our nearly three years of separation hadn't dulled our mutual attraction, and the time we spent together—a weekend trip to the eastern tip of Long Island, a jaunt to New England—felt good. No expectations, no debate of the great male-female issues. Just her wonderfully musical laughter, a friendly ear, a warm partner for a cold bed.

I told Teri I was sure Vin would make it, but she heard the truth: I'd been shaken to the core. She let me spout off about beating back the tumor through willpower and all the things I desperately needed to believe. As always, her beauty and steady support were balms for my eyes and soul.

She, too, was beginning to tire of the single life, but she had her own agenda, and it didn't involve marriage. She told me she was planning to apply to library school for admission in the fall. I told her I had no plans beyond helping Vin cope and finding a job, and there matters stood between us as the new year commenced.

going to the wall

I stumbled into London jet-lagged and conflicted, with fever and a cold. The next two days passed in a fog of air pollution and cold medications, and it wasn't until we boarded the train, headed for the ferry to Paris, that I got a grip on reality.

I was six thousand miles from home, with a man who was determined to join a Communist revolution, heading for a virtual Third World country where I couldn't speak the language. For the first time I encountered bottled water, and the consequences of not drinking it; croissants, and the derisive laughter of French waiters when I tried in stilted Mississippi/French to order; and a continent where left-wing politics were taken seriously.

All of a sudden Bill wasn't an anomaly. Now he was one of the guys, attended by laughing, back-slapping cronies who joined him in emotional renditions of "The International." I found myself increasingly isolated, sitting in corners of dark bars, sipping warm German beers and smiling politely at enthusiastically delivered bombast in languages I couldn't comprehend.

On the boat across the English Channel, Bill met a Frenchman named Tony who was walking around with a tattered copy of *Portugal and the Future*. Written by the Portuguese colonial war hero Antonio de Spinola, it had largely triggered the 1974 Revolution of the Carnations, which overthrew the remnants of Antonio de Oliveira Salazar's thirty-six-year dictatorship and replaced it with a Marxist-oriented regime. To be heading into a country that had recently embraced Marxism—though by 1978 it was already moving to the political center—caused Bill to ooze revolutionary zeal.

He came running up to me, a willing Tony in tow, almost orgasmic at having found a human being of like mind. He and Tony threw back beers and chain-smoked filterless Camels, dissecting the finer points of the Portuguese political situation. Their conversation was a mishmash of French, English and Portuguese with a little Italian thrown in when needed. I caught only one phrase, delivered by Tony with grandiose hand gestures. "You steek weeth me, *mon ami*. You and Madame weel see the rottink—how you say—under stomick of ze continent."

. . .

The day we left Paris on the train for Lisbon was the first time I became aware of the new shape time was taking. There were no more arbitrary schedules. I began to address each mental, emotional, physical and spiritual need as it arose. No one in this place knew of me or my people. They had no expectations of me—how I would fit in, what I would contribute. I was culturally and socially nonexistent. The vacuum swept through my brain like a fever. It was like being born again to emerge naked into a world not your own. Each minute was stuffed with learning.

I left our first-class cabin and walked the length of the train. Though Bill and I had eaten in the luxuriously appointed dining car, I saw that most of our traveling companions had brought their own food. Mounds of chicken bones and orange peels nested at the heart of each gathering of four or five people. Large bottles of homemade wine were passed from hand to hand, mouth to mouth, and bread crumbs clung to the dense black beards and mustaches of the men. Their hands were hard and callused, the cuticles torn and black as though they dug in the soil daily. Yet their eyes were as sparkling and bright as those of their dark-headed children.

I strolled past the entire gamut of conversational possibilities: men standing and pointing fingers at each other, hotly contesting some concept or other; women comparing lace tatting, running olive-skinned fingers over delicate patterns of ivory and white, the result of years of patient work; children pestering parents for sweets; husbands and wives discussing travel plans.

It wrenched my heart, and I felt suddenly alone. When I got to our hotel that night, I began a letter to Randy, one of many I wrote him in those first days abroad.

> *My Dear Randy,*
> *This is an experience for artists and romantics. There isn't a single tourist marker. No guards, no hours, no admission charges. Old fortresses and churches—slowly decaying and defiant with age—moving toward their destinies unhampered, unretouched. Sheep and cats and dogs wander through them. They sit on cliffs where everything can be seen: the ocean, the town, the bay, Lisbon, tops of other mountains. And you can live within their shadows for $300 a month, like a king.*

I tried to lose myself in a culture I found to be mysterious, intriguing and beautiful. But I was shocked to discover that I was capable of such a profound and stimulating journey with a man I no longer loved. Though I had hoped that Bill and I could restart our marriage once we were alone, it wasn't happening.

I admired his facility with languages and easy ways with people, but a chasm of grief and loss had opened in my heart that was so vast I sometimes gasped with the pain of it. Whatever it is in human beings that recognizes a mate, that brings you to realize a partner for life, I had realized it with Randy. I knew him beyond the eleven months we had spent in companionable industry in Jackson. It was like entering a strange house and discovering that every key in your pocket fits every lock in it. With Bill, even after six years, I was sometimes a lock-pick, forcing my way into chambers that were foreign to me. And he seemed to have no access to me at all.

Just before Christmas we moved into an apartment outside of a small beachfront village named Sesimbra. It was luxurious compared to its neighbors, a ring of low-lying, stuccoed cinder-block homes sprinkled along a dirt road that ran from a precipitous cliff to a small fishing lagoon. Everyone in the little settlement—if you can call a five-hundred-year-old collection of dwellings a settlement—kept pigs, chickens and rabbits. Each family had a stone washtub on legs, pulled in close next to the neighbors', where the women, always dressed in black, gathered once or twice a week to beat the laundry into submission, lathering the clothes with lye soap, rinsing them and hanging them under the eaves to dry.

The temperature was in the low forties, not that cold, but there was no heat and nothing ever really got dry. Moisture stood on our beautiful hardwood floors, glowing with wax and years of meticulous housekeeping, and beads of water ran down the white plaster walls. Our bed was heaped with goatskin blankets, and the landlord kept stopping by with more. That seemed to be all anyone could offer, but it wasn't enough. We stood the miserable conditions as long as we could, then Bill and I embarked on a holiday from our new life, heading south by train toward the warmth and sunlight of northern Africa.

January 6, 1979

Algeciras, Spain
Dearest Randy,
We started another journey four days ago, looking for some sun and dry weather and haven't found either one yet. So we are going on to Africa, continuing south until we feel warm again.
Later the same day:
The boat didn't sail because of a typhoon, so we're staying here one more night. We are booked into a real dive—the only

*thing available—with a Dutch diplomat, Bryan, and his
daughter, Leslie, who is 14. We had a wonderful meal with
them, but when we got back to the hotel, all the windows
were blown out of Bill's and my room. We tried to sleep in the
bathtub, then gave up. It was freezing!*

*So I went for a walk with Leslie. The wind roared around
us, pushing us forward, then whooshing from the front, almost holding us stock still in its grasp. Roofs were flying off,
signs collapsing, windows breaking. We started screaming,
hooting with sheer joy—not 14 or 27, just ALIVE.*

*People crossing, traveling, meeting here and there. I am
ecstatic tonight to feel so good.*

The Ville de France, a grand hotel in Tangier, was perched high on top of a
hill, surrounded by graceful palms and looking out over the Mediter-
ranean. As we walked into its wondrous tiled entrance and stood by the
crystal clear pool in the center of the lobby, I whispered to Bryan, "I don't
think we can afford this." But he just smiled.

"Wait here."

In a minute he returned with a room key and handed it to Bill. "It's all
taken care of," he said.

"Far out," Bill answered.

Our room seemed like a palace to me. It had high ceilings and a bathtub that was over six feet long with sparkling gold faucets. The towels were
as large as a bedspread. As I let my cares drift into the steam of the first
hot bath I'd had in weeks, Bill stuck his head around the door.

"All I need now is a little hashish. I think I'll go out."

"Bill, that's crazy," I wailed. "Bryan told me they have very harsh drug
laws in Morocco."

"But the hashish is supposed to be incredible," he countered. In a
minute I heard him leave. I began lecturing myself, determined that if he
got arrested, I wouldn't waste my life trying to extricate him from a Moroccan jail. From what I had already seen of Tangier, with its shrouded
women and tightly controlled oligarchy, the thought of Bill haphazardly
approaching people on the teeming streets looking for drugs made me
shudder. After bathing, I lay in bed, curled around a Balzac novel and the
knot in my stomach, hardly seeing the words. He came back around midnight with a chunk of hash as big as a brick, and a tale of being led
through dark, winding alleyways.

For three days, Bill and Leslie shared his hashish, and I saw the sights
with Bryan. He was a charming, handsome man, who listened politely
when I poured out my tale of woe. Then, as though something had just oc-

curred to him, he asked me, "Should I worry about leaving my daughter with your husband?"

It took me aback, but I wasn't worried about anything sexual happening. Bill was a basically decent man. Then it began to dawn that drugs might fall under the category of something worrisome to a parent, especially a diplomat. Bryan watched my face as I thought these things, and all I had to say was, "Hashish?" to make him bolt from the Kasbah. When I got back to the hotel, the manager met me at the door and told me our "reservations" had expired.

I called and found out we could leave immediately on the evening ferry. I didn't want to risk running into Bryan again, I was so embarrassed. But while Bill packed our bags, I wrote Bryan a note of thanks and an apology for repaying his kindness so poorly. Then Bill and I walked to the port.

When we came to a large public park, I gratefully dropped my heavy bag and sat down on a bench. "You didn't bring the hashish, did you?"

"Sure I did. They won't search me," he said. "We're Americans."

"Why try it? For what? This is your whole life—and maybe mine— you're talking about risking." Bryan had been with us when we arrived and we had been quickly shown past others whose bags were being searched. There had been drug dogs. Now we were on our own. "Oh no," I said, "what if Bryan's alerted customs?"

This got Bill's attention, too. He walked farther into the park and handed a surprised Moroccan man his stash. "Enjoy. Enjoy. It's on me," Bill said. The man grinned when he peeled back the foil and looked at what he had—over a hundred dollars' worth of hashish, a fortune for a poor Moroccan.

When we got back to Portugal, we found that our apartment—which we had left a mess—was immaculate. Not only were our clothes washed and ironed and put away, the bed was made, the floors were waxed and the walls had been wiped down. It was the same warmhearted kindness Portuguese people had shown us from the beginning, but after what had happened with Bryan, I didn't feel like imposing on the goodwill of strangers any longer. We gave up trying to live like peasants. We were simply powder puffs unable to coexist with the working class we had idolized.

Bill had promised me he would look for work after we spent a few weeks goofing off. But when he was offered a job teaching English at a local school, we discovered the salary wasn't enough to live on without dipping into our savings.

"It's better than nothing, Bill, until you find something else."

"It's exploitation," he raged. "I won't take it."

"But Bill, we only have enough money for a few more months, then we'll have to go home."

"Okay. Let's blow it all."

"What!? What are you talking about? I thought we were trying to make a life here. Are you saying we're just taking an extended vacation, then going back to Mississippi?"

"Well, I'm not working for slave wages."

I was furious. It ended the last of my illusions about our compatibility, and I spent the following weeks watching our nest egg vanish as we tried to live like middle-class Americans instead of the paupers we were.

We rented a modern apartment on the beach with central heat, electric stove and a washing machine. Some days, standing on the sunny roof with our clean sheets flapping around me and the Atlantic Ocean stretching to the shores of the United States, I ached with homesickness. On others I exulted in the beauty of my surroundings. But I was reaching the end of a ten-year journey that had begun with a letter. I was beginning to see that I had gone too far. Then I got another letter that gave me the will to find my way back.

> *Dear Ruth,*
>
> *I just got your letter from London and have already gotten a card from somewhere in Spain (beautiful city). I can't stand not to write you, so I'm mailing this into the void. I hope you get it, but no matter, there will be more.*
>
> *It's unbearable not to be able to talk to you.*
>
> *I love you, Ruth. I always will no matter what happens. A part of me will always be waiting for you to come home. This sounds so desperate but it's the way I feel. I long to be with you.*
>
> *All my love,*
> *Randy*

I had never believed he would say those words, and once I read them, I knew I had to get back to him. But how could I? There was no easy way for Randy, Bill and me to graciously transpose ourselves into more suitable lives. Bill and I had bonded as children, not trying to imagine the people we would become. We had simply melded together and lost our identities in each other. We were Bill-and-Ruth, a third being that would have to be destroyed. And I would have to decide to do it, a decision so difficult it seemed to make my heart stop.

I spent days wandering among the ruins above Sesimbra, trying to fathom what I should do and what I was capable of doing. One afternoon, as I sat with my back against the wall of an old fortification, writing Randy, I finally reached a decision.

January 23, 1979

My Dear Randy,

What a torture it's been, throwing up one mask after another, alternately withdrawing into torpor and exploding into frenetic hysteria, never really saying what I'm thinking to Bill, just fending off, fending off, a look that might reveal too much or a conversation that might hurt too much.

I feel like such a traitor. The choices are maddening.

I know these decisions aren't yours to make, that you can't protect me from the accusations of my own conscience if I don't ultimately make the right choices for the right reasons. But you are the only person I can talk to.

Reading your letters is like diving into fire, just like looking into Bill's hurting eyes. The horrible pain I feel when I see how hard Bill is trying to give me the room I need for growth—I think I'd rather do anything other than hurt him!

But my life with him has been based on so much compromise, made possible by my willingness to yield to his fanatical leanings, political ideals and his not uncaptivating search for adventure. But you have helped me see a peaceful, quiet, potentially constructive life. An artist's life. Observing, piecing together, putting images down, searching with tools of talent and integrity.

I wish I had more humility, a sense of resignation, those traits women have been taught forever. But the recognition of a kindred spirit, a person who can complement, encourage and assist in my most pressing goals—(Isn't that what being in love is?)—that recognition is driving me to a decision. Bill and I lack that enigmatic spark of true affinity for each other's desires.

I put my pen down and watched the sheep that had gathered around me as I silently scratched away, pen to paper. They had taken me for a rock, I'd been hunched over for so long. As I leaned back against the immense and ancient wall, they ran away.

I had made my decision. I was leaving Portugal, alone. A powerful but comforting sadness came over me. I welcomed it. It made me feel better about myself to be unhappy about leaving a man I'd once loved so dearly.

• • •

"Don't go," Bill said.

I watched an American woman, wrapped in a full-length mink coat, purchasing loose topazes from a duty-free shop. My mind skittered away from what I had to do: turn and walk into customs, get on the PanAm flight to Kennedy, leave Bill, end my marriage, go home.

I dragged my eyes back to his face. There was no anger there. It was washed white with sadness and fear. Yet, even on this day, he had stopped during our walk through the airport to purchase a local Socialist newspaper and was sneaking peeks at its headlines as I loaded my bags on a cart. I had never understood that part of him. I knew I never would. "I have to go," I said.

He reached for me and I for him, and we shared a gentle hug, a final kiss.

44. Ruth

fire and ice

Emergency lights flashed along the runway at Kennedy in New York as our jet dropped from snowy skies. I noticed a young mother with two children across the aisle. She had a rosary in her hands. Both children were tight by her side. Could this big plane really land on ice at three hundred miles per hour?

I pulled my seat belt snug and closed my eyes, a fatalistic sense of powerlessness washing over me, and for the first time in years I began to pray, groping for clarity. I waited for the welcome slide into warm, bright places, the feelings of hope I remembered from childhood prayers. But on this day I found myself stumbling blindly toward a dead end. The corners of my mouth drew down in concentration and I clasped my hands together tightly in my lap. It seemed important to get to the bottom of my fear.

At first, all I could think of was *Dear God, keep me safe. Don't let me die now. I want to be happy.* But some internal bully kept taunting me. *You're faithless and selfish. You're taking the easy way out.*

What's wrong with that? I shouted back. *Why can't I have a better life?* Suddenly I found myself praying for Bill; for the end to his aimless, meandering search for meaningfulness; for the beginning of something better for him. The plane forgotten, tears slipped through my closed eyelids and dropped onto my hands.

While we were in Portugal, Bill had become sexually enamored of me. Being suddenly idolized when I wanted to be left alone had confused me at first, but finally it made me sorry for him, for his lateness in having those feelings, for the added pain it would cause him when I was gone. I also relished a certain triumph in having finally seduced the part of him that had brought me so much sadness.

So I prayed for the strength to forgive him, before hurt and anger poisoned all the good things we'd done together. And I recalled that we had been too young at the start, and I should forgive myself, too.

But now I was an adult, much more aware of my own desires. And I was in love with another, caught in a gentle web of loving that was as easy as it was sensual, that was hopeful rather than hopeless. With relief I allowed sweet thoughts of Randy to wash away the bitter gall of a ruined marriage. The praying became almost effortless, a flooding of joy and light into my soul that ended once and for all any doubts I had. The jolt of yearning I felt for Randy in that instant almost unseated me. Or maybe it was just the plane finally touching down, because when I opened my eyes, the other passengers had assumed their workaday facades, jostling to get into the aisles and retrieve luggage, and wondering out loud about delayed connections. I sat still, letting everyone else exit before I did.

I was tired to the bone after over twenty-four hours of traveling, and still thousands of miles from Randy, who I assumed was in Atlanta waiting to meet my flight. When the plane was empty I rallied and got off, hoping to quickly find a phone and get in touch with him.

In the airport people were running frantically from one airline to another, looking for some way out. Rental car counters leased everything they had, then shut down. Lines of people waiting for telephones snaked up and down the corridors. I was an anonymous castaway in a twentieth-century shipwreck.

I stashed everything under some chairs except for Louie, who had been shipped to us in Portugal by Randy. ("You take him," Bill had said when I left, "and every time you look at him you'll think of me.") I put Louie on his leash and we went into the bowels of the airport to find the PanAm administration offices.

The staff there was pleased to see a person with a problem they could solve, and in a few minutes I was on a toll-free line in an empty office with a cup of coffee on the table beside me. I tried paging Randy in the Atlanta airport, which was as chaotic as Kennedy because of a freak Southern ice storm, but never got a response. With some reluctance I finally called his mother, Mary Louise. I had no idea how she would feel about her son's mad rush into treacherous weather to rendezvous with a married woman, but I knew if he was stranded somewhere he would have let her know. Her health was fragile and Randy shared a warm bond with her.

She was delighted to hear from me. "I just got off the phone with him," Mary Louise said. "He couldn't make it to the airport so he checked into a motel outside of Atlanta. Do you want the number?"

Gratefully I scrawled it onto a notepad. Then she said, "I'm glad you came back to him. He's missed you."

It was hard to talk over the lump that came up in my throat, knowing she had just given us her blessing. But I spent a few more minutes with her, hearing the latest Yazoo gossip and catching up on news about people who had once seemed hopelessly boring, but whose lives now represented the very height of peace and contentment to me.

Then I called Randy. We talked for hours, a verbal gusher of relief and joy that we no longer had to rely on letters that took ten days, or phone calls that cost hundreds of dollars and had to be planned days in advance.

"We're not together yet," he said, "but we're a lot closer tonight than we were last night."

One part of me couldn't believe he awaited me so eagerly. After all, I had married the first man I'd ever dated steadily, and before that every romantic encounter had been painfully short-lived. I wasn't accustomed to men being accommodating and tenacious. And Randy's land journey with his dog, Kenya, had been no less harrowing than mine in the skies—fourteen hours of treacherous driving through snow and ice while hapless Southern drivers spun into oblivion all around him. But he'd made it, and would keep waiting in Atlanta for me.

At the end of the call I didn't know what to say. "I love you" felt premature, and also inadequate to describe what had brought me winging across the Atlantic, leaving a husband in my wake. I finally tried to end the call by saying, "See you soon."

But Randy wouldn't let me go with that. "Uh-oh. I think a wall just went up. What scared you?"

"What do you want me to say?" I parried.

He grew silent. I knew he was as afraid as I of what we had set in motion, of this force in our lives that seemed stronger than both of us and that was already changing what we called reality. (I had foolishly believed "reality" was an immutable thing.)

I fell back on one of our standard lines. "I love you more than any man in this room, except maybe Louie."

"That much, huh?"

"Even more than Louie."

"That's a lot," Randy said, his voice husky.

I left the little office around 4 A.M. and heard that the weather would keep us earthbound at least two more days. But PanAm was going to bus its stranded patrons to hotels in the morning and foot all the bills. As thoughts of room service and American food began making my mouth water, it dawned on me for the first time that I was back in my own country, a penniless prodigal, but eager to be repatriated with all the rights and privileges I could lay claim to.

What would Jeff say, I wondered, *if he knew I'm finally embracing the laissez-faire American Dream?* But the thought of Jeff filled me with sadness. It had been so long since we'd been in touch.

While the night dragged into morning, I began an internal housecleaning—throwing out the detritus of wrongheadedness and poor judgment I feared had marred my life thus far, and emerging with a powerful emotional icon: the struggle for rootedness that Mike McCourt had urged me to pursue.

With Louie trotting beside me, I went on a quest through the airport, searching for the corridor, the door, the gate where Alice and I had taken leave of our New York loves. I wandered for hours, despairing once or twice of having enough recall of that day to accurately identify the location. But suddenly, clued by early-morning sunlight slanting through plate glass just as it had ten years before, I knew I had found it. I let pieces of remembrance fall into place and reattach themselves to the physical evidence of their occurrence; then I sat down, overwhelmed by the remembering.

Four teenagers had stood here considering the merits of impetuous marriage. But they had finally parted, displaced forever into their separate lives. Yet Mike's words to me later, his deftly aimed wounding of my heart, still reverberated. "Our roots are too deep, and too different."

Since then I had tried by every means I could to obliterate my roots, but instead they had grown deeper. All the years of lost wandering among city dwellers and radical politics, when my own heart knew the complicated soul of the tortured South with an insider's sure understanding, had brought me back to this spot. In spite of the violence and hatred and ignorance that had made Mississippi the most reviled state in the Union, I would return to it for good, because it was, after all, the only place to which I had ever belonged. This time I would look squarely at it, the despicable parts as well as the uplifting ones, and take responsibility where I could.

I realized a simple but stunning truth. Everything that had happened in this corridor in 1969 had been for the best. A romance with an impassioned young man had been sweet ephemera, leaving behind it only the hard task of being true to my beginnings.

But what of the friendship Jeff and I had shared? He had barged his way into my youth, in the barest last moments of innocence, and had taken firm root there as we shared the mysteries of our different worlds— children playing with fire, not knowing it could burn as well as enlighten.

I had his letters in my suitcase, where they had traveled with me from Mississippi to Portugal, and now back. Why had I brought them? Why had I guarded and kept them with me through all these years of our silence?

I looked at the runway, seeing again the two boys, Jeff and Mike, running onto the tarmac in a bolt of despair. Now it was covered in snow and ice. Then it had been shimmering with heat. I could feel the memory of that time carrying me back into possession of an intangible but profound friendship.

After a lot of food and a little sleep in my luxurious hotel room that afternoon, I called my mother to tell her I was back in the United States and had left Bill. She was living alone in the big house. But it was not a lonely life for her. Since the divorce, she had blossomed, taking trips with friends to Europe, visiting my sister Patty in Dallas, supervising Margie's college career and making canny picks in the stock market. Her love of golf and card games kept her busy when she was home, and it seemed one or the other of her children was always turning up.

That day she said what I needed and expected to hear: "Come home." Her great gift to her children is that she is always there, unconditionally, regardless of our failings, our wanderings, our imperfections. The house on Jackson Avenue, with its friendly ghosts and my sweet mother, has always sheltered love and acceptance.

I waited alone in the Atlanta airport. Where was Randy?

The flight had been uneventful, but interminable. Now my thoughts fluttered hither and yon, out of control, blithering into each other in disarray. *What am I doing? Has Randy gotten cold feet? Where is he?*

I'd talked to him that morning for over an hour, and he had been excited and affectionate.

Yes, but what will he think of me after so many months apart? Maybe he had idealized me into something more than the tall, slightly pretty woman I really was. Slightly pretty? *No,* I corrected myself, *I'm closer to barely pretty. Or just attractive. Not pretty at all. Just intelligent with nice eyes. Passable, maybe, on a good day.*

Nervously, I tugged at my clothes, trying to smooth out the wrinkles. I thought I was tastefully dressed, in a black blazer with a white blouse and jeans. And my hair was okay. Like Jo March in *Little Women,* I'd always had good hair. At least there was that.

I scanned the hurrying travelers, watching for his blond curls. I remembered the feel of his face beneath my fingers. The fluid play of muscle along his strong jaw. The amazing texture of his skin, which was like butter. And the strong, warm grip of his beautiful hands.

"Handsome," Randy had corrected me when I first commented on the beauty of them. "A man has handsome hands."

"Then they're beautifully handsome," I'd said, holding one of them up to the light. It was finely sculpted, but hard and translucent like marble.

More than anything, I had dreamed of Randy's hands while I slept so far from him in Portugal. His hands that could passionately hone details of color, shape and line in a painting, or gently comb my hair into a more becoming style.

The crowd was so thick around me that all I could see were feet. Then I glimpsed his brown boot, the one with the toe he had repaired himself using epoxy, and caught a glimpse of the blue-gray shirt that he had traded a painting for in Tennessee. His slow approach, a dance of neck craning and delicate side-stepping across the flow of traffic, seemed lovely to me. It appeared he was being drawn to my exact spot, and would not, no matter what, be able to avoid running right into me before he saw me. I reached over and took his hand. It tightened on mine and he pulled me up to him for a sweetly urgent kiss, tinged with laughter and tears. The yearning heartache, the longing and fear of months apart, ended with that simple kiss.

We stood in the bustling crowd, forcing it to separate around us, and held each other, in an embrace that has never cooled. Even after two decades we return to each other's arms with utter pleasure and assurance. That loving embrace is our emotional home, and when we are apart I feel orphaned.

"You look gorgeous," he said when we finally turned to leave the terminal.

Returning home was more complicated, and much different, than I expected.

Randy and I discovered that combining two adult lives was a long, delicate task of simultaneously nurturing our newfound love and building a framework for it to thrive in. He wanted to go back to the mountains. I clung to my roots. There was the problem of privacy for his painting and my need to heal. Finally, I rented a house in Jackson and he remained in his home in the country. We made weekly three-day excursions into each other's lives, slowly weaving the loose ends together. But it was almost five years before we finally married.

What I had thought would be the hardest problem of all, finding work, was solved within days of my return. The Mississippi Museum of Art's director, Jim Czarniecki, asked me to design a catalog for the USA International Ballet Competition, which is held in Jackson every four years. Though I was at first disappointed that he didn't offer me my old job back, it turned out to be a lucky break that brought me into contact with the great (Mikhail Baryshnikov and Robert Joffrey) and the not-so-great (Cliff Finch, then governor of Mississippi, who would one day announce his run for the presidency to the press while bathing in a heart-shaped tub in Las Vegas). And it was the beginning of the advertising agency Randy and I would grow together, Williams & Williams.

I woke up one day in the fall of 1980 to discover that the tangle of my life had pretty much sorted itself out. But something was still missing. When I opened my closet door, it struck me what it was: A box of Jeff's letters, yellowed with age and ragged from their travels, fell onto my head. I sat right down on the floor and began reading them, crying and laughing at first, then falling silent, pondering the people we had been. A few hours later, I picked up the phone.

I called the Merrick operator and was depressed to learn there was no listing for Durstewitz. And the other names—Feldman, Greenfield, Cohen—were impossible. There must have been hundreds of listings for each.

In the last letter I'd had from him, in 1974, he had just moved back to Oswego, so I began checking listings in cities in upstate New York. I found a Jeff Durstewitz in Buffalo. I carefully wrote the number on a pad and stared at it. It had taken only ten minutes to locate him.

I went for a walk. Drank a cup of coffee. What would I say to him? Then I sat down and dialed the number. *It's early evening,* I was thinking. *If this is his number he might not be home from work yet.* But before I could complete the thought, I heard: "Hell-o."

The voice. The deep, intelligent voice. The slightly impatient overtone, as if his mind was skipping on to things more important than a phone call. "Jeff?" I said. But I knew it was him.

"Wha—" a silence, a brief pause. "Ruth?"

"Yes, Jeffrey, this is Ruth Tuttle."

"I was just thinking about you—" he blurted out.

"You're lying," I laughed.

lost

and

found

45.   *Jeff*

contact

I was feeling a touch of the late-summer blues as I sat on my second-story porch in Buffalo and surveyed my meandering life. It was a cloudy day, but not cold or even cool. Still, something—perhaps the faded quality of the afternoon light—betrayed the coming of fall. The leaves on the elm in front of my house were yellowing, and I was facing another winter alone.

Loneliness had become my main companion since Teri had moved out, over a year and a half earlier, to establish a separate life in Pennsylvania. Her going had been as much my choice as hers; I knew I could have stopped her just by saying "Stay with me." But I hadn't said it, and one day a moving van had appeared at our door. We still visited regularly, but I missed her and feared I would lose her completely someday.

That thought took me naturally to Ruth, the great mystery of my life. I hadn't heard from her in almost seven years, but I couldn't forget her. Was she lost to me forever? Were she and her mad husband still trying to fix the world with the wrong tools, or had reality finally caught up with them? Just then the phone jangled me back to the present, and I reluctantly rose to answer it. Hearing Ruth's voice at that moment was as much a miracle as anything I've ever experienced.

At first I simply let the warm, unhurried tones of the South wash over me, a healing balm. It took a while to accept that it really was Ruth, my sister of the soul, and not just a gentle-voiced impostor. But who was the real Ruth now?

As we talked on and the picture became clearer, my initial reserve began to melt. It was the old Ruth who'd finally reached out of the abyss of time to take my hand once again, the Ruth I'd sorely missed. She told me of how she and Bill had come to a parting of the ways, and although I felt no rancor toward him, I was glad to hear that she would never again allow his obsessions to run her life.

Of course she'd changed in other ways, as I had. We were no longer cocky twenty-three-year-olds just beginning the adventure of adulthood. Now, with a lot of "sadder but wiser" under our belts, we were somewhat battered young adults warily eyeing the creeping approach of middle age.

She asked me about Kate, and I told her we had parted long ago and that I had returned eventually to Teri, but we had not been able to work out terms of a permanent union. I believed we loved each other, I told Ruth. But Teri was an intensely private person who didn't easily share her feelings. It seemed there was something missing, something that kept us both from going all out to make the relationship work. I said I didn't want to settle down without being sure we were doing the right thing for both of us.

Ruth, who'd been listening quietly, asked me point-blank: "Jeff, are you still dreaming of Alice?" I laughed at that old joke, but the truth was that a part of me still longed for the pure, young love I'd shared with Alice, a love without doubts.

Speaking of Alice brought us to Jerry and Feldo, and then to Vin. I cautioned her that she'd missed a lot of group history over the past seven years, and that some of it wouldn't be fun to hear.

"Don't spare me, Jeff," she said. "I want to hear it all."

I began with Kate's story, then moved on to the failed political campaign and the beginnings of Vin's nightmare. From there, the tale of how she had come to find me in Buffalo that day more or less told itself.

In early 1977 I had finally succeeded in landing a job in New York, helping a publisher on Park Avenue South put out employee newsletters for large corporations. The pay wasn't too bad, and the job would allow me to stay near Vin. But the day after I started, I knew I'd made a terrible mistake. The boss was a neurotic old tyrant, and when he fired me, several months later, it felt like a reprieve. I took my unemployment benefits and ran to the Adirondacks, where Vin joined me for a couple of weeks of swimming, hiking and canoeing.

After he left, I lived on my own in the great north woods for five months, fixing up my parents' old camp and sending résumés to every plausible job listed in *Editor and Publisher*. I loved the mountains, and part of me would have liked to stay there forever. But it was a desperately lonely existence, and I felt that life was passing me by. I needed to get my career—*any* career—back on track.

Blessings in Disguise

Ben and Jerry also were adrift. Ben had lost his job after the state swooped down on Highland Community School in the spring of 1977, putting it out of business with a list of code violations. Never one to dwell on reverses, he called Jerry in North Carolina and asked if he'd like to start a business. "Sure," said Jerry, who was tired of his job as a lab assistant. "What kind of business?"

"How about a pizza parlor?" Ben answered, probably thinking of Merrick's famous Sam & Tony's.

"Great!" said Jerry. "How do you make pizza?"

But they found that used pizza ovens were expensive, while rock-salt ice cream makers were not, so they decided to open an ice cream parlor instead. They set their sights on Saratoga Springs, which Ben knew from his college days, but that meant they'd have to sell something else to tide them through the bitter upstate winters. They decided on crepes, which were popular at the time. A natural chef, Ben honed his cooking skills while Jerry sent for a Penn State ice cream-making course they'd seen advertised on a matchbook cover. The crepes never caught on, but the five-dollar ice cream correspondence course was all they needed.

They took a low-rent apartment on Saratoga Lake during the summer of 1977, and since my parents' camp was only about sixty miles away, I visited them often. The three of us would range far and wide, scouting out used ice cream equipment, looking at menus and prices, getting tips from shop owners.

Whenever I visited, Jerry would tell me to open wide; then he'd stick a gob of their latest ice cream in my face. "Here, Dursht," he'd say, "taste this. I think Ben put too much flavoring in it, but see what you think." And usually the ice cream was very strongly flavored indeed, a legacy of Ben's childhood postnasal drip. His mother had used a powerful nose spray on him, he said, which had wiped out his nasal cilia. Hence the birth of Ben & Jerry's "euphoric" flavors.

They had no money to buy bulk flavorings in those days, so they'd send for free samples. One day, I got a tongue-boggling blast of carob-ginger when I walked in the door. The next time, it was orange-pistachio. This process, with some refinements, went on for years in the gleaming Ben & Jerry's lab in Vermont, where Ben was taster in chief.

They hired a lawyer to negotiate a lease for a downtown Saratoga location, but somehow one of the lawyer's friends ended up with it. Disappointed but undaunted, Ben and Jerry headed for their fallback location: a rundown but soon to be legendary former Mobil station in Burlington, Vermont. They told me later they didn't think the Saratoga storefront would have worked out, because it had no parking spaces. Their move, which seemed like a big setback at the time, turned out to be yet another demonstration of Ben's favorite proposition back then: There were no disasters, only blessings in disguise.

I got a few nibbles from the résumés I sent out that summer, but nothing solid. Feeling increasingly pressed as both the winter and the end of my unemployment checks loomed, I drove to Oswego to see some friends and apply for a job at its daily newspaper, the *Palladium-Times*. The editor said he had no openings, but he told me the *Buffalo News* was hiring. I laughed; given my job history, I felt I had as much chance of getting an offer there as I had of becoming an astronaut.

But Teri, who'd visited once or twice over the summer, was attending library school in Buffalo, so I decided to drive over and see her while applying at the paper. With nothing to lose, I was prepared to chain myself to the *News'* door if necessary.

I spent a day taking tests at the *News*, after which its managing editor, Woody Wardlow, asked me if I'd like to be a copy editor. "Sure," I said. "What's a copy editor?" He hired me anyway. It was an almost unimaginable career coup, and I pinched my thigh black and blue as I drove back to the mountains that night.

Teri and I moved in together after I resettled in Buffalo, but while we were generally happy, we couldn't reach an agreement about our future. At the end of 1979 she accepted a job offer from the library at Penn State in Altoona. I found myself living the swinging singles life once again, but the more I swung, the more single—and solitary—I felt.

Ben and Jerry had asked Vin to join them in the business during the summer of 1977, but he had passed on becoming a partner because of his precarious health. Still, he was more than willing to help them get up and running. They all moved to South Hero Island, Vermont, that fall to prepare for the grand opening of Ben & Jerry's Homemade Ice Cream and Amazing Crepes in nearby Burlington the following spring.

When I visited Burlington in April of 1978, a few weeks before the scheduled debut, I expected to see a gleaming shop all but ready for its first customers. Instead, I found a wreck of a former gas station haunted by three haggard wraiths who, upon closer inspection, turned out to be my friends. I didn't want to laugh out loud when Ben assured me that the store would open in two weeks, but I couldn't help smiling in response to Jerry's sardonic grin over Ben's shoulder.

When I asked the grim, paint-spattered Vin how the project was going, he just rolled his eyes and kept working. They couldn't stop to hang out with me, Ben said, but if I felt like pitching in, I could write them a press release to anounce the opening. Sitting on a waterless john in their half-finished bathroom, I scribbled optimistic phrases but doubted the store would be ready on time. *Maybe by July,* I thought.

They did open on the promised day, though, and the store drew rave reviews and long lines of customers. Even more amazing, given what they knew about running a business, was that it survived.

Vin worked at the store for a while, then left Vermont for a tutoring job in Great Barrington in the Berkshires of western Massachusetts. But it was hard for him to do steady work, because the paralyzing headaches and blackouts continued and his mind would simply shut down when mental or emotional stimuli became too strong. He tried to carve out a normal life for himself, but eventually the tumor became his silent partner, always limiting his options and pulling his strings.

Perhaps his worst experience was the morning he woke up to find a note on his pillow from a woman he'd been living with for several months. She loved him, the note said, but she wanted to have children, and she just didn't feel she could do that with Vin. He told me he understood and had forgiven her, but I knew it had hurt him to his bones.

The day after the Three Mile Island nuclear disaster in 1979, Vin and I were in the Adirondacks and heard on the radio that the authorities were looking for volunteers to help clean up the reactor core. After a loaded silence, he said, "I should go down there."

"What are you talking about?" I nearly shouted. I felt my world start to collapse whenever he seemed ready to give up.

"I don't have much to lose," he blazed back. "At least I could do some good."

"You can beat it, Vin," I told him, reminding him of Kate's recovery. "You can make yourself well, but you've got to believe that and focus all your will on it, or it won't work." That ended his talk of volunteering at Three Mile Island, but I knew he felt that "the BT," as he called his sinister guest, would get him eventually. The real challenge, as he saw it, was to lead a useful life in the interim.

As part of that effort, he had let it be known after his one-year checkup that the tumor was gone. No trace. In fact, it never disappeared, although it did shrink dramatically. But the white lie gave his friends and family reason to hope and gave him some much-needed breathing room.

"So his tumor is gone now?" Ruth asked hopefully. I said yes, and I really believed that.

"That's good," she said, "because I can't imagine how you could cope with losing Vin." When we hung up, I was filled with emotions I hadn't felt in years. I tried to tell her how I felt in a letter:

My Dear Ruth:

Where to begin? I think it's been nearly six years since I began a letter with "My Dear Ruth." When are you coming to visit? I feel we so much need hours and hours together, as much time as it takes to explain ourselves and come to know each other again. And I think there's probably no one else in the world whom I could relax with so fully. But maybe this is all nostalgia. Maybe we'll have a hard time over breakfast, or after the 6:30 news has gone off. But I don't think so. I just wonder if we'll really be recognizable to each other after all this while. I think we will.

. . . I just spoke to Vin and Jerry. They were both amazed I'd heard from you. Vin is fortified with a new negative CAT scan, which means his sword of Damocles has not begun to threaten him again. Jerry is looking for a warm vacation spot for January, so don't be surprised if two sun-starved Yankees turn up on your doorstep.

But this happy plan never came to pass, and within ten months I would realize just how dangerously ill Vin still was, and how lucky I was to have Ruth back in my life.

46. Jeff

he ain't heavy

"The *Bulletin*'s folding, man. The Inky is hiring hundreds of people to grab all the circulation before the suburban dailies get it. Get your ass down here—now!"

The low, raspy voice on the phone belonged to a friend of mine—Ceaser Williams, who had left the *News* a few years earlier and was now, in early 1982, working at the *Philadelphia Inquirer*. I found his summons hard to refuse.

The *Inquirer* had acquired legendary status by that time, racking up a series of Pulitzers and building a reputation as one of the best dailies in the country. Although I had done well at the *News* and was now an assistant chief copy editor, I had no roots in Buffalo. And I was eager to play in journalism's big leagues.

I landed a job on the *Inquirer*'s national copy desk, pulling off a career triumph that many of my peers would have done almost anything for. Yet I found that I wasn't feeling all that triumphant as I prepared to move from Buffalo to Philadelphia that spring. In fact, I was losing sleep over two things: my relationship with Teri and Vin's situation, which was deteriorating rapidly.

The subject of Teri had come up during a memorable visit by Ben, Jerry, Feldo and Vin a few months before. We were sitting around shooting the breeze in my apartment, and I began my old spiel about matrimonial qualms. This was a surefire laugh-getter, given that they'd been hearing it for years and were all living through variations of it themselves. Except Vin. He'd been disqualified from the marriage market, and he saw things with an outsider's clarity.

He cut me off in midstream and picked up a picture I'd taken of Teri. Then he turned to the others and said: "Look at this picture. She's gorgeous! If Durst doesn't make his move, I'm going to." He winked at me and added, sotto voce: "And she's so *huggable,* man. She's the most huggable woman I've ever known."

A few weeks later, still vacillating, I sent him a letter about my ideas for a two-year trial marriage. His reply, written despite the fact that the lethal star in his head had begun its sudden and final resurgence, is still tacked up on my bulletin board:

> *If you have the idea of a loophole, you may not do every-*
> *thing possible in a marriage. I think marriage is a great leap*
> *of faith, but if you're going to get angry at change, forget it.*
> *Change is the meat and potatoes of a deal with another per-*
> *son. And the dessert of love with another person, too.*
> *It's the choices we conscientiously make that are the*
> *really important ones. That's all. They are ours . . . and*
> *ours only.*
> *Take a leap.*

Several months later, on a hot spring day on Long Island, the sweat was beginning to form on my neck and brow as I waited to begin the solemn process that would return Vin to Mother Earth. The gleaming oblong box of hardwood and brass seemed unbearably heavy, and I was torn between a desire to be free of its great weight and my need to hold on, to delay the final parting as long as possible.

Teri and I had driven to Merrick from Philadelphia early that morning in a fog of anguish and denial, and I'd drifted through the proceedings on autopilot, as if I were a character in a bizarre, sunlit nightmare. But the coffin's weight was all too real, and it reminded me that we pallbearers—Ben, Jerry, Fred, Feldo, me and Kevin Mednick, Vin's best friend from Harpur—were waiting for the signal to bring what remained of Vin to the hearse for his last ride. Ronnie Bauch stood off to the side with his fiancée, and I remember thinking that it was too bad coffins didn't have more handles, because Vin had too many close friends for a six-handled box.

The sun beat down, bouncing off the coffin and into my eyes, which glazed over at the prospect of a life without Vin, my unfailing moral compass. The coffin seemed to carry not only his weight but the weight of grief of all who had come to mourn him—his father, mother and sister, who'd been a second family to me; his many uncles, aunts and cousins; the neighbors he'd grown up with in his modest North Merrick neighborhood near the parkway; and Birgit, the love of his life, who'd flown halfway around the world at the news of his death.

We'd all had a lot of time to prepare for this—the tumor had been discovered over five years before. Still, there was shock on every face. The simple fact was, he'd died at thirty-one. Who, even with the help of almighty God, could comprehend it?

As I stood there, aching in every fiber, I thought about the funeral service I'd just endured. It hadn't had much to do with the Vin I'd known, who probably would have preferred philosophy readings and a square dance. Contrary to what the priest said, he had not been one of the faithful, at least in the sense of being a churchgoer. He'd been a communicant long ago, but in later years he'd become skeptical—not of God, but of men who put on robes and announced holy truths like train schedules.

Always trying to get to the heart of matters, he had simply been too curious to be a true believer. He loved to turn things over in that many-chambered mind, approach them from all angles and apply tests of logic and belief until he had winnowed out the truth. It was, he half-believed, what had given him the tumor. "Too much thinking is bad for you, Durst," he'd say with a rueful smile. But even as he said that, we both knew he'd be thinking hard as long as he breathed.

He'd certainly thought about his exit, and he'd left explicit instructions about the parts of the final rites that he thought he could control. Among these was that Durst was to read some words over his bones. But the priest had other ideas. He had told Vin's parents that he alone, as God's representative, would speak at the church and at the grave.

Still, the scene at the funeral home earlier that morning had been pure Vin. The open coffin held his uncannily live-looking husk inside, dressed not in a suit but in jeans, a flannel shirt, turtleneck, sandals and socks. At his instruction, his favorite photos were placed around the coffin—some of which I'd taken, and some of which I was in. And there was his music. In addition to Samuel Barber's *Requiem*, Vin's playlist included a wry Michael Cross tune about a family of undertakers:

> *We earned our riches*
> *putting people in little ditches—*
> *six feet under the ground.*

But Kevin, whose job was to keep the tunes coming during the viewing and who was used to somber Jewish funerals, couldn't bring himself to play that one.

I stood in the sun, fighting back the need to collapse in grief and guilt. I hadn't been with him at the end, and it would take a long time to forgive myself for that. But at least I'd seen him two weeks before, in the terminal ward of Memorial Sloan-Kettering in New York City. He'd told me, in halting speech and by writing on the little pad he used when he couldn't speak, that he was about to blow out of there, no matter what counteroffensives the doctors were planning. I had broken down, because his words made me realize that death wouldn't be put off much longer.

We had hugged each other tightly. With tears streaming down my face, I had begged him to reconsider. "Vin," I said, "you've got to let them do whatever they can for you." But he smiled and gently shook his head. He knew I was pleading for myself, and that I couldn't help it. "Durst," he said slowly, looking directly in my eyes, "I'm ready to check out."

Then he motioned me to listen. On the other side of a white curtain was a middle-aged man dying of bone cancer. I had been shutting out the sounds he was making, but now Vin insisted that I hear them. The man was delirious, pleading with the pain as if it were someone he could reason with. With his voice rising and falling in anguished tremolos, he sounded like a soul in hell, begging and pleading with his tormentor to ease off, have mercy, just let him catch his breath. And he was suffering alone. No nurse, no doctor, no family—just a mortal and his mortally suffering self, praying for all he was worth to die.

I looked back at Vin, who wrote something on his pad. "I don't want to die alone. I want to spend my last days with the people I love." He said he was going to check himself out and go up to Vermont with his sister, Dolores. They'd stay for a while with Ben and Jerry, then head down to his parents' house in Merrick, where I would visit him after I'd gotten settled in my new apartment in Philly.

It was a great plan, even if it didn't work out the way he wanted. After nearly two weeks in Vermont, Vin and Dolores left for Merrick. But at Great Barrington, where he'd lived for the last several years, he went into a spasm so horrific that his sister couldn't recall it later without tears. It had started with a blinding headache, but she'd kept driving because terrible headaches were a condition of his life. But when he started to howl in agony, she looked frantically for an exit. A short while later, in the emergency room of Fairview Hospital in the Berkshires, Vin died, his shade rising into the gentle old mountains he'd loved.

I knew nothing of this as it was happening, but I felt his soul touch me as it left him. It was a sultry day in Philadelphia, and I was idling in my apartment before beginning my afternoon shift at the *Inquirer*. Suddenly I felt a strong urge to go to my desk and write about Vin. Later, I found out from Dolores that this had happened at the exact moment Vin died. As I wrote, I was surprised to see a eulogy taking shape on the paper.

When it was finished, I paused for some comic relief—a letter from Ben and Jerry that had come the day before, asking me if I wanted to buy stock in their now flourishing ice cream company. Ben said he thought it would make a pretty good, though "highly speculative," investment. I was smiling when the phone rang. It was Mr. Vito.

"Vin died this afternoon," he said between sobs. "We didn't get a chance to see him. We didn't get a chance."

· · ·

My great career coup had cost me my chance to be with him at the end, too, but I'd written the words he'd asked me to write, and now, clutching the coffin handle, I was determined to read them.

People in mourning move slowly, as if in physical sympathy with the newly dead, and my suffering right arm grew wearier as we six waited in silence for the stragglers to get into their cars, which would be our signal to proceed. But a horrible question had begun to nag me. Would I be the one to embarrass himself—and everyone else—by losing my grip on the mortal remains of my best friend?

This thing is so damn heavy, Vin, I said to myself. *It's gonna break my arm.* Then the words to a song began to fill my head:

The road is long, with many a winding turn . . .
that leads us to who knows where, who knows where?
But I'm strong—strong enough to carry him . . .
he ain't heavy, he's my brother.

It was a cut from an album Vin had given me for Christmas nine years before, the Persuasions' a cappella classic *Street Corner Symphony*. The luminous gospel harmonies that had turned a pop song into a powerful hymn of love and brotherhood washed over me again and again, giving me strength for this heaviest of loads. It felt like a miracle, but I knew it was just Vin taking care of me as he always had.

Tears formed in my eyes, but I didn't cry. *Got to get through this,* I told myself. Finally the undertaker motioned to us.

Later, I watched in a daze as the coffin was lowered into the ground. Words from a book and a heap of dirt: Was that really all there was to it? I kept scanning the faces on the other side of the grave, looking for him, hoping his eyes would catch mine and tell me what I wanted to believe: The whole thing had been a bad dream.

But if Vin was among us, as I'm sure he was, the almost tangible grief in the air obscured his presence. Slowly the crowd thinned and filtered into cars for the drive back to the Vitos' house. There, Mr. V. had told me, I could read the words on the sheets of paper I'd carefully folded that morning and stuck in my breast pocket.

In a small room with Teri at my side and the somber faces of Vin's close family and friends all around, I tried to sum up the message of his life:

"Vin's passing leaves us a heavy load of grief. But it also leaves us a crucial insight: Human life includes a vast potential for loss, and loss can come as quickly as tomorrow. It is what we do in the months, days and minutes before those losses that counts. Are we wasting time, or are we keeping focus on the infinite importance of each moment as we live it? For the past five years, Vin has been finding the proper course. Now, he has made it clear to us.

"When I last saw him, I was sunk in grief. But he smiled and said, 'Durst, we're so lucky. We're so lucky to have had this time . . . we've been able to learn so much.' "

47. *Ruth*

a gift

I reread Jeff's letter, thinking I had misunderstood something. Vinny couldn't be dead. He had been in remission—"cured," Jeff had said, the last time we spoke.

Why Vin? I asked myself. I still knew so little of life's paring pain as we all step, less and less lively, toward our conclusion. I thought divorce would be the worst tragedy of my life, and Vin's death was my first adult glimpse of other, more inevitable, losses.

But mostly I worried about Jeff. His friends, especially Vin, were the bedrock of his life, and I didn't know what aftershocks might reverberate following Vin's death. So, I wrote back immediately. But three weeks later, I still hadn't heard from him, and I became possessed by a fear, a suspicion, that he needed help.

I called him, but what I heard seemed to be more superficial bravado than substance. We laughed, played word games and caught up on news of our families. When I asked, "How are you doing, you know, about Vin?" he said, "Coping."

It was an unsatisfactory conversation, and I brooded after we hung up, awash in my inexplicable feelings toward this man I knew so well on paper, but with whom I had never had the same comfortable communication in person. I decided to go see him.

Randy and I were engaged at that time, finally living under the same roof three years after I'd come back from Portugal. But Jeff was, for him, no more than the thick envelopes I occasionally pulled from our mailbox and disappeared with for a while. He couldn't understand why I wanted to drive twenty hours, leaving work unfinished and clients adrift, to "check on a friend."

"Can't you call him?"

"I already have, but it didn't help. I've got to go up there." I noticed that Randy looked a little alarmed, so I asked, "Do you want to go with me?"

Relief flooded his face. "Yeah. I do."

We left the next day and drove straight through. By the time we turned into downtown Philadelphia, both of us were suffering from serious sleep deprivation. But we went straight to the basement of the *Philadelphia*

Inquirer—a gloomy, atmospheric place—where Jeff had asked us to meet him. He appeared right away, nervously skipping down the stairs and extending his hand to Randy. Then we hugged as Randy discreetly looked over a bulletin board and walked down the hallway.

In the eight years since we had last seen each other, Jeff had remained thin. Too thin, I thought. And, perhaps due to his erratic nighttime hours, he was also very pale. Gray was beginning to appear in his dark blond hair. When we pulled back, he said, "Still taller than me." I saw the old question in his eyes.

"And you're still shorter than me."

"Yeah, well, I think we need to get to the bottom of that," he laughed. "Maybe tonight."

Randy walked over to us.

"I like 'em tall," he interjected, putting his arm around me and pulling me next to him. I'd never heard him say that before, and I loved it, because I'm taller than Randy, too. Then, referring to an old joke of ours, he said, "But big women sure can eat. Can you join us for a late supper?"

Jeff crossed his arms and a familiar, cunning look came over his face. He looked me up and down like a prize mare. I braced myself. "Puts a strain on your budget, does she?"

"Hey, hey, hey," I chortled. "We've gone far enough with that!" With senses of humor crackling and sparking, we went to eat, though the quality of our pugilistic punning was almost enough to ruin even my appetite.

The next morning, I asked about Vin's funeral. "It was bad," he said, "as you can imagine. I was in shock. I really don't remember much about it." I didn't press him.

During the next two days we bustled hither and yon—touring historic landmarks, cooking in Jeff's tidy kitchen, taking a miserable walk to free his impounded car, even attending a Halloween party at his neighbor's. Our time together began to seem like an agony of chitchat. We never really talked. But I started to realize that something else was happening. Even if Jeff wouldn't let me tidy up his pain as I had foolishly thought I could, he and Randy were becoming friends. It was a gift I had hoped for, but hadn't really expected.

My gentle lover put aside his reserve and brought his guitar from the car, and he and Jeff played a discordant duet, Jeff the incorrigible rock 'n' roller and Randy the Muddy Waters bluesman. My ears ached with the awful sound of it. But with their two heads bent close together over their instruments, they looked entirely harmonious.

Before we left the next morning, Randy snapped a picture of Jeff and me sitting at his kitchen table with our arms around each other. He was dressed for work and I was still in my bathrobe. We were laughing. I sent a copy to Jeff a few months later, and he wrote an uncharacteristic response:

Well, I was raht puhleeused (how's my drawl? It's tough to raht a drawl, you know) to get that picture, although it made me wish I'd had the presence of mind to get into a bathrobe myself, so that it would at least look like I'd been intimate with such a chestnut-haired beauty. (Best not let Randy read that last part.)

I quickly hid the letter. The budding friendship between Randy and Jeff was too precious to risk over a misunderstanding.

48. *Jeff*

a big break

I nearly plowed into two other drivers as I navigated the dense traffic up and down South Burlington's main drag in search of the Ben & Jerry's Ice Cream plant. I had the address, and I knew I was in the right place, but nothing leaped out at me from the faceless commercial/light industrial strip.

Finally, after driving by it several times, I found the ice cream mecca wedged into the side of a truck-repair depot. It was the summer of 1982, and I was on vacation. Jerry had taken a sabbatical to Arizona, and Ben was off-site when I arrived. His office manager rummaged among the steep canyons of stuff on his desk to find a phone number where I could reach him.

"Chief!" I yelled over the plant noise when he answered. "How's it going?"

"UGH!" he yelled back. "Go-um hairy, Tribe. You see-um article?"

"What article?"

"The one in *Time* magazine."

"What? You mean . . . ?"

"Yeah!" Ben yelled. "We got some nice exposure."

Following his instructions, I found the "nice exposure" under a pile of papers. The cover story began with these words: "What you must understand at the outset is that Ben & Jerry's Homemade, of Burlington, Vermont, makes the best ice cream in the world."

"Ben," I stammered, "this is incredible. Do you know how many people read *Time*? Millions!"

"Yeah, it's a lot. The phone's been ringing like crazy since it came out."

Later, over dinner, he told me he'd received a call from some guy who'd then flown to Burlington in his own plane to see him.

"Really? Who was it?"

"I forget his name," Ben said. "John something. John Bron, Bron . . . Bron something."

I racked my brain. "Bronfman, Ben? John Bronfman?" I couldn't believe it: Ben had been dealing with a Seagrams heir.

"Yeah!" Seeing my reaction, he added: "What, is he some kind of a big guy?"

. . .

One day in late 1982 I caught an error in a *Washington Post* wire story that I was editing for the *Inquirer*'s Sunday edition, and its grateful big-name writer urged me to apply for a job at the *Post*. I felt flattered, and I toyed with the idea of trying to climb higher on journalism's totem pole. But I wasn't happy in Philly, and I knew I wasn't likely to be happy in Washington, either.

On one level, I was proud of myself for having made it at the *Inquirer*: I was working at the top of my profession, and the end product was among the best papers in the country. But my graveyard schedule was atrocious, the peer competition fierce—I was one of sixty-seven copy editors—and I wasn't enjoying big-city life.

I also couldn't stop thinking about the message of Vin's life and early death: You can't know how much time you have left, so it's foolish to waste time being unhappy. And after five years of writing headlines, which has more in common with the jeweler's art than the writer's, and of polishing other people's prose, I was ready for a change. I also had found that the simple act of heading north—to the Adirondacks and the Saratoga area, where my family had settled after leaving Long Island—lifted my spirits.

I was tossing and turning one night—the insane work schedule had syncopated my circadian rhythms—when a wild idea hit me. I had heard from my brother, Jim, that Ben & Jerry's Homemade was looking for a franchisee in Saratoga, and I knew that Jim was looking for a way out of a dead-end retailing job. I sat bolt upright in bed, turned on the light, and called Ben. It was about three in the morning, but this idea wouldn't wait.

On July 1, 1983, my brother and I—exhausted from two nonstop months of turning a dilapidated gas station into a sparkling ice cream parlor under Ben's firm direction—were serving our first customers in Saratoga Springs. Not wanting to take any chances that our soda fountain wouldn't be ready on the big day, Ben had plumbed it in himself. Jerry had manhandled the planter boxes, made from railroad ties, into position. There were still huge piles of sand and debris in front of the building the day before the grand opening, but they were gone by the time we started scooping. There were lines out the door from day one.

That first summer was half exhilaration, as the store became a tourist attraction, and half nightmare, as one problem after another threatened a literal meltdown. Once, when Jerry dropped in to visit, I was so frazzled that I started raving as soon as I saw him. He threw his arms around me in a friendly bear hug until I was quiet. "Dursty, Dursty, Dursty," he crooned, rocking me gently, "it's all right. Don't go crazy, okay?"

Gradually, though, we got a grip on it, and within a few years my income had almost doubled from what I'd been making at the *Inquirer*. Ben hired me in early 1984 to write press releases and marketing copy for Ben & Jerry's on a freelance basis, and I also bought stock in the company. When Ben sent my stock certificate, he enclosed a note to the effect that it just might turn out to be the best investment I had ever made. In fact, holding the stock was like having a money tree in the backyard, and it kept me solvent despite my best efforts to ruin myself over the next few years.

Running a small business—even one involving a fun product like ice cream—can be a horrible grind. You're your own boss, but you're also your own slave. I learned that first summer that I had "retail feet," which meant I couldn't stand for more than a few hours without steady pain. But I had no choice but to stay on my feet for upwards of twelve hours a day.

Then there was the late-summer afternoon when I found myself alone behind the counter facing several dozen customers. I had been scooping like a maniac all day, and my arm simply seized up, leaving my right hand a useless claw for several minutes. I hurriedly massaged the stricken arm with my left hand and asked everyone's patience. They all got their ice cream eventually.

I also found that you can cut yourself on ice cream that's been taken directly from the deep freeze (which can lead to a condition known as "cherry in the vanilla") and that my back hadn't been made for the job of stocking twenty-pound tubs coming off a truck in double time. In 1986, I had the surreal experience of filing a workers' compensation case against myself.

One of the things that made it all worthwhile in the early days, though, was being in on the birth of a much needed, if subversive, innovation: the fun corporation. At my first franchise meeting, in 1984, Ben put on his swami outfit—a sheet wrapped around his substantial girth and a pillowcase piled on his head like a turban—and emerged as Habeeni Ben Coheeni, famous mystic. Jerry donned a pith helmet and safari jacket and explained to the astonished franchisees and suppliers that he had discovered Coheeni in a metabolic trance at the ancient temple of Rishikesh. This trance, he told the hushed crowd, was strong enough to protect him from physical harm.

I'd seen this trick before—they'd done it impromptu at my store one night to the amazement of bystanders who had no idea who they were—but Ben's parents, who were at the meeting, hadn't. As Jerry swung a sledgehammer high above his head and brought it down with a crash, breaking a cinderblock on the naked belly of his blissfully chanting partner, Ben's mother let out a little shriek. But the block had absorbed the blow, and they took bows amid wild cheering.

I strove to capture this exuberance in my press releases. When the company's promotional RV, the Cowmobile, went up in smoke outside of Cleveland one day in an engine fire, I wrote a release that began: "It was kind of like a giant baked Alaska." It was picked up by media all over the country, even in places where they'd never heard of Ben & Jerry's.

By 1987, franchise meetings were much more businesslike, which was understandable—the company had grown exponentially, and the stakes were much higher. But a tone of high seriousness bordering on religious fervor had crept into the proceedings, and a dialectical transition away from Groucho Marx and toward Karl seemed to have begun. Ben had noticed that the world needed saving, and it was very hard to imagine him as Habeeni Ben Coheeni anymore.

I had hardly had a chance to catch my breath in the first four years, but now I found myself thinking more and more of returning to journalism. The thrill of getting a business up and running was over, and I knew there would come a time when my résumé, even with my stint at the *Inquirer* at the top, wouldn't get me a newspaper job. And although I agreed with Ben's idealistic goals, I wasn't at all sure that his methods made sense.

Savvy Wall Street types had come to the conclusion that Ben was a promotional genius whose social responsibility shtick was nothing more or less than a way to boost sales and the stock price. I knew better—Ben's motives were always humanitarian, even if his initiatives often boiled down to huge publicity coups and little else. By 1988 or so I felt I had to warn him, as his publicist and his friend, that social responsibility could easily become a double-edged sword, because it is the nature of the news business to discover, trumpet—and sometimes invent—contradictions. A "holier-than-thou" company would be held to impossibly high standards.

He tuned me out, which I found very frustrating. To some extent, it was a matter of differing perspectives—Ben's relentlessly close focus to my wide angle. But the irresistible personality that had built an empire out of almost nothing had locked on to something, and he barreled along, constantly looking for ways to tie the profit motive to his own brand of social responsibility. This—not ice cream or merchandising—was his true life's work, and he would boldly take it where no one had gone before. Later, as I feared, he suffered terrible blows in the press. But he was always ready to take the heat for his ideals. And he and Jerry—Vermont's finest and two of the best people I know—were also ready to take it in stride when I found my path diverging from theirs. I stopped writing for Ben & Jerry's in 1989, but we have remained close friends.

I had given up my job at the *Inquirer* thinking that I could start a business with my brother and leave it after a year or two, going off to do my own thing—freelance writing, perhaps, or political commentary—with financial support from the store. But that expectation had been unrealistic, and in the end it would take eight years to break free of the ice cream business.

49. *Ruth*

a family reunion

Jeff and Teri were married in 1985, and I flew to Saratoga Springs for the wedding. Randy, who had wanted to come with me, stayed to finish an ad campaign for a client. Though our business wasn't a Wall Street darling like Ben & Jerry's, it was growing fast. After seven years it was sometimes all we and our four employees could do to keep up with the workload. But I had other things to think about that day. For the first time since my miscarriage, I'd missed a period. I thought I might be pregnant.

As clouds slipped by my window and the large man next to me took more than his fair share of the seat, I seldom looked up from my book, Joseph Chilton Pearce's *Magical Child*. But I took frequent deep breaths to calm the excited fluttering of my heart, which that day was full.

I'd come to think of my early miscarriage as an aberration, though I had often wondered why, in more than ten years, I hadn't gotten pregnant again. But I was still only thirty-four. *Far too young,* I thought, *to worry about my reproductive health.* The happiness of my marriage had perhaps endowed me with a sense of invulnerability.

After Randy and I had wed in 1983, we renovated an old house to live in and another one to work in and had since enjoyed the hectic married life of two artists. It was a life that was often cluttered—we both had so many projects—but that was also energized by the high, thrilling whistle of our passions. By the time the plane landed, I had fully imagined our child, and its innocent acquisition of the world under our inventive guidance. We would be adventurers together. Our child would never know the fear of parents at war with each other, or the hunger of a mind denied what it needed to grow. Then, almost bursting with the richness of my life, I walked briskly from the plane and began to think about why I was there.

I didn't expect to spend much time with Jeff on this trip, the first time I'd seen him since Philadelphia. He was the groom, and I knew he'd be busy. But I hoped to get reacquainted with Jerry and Dave, who would be there, too. And to finally meet the full cast of characters, like Ben and Fred and Ronnie, that Jeff had been telling me about for so long. I drove, too fast, from Albany to Saratoga Springs, and went straight to Jeff and Teri's home, with a bottle of good champagne, their wedding gift, on the seat beside me.

As family and friends washed around us, Jeff and I spent a precious few minutes saying hello, and I was struck by his calmness. After so many years of agonizing, he finally seemed happy in the role of groom. Then I turned to look over the crowd in the living room. Most of the faces I saw were unfamiliar, Teri's relatives or friends of theirs of whom I'd never heard. I introduced myself to her parents, then went to my hotel, knowing I wouldn't see Jerry and Dave until the next day at the wedding.

I was nervous. It was the first time in sixteen years that we four would be together. From Coach Rush's lawn in Yazoo City to Jeff's wedding in Saratoga Springs was a big leap. Would the magic of 1969 return? Or would they recall me only as a tall, gawky girl, too quiet, too intense, long ago dismissed from memory, while I had held them in shining stasis, the gallant Northerners who had pierced the shell of my insulated world?

The next morning I went to the courtyard of the splendid Adelphi Hotel, where the wedding was being held, and found a seat. I waited. I didn't recognize anyone. Then I saw Ben and Jerry hauling a video camera and a tripod down the far side of the room. Jerry looked up and waved, I thought, to me. But in a minute I realized it was to someone behind me.

"Yo, Feldo," Jerry called out, and I turned to see Dave striding down the aisle, resplendent in a black suit with wide pinstripes, a black shirt and a black tie. I had no trouble recognizing him. He was just in from California, but he looked like a wise guy from Little Italy. With his curly black hair and piercing eyes, he was as flamboyant as ever.

He glanced at me when he walked by, and I smiled. "Hi, Dave."

"Hi, ah, Ruth! Hey, Jer, it's Ruth!" Dave yelled across the heads of other guests as he stood on tiptoe and pointed to me, grinning in my chair. Jerry's mouth dropped, and he hurried over. They were amazed that *I* remembered *them*. We exclaimed and hugged for a few minutes, then we all went to our separate places to watch our friend marry his beautiful bride.

Teri swept in on the arm of her father. Her hair was braided into a crown on her head and entwined with baby's breath. She wore what appeared to be a family heirloom, a lace-encrusted wedding gown, but by far the most beautiful thing about her was her smile, which was radiant. I had met her for the first time only the night before, and she had hugged me warmly, saying she had always looked forward to meeting me. I thought Jeff had waited far too long to plight his troth to such a wonderful woman.

During the reception, Jerry, Dave and I relived their visit to Yazoo City—with Ben listening in rapt attention—and I could see the traces of our shared adventure in their faces.

"I tell the story all the time," Dave said, and Jerry nodded in agreement. We were huddled together at a table by the bandstand, and I felt I would never get enough of reminiscing. When the dancing started, I tried to teach Jerry and Dave to waltz, and then we all joined hands and raced around the room with the other guests in a giant spinning circle dance, until everyone in the room collapsed, exhausted.

Later, I sat alone and watched the guys—Dave, Jerry, Jeff, Ben, Fred and Ronnie—musically whaling the somewhat astonished guests with violin, harmonica, kazoos, a jug and vocals. This reprise of their high school group—Grandma's 123-Toed Jug Band—reminded me of the day in Yazoo City when we all dragged Grand, singing the Lovin' Spoonful's "Jug Band Music," I wearing Jerry's knit cap in the front seat of Dave's VW, and Alice draped across Jerry's and Jeff's laps in the back. I found these people still firmly rooted in my heart, right next to my Mississippi ancestors. I felt as though I was staring through a karmic veil at the family I had known in another life and had somehow been flung far away from in this one. When the performance ended, I joined the other guests in hooting and clapping for the band.

Later that day, back at Jeff and Teri's house, I met Vin's parents and Jeff's father for the first time. Then I found myself sitting alone. I realized that although I thought of these wonderful people as a kind of family, I was an enigma to them. No one knew what to make of me. I grew uncomfortably aware that I had offended some of the women, who might have interpreted my joy at seeing their husbands and boyfriends as the designing wiles of a jezebel. In fact, I was in the same quandary Jeff had experienced in Yazoo City. Just as he had stumbled unawares into a tightly knit society of long-standing interpersonal relations—and had been judged a jackanape—so had I at his wedding. He and I were still, after all these years, facing a chasm between our two worlds. When would we succeed in building a bridge?

Our letters had become only an echo of the past. Unless we were able to be part of each other's lives in a real way, I could see that the chasm would finally engulf us. I went over to Jeff, who was smiling quizzically, his feet firmly planted and his arms crossed, while he and Ben engaged in a marketing tug-of-war.

Ben, whose promotional genius never seemed to take a breather, had picked this as the ideal venue for a discussion about a new idea. He leaned over Jeff like a coach conferring strategy to his quarterback.

"A Dog Day in August," I heard. "Ice cream cones free to dogs," Ben rasped in Jeff's ear, his deep voice rising and falling as the plan took shape. But Jeff was dubious.

"They'll be barfing and shitting and fighting all over the front of the store," he protested.

Ben was adamant, and he finally got Jeff to agree. However, a few months later when I asked how the promotion had worked, Jeff admitted

he hadn't done exactly what Ben had wanted. Instead of ice cream he offered free dog biscuits and a donation to the humane society for dog owners who bought a cone for themselves. It was a bust. But Ben's original
concept won a national advertising award that year, and Jeff, maybe as a
penance, wrote the press release announcing it.

When their conversation was over I tapped him on the shoulder, and he
turned to me. I said, "The wedding was lovely. I've got to be going."

"Thanks for coming. I'll write."

We hugged a long time, then he was whisked away.

On my way out, Dave stopped me and asked if I'd like to join him and
the others the next morning for breakfast. "Why don't you call me later
and tell me the details? I'd love to do that." I was talking fast, because I
was desperate to go. I was feeling ill and unsteady. When I got back to my
room, I found out why. I was bleeding heavily.

I spent several hours on the phone with Randy and my doctor in Jackson, who told me to go to the emergency room if I was in pain. But since I
was probably only five or six weeks along, he thought I could wait until I
got home to come in and see him. "It sounds like another spontaneous
abortion," he said. I thought of calling Jeff and Teri to get the name of
Teri's ob-gyn, but couldn't bring myself to intrude on their wedding night.

By morning I hadn't slept and was lying in bed with black spots swimming in front of my eyes, wondering how I was going to be able to drive
myself back to Albany to catch a one o'clock flight. Then the phone rang.
It was Dave. Just hearing his voice—he had grown into a remarkably con-
siderate and sensitive man—made me feel better. I didn't mention my
predicament, except to say I'd had a bad night and I didn't feel like meeting them after all.

"It'd be so nice to have you join us. We haven't had much of a chance
to talk."

I hesitated only a moment before I said, "Well, okay. I'll meet you at
the restaurant in half an hour."

Somehow, I managed to get bathed and dressed and checked out of
the Adelphi. An hour later I walked up to the table where Dave was still
waiting for me with Jerry and Elizabeth, Ben, and Fred and Alalia. Dave
stood up so I could slide into the booth between him and Ben, but before I
was even settled, the rest of the group left in a silent flurry. Fred stayed a
few minutes, then he left, too. Dave looked slightly guilty and Ben sat
silently to my right.

I ordered toast and coffee, and while we waited, Dave told me about
his volunteer work with people who had terminal illnesses. We got into a
rather morose discussion of death, which was foremost in my thoughts
anyway, and suddenly, to my astonishment, I burst into tears. Great waves
of grief swept over me, even as I struggled to contain them, and at one

point both Ben and Dave were holding me up. I sobbed incoherently, and I'm sure they thought I was losing my mind. Other patrons were turning around to see what was going on. After a few minutes I was able to calm down, but they had to half carry, half lead me to the front of the restaurant where I stood, weak-kneed, while Ben paid the bill. Then we went outside. I was amazed to see the rest of the group still there, sitting in Ben's car, waiting for him. *Why did they leave in the first place?* I wondered.

Dave was saying that someone should drive me to the airport. But by then I was overwhelmed with embarrassment, and I made a huge effort to convince him I would be fine. I wanted to be by myself. I leaned into Ben's Saab and hugged Jerry. Everyone else nodded politely. Smiling as warmly as I could, I said it had been a pleasure to meet them. Then I turned to Dave and Ben, who each gave me a kiss. Dismay showed plainly on their faces as I drove off.

I arrived home believing that I had been more of a liability than an asset at Jeff and Teri's wedding. The sense of being an outsider, perhaps even an interloper, rankled. I knew so little of him and his life, and he of mine. But we kept writing, though not as frequently as before.

July 2, 1986

My Dear Ruth:

Yes, it is I, the prodigal correspondent. We both know the bitter truth in our hearts: I am irresponsible.

I realized that to the depths of my soul after hearing from Feldo last weekend. He said he has written to you several times since he saw you at the wedding. Feldman, that most erratic of letter writers: It was too much to bear. So here I am, a hangdog waiting for a whipping. If I've earned unflattering comparison to the Feld as a correspondent, then by God in Heaven I must write. Well, really it was your last letter's fault. Too much to absorb, old friend. Too many insights and revelations. I feel so lucky to have letters from you. I mentioned this feeling to the Feld and he smirked, "Yeah, she gives good letter." (So write ALL your letters to sensitive, appreciative ME.)

August 29, 1986

Dear Jeff,

I hesitate to get caught in the vestiges of male adolescent rivalries—so suffice it to say that you are Number One in the letter department, contingent on continued good behavior.

When I didn't hear from you I was worried that I had

*offended you, or created an uncomfortable situation when I
arrived at your wedding unescorted. Silly me, I said to myself.
I'm an old married lady. But one never knows. We have had
such an unorthodox relationship for so many years that I
thought maybe it had finally become too bizarre for us to continue. It gave me many unhappy hours. But then your letter
came and I finally felt we would be able to go on with our
dialogue. I wrote Dave trying to get a sense of closure on your
wedding. I couldn't believe how emotional the whole experience was for me. Not just the wedding but seeing all of you
together as a group, for the first time since you were in Yazoo.
Meeting this magnificent trio of my youth, in the flesh: they
dance, they talk, they eat, they laugh. It was like something
ghostly—like legends had engulfed me. The distance between
all of us, and the closeness. It schizzed me out, Jeff.*

October 27, 1986

My Dear Ruth:
    *Where to begin, o my Mississippi muse? I think you put
your finger right on it when you said there must be an excess
of emotion between us that gets in the way of prompt correspondence. Remember when we used to dash off four-page
letters several times a week? When I think of those feats of
epistle slinging . . . We must have been possessed, in a sense.
A sublime possession for as long as it lasted and despite (or
maybe because of) how little we understood it . . .*

50. *J e f f*

the 400 blows, part one

I'd been dabbling in stocks since the late seventies, but had never built much of a portfolio except in Ben & Jerry's. But in 1987 my accountant said I should diversify, after the stock had gone public and made me a bundle. I soon began to place larger orders and call amateur fellow equities analyst Ronnie Bauch late at night to confer on this or that hot tip. Gradually, I began to fall into a fatal trap.

While I had started the year as a pure speculator, dashing in and out of stocks to pick up a few bucks, by the middle of that summer I'd begun to notice that every time I sold something, it shot up to new heights. Why, I asked myself, didn't I just buy and hold instead of churning my own account?

At the end of the summer, Ron called and left an oracular message on my answering machine. "Dursht," it said, "the end is near. You hear me? Get out."

I teased him about it a week or so later, at a rollicking meeting of the old boys in New Hampshire: "Come on, Ron, don't be a chickenshit! We just have to be a little more careful with our picks now."

On that October day when the bottom fell out, I was sitting on a fairly large portfolio with relatively little debt against it. The drop was dizzying, sickening, and my stomach tied itself in knots that night as I watched grim TV commentators drawing parallels to 1929.

Teri and I, who were living the blissfully carefree life of DINKs (double income, no kids) at the time, had kept our finances largely separate. This was good in one sense: She hadn't been doing any trading and so had no losses. The downside was that she didn't have much to say when I tried to discuss the situation with her. The disconnect symbolized our relationship then: tandem lives, living in the same house but barely touching when it came to the kind of open communication that is the lifeblood of a good marriage.

On the morning after the crash, I woke up feeling certain about one thing: Fortunes were made at such times by people with the guts to buy rather than sell. So I bought a long list of great stocks. But that day saw what the market pros call a "dead-cat bounce"—a reaction to the crash that merely presaged more to come. On the next day I watched in shock as my new picks fell like stones. The moment of truth came in the form of a "margin call" the next morning. The brokerage wanted a big check to cover the money I'd borrowed to buy the stocks, or it would start selling.

I sat alone in my tiny cell of a home office and tried to think rationally, but after staring at the price notations I'd scribbled on a notepad and going over my options, I kept arriving at the same bleak choices: send the money or sell. Each call to the broker—when I could get through—brought more bad news, and the wisecracking pros I'd been dealing with now sounded slightly panicky. In the end, I folded my hand and sold, locking in big losses. If I had chosen to meet the margin call and keep the portfolio intact, I would have been rich within a year.

At the end of that wild week, amid a crescendo of doomsaying from "told you so" commentators, I tuned in to *Wall Street Week with Louis Rukeyser*. Ron had told me that only chumps watched it, because the picks made by Lou's hot-shot guests always spiked before the show, and because Rukeyser had recently roughed up Ron's technical guru for predicting long-term financial carnage.

I wasn't looking for stock picks or strategy that night, though. I was looking for consolation. And Rukeyser gave it. Life goes on, he said, and the economy wasn't likely to grind to a halt no matter what the "gloom and doomsters" said. If your wife, your kids, your friends loved you before the crash, they still loved you now, no matter how much money you had lost. For the first time in five days, I slept soundly that night.

But the heavy losses had shaken my confidence, and, as I tried to regain my footing over the next month or so, I committed another classic error. Instead of doing nothing, I dived into the "safe" real estate market.

Bain Road

David, our first child, came into the world in June of 1988, but I was so caught up in property and business dealings that I almost didn't notice his arrival. Instead of clearing the decks for the domestic hurricane that is a first baby, I had begun to rehab an old farmhouse I'd bought at the end of 1987. Now, Teri's swollen womb had suddenly yielded up a tiny proto-person with urgent needs and a yowling voice to make them known. Pulled in so many directions at once, I felt myself coming apart at the seams.

But the baby was mild and quiet when I held him for an hour or so on the first night of his life, trying to fathom the unlimited potential in his wide brown eyes and immersing myself in the awe of his birth. Here in my hands, I realized, was the best possible reason to make sure all my ventures came out well. Trying to hold that thought, I headed back into the rat race the next day.

I got a foreshadowing that I'd made a mistake with the farm property a few weeks later when Campbell Black, my old professor friend who'd since become a successful novelist, came to visit. He laughed darkly when he saw the road sign on the way to the old house.

"Bain Road, Durstewitz," he croaked. "Bane, indeed. It'll be the bane of your existence, I'm afraid." He had just been through a money-pit disaster in Arizona, and he said he recognized all the symptoms when he saw the house. But I laughed off his jibes and forged on. By that time, it was too late to turn back anyway.

I had bought the house after making a deal with Jim Post, my old friend and roommate from Oswego. He'd been living at a commune in the Finger Lakes for the last twelve years and was looking to make a new start with his girlfriend, Petra Kanz. They had no money, but he was a highly skilled craftsman, and she was willing to do laborer's work. It seemed they would make perfect partners in the Bain Road venture; I would supply the capital, and they would do most of the work. When it was done, they'd have the beginnings of a nest egg and Teri and I would have a country retreat. That was the plan, at least.

The four of us had scouted out the house in Argyle, a hamlet in the gorgeous rolling dairy country about twenty-five miles northeast of Saratoga, and it actually was a rare find—a time capsule from the mid-1800s except for some "remuddled" rooms. But its antique charm hid some serious problems.

I had bought the property from a slick marketing company that had picked it up for a song from a farmer who was about to go bust. The company had sliced and diced the old farm into parcels specifically designed to separate yuppies with rural yearnings from their eighties gains. I knew of the company's reputation and thought I had protected myself with some hard bargaining. But as soon as the snow melted in March, I hiked up the steep hill behind the house and had a sickening realization: The wooded acreage that had looked so enticing from the road was so vertical as to be almost useless.

And the boundary lines, which I hadn't bothered to walk off, had been generated on a computer from aerial photographs and had nothing to do with natural contours or the old stone fences that crisscrossed the property. The locals derisively called the resulting deep, narrow slices of land "spaghetti strips."

Jim and Petra had agreed to start the work by May 15, but they arrived in Argyle about a month late. This delayed a key element of the plan: turning three rooms of the house into a one-bedroom apartment that they could live in when winter came. It was an easy problem to forget during the sweltering summer of 1988.

Soon after he got started, Jim told me that immediate action was necessary to rebuild the foundation and improve drainage in the back, where the house was slowly settling into a wet area. We had seen that the foundation needed work when we first looked at the house, but it hadn't looked like an emergency situation.

"Can't we do the apartment first," I asked, "and tackle that next year?"

"It really wouldn't make sense," he said patiently. "If we build on a bad foundation, we'll only have to redo it all later, because everything will be thrown off." Even I could see the logic of this, but it would again delay the apartment work.

"Don't worry," laughed Jim, who'd once lived in an old VW bus for months, "we'll be all right." But the lack of running water that winter turned out not to be all right with Petra, who one day, as Jim sat by, hotly accused me of exploiting them.

It was an intensely painful moment, because although I certainly hadn't wanted to see them living in such crude conditions, yet another financial setback had made it impossible for me to afford extra hands to speed the work. I'd gone to my store in Saratoga one day in early April to find a registered letter from the landlord informing me that the lease was up and that he had a buyer for the property. I'd lost track of the renewal date, which had changed since we'd opened, and my brother and I suddenly found ourselves bidding for the small downtown parcel against big developers who were trying to buy the whole block.

By the end of 1988, we had won—but at a sky-high price. The only way to pay the huge mortgage was to squeeze costs until they—and we—squeaked. Teri had downshifted to part-time hours when David was born, meaning that our two-paycheck family now had to make do largely on one severely stressed check.

Much more serious, however, was the damage to our relationship. A first-time mother recovering from a C-section and dealing with a finicky baby, Teri badly needed my help and emotional support that summer. But I was so intent on putting out the various fires I'd started that I didn't see the desperation in her eyes. Imperceptibly, the gulf between us widened. And another test was on the way.

One evening in October, the three of us were sitting in front of the television after supper. I wasn't really watching; my mind was a blur of numbers, details, crises, negotiating points. Teri, who was holding David on her lap, also seemed preoccupied. She looked at me somewhat anxiously, as if she had earthshaking news but wasn't quite sure how to break it. She started to say something, then stopped as the earth—and our house—actually began to shake. It wasn't the first time we'd experienced a tremor, since Saratoga Springs sits on a fault line. But when she finished speaking, what she had said hit me like an earthquake.

"Tell Daddy what we found out at the doctor's office this afternoon, David. Go ahead, tell Daddy." David, four months old, gurgled and cooed.

"That's right! You're going to have a little brother or sister."

A Christmas Carol

After our initial panic we had decided to accept Teri's pregnancy gratefully, as a gift, and prepare as best we could. Emily arrived in June of 1989, and the two babies made such a beautiful pair in their double stroller that we were ashamed of our doubts. And we realized she'd taught us an important lesson—bad times can bring wonderful things. Besides, we'd always wanted a boy and a girl. Now that we had the ideal family, though, the question was: Could we support it?

Somehow the store made its huge balloon payments, and by 1990 my brother and I decided to sell the franchise while keeping the property for rental income. The negotiations took five difficult months, but when the sale was complete in June of 1991, it felt like Paris on Bastille Day. For the first time in eight years, I would be free to enjoy a summer rather than working through it. But there was one piece of unfinished business: Bain Road.

Jim and Petra had moved on after the money ran out, and the project had lain mostly dormant for two years, a huge drain. I hired a new contractor with money from the sale of the business, and the house again rang with the sounds of hammers and saws. Of course, costs soon went way over budget.

I had begun to test the employment waters by this time, but with almost no income and my job prospects dwindling as the economy headed into a deep recession, I felt it made sense to do as much of the work on the house as I could. My carefree summer quickly became a grind of ten- and twelve-hour days as I prepped, primed and painted the new walls. Meanwhile the real estate market had collapsed, and I found myself shoveling more and more money into a losing cause. But with the house so near to completion, walking away seemed crazy.

The interior was finished in late September, and all the work and worry finally began to seem worthwhile. I found a good tenant, but then the bane factor kicked in again. She canceled the day before she was to move in. In desperation I rented to an economically marginal family, and within three months they were defaulting on the rent and ruining the house.

By December I'd been without a paycheck for six months and had no firm prospects. Two journalism jobs that looked promising had gone to minority women at the last minute. And an editor at one paper, a man with whom I'd been having a lively chat about mutual acquaintances at the *Inquirer*, literally turned on his heel and ran away when I mentioned I was looking for work. Trying to get something going, I called the Albany bureau of the *New York Times* and got on its stringer list.

Miraculously, the *Times* called the day before Christmas looking for a freelancer to handle one of those awful stories that always seem to happen during the holidays. A house had burned in a little mill town along the Mohawk, claiming the lives of five young children in one family. And this was the second time in only a few years that the town had suffered a similar tragedy—a knockout story. Would I be able to go right over there?

"Of course," I said. The editor in New York said she would call back soon to let me know if it was a go or not. As I waited, I couldn't help but smile: the *New York Times*! And, if it was a slow news day, as major holidays usually were, the story might even get front-page treatment—or at least the metro section cover. I might get a byline if I was really lucky, and a story in the *Times* would shine like a jewel among my clippings. When I told Teri about the call, I expected a big smile and a hug. But she looked at me aghast.

"They want you to go over there on Christmas Eve and talk to people who've just lost five children and their house in a fire? That sounds horrible!"

By the time the editor called back to say they'd decided to send a reporter from New York, I'd made up my mind to turn down the assignment anyway.

Things look pretty bad, I thought to myself after I hung up the phone, *but at least we have two wonderful, healthy children, and we're all going to be together for a happy Christmas.* And it was a fine Christmas, except that we were having an annoying problem with David.

51. *Ruth*

intimate violence

Sunlight flickered through lofty tulip poplar leaves and dappled the coverlet I was smoothing onto the antique cherry bed in our foster child's room. Its intricate hand-sewn appliqués of blue and pink baskets felt bumpy under my hand, and I thought of the day Bill's mother had given it to me.

"My mother made this," she'd said as she pulled it from a chest in her attic. Then, laughing, she recounted the tribulations of being a middle-class housewife during the "White Sheet Wars" in Buffalo, when she'd labored to produce the whitest linens in town, and hung them on the clotheslines for her neighbors to envy. It had seemed like silly drivel to me then, caught up as I was in the important business of ending a war. But now, I surprised myself by feeling envious of those simple domestic pleasures, of the clearly drawn demarcation between career and family—that is, the man's career and the woman's family.

I had somehow ended up with an overload of career and no family life. A sign, I guess, that I had won at least one feminist battle. I recalled a quote that Randy was fond of: "A fanatic is someone who's lost sight of the goal but redoubled his efforts to attain it." It was an apt assessment of my life up to that point.

I had been willing at one time to go hungry, to live frugally, to encamp each night in a different dirty room—all for the ultimate goal of a better world. Sacrifice had been my lifeline, and I'd hung my personal dreams and talents out to dry on it like my mother-in-law's sheets. But now, when the crowds and the thrills were long gone and the angry young men and women had vanished into their lives of obscurity and accumulation, I was paying too dear a price, I believed, for indulging in youthful phantasms rather than domesticity.

As Willie Morris wrote in *New York Days*, "The Almighty has always been Southern in that regard: Get on early with the pristine charter of procreation." Foolishly, I had expected my body to perform its reproductive duties on demand, no matter how many years marched by. If one pregnancy didn't work out, another, more convenient one, would.

Maybe if I had just been more focused *on it,* I thought. But what was the use of replaying that old tape in my head? I finished making the bed and looked around the room. It was finally perfect, a room any girl would love. Randy had built a beautiful mantel for the fireplace, and I had lined it with dark green marble. His paintings of trees and mountains seemed to float dreamlike on pastel walls, and the heavy old bed stood solid as creation with the coverlet hanging just so around its hand-carved legs. Lace curtains fluttered in the windows, and the floor shone with polish.

I went into the room's small, private bath and leaned over the marble sink to splash water on my face. Then I took some deep breaths, trying to still the uncomfortable rhythm of my heart—that now-familiar ga-ga-ga-thump, the butterfly beat of mitral valve prolapse, with its little message of mortality.

"Nothing to worry about," my GP had assured me. "You'll die of a million other things before this does you in."

I'd stared at her for a moment, shocked at a doctor speaking of death in reference to me. Why, I could remember my fourteenth birthday like it had happened that morning: I had stood in front of the bathroom mirror in Yazoo City, looked myself in the eye, and said, "Ruth Tuttle, you're gonna live forever. Anything, *anything* you want to do is possible." I'd laughed my best immortal cackle, enjoying the way it lifted my rosy upper lip under the tip of my nose, creating only the barest hint of laugh lines around my eyes.

Now, twenty-two years later, I leaned toward the mirror and smiled a test smile, noting the paleness of my lips and the parchment of wrinkles that had begun to spread under my eyes. Disgusted, I glared at the bright bulbs surrounding the mirror. *It's just bad light,* I thought. *Thirty-six. That's not so old. Besides, they'll have a cure for wrinkles by the time I need it.* Then, looking myself full in the face, I said, "You idiot. You *still* believe in eternal youth."

Wrinkles, when I had once thought anyone over thirty should be put out of his or her misery, were a shocking sight, and would inspire me to try all manner of creams. I was beginning to see the folly of the Boomer mind-set, that our generation by flexing its demographics could incite the marketplace to conquer disease and aging. But it was not wrinkles that finally forced me to face reality. It was insidious biology as it robbed me, the already late starter, of the years I'd thought I had left in which to conceive a child.

I'd watched as other women, years older than I, had healthy babies. (My own mother gave birth to Margie when she was forty.) But I had been dealt another hand altogether. At thirty-four I had begun perimenopause.

"I can't tell you how much longer you'll be able to conceive naturally," my compassionate doctor, Bryan Cowan, told me. "You may have intermittent periods of fertility for several years. Or you may enter menopause almost immediately. We have to get very aggressive."

But after months and months of hormone injections, I had only achieved fertility once, then had seen the bloody end two weeks later. Desperate, reaching for the best medicine could offer me, I considered using the eggs of another woman. But to give birth to another woman's child? Not to have my own child? Not to have the blood of Cherokee Indians and Scottish high-landers, Texas roughnecks and Virginia minutemen in *my* child? I fought to achieve another perspective, trying to force myself to take this one last chance, until Randy told me in a burst of emotion that he didn't want to have a child from any woman but me.

"We have each other," he said. "Isn't that enough?" I could see he didn't feel the same loss I did, and I was grateful for that. I looked in his eyes and realized he was my family, and I was his, though we would never have children.

Hormone replacement therapy would eventually calm torturous hot flashes and give me a mental acuity I hadn't felt for a long time. But it would never repair the emotional hurt that bled and bled and bled its sorrow into every holiday, every shopping trip, every visit with friends or family when I saw the innocent faces of children. I believed at first that I would go howling to my grave with the pain of it, and on those days all I could do was cry in my dear Randy's arms.

Lisa

Though I may never make peace with not having my own child, I did finally realize that there were other children I could embrace. And that was how I met Lisa, who was desperately looking for someone to love her at the tag end of a childhood marred by years of abuse.

When I'd picked up the phone in December 1984 to call the Methodist Children's Home, it was on a whim. The thought of another Christmas as Aunt Ruth, watching Margie's child, Maggie, and Randy's nephew, Jaron, around the tree, filled me with a kind of terror. But this Christmas would be different. I'd borrow a child, one who had no place else to go, a child I could shower with gifts.

When the receptionist answered, I said, "My husband and I would like to open our home to one of your children for Christmas."

Are you crazy? I thought while I waited for a social worker to come on the line. I hadn't mentioned this wild scheme to Randy. I hadn't even thought of it until five minutes before. But fate was already smoothing the way.

A young woman came on the line. She was Sherry Meeks, who had been one of Margie's best friends in Yazoo City. We caught up on news about mutual friends for a few minutes; then I told her why I'd called.

"You know, normally I wouldn't even consider this, but I do know you and I have a girl who's unhappy with the people she usually visits at Christmas. She asked me just a few minutes ago to see if I could find her another place. I told her it would be impossible, but now you've called."

She paused to give me a chance to respond. It was a girl, and that pleased me. "What's her name?"

"Lisa. She's sixteen. Did you want a younger child?"

Though I had imagined a much younger child, I quickly said I had no preference and asked her to tell me about Lisa.

"Well, she's unusually well adapted considering her history, which I can't discuss with you. No behavioral problems, but she comes from a very disturbed family. Very disturbed." She paused again, a silent invitation for me to gracefully back out. I stayed quiet. "She gets attached to anyone who is good to her, so she's had a lot of disappointments. If you can't make a long-term commitment to be her sponsor, I don't think we should pursue this."

I told Sherry my reproductive history and vowed to be like the Rock of Gibraltar for Lisa, the knowledge of whose very existence was already starting a humming in my heart. Sherry arranged for me to meet her the next morning, and we got off the phone.

I raced to our office on North Street, where Randy was working on a design project for a local business magazine. As usual he was under an impossible deadline and was anxious for me to pitch in and help.

"Something's happened," I blurted out.

He looked up at me, alarmed. "What's wrong?"

Breathlessly I poured out the morning's events, only vaguely aware of how wild a scheme I was describing to him.

"Whoa, now. Just sit down and catch your breath." I sat, but it was Randy who seemed to be having trouble breathing.

Finally, he said, "You mean we're going to have a teenage girl for Christmas? A girl with some kind of tragic past? A girl we've never met?"

"Not just for Christmas, Randy. We'll be her sponsors. Holidays, weekends, summers, camp, college, weddings, births." I spun out the years like a road map. But Randy's face told me he thought it was a map to hell.

"She's got no one else," I pleaded.

Randy leaped from his chair. "This is just a wild flight of fancy, isn't it? This girl is probably really fucked up. What were you thinking?"

"Can't we at least give it a try?"

"I need a minute. I can't dive into things like you do. Just give me a minute." He went to get a cup of coffee while I sat and waited. When he came back, Randy took me in his arms and said, "I'll give it a try. Let's see how Christmas goes."

· · ·

Lisa walked into the lobby of the Methodist Home, her little face tilted upward in an independent gesture that was somehow at odds with her small body. Barely five feet tall, she looked like a child of ten. In fact, I doubted this girl could even be Lisa. She had an innocent hopefulness that belied her circumstances. Her long, dark hair heightened the effect of childishness because it was pulled back with plastic butterfly barrettes, but she had tied a multicolored scarf around her waist that gave her a stylish flair. She was delightful. I fell head over heels for her, for her hope, her courage, her optimism.

On Christmas Eve, Randy and I made an elaborate supper, chopping and grating and baking everything we thought a teenager might like. We wanted to make Lisa feel welcome, but it dawned on me that all of our hustle and bustle might be making her feel left out instead. She sat idly at the kitchen table, staring at us blankly.

"You can help if you want, you know. You're not a guest."

"I know. But I like watching."

"Why?"

"It's so normal." She smiled her shy smile, which we'd already discovered hid a mischievous and outgoing nature. (Earlier that day in our living room she had burst into an astounding one-girl song and dance performance of a Broadway tune.)

"Of course it's normal," I said. "What do you expect at dinnertime?"

She giggled a little. "Oh, you'd be surprised."

I iced cupcakes, waiting for her to go on, but she didn't. "You don't want to let us in on the joke?"

A long, trilling laugh burst from her. "Okay, but you asked for it."

Randy and I looked at each other. Maybe she was starting to trust us.

Lisa began to speak, her eyes darting to our faces every so often, while the story came out in funny little chirps and bleeps, punctuated by her girlish laugh at the oddest moments, as though she could charm the truth away. Soon Randy and I stood transfixed, food chores forgotten, and listened.

"My mother had a thing about food. I mean, she could get mad about *anything*—she used to beat me for wetting the bed—but food was her *big* thing. Sometimes she wouldn't give us anything to eat. Sometimes it went on for a long time, maybe days, I don't really remember because I was so little. But I do remember having to sit and watch her and my dad eating steaks and being *really* hungry. When I cried, she dragged me and Patty, my sister, to the kitchen and forced us to eat a mixing bowl full of oatmeal, a whole pizza, six peanut butter sandwiches, a whole cucumber, a dozen cookies, until we got sick.

"But the worst time was one day when I sneaked a can of fruit salad. I threw the empty can out the window, and she found it. She whipped me and locked all the cabinets and the refrigerator. A few days later she tried to make us eat a lot again, and we hid what we couldn't eat in the washing ma-chine, and forgot to throw it out later—we were just little kids, you know."

"How old were you, sweetie?"

"I guess I was six then. But here's the funny part. She came home and put a load of wash in first thing, and when she found that food all mushed up in her clean clothes, she really lost it. Beat me up pretty bad. Whoo!" Lisa laughed. "That's when the welfare people took me away from her and put me in a foster home."

"Was it better?"

"Not really, hee-hee. Not really." I was afraid she was going to get hysterical.

"Honey, you don't have to talk about this."

"No, I can't stop now. Just let me say it."

I looked at a photo of a much younger Lisa I'd put on the refrigerator. It had seemed important to her that we have this image of her childhood. She was a preschooler in the picture, a pixielike little girl with a gap-toothed grin and short ponytails that stuck out from the sides of her head. I flinched at the image of that delicate child beaten, her tiny bones broken.

"What did your daddy do? Didn't he try to help you?"

"No. He's a lot older than my mother. She beat on him, too, sometimes."

"Your brother? Wasn't he a teenager then? Didn't he help?"

"Hah! He helped *her*! Not me. He was *worse* than her. He had sex on the brain, and tried to have it with me." This last she said in a whisper. "But he didn't ruin me, not in that way. You know what I mean."

I didn't, but I nodded. I suspected she meant she was still a virgin, a small victory over the intimate violence of her childhood.

"When I went to the foster home, they only wanted me to work. They had lots of other kids. The man, whoo, he was mean. And he beat me up almost as bad as my mother. So I got sent to another home.

"That one was pretty good. They really wanted a child and all, couldn't have one themselves. It was a nice place for a while. Pretty clothes and a regular school. And Sunday school. I even made some friends. But then my mother— I mean the woman, she got pregnant. Just like that. Out of the blue. And things changed.

"I tried to love their baby. I think I was eight when he was born. I could have helped take care of him, but they didn't like me near him. And when he got older he was a handful, got into my stuff, got me in trouble. I ended up hating him. And," she took a long ragged breath, then smiled as if to reassure us, "they sent me away.

"I could have gone to another foster family, but I'd had enough, you know? So I asked the social workers to send me back to my real mother. I'd been seeing her in supervised visits and she had promised me gifts and things if I'd come home."

"And the social workers let you go?"

"Yeah, when I was ten, and things were okay for a while. But then she got all weird again. Blamed me for putting the authorities onto her when I was little. She started beating me with everything—belts, switches, fly-swatters, her hands. It was so bad I had to wear long-sleeved wool sweaters in the summer to hide the bruises. Then she accused me of stealing food again—I think Patty had eaten an olive. She beat me up real bad that time and locked me in my room and left me there for five days—even on Christmas Day! no presents or anything!—until Patty climbed out a window and went for help." This last was said in a rush.

"So Patty and I were sent to the Methodist Home when I was twelve, and it's been an okay place. The twins were sent to live with relatives in New York. My brother stayed with my parents and they had another baby."

"Did that baby get taken away, too?" Randy asked.

"No, I think my mother treats her okay. It was just me she hated. I don't know why."

"What about adoption? Didn't that ever come up?"

"Yeah, I had a chance once. When I was younger—nobody wants older kids, you know, just the cute little ones—but my parents wouldn't sign the papers. So, here I am."

For long seconds we were all quiet, then Randy—whose blue eyes had grown dark while she talked—stepped over to Lisa's chair and gently laid his hand on her shoulder. "Yeah, here you are, thank God."

Through tears, Lisa smiled at us. Then she walked over and started arranging the cupcakes on a plate.

Whenever she was with us, we tried to make her life like a fairy tale—at least the happily-ever-after part of one—with the lovely bedroom and nice clothes, surprise gifts and always an open door and an ear to listen. She began to lose her little-girl look and to take an interest in school, where she was two years behind her age group. When she was seventeen she had her first date, at her ninth-grade graduation dance, and wore a dress that we had shopped for all over town. It was way too expensive for a junior high dance, and I knew it would only be worn once, but I bought it anyway. Layers of white lace ruffles fell from her tiny waist and the scoop-necked bodice gave her an air of sophistication. She was radiant when she left our house with her date, who looked thunderstruck to have such a beauty on his arm.

At Murrah High School she made the varsity cheerleading squad, the first child from the Methodist Home who had ever attained such an honor. Then she went on to become the first person in her family to get a college degree, a B.S. in fashion merchandising. But all of those things she did on her own, buoyed by her ebullient and irrepressible nature and perhaps the knowledge that Randy and I would always be there for her.

The Memory

I thought of Lisa's smooth and luminous complexion and looked at myself in the mirror again. The contrast between her youthful, effortless beauty and my own fading-rose face brought me up short. Where had it all gone?

And like a smack to my soul, something else welled up. It was a memory that had recently begun to torment me. For years I had lived in blithe forgetfulness, never being troubled by its legacy. But Lisa had made it come alive again with an innocent remark. A compliment. "I wish you'd been my mother. I think I would have turned out better."

It was as though she was regretting all the formative moments, the gaps in her childhood, the pain and abuse that had left scars long before I knew her. It made me realize once again that I would never be a mother, never provide the thoughtful guidance and love that help a child grow from birth to adulthood. The memory, a horrific thing, began to reverse all the hard work I had done to accept being childless.

It was a memory of a bright, cool morning in November 1974, a morning that had made Wisconsin seem like paradise. I was lying on the couch with my hand on my abdomen, imagining the tiny thing living in there, trying to think of it as an interchangeable part, something to be returned to the store, where it would wait until I was ready to reclaim it.

I'd been taking birth control pills since Bill and I met, but during our trip to California I had run out, and now I was pregnant. I felt a nagging regret that the pregnancy had happened at such an inconvenient time, and a deep sorrow that I couldn't have the baby. I knew I would love it, if it was born. But a baby—Bill and I were hardly more than children ourselves, children still playing in the fields of marital mayhem. *This little seed just had bad timing*, I told myself. *A few more years, and things will be better.* I got up and began to dress, but tears kept coming.

Bill went with me to the clinic. Only one other woman was in the waiting room, a middle-aged matron who seemed out of place. I thought perhaps she was waiting on her daughter. When I asked, she said, "No. *I'm* pregnant. I already have five children, and a sixth would be a hardship on everyone." But her husband didn't know she was there. "He'd never go along," she whispered.

"You're alone?" I asked. She nodded. Bill and I offered to give her a ride home, afterward. She grasped my hand and we hugged each other, then the nurse called my name.

"How long will it take?" I asked her. I hoped to hear it would take so long that Bill would miss his first class. We'd have to postpone.

"Only a few minutes. Are you ready?" I went with her, the Valium she had given me earlier beginning to dull my anxiety.

Cold, hard instruments did their work quickly, while the soft-voiced nurse stood by my side and held my hand. As I lay there, I thought of a friend who had almost died from a botched illegal abortion in 1970. That day I'd wrung out towels and mopped blood for over an hour, while she writhed and moaned, before I finally called an ambulance. When my own safe, sterile procedure was over, the nurse picked up a small stainless steel dish and laid a white cloth over it. I asked her to show it to me. The dispatching of an inconvenient child seemed almost too efficient.

"It's nothing you'd want to see," she said, her eyebrows raised. She handed me a packet of birth control pills. "Only a little tissue and blood. You rest now."

I didn't press her, but later I regretted not looking. Perhaps it would have helped me to see that little bit of tissue. To know it was not a murdered baby. To know I couldn't have seen hands or eyes or feet, because in my heart I have come to believe I left my only child on that cold tray.

When I got back to the waiting room, Bill said the other woman had changed her mind and left. "One more won't make that much difference," she'd said.

The most intimate moment Bill and I ever shared actually occurred ten years after we were divorced. I was in Lisa's room, helping her unpack the mounds of dirty laundry she'd brought home from college, when the phone rang. He was calling, as he still does from time to time, just to talk. He wanted to reminisce about the war and long-lost friends and, usually, our long-lost love.

"Why haven't you guys had any kids?"

"It just never happened." I knew I sounded too curt, but I couldn't help myself.

"Remember when you were pregnant in Madison?" My heart did its nervous tremor. I brushed a stray hair out of my eyes and saw Lisa standing in the doorway, trying to get my attention. *Just a minute,* I mouthed at her, feeling a rush of affection and gratitude that she was now so firmly placed in the center of my life. *No hurry,* she mimed back at me.

"I try not to remember." My voice, barely a whisper, was ragged. That surprised me, because for years I'd been emotionless with Bill, who I thought was responsible for all the pain of our marriage.

"Remember how I used to love those little tykes at the Head Start program in Jackson?"

"Well, what's stopping you from having your own? Men can have children whenever they want."

"My old lady, Linda, doesn't want to start over. Her kids are grown.

And I can't just go out and knock up a young piece of ass." He started to laugh, the piercing hyena laugh that always accompanied one of his outrageous comments. "Well, I could, but Linda would kick my butt."

"Then she's a better woman than I am. I never could get you to keep your hands off of poontang."

"God, I miss you, Ruthie." Suddenly tears were lurking under his voice. "Where did it all go? The passion? The love? We gave up our one and only child, you know. Our one and only."

I couldn't speak. Sorrow began clawing its way past my palpitating heart and came out in heaving sobs. For a few healing minutes Bill and I grieved together for a child long lost to our arrogance. Then I said, "Try to forget it, Billy. We can't change the past."

"But I'd like to," he said. "I'd really like to."

52. Jeff

the 400 blows, part two

A few days after Christmas in 1991, I found myself looking into the wide, fearful eyes of my beautiful three-and-a-half-year-old son and wanting to cry. But I couldn't, because I knew it would only upset him more to see his daddy break down. His pediatrician had just told us that David had Type I diabetes and would be dependent on daily injections of insulin from then on.

"Don't worry," she said, trying to be helpful. "They'll teach you all about the shots and the diet and everything at the hospital."

Seeing the despair on my face, she added: "It looks like you caught it pretty early, though. So there shouldn't be too much damage to his system."

Thank God for small favors, I thought to myself.

That morning had begun in a stop-action hustle as we strove to get ourselves and our tots—David and two-and-a-half-year-old Emily—ready for the trip to Uncle Ben's house in Vermont. Most of the gang would be there—Ben, Jerry, Fred and Feldo and their wives, along with "the cousins," as we called the children. David's birth had kicked off something of a population explosion—Jerry and Elizabeth's son, Tyrone, had been born a few months later, closely followed by Ron and Sandy's son, Benjamin. Feldo and Rita's daughter, Katie, had arrived next, with Emily following her. Ben and Cindy's daughter, Aretha, had come last. We were all looking forward to getting the group together in a setting that would give the toddlers and babies plenty to do, and I badly needed to commune with my old friends at the end of yet another awful year.

We had been concerned about David for a while. He was still in diapers, which was frustrating, but that wasn't the main problem. It seemed that he was urinating constantly. We thought this was his reaction to our determined efforts to get him toilet trained, and we weren't sure how to respond. His face, as our Christmas-morning video had recorded, was oddly flushed, as if he had a cold. But there were no sniffles or earache. And he wanted to drink, drink, drink, yet the endless cups of apple juice never seemed to satisfy him. My mother, who'd been diagnosed with Type II (adult-onset) diabetes in her forties, thought she recognized the symptoms, but the "d" word had been almost too terrible to speak, and she hadn't pushed the idea.

Fred had called from Ben's house and asked when we thought we'd be arriving.

"We're not making much progress," I said with a rueful laugh. "It seems every time we get a dry diaper on David, he wets again. We'll never get out of here at this rate." I paused before asking: "Do you think it might be diabetes?"

Fred put on his doctor's hat and asked me about David's symptoms. He said there were other things that could cause similar problems and urged me to take David to his pediatrician's office before we hit the road, just to ease our minds.

My chat with Fred, which had occurred less than an hour before, now seemed like a relic of a former life as I sat reeling in the examining cubicle with David. I was proud of him; he'd hardly cried when the doctor pricked his finger to take a blood sample. I saw him eyeing me worriedly and I tried to smile.

"Don't worry, D," I said. "We'll go to the hospital, and you'll be fine."

If I had known what was to come—the screaming as the IV nurse struggled to find a vein in his little arm, the shock when he realized he'd have to spend the night in a cagelike bed in a strange-smelling place where all the children were sick—I couldn't have said those words. But I had no idea how bad that week would be.

"We're going to the hospital?" he asked gravely. Now I regretted telling him so many times that he'd have to go to the hospital if he didn't stop doing this or that dangerous thing.

"Yes," I answered with as much reassurance as I could muster. "I'll stay with you, and you'll be feeling much better soon."

That much was true—by the end of that week, David's blood sugar would be back in the normal range, and Teri and I would be graduates of a crash course in pediatric diabetes management. By the time we took him home from the hospital the day after New Year's, he looked and felt much better. But we were devastated.

David's diagnosis seemed, at the time, the coup de grâce after a terrible four-year period that had begun just as Teri and I were surfing the crest of the eighties boom. Later I would come to think of this hellish time as *The 400 Blows*, after the Truffaut movie about the travails of growing up. It put a huge strain on our marriage, especially since much of our misery was the direct result of mistakes I had made.

One day, about three months after we brought David home from the hospital, he and Emily were talking about his dietary restrictions at the kitchen table. This was a very sensitive topic, since they didn't apply to her. I was listening warily as I bustled about getting ready to go to my night job—one of two I held at the time. I wasn't making much money, but things were looking up.

Teri was listening to the kids' conversation, too, and our eyes met. We had become emotional strangers by then, never seeking help from each other, but she didn't want to face this kind of scene alone. I sympathized, but I also didn't want to be late for work.

Up to this point, David and Em had discussed his condition very little, at least in front of us. And we, amid our parental agony of shots, testing, rigid scheduling and thorny food issues, had determined not to allow the cult of the "poor little diabetes boy" to get started, because we knew that self-pity would do him even more harm than the condition itself.

David sighed soulfully and said, "Oh, why did I have to get diabetes?"

Emily, playing with her applesauce, answered quickly, parroting our standard line: "It just happened, D."

"If I could," David said after a pause, "I would give it to you."

"NO!" Emily shouted. I held my breath, sure that David would follow up with a loud lament about how unfair it all was. But they looked each other in the eye for a moment. Then they laughed—that lovely, indescribable sound the angels use to communicate the possibility of heaven to parents. And, for perhaps the first time since those terrible days in the hospital, we laughed, too.

53. Ruth

imagining mississippi

Since our marriage in 1983, Randy and I had worked like draft horses in dual harness, and it had paid off. We'd also learned the survival skills of well-to-do Mississippians, taking two-week sabbaticals to Vancouver or New York or Santa Fe. But every time I stepped out of the Jackson airport into the brilliant sunset of a Mississippi evening, I knew I was home. For a few days afterward I'd marvel at the cleanness of the air and the gentle rhythms of the people, in this place where every nuance carried the after-glow of remembered happy associations. But eventually, like an allergy to a much-loved food, the other Mississippi would afflict me, the one I'd once fled and that I continued to struggle to understand.

Occasionally I'd see news reports of antiwar activists as they came out of hiding or were arrested, middle-aged householders ready to pay for the crimes they'd committed as zealots. Though I'd never set off a bomb, I also lived in hiding from my radical past, carefully cultivating an image of con-servative prosperity. Once, I sat silent and uncomfortable during lunch with clients at the University Club and listened while one of them ridi-culed his brother for having "squandered" his life in hippiedom during the sixties and seventies. "And that ol' boy still talks like it was the best time of his life, 'stead of the stupid waste of time it really was. Our man, Dick Nixon, would have ended the war regardless. He warn't no idiot." There was a ripple of laughter around the table.

As I smoothed the jacket of my Christian Dior suit, I briefly considered pointing out that the effects of the antiwar movement had stretched far beyond the Vietnam War. But my appetite for a soapbox was long gone, so I steered the conversation back to the ad campaign we'd been discussing earlier.

"You know the ad business, Ruth. Just do us up a plan," the man's partner said.

Knowing this woman would have her own ideas in the end, no matter what I came up with, I mentally increased the percentage of their budget that would go into my own bottom line. Then, dispensing with business, I said, "Looks like Peyton Manning's made the right choice. I hear my alma mater snagged him."

Silence fell over the table. Now we were talking about something *really* serious. As white-coated black waiters brought coffee and dessert, the elegant room echoed with the outrage of Ole Miss diehards, scorned by the progeny of their greatest hero, Archie Manning, who had made his name and fame in the late sixties.

Soon I was laughing at the ruckus as other patrons began shouting their opinions. "How dare you?" one of them yelled at me, a twinkle in his eye. "How *dare* you steal Peyton from us? You know how *garish* he's gonna look, all done up like a pumpkin in Tennessee orange?"

I'd been to only one football game at UT, and that one was memorable only because my date, a 250-pound ex-linebacker, threw up on me as we left the stands. But my lunch buddies were still reveling in the supercharged football Saturdays of their youth.

"Hotty, toddy, gosh almighty," one of them began to chant, stamping his feet on the floor in time with the famous Ole Miss football challenge. "Who the hell are we?"

"Ole Miss by damn," a dozen voices finished up, and the dining room exploded with clapping.

"Give us a Volunteer cheer," my client asked me, breathless from the impromptu pep rally.

Down with the pigs, I thought to myself. "Go, Vols," I said, raising my fist for emphasis.

We left the restaurant in high spirits.

Racing to Power

"One man stands out," a black woman said, her voice underlaid with the deep harmonies of gospel music. I put down *The Clarion-Ledger* to watch the television spot we'd just finished the day before. John Horhn was on the screen, handing out diplomas to young black women. Or admiring a newly erected statue of Medgar Evers. Or working intently at his desk, looking quietly efficient in a perfectly tailored suit. He was my candidate and my friend, running for the state senate in a district with a strong Republican minority, and it would be a challenge to get him elected.

But after a successful career in state government during which he had often had the ear of the governor, John was well known in the white community as well as the black, an accomplishment that had earlier propelled Mike Espy into Congress. When he called to tell me he was going to run in the Twenty-sixth District, I immediately offered my services in developing campaign materials and media spots. Then, as I wrote to Jeff, one thing led to another.

*Wouldn't Mike McCourt have been surprised to see me,
the only woman and the only white person there, elected as
chairman of John's finance committee? Of course, I think the
other members of the committee—all successful and influential black businessmen—knew that I was the only one of us
gullible enough to accept the position.*

In spite of what I wrote Jeff, I was pleased with the symbolic content of the
committee's little election, and in subsequent meetings found myself
deeply moved as I sat with that group of black men. I thought of relatives
who had once supported the symbol of Mississippi bigotry, Theodore
Bilbo, and who couldn't have imagined their descendant plotting political
strategy to elect a black man. Or imagined the likes of these black men—
Ted Jones, a dentist, LeRoy Walker, the owner of a half dozen McDonald's
franchises, Art Pullam, founder of a successful temp agency, and Malcolm
Shepherd, an economic development planner.

During one meeting, Art told me about his stint in Vietnam, saying,
"Back then, the military was a major career avenue for black men." It
struck me that he'd risked his life for a future, while white boys refused to
give up secure futures in order to risk their lives.

But though these men were seeing Martin Luther King's dream realized for themselves, in some parts of Jackson, every week, a black person is
killed by another black person. The nation's prisons are full of black men.
And African American families consist more and more of only a grandmother, aunt or mother with sole responsibility for the raising of the children. Because of this, I began to see the men around that boardroom table
as high-wire artists on a social tightrope, symbols of what is working in
black America. They are one of the most valuable resources of the New
South.

I listened closely when they analyzed seemingly innocuous actions of
their white associates. "It's racist," one would say. "No," another would answer. "That's not racist. Let me tell you about racist. . . ." For the first time
I understood their daily battle with racism, and saw it in contrast to my
own leisurely grappling with the concept of it.

John won the Democratic primary, defeating two other black candidates, and we began to focus on the general election, in which he'd have to
defeat a white Republican. It was costing a lot more than we'd expected,
but money continued to come in from all segments of the district, and we
felt optimistic.

Sometimes John would stop by to discuss strategy, or simply to share a
funny story about his day, but he was always in motion, his agile mind
striking one topic or another and mining its worth, then quickly moving
on. It was the beginning of a friendship with another remarkable man.

A few weeks into the campaign, a prominent white attorney offered to hold a fund-raiser at his home. John gladly accepted his offer and left the planning up to him and his wife. We thought no more about it. Then, two days before the event, John happened to see one of the invitations. He called me immediately. "You're not going to believe this invitation," he said. "And it's already been mailed."

My heart sank. Was it a typo? Was the date wrong? Was his name misspelled?

"They're giving a watermelon cutting party." For a minute I was stunned. But I heard the laughter in John's voice.

"Oh, John. I know they just didn't think. What a cliché."

"White folks," John said, laughing. "You white folks."

He won the election with over 60 percent of the vote, and quickly became chairman of the legislature's powerful economic development committee where he has been controversial and often knocked heads with then Republican Governor Kirk Fordice.

Recently, we took a few hours to catch up. Sitting at my kitchen table, we opened a bottle of good wine and—as we always do—fell into the kind of intense conversation that wakes one's mind and puts everyday worries to sleep.

"Anwar Sadat was as black as my junior high school principal. But do white people call Egyptians black?" A trained and talented actor, John fell into a caricature of a stereotypical Southern white woman. "Egyptians weren't black. Aristotle didn't study under a nigra." His eyes rolled back in his head in a feigned swoon.

"But John," I said, "if Vietnamese immigrants can lose everything, move to this country as paupers and be well off in only twenty years, why haven't African Americans been able to do it in more than two hundred?"

"Because we're bankrupt," he said, his eyes flashing. "We're emotionally, financially and psychologically bankrupt. There are liens on our culture, liens on our family structure, our history. In every sense that society accords you a sense of richness, we have been methodically bankrupted.

"You're not really considering what slavery did to black people. We were dragged to a strange country and forced to give up *everything*. And not just give it up, *to replace it immediately* with new concepts of beauty, language, order, right and wrong, religion. We're trying to imagine our future when we still haven't found our past."

He turned blazing eyes on me. "Too many of us aren't looking for that past, either. How can we? It's a challenge just to get to tomorrow, and whatever resources there are go for instant gratification." He assumed the persona of a gangbanger, a sudden slippage into another person's skin that disturbed me until I realized he was role-playing again. Anger and hatred, arrogance and ignorance filled my kitchen when he said, "Gonna get it now. Gonna enjoy it now. Forget the future. It's about me, and my time is *now*."

Then, becoming John again, he straightened his tie. "Look how much you've gotten just from a sense of belonging, of knowing your history. How many times has that history given you direction?"

"But what's the end result going to be?" I asked.

"It already *is*. It's rage against our own environment. Black killing black. We hate ourselves because we don't *know* ourselves." Looking desperately sad, he murmured, "Maybe there are no selves left to know, only what our children see on television and at the movies. Spirits are destitute, not just pocketbooks, and the rage will continue until that spiritual void is filled."

He paused a minute and said, "The main solace I feel comes from knowing that my ancestors survived seemingly insurmountable conditions, and most of them found ways to succeed. My hope is that soon their descendants will find that same desire to excel."

Mississippi may be closer to hell than anyplace else in the world for some people. But I see it on the brink between heaven and hell, grounded by the horrors of its past, yet trying to soar into the future on the optimism of its citizens.

This creates a paradise for writers, who thrive on contradictions, and Mississippi has more than its share of great ones. Once I stood behind Eudora Welty at the checkout in Jitney Jungle and watched her count out exact change. The young woman at the cash register fidgeted and tapped her long, false nails on the counter. Each one had a tiny heart painted on it in a different color of glitter. Seeing Miss Welty's dovelike hands sorting change next to these extravagant nails was like looking into a cultural abyss.

Finally, just as the girl's patience seemed at an end, Miss Welty handed her the coins. A gentle smile warmed the writer's plain face, giving only a hint of the outrageous beauty she carried inside her. The girl threw the change into the drawer and tore off the receipt with an air of exasperation.

When it was my turn to pay, I asked the girl if she knew who the old lady was.

"No, who is she?"

"Eudora Welty," I said. "A great writer."

"So?" She threw the question at me like a challenge.

"Would you like to read one of her books?" I asked her. "I'll give it to you."

"I don't need you to be giving me no white folks' books," she retorted, and a little heartbreak stayed with me all day.

. . .

Mississippi has brought me wonderful friends, and painful isolation. I have driven down its high-banked country roads entranced by the overhanging oaks, sweet gum and sassafras trees, only to discover later that horrendous acts of torture and murder were committed on those same roads against black people in times not so long gone. I have tried to banish this knowledge, to prevent it from spoiling my day, but it stays with me.

JoAnne Prichard, the teacher who fought by my side against Coach Rush and Mr. Richardson in high school, who became the managing editor of the University Press of Mississippi, and married Willie Morris in 1992, once showed me a collection of photographs of lynchings that happened in Mississippi in the 1930s through the 1950s. I knew I didn't want to look, that I would never erase them from my mind. But curiosity, and perhaps a hope that there would be only one or two *actual* lynchings, that the horror had been exaggerated, caused me to take the stack of photos from her hand and examine them.

My stomach began to churn as I turned them over and looked deep into the bulging eyes of young men. I ran my fingers over images of limp and bloody and dead bodies. They were bodies of men who had carried heavy loads. Muscular. Well made. Bodies that had only hours before been capable of speed and grace. Of physical labor and love.

One man's head was completely severed from his gaping neck by the rope. Blood and gore streaked another's dusty body. And these were in only one county in Mississippi, only one state of a dozen in the South. *How many others were murdered?* I wondered.

The victims' clothes were torn and patched many times, like the clothes of so many black people I remembered from my youth. They had nothing except their lives, and those had just been taken by white men who stood by the lifeless, hanging bodies like hunters who had bagged a deer.

It reminded me of conversations my older relatives had been fond of, puzzling out philosophical questions like "Are nigras human beings? Is there a nigra Heaven and a white Heaven?"

Why do we all—black and white, victims and persecutors and descendants—turn away from the truth of our pasts? We must learn it, and hate it, and gratefully measure our distance from it, again and again. When you live in Mississippi, the past is the one thing you cannot escape. But many of us, both blacks and whites, are doing what we can to bring justice to bear against it.

In 1994, the murderer of Medgar Evers was finally convicted, thirty-one years after the crime. In 1998, one of the murderers of another 1960s Mississippi NAACP leader, Vernon Dahmer, was convicted. And on January 11,

1999, the *Clarion-Ledger*'s lead story was "Widow Wants KKK Prosecuted: Justice Overdue in 1964 Slayings of Three Civil Rights Workers." Perhaps the most infamous Mississippi lynch mob of all—the murderers of Michael Schwerner, Andrew Goodman and James Chaney—will eventually receive the punishment they've eluded for so long. And we good citizens of Mississippi will once again file into a courtroom to stare in horror at the bland, grandfatherly faces of hate-warped night riders who have outlived their depraved era.

54. Jeff and Ruth

catching up

February 1, 1993

Dear Ruth,

Yazoo City. There I was, casually flipping through my Saturday **New York Times**, when what should I espy (Espy?) but Haley Barbour. What IS it about Yazoo City people? One of these days I'm going to visit again.

"Probably not, Jeff," you're thinking. But it just might happen, although the idea of up and doing something on my own, for myself, seems quaint and a bit laughable now that I'm "Daddy" to two weenies. Who were we then, Ruth? Who are we now? Are the two sets at all related?

It's a relief to be out of the ice cream business. I'm working for a nationwide fee-based financial counseling firm as an editor-writer. It's interesting work, and reasonably remunerative, though it doesn't duplicate the cheesy romance of the daily pulp factories of my past. It's the newspaper people I miss most of all, though I certainly don't miss the lousy hours and laughable pay. David is doing well and we're doing reasonably well in terms of dealing with his condition. But the whole thing is damnably complicated and nerve-racking—so many variables, and the stakes are so high. We're still hoping for a major breakthrough in the treatment of Type I diabetes.

Feldo is in Australia now promoting a joint venture. Jerry is a busy (too busy) ice cream executive.

January 8, 1994

Dear Jeff,

What a magnificent family! David and Em look like twins. They are beautiful children.

I'm so glad our correspondence has returned from the dead. I take full responsibility for the close call, Jeff, as you

are always so prompt in writing back. Maybe now, in our forties, we will be able to find more time.

In September I flew to Virginia for one of Willie's **New
York Days** book parties. If you haven't read the book, you
should. You'll really enjoy it. Harriet DeCell is quoted for a
full page.

The party was a lot of fun. I didn't know anyone, but I
must have met the entire roster of people who have ever appeared on PBS and most of Clinton's White House staff.

If you read the book let me know what you think of Willie's
assessment of our generation. I felt positively chilly towards
him after I read it, but it did get me thinking about my "lost"
decade, the '70s, and some significant regrets I have. I know I
lost every shred of intellectual integrity I possessed, but I
think the '90s may see my rebirth to some of those intellectual
possibilities. At least I've learned discipline from running a
business. Now if I can rediscover creativity . . .

                                        February 14, 1994

My Dear Ruth,
Well, old friend, it's been 25 years since we began this
and I can't tell you how exciting it still is to get a letter from
you. There's really no friend like an old friend, and I don't
have any other old friend as unique as you. I realize I'm going
out on a limb here, considering who some of my old friends
are, but it's the truth. You may be shaking your head and
wondering, "Why IS he going on like this?"

Well, it's just plain joy at finally having put time, energy
and emotion in one place. I can't just dash off a letter to you,
especially on our 25th (and Valentine's Day to boot).

I was lying in bed after tucking the kids in when I started
thinking of you and Alice and everything that happened at the
dim dawn of consciousness when we were 17. I still can't
understand it. It was magic, unearthly in some way. Have I
ever lived as much since then? Arguably not, though that
slights a lot of other significant moments. But how many people have such an adventure that doesn't end in disaster? Far
from disaster, it is a treasure that still links us so firmly to
each other.

I still think of Alice and marvel at the idea that she will
be 42 this year. Is that possible? She'll always be a gorgeous
child in my mind. You haven't told me anything about her in

ages. Are you trying to protect me in some way? I hope nothing awful has happened to her—that would be hard to take. Did she ever remarry? How old are her kids now? Is she somehow linked to Haley Barbour, and busily soliciting funds to dethrone King Bill in '96? Is she still as removed and distracted as Ophelia before her fatal end?

Of course I still love her, or at least the part of me that's still 17 and reckless and invincible still loves that 16-year-old apparition. I know it's not really her—it's an image, an impossible dream, a vision frozen in aspic. But it's still so vivid that sometimes I think I need to see her, so I can put that ghost to rest.

April 24, 1994

Dear Jeff,

When I read your last letter I realized how optimistically vulnerable we both were in 1969—the spontaneity, the trust, the leap of faith—and how gently we must treat each other now.

We never have asked too much of each other. We have been spared the daily grind of living, but maybe it's time to test our friendship. I hope we can write more frequently. I have always found your mentality to be uplifting and precious. To me you are the eternal liberal New York boy—quick-witted, brilliant word meister, thrill-seeker, single-minded and tenacious.

I haven't seen Alice in five years, at least. You know we were never good friends. We just shared that one powerful summer. But I do see Harriet often so I hear news of Alice. In fact I saw Harriet at JoAnne's 50th birthday party.

Harriet is, at 64, taking on another new challenge. She's the interim executive director of the Hinds County Library System—taking the job in the middle of a political firestorm until they find a permanent director. She always liked a fight (as you know).

Anyway, Alice remarried three years ago. She lives here in Jackson and is the mother of two children from her first marriage, and has a two-year-old from this one. Her husband is a third-generation attorney in a venerable old family firm. When I saw Harriet they had gone to Vail for two weeks with all the kids. I think Alice is happy, and there's nothing bad to report. All your worries were groundless.

August 21, 1994

Dear Ruth,

I'm glad you finally calmed my fevered ruminations about Alice. There is still that certain fascination that roils the waters, like bubbles in a silted pond, at the oddest times.

It was, I confess, a bit of a letdown to hear that she finally did pretty much what she was destined to do in the first place. The trouble with knowing this is that it skewers once and for all my knight-in-shining-armor fantasy. What's truly shocking, though, is to think she is older than her mother was when she gave me that memorable tongue-lashing on the way to Kenny Waldrop's house.

Harriet seems to be by far the most interesting character, though. Do you think she would deign to meet with me if I came down your way?

December 11, 1994

Dear Jeff,

I'm sitting at my dining table watching Randy and the hired man, Henry, rebuild a fence line. A gorgeous tangle of Mississippi woods frames their labors and a flock of sparrows on the patio are feasting on sunflower seeds. This is a watershed moment. The business has become a kind of self-renewing engine and our employees are wonderful. We had always thought we would sell it, but this may be better.

Anyway, here I stand at the pinnacle of my life with nothing to do but contemplate my mortality. Do you have any suggestions about where I should go from here?

December 23, 1994

Dear Ruth,

Why don't you start writing that book we've always talked about?

December 28, 1994

Dear Jeff,

Why don't we write it together?

55. Jeff

south toward home

The close air in the small jet's cabin felt like an extra layer of clothes as I hurtled down through the clouds toward a rendezvous with my own youth. My sense of excitement and awe accelerated as the plane slowed for its landing, and although I was vaguely conscious of the change in air pressure as we descended, and of the buzz of activity around me as flight attendants hurried to get seats in the upright position and the snack cart stowed, the main thing on my mind was the fact that I was finally, after twenty-six years, returning to Mississippi.

How many times, in how many letters, had I promised Ruth that I would soon revisit my Southern home of the heart? It had become a kind of ritual over the years: "I can't wait to get down there, Ruth. See you soon." "I'll call you next week about details." "It'll be great to see you again next month. You'll have to give me a tour of Yazoo for old times' sake." But although we'd seen each other five times since August of 1969, I'd never managed to make it back—until now.

The cabin chime rang, signaling our final descent. I could hardly breathe as I craned my neck, peering eagerly through the clouds for clues as to what I might encounter. Would I recognize the Jackson airport when it finally became visible, or would there be a disconnect between my scant, hazy memories from 1969 and the reality of today?

On my knee was a well-thumbed copy of Willie Morris's *Yazoo*, the copy I'd bought after Ruth recommended it half a lifetime ago. I'd been reading it for the past few days, keenly following the volatile situation in 1970, when the integration crisis and boycott had threatened to explode in anger and blood, as if it might tell me some crucial thing I'd missed the first time. I'd stopped reading at the familiar passage about Alice DeCell, the only student in Yazoo City High School who'd read *Soul on Ice*.

Alice, sweet Alice—would I get a chance to see her again? Ruth had had lunch with her the week before and reported that she was still stunning, "without a line on her face." But Alice seemed to take a dim view of our project; she was busy with her career and with raising a family, and she didn't care to have an adolescent flame turn up in the middle of her life like an old rumor.

Inevitably, such thoughts led to the last days I'd spent in Mississippi, just after my eighteenth birthday and just before I went to college, my head still spinning. I'd never been tongue-lashed so efficiently, and I'd never felt so wronged.

That had been my last taste of Yazoo, but bitter as it was, it hadn't erased its golden mystique. I had always wanted to immerse myself again in the warm music of Southern speech and feel the Mississippi sun on my face. The memory of Yazoo itself was like a magic carpet that took me to a mythical place, the El Dorado or Brigadoon of my youth, an elusive paradise I had always wanted to get back to. But how much of it had been real?

Well, I *had* actually dragged Grand with Feldo and Jerry and Ruth and Alice; I wasn't the only one who remembered that. I'd gone off to Short Creek for an afternoon with Alice's friends; I'd swapped puns with Feldo and a tipsy millionaire, Herbie Holmes, in the Piggly Wiggly parking lot; and I'd shaken the Whalin' Stick out the window of the Devilbug on Coach Rush's lawn. I'd survived that fearsome cop in Forest, and spent a week in the Tuttles' big old Victorian on Jackson Avenue, marveling each day at the neatly pressed and folded stack that Rita had made of my clothes.

I'd gone horseback riding with Alice, holding hands and stealing kisses that last sweet afternoon before the deluge . . . hadn't I? Or had it all been an extravagant fancy? No, I told myself. It *was* real. I had the letters and the memories—and the quickening pulse, twenty-six years later—to remind me. And there was an indisputable fact waiting for me at the airport—truth in the form of Ruth.

The last time I'd seen her had been almost seven years before, at Feldo's wedding. I'd met her husband, Randy, only twice, but now I'd be spending four days in their home. I wasn't really worried about the visit, because I knew Randy was a sweet-tempered, understanding soul who, like Teri, accepted what Ruth and I meant to each other and didn't feel threatened by it. Still, I wondered: Would there be some awkwardness between us? Would his patience wear thin after a few days of hosting this near stranger from his wife's dim past?

The plane was coming out of the low clouds now, and I could see the boxy airport buildings in the near distance, rushing up as they had that sunny day in August 1969 when the Waldrops had treated me like kin rather than a wild waif on a desperate mission of the heart. It struck me, whizzing along between the gray clouds and the dun earth, that I was landing not only in a faraway place but in a faraway time.

My reverie ended with a subtle jolt as the plane touched down, and within minutes I was heading toward the terminal, straining for a glimpse of Ruth and Randy. Then I saw them, their smiles mirroring mine. Throwing down my bags, I hugged Ruth hard, the two of us clinging to each other like lost children. Randy stood by, obviously touched. I was too full of emotion to do anything but babble at first. Ruth wore a dazed smile, as if I were a benign impossibility.

Later, at their home, we gazed in awe at a hunter's table filled with our own letters in chronological order, the primary source material for the recollections we had begun to form into a book. We laughed, cried and cringed as we went through them, marveling at how two such heedless youths had managed to survive. I'd also brought along a few of Alice's letters, and Ruth was struck by their intelligence and maturity. Then we looked at each other: Alice. Ruth had told her I was coming down, but neither of us had heard from her, and I was keen to know what she—and her mother—thought of our project.

The next morning we called Alice at her office and left a message, expecting not to hear back from her. Then we called Harriet, who invited us to her house for coffee. Just after Ruth hung up, the phone rang; it was Alice. She said she hoped we could join her for lunch at the Elite in downtown Jackson, and we said we would drive there directly from Harriet's. "Well, Jeff," Ruth said, "it looks like you're going to meet Alice again at last." She didn't say it, but I knew she was wondering: *Will I have to pick up the pieces?*

In a way, as I'd told Ruth half jokingly before coming down, it was Harriet I wanted to see more than Alice, because she'd never given me a chance to explain. As for Alice, I didn't think two married-with-children warhorses like us would hold much allure for each other.

I was a bit nervous as we walked up to Harriet's home, which was set back from the street in a beautiful Jackson neighborhood. Would she be friendly toward me? Severe? Would she bring up "the subject" herself, or would she leave that to me? Either way, I was sure it would arise.

Harriet welcomed us with a smile at the front door and introduced us to her husband, John Kuykendall. We were, she told him, writing a book about our longtime friendship. Then she led us to a spacious den at the rear of the house, and for a moment I flashed back to the DeCell home in Yazoo City. But I didn't say anything; I was prepared to wait for the right moment.

Harriet served us cake and coffee, then asked me what I did for a living. For the next hour, she kept up an unremitting barrage of emotionally neutral conversation, then escorted us to the door and wished us luck on our book. Ruth and I found ourselves staring at each other on her front stoop.

"She did it again!" I said. "She didn't let me get a word in edgewise." Ruth laughed and said, "You had no idea what you were up against twenty-six years ago."

On the way to the restaurant, I was staggered by what I was about to do. How would Alice look? What would we say to each other? Based on things she'd said to Ruth, I assumed she would treat me a bit like toxic waste, keeping a cautious distance and cutting our meeting as short as possible. We were several minutes late as we walked into the restaurant, and I felt sure Alice had bailed out. But as we approached the front counter, there she was—and in a split second we were hugging each other, our eyes moist and our throats dry.

As Ruth had said, Alice was still very attractive—although no longer the miraculous vision of my memory. Her skirt was faded, her blue sweater was worn and her hair had lost its almost magical luster. She was, after all, a forty-three-year-old mother of three, and a working woman to boot; no one is immune to the effects of twenty-six years of cares and responsibilities. But as we headed toward our table, I found myself walking on air once again.

We sat and talked about old times as I drank her in, studying every detail amid the clangor and bustle of a busy lunch trade. She didn't recall much in the way of specifics from those days, she said, but she clearly remembered the pain of my last visit to Yazoo. In the end, she said, she'd had no choice but to put it behind her.

Alice had to get back to work after lunch, but she invited us to meet her children later that day at Van & Lillie's, the only restaurant in town that served Ben & Jerry's ice cream. We agreed, amazed that she seemed to have forgotten her reservations about me and our book. On our way back to the car, Ruth noticed that I was walking slowly, as if in a daze. "Are you okay?" she asked. I nodded, but later, back at her house, I was nearly overcome by the sadness of it all.

Two kids had loved each other with the bright, intense ardor of youth, yet somehow it all had devolved into a loss that still rankled, all these years later.

Ruth was afraid I'd fallen in love with Alice all over again as I wandered for hours in the fields and woods behind her house with her dogs, but I hadn't. I'd simply found myself wishing that I could have gone back in time and changed things a little so that our love, doomed from the first not by distance or parental opposition or clashing cultures but by our irreconcilable natures, could have died the natural death it deserved.

As Alice herself had written just after our debacle: "The reality is that when I get married . . . I'm going to marry a basically conservative, Southern boy."

In the end, it was hard to deny myself the bitter satisfaction of having felt cheated, for all those years, of Alice's love. But the truth, as the Bible says, shall make you free.

Later, in the months and years it took for this book to be born, I began to feel the effects of that freedom. Finally, the haunting was over, the apparition from the past was exorcised, and I realized that, between the two Mississippi girls I'd met in 1969—the one I'd dreamed of and the one who'd become, against all odds, my bosom friend—I'd ended up in the right relationship with the right one. As I told Ruth in a letter, I valued her insights above everything else we were to each other. "One very important thing you are for me," I wrote, "is a successor, as much as anyone can be, to Vin. There are some resonances of the exchanges I had with him in the exchanges I have with you. It's a very great gift for me."

And I found I was ready, as I had never quite been before, to focus on Teri and on repairing the emotional damage we'd suffered. Now I was prepared to take the lessons I'd learned to heart and to make our marriage work. Dreams are sweet, but you can't build a life on them.

Teri and I are still working out the consequences of those four trying years—a time when we should have opened to each other more, but kept too much bottled up inside. In the end, we both had hard lessons to learn about accommodating our two very different selves within a loving framework, and for a while it looked as if we might be driven apart under the pummeling of the four hundred blows.

But in the end we chose to try and grow together, a dauntingly difficult process at the best of times. We realized that our love, begun when we were scarcely more than children ourselves, must survive, because the stakes—as represented by two wonderful kids—are too high to let it die.

56. Ruth

the nature of friendship

It was there from the beginning: a dare—whispered through the greeting "Dear whitey, honky, WASP, bitch"—to see into the heart and mind of a boy from a foreign land, and to discover that they resonated with my own. And to experience it all through words: written in calm repose, or dashed off in rushed nonchalance; wrung from anguish, or lackadaisically penned in boredom.

God, or dispassionate time, has been kind to us, and prevented the years from separating us, until we are finally part of each other's lives. I have daydreamed about him, again and again, my faithful correspondent. But it was only in the past few years that we achieved the full potential of our friendship. After the years of nurturing, it now grows like a delightful weedy plant through our lives, yielding unexpected bounty at unlikely times.

Technology has helped—we're still two thousand miles apart—but we fire faxes and e-mails back and forth almost daily. And occasionally I find a letter from him, buried in the heaps of catalogs and commercial garbage people today call "mail," and eagerly reach in to retrieve it, to feel the old, remembered enchantment.

Emotions never die. Those words have become a mantra to us, explaining the need to bring our friendship to life on these pages. It was emotions—not dusty or worn, but as fresh as they were in 1969—that gave us the sudden mutual ability to forget sleep and to write, write, write deep into many nights.

I thought, at seventeen, that loneliness and fear were unique to me. Then I learned with time and hard experience that we all carry them like razor blades hidden in the soft folds of our lives; that there are some people who can help us realize life doesn't have to be a solitary journey; that the name of their magic is friendship.

When Jeff finally came back to Mississippi in 1995, I stood in the Jackson airport feeling seventeen again, engulfed by the same emotions that had led me in 1969 to make a link with a boy so far removed. But I was moved by something else, too, because now our lives were meshed.

We were writing a book, in a real sense the child of our relationship, which, like all children, would eventually find its own way into the world—touching others or vanishing into obscurity. But the creating belonged to us, a journey we would make together.

Then Jeff was in front of me, and we hugged, and hugged again.

"You're still taller than me," he said, his eyes questioning, pressing me once more to help him figure out the old puzzle of our miscommunication.

"Not by much," I answered, my same standard answer.

"Please try to remember," Jeff prodded me, putting his hand on my arm. "Didn't you know you were taller than five-eight?"

"Didn't you know you were shorter than five-eight?" We briefly stared a challenge at each other before walking on.

"Does it really matter now?" Randy asked.

Jeff and I looked at each other and grinned. "Yes," we both said.

"Y'all are nuts." Randy picked up Jeff's bag and took my hand. We walked out of the airport through beams of sunlight that crisscrossed the hallway, and several people spoke to us. But I was bobbing along on a sea of remembrances and affection, oblivious to everything except the two men walking on either side of me.

That night I told Jeff the truth, that even though I'd said I was "about five-eight" in 1969, I'd known I was taller. "But I'm glad I said it."

"Me, too," he answered. "If you hadn't, I wouldn't have come to Yazoo City. It would all have been over before it started."

"But you weren't five-eight, either, were you?"

"I *thought* I was. No, I definitely believed it."

"But?"

"Feldo swears I wasn't. I guess he's right."

It seemed that once we started talking, we couldn't stop. We talked for four days before we came to the end of it—a breathless pause as we sat across the table from each other, all our letters spread out between us.

I leaned over the yellowing piles and laid my hand on Jeff's. I needed that moment of physical contact, the first time I'd ever held his hand. His blue eyes caught mine in a long, sweet look. It popped into my head that we had never fallen out of love for each other, not since those first weeks of giddy letter writing that had brought him to Mississippi. That our love for each other had simply changed in whatever way it had to, keeping us together.

"What would I have done without you?" he asked. *Or I without you.*

I smiled at him and blinked back tears. He hurriedly pulled a hand across his own brimming eyes and left the room to get a cup of coffee. In a minute I heard Jeff and Randy in the kitchen, talking about buying an ultralight plane together. Through the window I could see a line of crows sitting on the fence, preening their feathers and blinking in the sun. Their black eyes were hooded and wise. Then one by one they flew away, and I counted silently to myself:

One for sorrow
Two for joy
Three for a letter
Four for a boy
Five for silver
Six for gold
Seven for a story that's never been told.

acknowledgments

There's really no such thing as writing. There's only rewriting, a seemingly endless process of trial and error, hope and despair, fashioning and smashing the words until they finally make sense. And while the popular image of the scribe is of a solitary person burning the midnight oil, in fact it took scores of people—maybe hundreds, if we could remember them all—to help us through the five-year creation of this book.

I particularly wish to thank my longtime (but who's counting?) sweetheart and spouse, Teri, who made great sacrifices to help bring this story to fruition. Without her understanding and cooperation, it could not have been told. Thanks, too, to our children, David and Emily, for respecting Dad's often-closed office door.

Campbell Black, my old friend, adviser and fellow sojourner on the road from Oz, inexplicably failed to make specific suggestions for improving the early manuscript I sent him, although I had expected him to respond with dozens. Instead, he called from Ireland to say he'd read the whole thing (600 pages!) in a few days and that it had touched him deeply. Coming from a great writer and a world-class curmudgeon, his reaction made me realize, as I hadn't before, that we were on to something.

Thanks also are due to so many old friends, beginning with Dave Feldman, Jerry Greenfield, Ben Cohen, Fred Thaler, Ronnie Bauch, Wayne Walcoff and Alice DeCell Wise, who generously let us plunder their memories for the nuggets that make this story live and who read and reread chapters as we produced them to help us get things right. And to Randy Williams, in whom I was blessed to find yet another soul brother.

Thanks, too, to former guitar hero and now ace L.A. lawyer and scriptmeister Ted Gerdes, who enthused over the manuscript in his laid-back way, another sure indicator that we were on the right track. And especially to Dolores Vito, my second sister, who gave us her blessing and allowed us to use Vin's letters. Without Vin and his family, my life would have been infinitely poorer, and Vin's letters have been an inexhaustible wellspring of inspiration. Thanks again, *fratello mio*—your spirit is always with me.

We're also very much beholden to Richard Russo, whose unflinching appraisal of the "finished product" back in 1997 made us realize how much more work it still needed. The resulting changes improved this book immeasurably.

Thanks, too, to all those who read chapters and manuscripts at various stages and/or kept us going with their support and encouragement. I particularly want to thank: my father and mother, Wes and Addie Durstewitz; my sister, Deb Durstewitz; and Jim and Antoinette Vito, Kevin Mednick, Jim Post and Mitch and the late, great Sandy Kupperman.

Also, Birgit Hollbrügge, Norma and Fred Bartle, Jim and Judy Guldenstern, Kathleen Mooney, Fred, Fritzi and Nina Feldman, Kelly Pennacchia, Susan Male, Crista Ellis, Pat Yazum, Dave Ernst, Ceaser Williams, James Austin Moran, Rita Oliverio, Fred Lager, Don Vanouse, Craig Gall, Paul Grau, Dave Sterns and nonpareil copywriter Curtis Au. Special thanks to Chris Hebblethwaite and Marion Green of Oswego State's Penfield Library for research assistance above and beyond the call of duty, and to Dr. Dave Gabay, who managed to straighten out my spine every time I put a writer's crimp in it.

And last but not least, to Apple, upon whose stalwart Macs this whole book was written.

JEFF DURSTEWITZ

Saratoga Springs, New York, August 1999

Many thanks go to my husband Randy, who is my heart. I know there were times when I asked too much, but you never failed to respond with love, respect and boundless integrity.

Every person who read and commented on this book during its many transformations, enriched it. The generosity of family, friends and strangers, those in the publishing world and outside of it, has been remarkable.

JoAnne Prichard Morris shepherded us from the earliest days, through countless readings and rereadings, with invaluable advice and commentary. She and her husband, Willie Morris, were ever my true friends and counselors. Willie's audacious words of encouragement gave us an inspiring view of faraway literary horizons. When he passed away suddenly on August 2, 1999, his ardent spirit seemed at first lost, but now I find that it lives on in the many lives and hearts he touched with his own.

Willie's death was not the only searing loss of the summer of 1999. On May 24, our editor at Bantam Books, Beverly Lewis Eames, collapsed and died. She was a remarkable woman, in full bloom at the heart of many lives, including ours, and we felt her death as a shocking blow. I hope we have lived up to her standards.

Christine Brooks, who took over as our editor after Beverly's death, has steered us toward the final goal with admirable grace and skill. We are deeply grateful to her. Our unflappable agent and friend, Al Zuckerman, believed in the book, and improved it with his editorial and professional advice. He has been our rock. Many thanks to Teri for coming along on a journey that was always uncharted and sometimes rocky.

I also wish to thank the following people who read the manuscript and provided factual information and/or moral support: my mother, Margaret Tuttle; my father, Douglas Tuttle and his wife, Nina; my sisters Margaret Tyer and Patty Arostegui, my brother Doug Tuttle and my niece Maggie Corley; Tina Robinson, Bill Poulsen, Harriet Kuykendall, Stew Albert, co-editor of *The Sixties Papers,* an anthology of sixties writings, Carroll Bible, Bob Williamson, Patty Seward, Belinda Backstrom Roark, John Horhn, Sid Salter, Rebecca Pittman, Nancy Gavan, Cindy Clark, Dave Clark, Ben Williams, Gayle Richardson, Tracey Parrish, Barbara White, Nancy Williams, Dora Carl, Lea Huxtable Barrett, Debbie Nicholas, Suzanne Gold Cooper, Sarah O'Connor, Charlie Brenner and the staff at the Eudora Welty Library in Jackson and William B. Englesbach and the reference staff at Hoskins Library at the University of Tennessee. The 1990 graduate thesis of Susanna Taipale was invaluable in helping me reconstruct events in Knoxville from 1969–1971.

RUTH WILLIAMS

Flora, Mississippi, August 1999

about the authors

Jeff Durstewitz lives with his wife, two children and two feline personalities in Saratoga Springs, New York.

Ruth Campbell Williams and her husband Randy live a rural idyll in Flora, Mississippi with their three dogs, two horses and a cat. From time to time they reside in an isolated cabin on a lake in Harrop, British Columbia.

Visit the authors' website at www.youngerthanthatnow.net.